T0235365

Lecture Notes in Computer Science   9258

Commenced Publication in 1973
Founding and Former Series Editors:
Gerhard Goos, Juris Hartmanis, and Jan van Leeuwen

More information about this series at http://www.springer.com/series/7409

Giuseppe Di Fatta · Giancarlo Fortino
Wenfeng Li · Mukaddim Pathan
Frederic Stahl · Antonio Guerrieri (Eds.)

Internet and Distributed Computing Systems

8th International Conference, IDCS 2015
Windsor, UK, September 2–4, 2015
Proceedings

 Springer

Editors

Giuseppe Di Fatta
School of Systems Engineering
University of Reading
Reading, Berkshire
UK

Giancarlo Fortino
Dipartimento di Ingegneria Informatica,
    Modellistica, Elettronica e Sistemistica
University of Calabria
Rende
Italy

Wenfeng Li
School of Logistics and Engineer
Wuhan University of Technology
Wuhan
China

Mukaddim Pathan
CSIRO ICT
Acton
Australia

Frederic Stahl
School of Systems Engineering
University of Reading, Whiteknights
Reading
UK

Antonio Guerrieri
Dipartimento di Ingegneria Informatica,
    Modellistica, Elettronica e Sistemistica
University of Calabria
Rende
Italy

ISSN 0302-9743   ISSN 1611-3349   (electronic)
Lecture Notes in Computer Science
ISBN 978-3-319-23236-2   ISBN 978-3-319-23237-9   (eBook)
DOI 10.1007/978-3-319-23237-9

Library of Congress Control Number: 2015946745

LNCS Sublibrary: SL3 – Information Systems and Applications, incl. Internet/Web, and HCI

Springer Cham Heidelberg New York Dordrecht London

Printed on acid-free paper

Springer International Publishing AG Switzerland is part of Springer Science+Business Media
(www.springer.com)

Preface

IDCS 2015 was 8th annual event of the conference series dedicated to the Internet and distributed computing systems and was held in Windsor, Berkshire, UK. The previous seven successful editions include IDCS 2008 in Khulna, Bangladesh, IDCS 2009 in Jeju Island, Korea, IDCS 2010 and IDCS 2011 in Melbourne, Australia, IDCS 2012 in Wu Yi Shan, China, IDCS 2013 in Hangzhou, China, and IDCS 2014 in Calabria, Italy.

The Internet as ubiquitous infrastructure and the widespread use of mobile and wireless devices have laid the foundation for the emergence of innovative network applications. In addition, the advances of sensor technologies are facilitating cyber-physical systems, i.e., the integration of the digital world with the physical environment, and the advent of the Internet of Things. Large-scale networked systems, real-time data streams from sensors and widespread use of mobile devices are contributing to the big data phenomenon. Intelligent and efficient approaches are required to turn the wealth of data available from the network into useful and actionable knowledge.

IDCS 2015 received innovative papers on emerging models, paradigms, applications, and technologies related to Internet-based distributed systems, including Internet of Things, cyber-physical systems, wireless sensor networks, next-generation collaborative systems, and extreme-scale networked systems. The audience included researchers, PhD students, and practitioners who have a general interest in the different aspects of the Internet and distributed computing systems with a more specific focus on practical and theoretical aspects of the cyber-physical systems built with the integration of computer networks, distributed systems, wireless sensor technology, and network applications for complex real-life problems.

IDCS 2015 received a large number of submissions from 20 different countries: 19 regular papers and seven short student papers were accepted after a careful review and selection process. The selected contributions covered cutting-edge aspects of cloud computing and Internet of Things, sensor networks, parallel and distributed computing, advanced networking, smart cities and smart buildings, big data, and social networks.

The conference also featured two keynote presentations: the first presentation on "Coordination Mechanism in Multi-Layer Clouds: Architecture and Applications," was given by Prof. Omer F. Rana, School of Computer Science and Informatics, Cardiff University, UK; the second presentation on "Cloud Computing in Healthcare and Biomedicine" was given by Prof. Mario Cannataro, Bioinformatics Laboratory, Department of Medical and Surgical Sciences, University Magna Graecia of Catanzaro, Italy.

The conference was held at the Cumberland Lodge, which is a 17th century house that combines charming English hospitality with 21st century facilities. The conference venue is immersed in the Royal landscape of the Windsor Great Park, at walking distance from Windsor Castle and within its parkland. The conference activities included an excursion to Bletchley Park and the National Museum of Computing. Bletchley Park is the historic site of secret British codebreaking activities during WW II, workplace of Alan Turing, and birthplace of the modern computer. The National Museum of Computing is dedicated to the history of computing and includes Colossus, the world's first programmable, electronic, digital computer.

IDCS 2015 included a workshop for PhD students to give them the opportunity to present their project work: their contributions are included in the proceedings as short student papers.

We would like to thank the University of Reading and, in particular, Prof. Ben Cosh, Dean of the Faculty of Science, for providing four student grants to support the participation of PhD students from overseas countries.

The successful organization of IDCS 2015 was possible thanks to the dedication and hard work of a number of individuals. In particular, we would like to thank Antonio Guerrieri (publications chair) for his commendable work for the conference publicity and proceedings. We also express our gratitude to the PhD students of the University of Reading, Alexander Luke Spedding, Mosab Ayiad, and Anas Al-Dabbagh, who offered their voluntary support during the conference.

September 2015

Giuseppe Di Fatta
Giancarlo Fortino
Wenfeng Li
Mukaddim Pathan
Frederic Stahl
Antonio Guerrieri

Organization

General Chair

Giuseppe Di Fatta   University of Reading, UK

Program Chairs

Wenfeng Li   Wuhan University of Technology, China
Giancarlo Fortino   University of Calabria, Italy
Mukaddim Pathan   Telstra Corporation Limited, Australia

Local Program Chairs

Rachel McCrindle   University of Reading, UK
Lily Sun   University of Reading, UK

PhD Workshop Chair

Frederic Stahl   University of Reading, UK

Publicity and Industry Chair

Dom Robinson   Innovations, id3as-company, UK

Publications Chair

Antonio Guerrieri   University of Calabria, Italy

Steering Committee - IDCS Series

Jemal Abawajy   Deakin University, Australia
Rajkumar Buyya   University of Melbourne, Australia
Giancarlo Fortino   University of Calabria, Italy
Dimitrios Georgakopolous   RMIT University, Australia
Mukaddim Pathan   Telstra Corporation Limited, Australia
Yang Xiang   Deakin University, Australia

Program Committee

Gianluca Aloi	University of Calabria, Italy
Hani Alzaid	King Abdulaziz City for Science and Technology, Saudi Arabia
Doina Bein	The Pennsylvania State University, USA
Alfredo Cuzzocrea	ICAR-CNR, Italy
Claudio De Farias	PPGI-IM/NCE-UFRJ, Brazil
Maria De Souza	The University of Sheffield, UK
Declan Delaney	University College Dublin, Ireland
Giuseppe Di Fatta	University of Reading, UK
Marcos Dias De Assuncao	Inria Avalon, LIP, ENS de Lyon, France
Abdelkarim Erradi	Qatar University, Qatar
Zongming Fei	University of Kentucky, USA
Giancarlo Fortino	University of Calabria, Italy
Stefano Galzarano	University of Calabria, Italy
Maria Ganzha	University of Gdansk, Poland
Saurabh Kumar Garg	University of Tasmania, Australia
Luca Geretti	University of Udine - DIEGM, Italy
Hassan Ghasemzadeh	Washington State University, USA
Mick Hobbs	Deakin University, Australia
Soumya Ghosh	Indian Institute of Technology, Kharagpur, India
Raffaele Gravina	University of Calabria, Italy
Antonio Guerrieri	University of Calabria, Italy
Ragib Hasan	University of Alabama at Birmingham, USA
Mohammad Mehedi Hassan	King Saud University, Saudi Arabia
Jaehoon Paul Jeong	Sungkyunkwan University, The Republic of Korea
Dimitrios Katsaros	University of Thessaly, Greece
Ram Krishnan	University of Texas at San Antonio, USA
Hae Young Lee	Seoul Women's University, The Republic of Korea
Wenfeng Li	Wuhan University of Technology, China
Antonio Liotta	Eindhoven University of Technology, The Netherlands
Jaime Lloret	Polytechnic University of Valencia, Spain
Valeria Loscri	Inria Lille Nord-Europe, France
Carlo Mastroianni	ICAR-CNR, Italy
Kashif Munir	KFUPM, Saudi Arabia
Enrico Natalizio	Universitè de Technologie de Compiègne, France
Marco Netto	IBM Research, Brazil
Sergio Ochoa	Universidad de Chile, Chile
Andrea Omicini	Università di Bologna, Italy
Ekow Otoo	University of the Witwatersrand, South Africa
Pasquale Pace	University of Calabria, Italy
Carlos Palau	UPV, Spain
George Pallis	University of Cyprus, Cyprus
Marcin Paprzycki	IBS PAN and WSM, Poland
Mukaddim Pathan	Telstra Corporation Limited, Australia

Contents

Distributed Computing

Parallel Computing

Advanced Networking

Big Data and Social Networks

Cloud Computing and Internet of Things

Cloud Shield: Effective Solution for DDoS in Cloud

Rajat Saxena$^{(\boxtimes)}$ and Somnath Dey

Cloud Computing Lab, Department of Computer Science and Engineering,
Indian Institute of Technology Indore, Indore, India
{rajat.saxena,somnathd}@iiti.ac.in

Abstract. Distributed Denial of Service (DDoS) attack is a complex security challenge for growth of Cloud Computing. DDoS attack is very easy to apply, difficult to prevent and hard to identify because attacker can spoof the IP address of itself for hiding the identity of himself.

In this paper, we present a Third Party Auditor (TPA) based efficient DDoS detection and prevention technique which has the strong identification factor based on these weaknesses. It has less overhead at the user end. Thus, we target various aspects of prevention of DDoS attack in the Cloud environment.

Keywords: Cloud computing · DoS attack · DDoS attack · Third party auditor (TPA) · Dempster shafer theory (DST)

1 Introduction

Cloud computing [1,2] is defined as services and applications that are enforced on a distributed network using virtual resources and accessed by common networking standards and Internet protocols. It is distinguished from the traditional system in the conditions that resources are virtual and limitless and implementation details of the physical systems, on which software runs, are abstracted from the user.

However, Denial-of-service(DoS) and Distributed Denial of Service (DDoS) attacks are two major security restrictions for functionality and availability of Cloud services. In DoS attack, an intruder tries to prevent authorized users from retrieving the information or services. DDoS is an advance version of DoS attack. DDoS is a collaborative attack on functionality and availability of a victim cloud through multiple corrupted systems. In DDoS attack, multiple corrupted systems are utilized for targeting and corrupting a victim cloud to produce a DoS attack. The approach of attack is "distributed" because multiple systems are used by the intruder to launch DoS attack. In the process of DDoS attack, victims are all, victim cloud as well as multiple compromised systems. The main objective of DDoS attack is debacle damage on a victim cloud. Commonly, the undisclosed intension behind this attack is to restrict the available resources and dissolute the service which is highly demanded by the victim cloud.

G. Di Fatta et al. (Eds.): IDCS 2015, LNCS 9258, pp. 3–10, 2015.
DOI: 10.1007/978-3-319-23237-9_1

Thus, it commits harassment of the victim due to huge financial loss. The attacker also malfunctions the confidentiality of the victim and uses their valuable data for own malicious purpose. Apart from all these, acquires the popularity in the hacker's community is also an ambitious reason for these attacks.

In current situations, all the malicious attackers which are affected by the intruders, are send a large number of malicious packets directly to the victim cloud servers. As a result whole network is flooded with attack messages instead of legitimate packets. Thus, availability of cloud storage servers for the legitimate users would be null, because Cloud storage server have been crashed out from attack packets. It is also possible that attackers can manipulate the content of the legitimate packets. This would damage the services of victim Cloud server.

Some examples of DDoS attacks are following. A massive DDoS attack [3,4] occurred on website of yahoo.com at February 7, 2000. In this attack, even though yahoo.com have much extensive computing and bandwidth resources than any of the attackers, yet yahoo.com server collapse for 1.5 h. In 2008 [5], BBC, eBay and Amazon.com are suffered from DDoS attack. In 2010, transactions through PayPal.com are suspended by WikiLeaks website. In 2012 [5], Sony, US, Canadian and UK government websites knocked down by anonymous. In 2013 [8], Czech financial sector, stock exchange and national bank websites are destructed by enormous DDoS attack.

Recent analysis observes a giant amount of financial losses due to DDoS attack every year. According to the Computer Crime and Security Survey [6], the Computer Security Institute (CSI) and Federal Bureau of Investigation (FBI) survey [7], annual loss of financial corporations are increases day by day. A survey by Arber network [8] exposed the fact that approximately 1,200 DDoS attacks occurred per day. It is also disclose this interesting fact that the scale of DDoS attacks have been growing drastically since 2001. In year 2013, the largest recorded DDoS attack against a single target reached 150 gigabits per second, as against 40 gigabits per second in the year 2008 and 24 gigabits per second in year 2007.

Key elements that motivated us for providing a solution to DDoS attacks are revenue loss, slow network performance, service unavailability and loss of customer trust in service providers. Thus, we require a powerful and efficient technique to detect and prevent DDoS attack in cloud environment. For this purpose, we need to find out which type of tools are required to implement this attack and what are the weakness of these tools.

2 Proposed Scheme

We propose an effective approach to detect and prevent the victim cloud servers from any type of attack. First, we take a workstation as a TPA for observation of the all packets reached to cloud servers. It is an independent and trustworthy entity which logs all legitimate as well as malicious packets on the behalf of all cloud servers. We called this entity as "Cloud Shield". Figure 1 shows the architecture of proposed Cloud Shield.

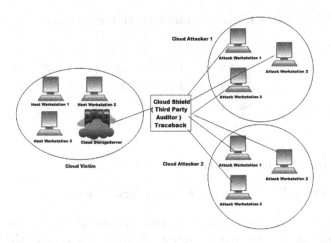

Fig. 1. Our proposed scheme

Cloud Shield is able to traceback the origin of the attack based on Dempster Shafer Theory (DST) to analyze all packets. This DST analysis is depended on 3-valued logic.

2.1 Dempster Shafer Theory (DST)

DST [9] is powerful method for mathematical diagnostics, statistical inference, decision analysis and risk analysis. For DST, probabilities are assigned on mutually exclusive elements of the power sets of state space (Ω) (all possible states). The assignment procedure of probabilities is called basic probability assignment *(bpa)*.

According to DST method [10] for a given state space (Ω) the probability (called mass) is allocated for t set of all 2^Ω elements, which are all possible subsets of (Ω). The DST operations with 3-valued logic provides Fault Tree Analysis (FTA) [11]. For example, if a standard state space (Ω) is (True, False), then 2^Ω should have 4 elements: Φ, True, False, (True, False). The (True, False) element describes the imprecision component, which is introduced by DST. This elements refers the value either true or false, but not both.

We have the following relation for DST as the [sum of all probabilities] $= 1$ and $P(\Phi) = 0$:

$$P(True) + P(False) + P(True, False) = 1 \qquad (1)$$

Thus, for analyzing each VM corresponding to the victim, we use FTA, which is perceived by boolean OR gate.If we choose set A = $\{a_1, a_2, a_3\}$ as an input set and B = $\{b_1, b_2, b_3\}$ as output set. Then Table 1 describes the Boolean truth table for the OR gate. From Table 1 we get:

$$P(A) = (a_1, a_2, a_3) = \{P(True), P(False), P(True, False)\} \qquad (2)$$

$$P(B) = (b_1, b_2, b_3) = \{P(True), P(False), P(True, False)\} \qquad (3)$$

$$P(A \vee B) = \{a_1b_1 + a_1b_2 + a_1b_3 + a_2b_1 + a_3b_1; a_2b_2; a_2b_3 + a_3b_2 + a_3b_3\} \qquad (4)$$

Table 1. Boolean truth table for the OR gate

	b_1		b_2	b_3
$\vee$	T	F	(T,F)	
a_1 T	T	T	T	
a_2 F	T	F	(T,F)	
a_3 (T,F)	(T,F)	T	(T,F)	

Putting the value from Eq. (1) into Eq. (4)

$$P(A \vee B) = \{a_1 + a_2b_1 + a_3b_1; a_2b_2; a_2b_3 + a_3b_2 + a_3b_3\} \tag{5}$$

In last, our solution uses Dempsters combination rule, which fuse evidences from multiple independent sources using a conjunctive operation (AND) between two *bpa's* P_1 and P_2, called the joint P_{12}

$$P_{12}(A) = \frac{\sum_{B \cap C = A} P(B)P(C)}{1 - K} \tag{6}$$

The factor $1 - K$ is called normalization factor and it is constructive for entirely avoiding the conflict evidence, When A $\neq \Phi$; $P_{12}(\Phi) = 0$ and $K = \sum_{B \cap C = \Phi} P(B)P(C)$.

Thus, by Eq. (6) we can easily analyze the DDoS flood attack from any topology or any type of resources the attacker have.

2.2 Our Implementation

Cloud Shield is a private cloud which is configured with front end server and three nodes (or VMs). The first step in our implementation involves deployment of a private cloud using Cloudera CDH 5.3.0-0 [12]. The other three nodes are selected and managed in "networking mode" of Citrix Xen Server 6.2.0 [13], because it provides the advanced features of virtualization. The depiction of Cloud Shield is given in Fig. 2.

We divide whole working of Cloud shield in three parts.

1. **Detection Phase:** This phase is handled by three nodes in which we assume that snort based on DST is installed and configured. It detects the packet floods and stores in the MySQL database. It also stores the attack alerts gathered from VM based IDS.
2. **Conversion Phase:** In this phase, front server convert alerts into basic probabilities assignments (bpas) based on the attack alerts. In our work, we utilizes 3-valued logic {True, False, (True, False)} in DST operations for successful detection of TCP-flood, UDP-flood and ICMP-flood attacks. Thus, we analysis of TCP, UDP and ICMP packets. Algorithm 1 provides conversion of alerts received from VM's into bpas.

Table 2. Boolean truth table for Dempster's combination rule

	$P_{V_1}(T)$	$P_{V_1}(F)$	$P_{V_1}(T,F)$
$P_{V_2}(T)$	$P_{V_1}(T)\ P_{V_2}(T)$	$P_{V_1}(F)\ P_{V_2}(T)$	$P_{V_1}(T,F)\ P_{V_2}(T)$
$P_{V_2}(F)$	$P_{V_1}(T)\ P_{V_2}(F)$	$P_{V_1}(F)\ P_{V_2}(F)$	$P_{V_1}(T,F)\ P_{V_2}(F)$
$P_{V_2}(T,F)$	$P_{V_1}(T)\ P_{V_2}(T,F)$	$P_{V_1}(F)\ P_{V_2}(T,F)$	$P_{V_1}(T,F)\ P_{V_2}(T,F)$

3. **Attack Assessment Phase:** This Phase is conducted inside the front-end server and it resides in the Cloud Fusion Unit (CFU). It fuses the converted *bpa's* and based on normalized factor it assess the attack. Thus, it uses Dempsters combination rule for obtaining combined results of VMs for observing the impact of DDoS flood attack. This is used for maximizing the DDoS true positive rates and minimizing the false positive alarm rate. P_{V_1,V_2} is calculated from the Eq. (6) and Truth Table presented on Table 2.

2.3 Service Model of Cloud Shield

We have identified the basic symptoms of a DoS or DDoS attacks. These symptoms are system speed gets reduced and programs run very slowly, large number of connection requests from a large number of users and less number of available resources.

We have also resolved the IP spoofing issue. In case of IP spoofing, an attacker tries to spoof the users that the packets are coming from reliable sources. Thus, the attacker takes control over the client's data or system showing himself as the trusted party. Spoofing attacks can be checked by using encryption techniques and performing user authentication based on key exchange technique. Technique like IPSec helps in mitigating the risks of spoofing. We have analyzed this and implemented multi factor authentication, which reduces the possibility of IP spoofing.

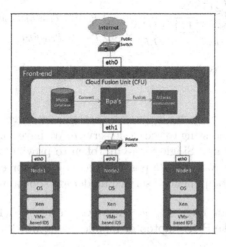

Fig. 2. Cloud shield

Algorithm 1. Conversion of Alerts into BPA's

Input: Alerts received from VM's .
Output: Probabilities.
$\{P_{UDP}(T), P_{UDP}(F), P_{UDP}(T,F)\}$.
$\{P_{TCP}(T), P_{TCP}(F), P_{TCP}(T,F)\}$.
$\{P_{ICMP}(T), P_{ICMP}(F), P_{ICMP}(T,F)\}$.

1: **for** each VM node **do**
2:     Capture {UDP; TCP; ICMP } packets.
3:     **for** each packet X $\in$ {UDP; TCP; ICMP } **do**
4:         Query the alerts from the database when a X attack occurs for the specified VM node.
5:         Query the total number of possible X alerts for each VM node.
6:         Query the alerts from the database when X attack is unknown.
7:         Calculate the Probability (True) for X, by dividing the result obtained at step 1 with the result obtained at step 2.
8:         Calculate the Probability (True, False) for X, by dividing the result obtained at step 3 with the result obtained at step 2.
9:         Calculates probability (False) for X: 1- {Probability (True) + Probability(True, False)}
10:     **end for**
11:     Calculate the probabilities for each VM by the FTA given in Fig. 3. Figure 3 only shows the calculation of the probabilities (i.e. $P_{V_1}(T), P_{V_1}(F), P_{V_1}(T, F)$) for the first VM node.
12:     With the help of FTA the values of belief (Bel) and plausibility (PL) for each VM is calculated as follows :
13:     $Bel(V_1) = P_{V_1}(T)$
14:     $PL(V_1) = P_{V_1}(T) + P_{V_1}(T, F))$
15:     This Calculation is done also for VM node V_2 and V_3.
16: **end for**

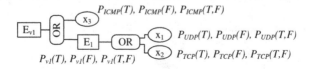

Fig. 3. Fault tree analysis for one VM

Our service model provides secure connection and convenient exposed Open APIs to the user for accessing to the cloud service. We have consider cloud orchestration environments and Single Sign-On Token to provide seamless experience to user. Furthermore, we provide possible technologies for cloud collaboration. The details of each component of service model are shown in Fig. 4.

1. **Client:** Client can retrieve the resources with the help of web browser enabled devices like PDA, laptop or mobile phone which require multi factor

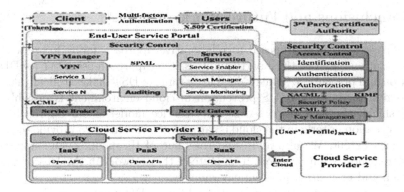

Fig. 4. Service model of cloud shield

authentication. Multi-factors authentication is done based on the certificate issued by Cloud Shield.

2. **Users:** In this component, client which enables the multi factor authentication, is able to get X-509 certificate for the user interaction.
3. **End-User Service Portal:** When clearance is granted, a Single Sign-on Access Token (SSAT) could be issued using certification of Client. Then the access control component shares the user information related with the security policy and verification. User could use services without limitation of service providers.

   – **Service Configuration:** The service enabler makes provision for Cloud Shield service using user's profile. This user's profile is provided to the service management in cloud service provider for the integration and interoperation of service provisioning requests from user. The Service Provisioning Markup Language (SPML) can be used to share user's profile. The asset manager requests user's personalized resources withuser's profile SPML to cloud service provider and configure service via VPN connection.

   – **Service Gateway, Service Broker:** A service gateway manages network resources and Virtual Private Network (VPN)on the information life-cycle of service broker.

   – **Security Control:** The security control component provides significant protection for access control, security policy and key management against security threats.

   – **VPN Manager:** An automated service monitoring systems guarantees the high level of service performance and availability.

4. **Cloud Service Providers (CSP):** This component is used to provide any type of resource as a service for an users.
5. 3rd **Party Certificate Authority:** This component enables trust between user and CSP to authenticate with each other and exchanges of service with each other.

3   Conclusions and Future Work

In this paper, we have proposed a collaborative approach for DDoS detection and prevention based on third party auditors. This approach uses DST for DDoS detection and prevention. Three valued logic value of DST makes it ideally suited for cloud storage. Easy DDoS prevention in cloud environment is possible by Cloud shield. We have discussed security service model of our approach and their prevention criteria in the cloud environment. This helps to provide security with much extent. We also addressed the issue of IP spoofing. Our approach shows tremendous improvement from state-of the art work in the area of DDoS detection and prevention in cloud environment.

This technique supports to prevent the different DDoS attacks with less overhead. In future, we will able to include performance and security comparison of this technique with other techniques.

References

1. Saxena, R., Dey, S.: Collaborative approach for data integrity verification in cloud computing. In: Martínez Pérez, G., Thampi, S.M., Ko, R., Shu, L. (eds.) SNDS 2014. CCIS, vol. 420, pp. 1–15. Springer, Heidelberg (2014)
2. Ruj, S., Saxena, R.: Securing cloud data. In: Cloud Computing with e-Science Applications, pp. 41–72. CRC Press (2015). ISBN:978-1-4665-9115-8
3. Garber, L.: Denial-of-service attacks rip the Internet. IEEE Comput. **33**(4), 12–17 (2000)
4. Yahoo on trail of site hackers (2000). http://www.wired.com/techbiz/media/news/2000/02/34221
5. Powerful attack cripples Internet (2002). http://www.greenspun.com/bboard/q-and-a-fetch-msg.tclmsgid=00A7G7
6. Australian computer emergency response team, Australian Computer Crime and Security Survey (2004)
7. Gordon, L.A., Loeb, M.P., Lucyshyn, W., Richardson, R.: CSI/FBI Computer crime and security survey (2005)
8. Arbor networks, Worldwide Infrastructure Security Report, vol - IV, October 2008
9. Siaterlis, C., Maglaris, B., Roris, P.: A novel approach for a distributed denial of service detection engine. National Technical University of Athens, Athens (2003)
10. Siaterlis, C., Maglaris, B.: One step ahead to multisensor data fusion for DDoS detection. J. Comput. Secur. **13**(5), 779–806 (2005)
11. Guth, M.A.S.: A probabilistic foundation for vagueness and imprecision in fault-tree analysis. IEEE Trans. Reliab. **40**(5), 563–569 (1991)
12. Cloudera (2014). http://www.cloudera.com/content/cloudera/en/downloads.html
13. XenServer (2014). http://xenserver.org/open-source-virtualization-download.html

Towards Modelling-Based Self-adaptive Resource Allocation in Multi-tiers Cloud Systems

Mehdi Sliem[1]([⊠]), Nabila Salmi[1,2], and Malika Ioualalen[1]

[1] MOVEP Laboratory, USTHB, Algiers, Algeria
{msliem,nsalmi,mioualalen}@usthb.dz
[2] LISTIC, Université de Savoie, Annecy le Vieux, France

Abstract. Achieving efficient resource allocation is one of the most challenging problems faced by cloud providers. These providers usually maintain hosted web applications within multiple tiers over the cloud, leading to an overall increased complexity. To answer user requests, meet their Service Level Agreements (SLA) and reduce the energy cost of the data center, cloud systems are being enforced with self-adaptive features such as self-scaling, to efficiently automate the resource allocation process. However, the main concern is how to choose the best resource configuration to reach these objectives of Quality of Service (QoS) with a minimal amount of resources consumption. In this context, we target to use performance modelling and analysis, to forecast the system performances and deduce the most appropriate resource configuration to be applied by the autonomic manager. As a first work to define a modelling based resource allocation autonomic manager, we present, in this paper, the modelling and analysis process, allowing to predict the efficiency of the self-adaptive systems relating resource allocation in the context of multi-tiers cloud systems. We used Stochastic Petri Nets modelling, enforced with a reduction method to avoid a scalability issue. A set of experiments illustrates our approach starting from modelling to performance evaluation of the studied system.

Keywords: Cloud computing · Autonomic computing · Performance modelling · Resource allocation · Petri net

1 Introduction

Today's data centers are subject to an increasing demand for computing resources, as they host complex, large-scale and heterogeneous distributed systems. This is also true in Cloud systems. Particularly for multi-tiers applications, resource management is critical, as sometimes, performance bottlenecks may appear when insufficient resources are not available in one tier, leading to a decrease of the overall profit. This growing complexity stresses the challenging issue of appropriate resource management, especially when a cloud provider has to maintain Service Level Agreements (SLA) with its clients. The main concern to achieve efficient resource allocation is then to find the minimal amount

© Springer International Publishing Switzerland 2015
G. Di Fatta et al. (Eds.): IDCS 2015, LNCS 9258, pp. 11–18, 2015.
DOI: 10.1007/978-3-319-23237-9_2

of resources that an application needs to meet the desired Quality of Service without degrading system performances.

To face this challenge, decisions made by a provider with regard to the deployment of a tier application in the cloud and resource allocation, can be strengthened with a scale-up/down operation. Scaling up/down consists of adding/removing resources to individual virtual machines. However, when the application is implemented following a multi-tier architecture, this will directly impact both the application performances and the providers operation cost. To overcome these issues, the concept of autonomic computing [1] has been proposed to dynamically build the adequate configuration on the monitored system. Autonomic computing commonly describes computing systems that are able to manage themselves. In the context of resources allocation, self-management usually provides two main properties: self-configuration to reconfigure the system according to high-level goals and self-optimization to dynamically optimizes the resource use.

However, a beforehand study of the self-adaptive resource allocation is required, to correctly adjust the scaling parameters of the autonomic manager. This helps to implements the system with more optimized performances. For this purpose, it is interesting if decisions of the autonomic manager are made on the basis of an "a priori" knowledge about predictive behaviour and performances of the chosen resource sharing configuration. IN this context, formal methods are strong tools for system performance prediction based on modelling. Mathematical models, such as Petri nets, are well suitable for modelling distributed complex systems.

We aim, in our work, to contribute in developing modelling and analysis approaches and tools that allows strengthening autonomic systems [8]. To reach our goal, we introduced in [8] a case study for modelling resources allocation in self-adaptive systems. In this paper, we extend the approach for a more detailed modelling of the workload behaviour and computer additional performances indices. We then, extended and dedicated our approach to autonomic multi-tiers cloud systems, addressing resource self-scaling. Our approach is based on a Stochastic Petri Nets (SPN) modelling, with the use of the GreatSPN tool [3] for performance analysis of obtained models. The scalability of our approach is, then, considered using a proposed Petri net reduction method.

The paper is organized as follows: Sect. 2 discusses related work. Then, Sect. 3 presents our case study. Our reduction method id then explained in Sects. 4 and 5 discusses some experimental results. Finally, Sect. 6 concludes the paper and gives some future work.

2   Related Work

Modelling autonomic systems has gained many attention during the last decade, investigating mainly solutions for the distributed resource allocation problem, to satisfy client Service Level Agreements (SLAs). Among these proposals, some authors used mathematical and performance modelling/optimisation approaches

in the general context of autonomic computing, and optimized resource allocation algorithms for the special case of cloud systems.

Litoiu [7] used queuing networks instead of a single queue model. He investigates performance analysis techniques to be used by the autonomic manager.
The workload complexity was studied, and algorithms were proposed for computing performance metric bounds for distributed transactional systems. Workloads
are characterized by their intensity representing the total number of users in the
system, and their mixes which depict the users number in each service class.

In the field of cloud computing, an SLA-based resource allocation for multi-
tier applications was considered in [5]. An upper bound on the total profit was
provided and an algorithm based on force-directed search was proposed to solve
the problem. Processing, memory requirements and communication resources
were considered as three dimensions in which optimization is performed.

In [4] identifies open issues in autonomic resource provisioning and presents
innovative management techniques for supporting Software as a Service (SaaS)
applications hosted in Clouds. The authors present a conceptual architecture
and early results highlighting the benefits of Clouds autonomic management.

Most of the cited proposals are based on the use of formal modelling for an
autonomic online optimization [2,6,9,10], basing generally on queuing models,
or of optimization algorithms. Few work, however focused on the efficiency of
autonomic components to achieve adequate resources management. In this direction, we use, for our modelling, SPN rather than queueing models, to be able
to express most properties of nowadays complex systems. In addition, we model
the complete autonomic system behaviour including the resource management
and the self-adaptive component. This will allow to analyze the efficiency of the
autonomic manager and identify the best configuration to apply.

3   A Self-Adaptive Resource Allocation Cloud Platform

To illustrate our modelling and analysis approach, we present, in this section,
a typical example of a resource allocation cloud system strengthened with a
self-scaling property.

This system consists of an autonomic cloud server receiving user requests
and distributing a set of resources to these requests through a resource allocation process. Requests in our example, are served following a FIFO policy, so
conflicting requests are served according to their arrival order. As a first work,
we consider here only one service class for user requests. Studying several service
classes requires more investigated models, namely high level models. However,
the same modelling methodology can be used to predict performances, considering, in addition, specific colour classes.

The main managed element in this cloud autonomic system is the resource.
A resource may be any element used or invoked during the processing of a user
request: it may be a server, a processor cycle, a memory space, a virtualized
memory, a used device, a network bandwidth, and so on.

The received requests are put by the system in a queue for their processing.
The requests processing is carried out by first taking a request from the requests

queue, and allocating it the required amount of resources from the resources pool. Each user request consumes, hence, resources for its operation. If the needed number of resources isn't available, the current requests are kept pending in the requests queue, waiting for the release of the required amount of resources.

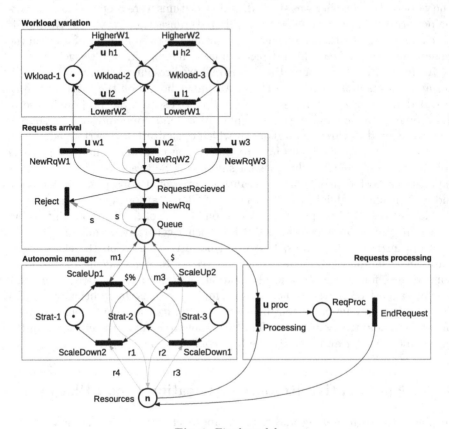

Fig. 1. Final model

Once the processing finished, the resource is available again, to be allocated for other purposes. When the workload is high, a saturation state may be reached quickly, making the system unable to process new request arrivals. We assume, then, that the system uses an autonomic scaling up/down strategy, to increase the system scalability, implemented in an autonomic manager.

Meanwhile, the self-adaptive manager adjusts the amount of available resources for the processing of the queued requests. For this, the main system and its environment are continuously monitored to analyze the workload variation and the number of pending requests. When the number of available resources is inappropriate in relation to the current demand (too low/ too high), the self-adaptive subsystem switches the current configuration to a more suitable one. This process is carried out by adding/removing resources from the resources pool. In addition, we want to plug a modelling analysis module into this self-adaptive manager, to choose the best suitable resource configuration. This will allow to obtain a more trusted and optimized system with regard to performances and resources consumption cost.

We build a model for each component of the platform, using stochastic Petri nets. The obtained sub-models are combined to build a global model of the whole system behaviour. Finally, on this global model are directed a set of experiments for predicting performances of the configuration under study.

4   Analysis of a Multi-tiers Autonomic System Model

When dealing with several tiers, the obtained model becomes rapidly important which make it difficult and even impossible to analysis. To overcome this issue, we propose an analysis process based on a Petri net reduction principle:

Let S be the autonomic system under analysis, being composed of n tiers T_i, $i = 1..N$. To analyze this system, we propose to perform this task gradually in several steps. Each step studies a tier model, connected to "abstract views" of other models, rather than connecting the complete tiers models. Let us, first, define what is an "abstract view" of a tier.

4.1   Abstract View of a Tier

The *abstract view* of a tier is a macro representation or *macro-view* that aggregates its behavior to a minimal equivalent Petri net keeping interactions with other tiers.

Definition 1 (Abstract view of a tier). *Let M_i be the SPN model of a tier T_i. The abstract view $A(M_i)$ of the tier T_i is composed of a timed transition TierProcessing, modelling the activities of the tier, this transition summarizes all the Petri net connected between the place Queue and transition Processing in Fig. 1. This technique has as benefit to significantly reduce the state space of the SPN.*

To the transition is associated a firing rate inversely proportional to the response time of the n requests marking the input place, that means:

$$\theta(t, M) = 1 \div ResponseTime(M)$$

4.2   Analysis Process

The analysis process proceeds as follows:

- First, we build the model of each tier T_i. We denote the obtained model M_i.
- We isolate the model M_N of the last tier. A complete analysis of this model is, then, performed to compute the mean response time of the tier under different initial markings and transitions rates.
- We move to the analysis of the model M_{N-1} of the tier T_{N-1}. To do that:

- We isolate the model M_{N-1} of the tier $N-1$, beginning from the *Requests* place of the tier, as if it is the 1st tier.
- The analyzed tier's model M_N is replaced by its abstract view $A(M_N)$.
- The abstract model $A(M_N)$ is connected to the model M_{N-1}, according to the system specification.

  This step gives a new aggregated model, denoted $AGGR_{N-1}$ representing the two tiers T_N and T_{N-1}. The analysis of this aggregated model will result in a reduced number of states.
- We analyze the obtained model $AGGR_{N-1}$, and compute the mean response time of the tier T_{N-1} under different initial markings.

– We move to the analysis of the model M_{N-2} of the tier T_{N-2}. The reduction is applied again on the model $AGGR_{N-1}$, reducing the two last tiers with a new abstract model $A(M_{N-1})$. We repeat the construction step of the aggregated model of the tier T_{N-2}, then the analysis step.

– The previous steps are repeated until all tiers are considered. The recursive reduction of each analyzed part of the system ensures to keep a reasonable state space of the obtained Petri net, regardless of the total number of tiers in the system. The final aggregated model analysis (of $AGGR_1$) gives then performance and reliability metrics of the whole system, avoiding a combinatorial explosion of the state space number.

This analysis technique ensures the scalability of our methodology, and guarantees faithful results with regard to the unreduced model. In the next section, we illustrate our methodology with a set of experiments applied to an illustration example, the targeted.

5   Illustration

We directed a set of experiments on the constructed model for a 2-tiers system. The analysis of the obtained model was done using the GreatSPN package [3], on an Ubuntu linux 12.4 LTS workstation with 4 GO of RAM. Perl scripting was used to automate the tests with GreatSPN under different configurations, by varying the workload intensity, the available resources number, the threshold of self-adaptation launching and the amount of resources scaled.

Figure 2 shows the mean response time of requests processed by the system, under the variation of *param* 1 and *param* 2. The threshold of monitored requests and the amount of scaled resources represent the two main parameters influencing the autonomic manager efficiency. The figure shows an inversely logarithmic evolution of the response time, as the number of scaled resources increases, while the obtained results are slightly more important for a lower reconfiguration threshold. A stagnation is then noticed at the final part of the graph where the response time remains slightly the same for the different threshold values. This metric helps in identifying the configuration points where no impact is induced on the system performances.

For the same parameters, Fig. 3 gives the amount of resources used by each system configuration. This metric is a main value that should be optimized in

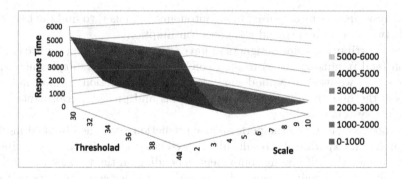

Fig. 2. Mean response time varying the autonomic manager parameters

a resource allocation system, as a high number of active resources increases the energy consumption and the system operation cost. First, a higher scaling implies obviously more resources use; Although, from a certain threshold of scaling, the consumption decrease and stagnate at a same point, this is due to the improvement of performances that leads to less reconfigurations, which implies less resources consumption. In the other hand, the consumption decrease linearly according to the reconfiguration threshold increasing.

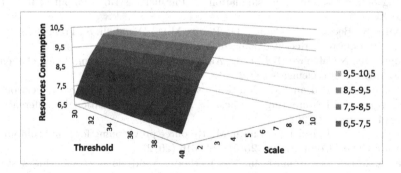

Fig. 3. Resources consumption varying the autonomic manager parameters

These experiments show that the use of our modelling approach helps in identifying such well suitable adjustments, according to particular workloads intensities and parameters adjustments. The computed metrics can then be used to efficiently configure the targeted system to ensure an appropriate solution between costs and quality of service.

6   Conclusion

Quality of service and energy management is one of the main issue of today's cloud applications, especially web applications usually designed following a multi-tier architecture. In this direction, we presented, in this paper, a modelling and analysis approach to be used in an autonomic manager, to find the best balance between performance and resources consumption.

This contribution helps designers in forecasting the most appropriate configuration (and parametrization) to apply on a system before its deployment. For this purpose, we used SPN modelling along with a reduction method in order to model the main components of such systems and predict performances and ensure the system scalability.

To show how to reach the performance prediction goal, the obtained models were analyzed. Experimental results highlighted how to identify the most suitable parameters for the self-scaling component depending on the workload evolution.

Finally, our modelling approach requires us to develop appropriate tools implementing the proposed performance modelling and analysis, to be done automatically. This will allow to exploit concretely our modelling to build trustworthy and reliable systems.

References

1. Autonomic Computing: Principles, Design and Implementation. Springer International Publishing (2013)
2. Amorettia, M., Zanichellib, F., Conte, G.: Efficient autonomic cloud computing using online discrete event simulation. J. Parallel Distrib. Comput. **73**(1), 4–13 (2013)
3. Baarir, S., Beccuti, M., Cerotti, D., Pierro, M.D., Donatelli, S., Franceschinis, G.: The greatspn tool: Recent enhancements (2009)
4. Buyya, R., N.Calheiros, R., Li, X.: Autonomic cloud computing: Open challenges and architectural elements (2012)
5. Goudarzi, H., Pedram, M.: Multi-dimensional sla-based resource allocation for multi-tier cloud computing systems. In: IEEE 4th International Conference on Cloud Computing (2011)
6. Hu, Y., Wong, J., Iszlai, G., Litoiu, M.: Resource provisioning for cloud computing. Future Gener. Comput. Sys. **25**(6), 599–616 (2012)
7. Litoiu, M.: A performance analysis method for autonomic computing systems. ACM Trans. Auton. Adapt. Sys. **2**(1), 3 (2007)
8. Sliem, M., Salmi, N., Ioualalen, M.: An approach for performance modelling and analysis of multi-tiers autonomic systems. In: The 28th IEEE International Conference on Advanced Information Networking and Applications (2014)
9. Tchanaa, A., Tranb, G.S., Brotob, L., DePalmaa, N., Hagimont, D.: Two levels autonomic resource management in virtualized iaas. Future Gener. Comput. Sys. **29**(6), 1319–1332 (2013)
10. Yuan, H., Bi, J., Li, B.H., Chai, X.: An approach to optimized resource allocation for cloud simulation platform. In: 14th International Conference on Systems Simulation (2014)

Web2Compile-CoT: A Web IDE for the Cloud of Things

Claudio M. de Farias[1]([✉]), Paulo G.S.M. Júnior[1], Marina V. Pereira[1],
Italo C. Brito[3], Igor L. dos Santos[1], Luci Pirmez[1], Flávia C. Delicato[1],
and Luiz F.R.C. Carmo[1,2]

[1] Programa de Pós-Graduação em Informática, Universidade Federal
do Rio de Janeiro, Rio de Janeiro, RJ 21941-901, Brazil
claudiofarias@nce.ufrj.br,
{pgeovanejr,igorlsantos,luci.pirmez,fdelicato}@gmail.com,
marinavianna@poli.ufrj.br, lfrust@inmetro.gov.br
http://www.labnet.nce.ufrj.br/
[2] Instituto Nacional de Metrologia, Normalização e Qualidade Industrial,
Duque de Caxias, RJ, Brazil
[3] Colégio Pedro II, Rio de Janeiro, RJ 20921-440, Brazil
italo2v@gmail.com

Abstract. This paper presents Web2Compile-CoT, a WebIDE for
developing Cloud of Things (CoT) applications. The Web2Compile-CoT
was built grounded on the paradigms of integrated development environments, based on web technology, and cloud computing. So it provides
to the scientific community (students and researchers) an ubiquitous
development environment that does not demand any configuration or
download of applications to work properly, but requiring only updated
Internet browsers. Web2compile-CoT works with Contiki and TinyOS
sensor operating systems, and it is able to interact with IoT-lab, a sensor testbed for CoT applications. We evaluated Web2Compile-CoT in
terms of System efficiency and effectiveness. With Web2Compile-CoT we
can reduce the average time for development of an application in classrooms from four hours to 30 min. In addition, due to IoT-lab integration,
Web2Compile-CoT supports classrooms with more than 50 students executing experiments simultaneously.

Keywords: WebIDE · Testbeds · Wireless sensor networks · Internet
of things · Cloud of things

1 Introduction

In the current scenario of Information and Communication Technologies (ICT),
a growing number of increasingly powerful intelligent devices (e.g. smartphones,
sensors and home appliances) is joining the Internet. This trend significantly
impacts the amount of generated traffic with respect to, for instance, data sharing, voice and multimedia, and foreshadows a world of connected intelligent

© Springer International Publishing Switzerland 2015
G. Di Fatta et al. (Eds.): IDCS 2015, LNCS 9258, pp. 19–30, 2015.
DOI: 10.1007/978-3-319-23237-9_3

devices, or "things" under the perspective of the Cloud of Things (CoT) [1]. Among such intelligent devices in CoT, the wireless sensors stand out. Wireless sensors are small sized, and enable the monitoring of physical and environmental variables, such as temperature, humidity, noise and movement, of objects with high degree of accuracy [2]. Such wireless sensors can be grouped into a Wireless Sensor Network (WSN).

The development of educational WSN applications for the CoT environment is a promising field, however there are still challenges in it to be addressed. We can highlight, mainly: (i) the current high financial cost of wireless sensor hardware and (ii) the complexity of the installation and maintenance of development environments. For instance, the MEMSIC MICAz sensor platform [3] requires a sensor network operating system for being programmed, such as TinyOS [4] or Contiki [5]. For installation and configuration of the development environment of such operating systems in a local user machine, a complex procedure is required, demanding knowledge and time from the user to be performed.

The objective of this study is to provide an extension of a Web IDE [6] for WSN known as Web2Compile [7]. This extension enables the development of CoT applications, and is called Web2Compile-CoT. The Web2Compile-CoT is a solution that accelerates the learning of CoT application development, since the students do not need to perform complex procedures, neither upgrading their personal or laboratory computers, for installing the development environment required for learning.

The main contribution of Web2Compile-CoT is to enable any user to develop applications for the CoT with a simple web interface that requires only an updated Internet browser for properly working. The Web2Compile-CoT is intended for users in several situations, such as: (i) users who do not have the time or expertise to perform the installation or configuration of the CoT development environment (for instance, students in a laboratory during a CoT application development class), (ii) users which face restrictions on downloading, installing or running the CoT development environment in its local machine (such as insufficient machine RAM, storage, bandwidth and processing specifications, or security configurations that forbid the user to install programs in its local machine), (iii) users who do not possess physical sensor devices, such as MICAz sensors. The Web2Compile-CoT also offers integration with testbeds, such as the Iot-lab [13], allowing users to deploy (over the cloud) their developed CoT applications on real sensor nodes.

The remainder of this paper is organized as follows. Section 2 discusses related work. Section 3 presents the proposed tool (Web2Compile-CoT) and its software architecture. Section 4 presents experiments and their results. Section 5 concludes our work and shows future directions.

2   Related Work

Recently, several applications are being developed following the web 2.0 paradigm, as it is the case of Web IDEs. Most of Web IDEs have the sole purpose of facilitating the developer tasks, and among their most interesting features there are: (i) provision of an IDE aimed at the specific aspects of a given programming language syntax; (ii) provision of an internal compiler for running the developed programs online; (iii) provision of server authentication services for users to store their programs for later use. Among the existing Web IDEs we can highlight Arvue [8], WWWorkspace [9], eLuaproject [10] and eXo Cloud IDE [12].

Arvue [8] allows the easy development and publication of applications, as well as their web hosting as a service. The application programming is performed in the web browser using a project interface (interface designer) and an integrated code editor. The developed programs are stored in a version control system provided by the own Arvue, and can also be published in the cloud. Arvue was developed using Vaadin, an open source Java framework for building web applications. According to [8], the goal of Arvue is to present a useful editor for a single task: creating and publishing small Vaadin applications for iPhone. Unlike Arvue, our work does not have its main focus on providing a well stablished development/programming interface. Our work focuses on generating compiled programs for deployment on sensor hardware. In addition, it is important to mention that Arvue is not directed to the development of WSN/CoT applications.

The WWWorkspace [9] is based on a Java integrated web development environment built on top of Eclipse IDE. It allows its users to upload their work space and code from any personal computer with an available web browser. However it is worth mentioning that, unlike other tools, for using WWWorkspace, the user must download a program from the developer's site, which contains all the files needed to run the application, including a Jetty server, Eclipse plug-ins and DOJO JavaScript library. In contrast, our proposal has a server acting directly as a compiler of the developed programs, exempting the user from the need to download plug-ins from the internet. Our work also differs from WWWorkspace because it is related strictly to the development of applications for WSN/CoT.

The eLua Project [10] aims to introduce the Lua programming language to the world of embedded software development. Lua is the perfect example of a minimalist, but fully functional programming language. Although usually advertised as a "scripting language" and used in accordance, especially in the gaming industry, it is also fully capable of running independent programs. The small resource requirements of Lua make it suitable for a large number of families of microcontrollers. Like other Web IDEs, the eLua Project's goal is to have a fully functional development environment in the microcontroller itself, without the need to install a set of specific tools, or performing environment configurations. In contrast, our work is not directed to support the development of embedded applications, it is directed only for supporting WSN/CoT application development.

The eXo Cloud IDE [12] is a web-based development environment that enables collaborative development of applications that can be deployed directly into an Heroku Platform as a Service (PaaS) [11] environment. Heroku is a web-based platform for supporting the languages Ruby, JavaScript (including Node.js), and, more recently, Java (support is included for web applications).

The deployment directly within a PaaS environment allows rapid migration from development to deployment. The eXo Cloud IDE also contains a real-time collaborative editor for use with up to five developers. The eXo Cloud does not have the objective of supporting WSN/CoT application development.

In the context of testbeds, IoT-lab [13] offers several tools to deploy, over the internet, compiled WSN/CoT applications on a large-scale WSN infrastructure mounted over several French universities. These applications can be installed on different types of sensor hardware and can be developed for most common WSN operating systems, including Contiki. Unlike Web2Compile-CoT, the IoT-lab does not provide tools for editing, creating and compiling application code.

The predecessor of Web2Compile-CoT, Web2Compile [7] is a Web IDE for developing WSN applications that allowed users to develop code online using the TinyOS operating system [4]. Unlike Web2Compile-CoT, the Web2Compile did not offer integration with any testbed and did not allow the development of code using the Contiki WSN operating system.

Apart from all the presented works (except for Web2Compile), Web2Compile-CoT is focused in the WSN development, presenting tools for network development and simulation. A difference between Web2Compile and Web@Compile-CoT is the use of testbeds. Integrating Web2Compile to testbeds allowed the developers using Web2Compile-CoT to deploy code to real nodes and test it instead of using only simulations.

3   Web2Compile-CoT

Web2Compile-CoT is a Web IDE focused on the development of applications for WSN/CoT. Following a client-server and web-based architecture [14], the architecture of Web2Compile-CoT consists of client computers and a web server.

In the web server an operating system for WSN is hosted, and the respective WSN development environment is configured and ready to run simulations and compilations. The user will have the option of developing applications on the client machine or through the system web page. When opting for the development on the client machine, the user can choose to upload the application development files, as needed.

3.1   Architecture

Regarding to the logical architecture, Web2Compile-CoT is composed of two components (*Execution Manager* and *Interface Manager*), two subsystems (*Compile Manager* and *Testbed Manager*) and two databases (*Platform database* and *Testbed database*) as presented in Fig. 1.

The *Execution Manager* manages the operation of the other components and subsystems and coordinates all the actions performed in the WebIDE. So, it is responsible for performing several tasks. It receives the data sent by the *Interface Manager* and sends these data to the *Compile Manager* or the *Testbed Manager*, based on data received from the user. If the user desires to simulate or

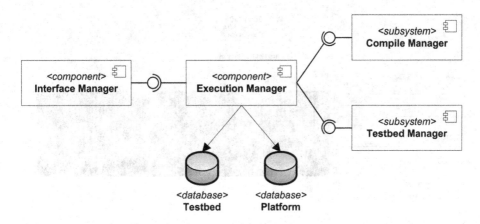

Fig. 1. Web2Compile-CoT Architecture

to generate a sensor image, the *Execution Manager* queries the *Platform Database*, which contains all platform parameters, such as their identifiers, commands to be performed and the output to be delivered. Then it delivers this data to the *Compile Manager* subsystem. Otherwise, the *Execution Manager* queries the *Testbed database* about the testbed details (such as device types, platforms supported) to deploy the code in the testbed. The *Execution Manager* is also responsible for collecting the output from the *Compile Manager* and The *Testbed Manager* subsystems and send it to the*Interface Manager*.

The *Interface Manager* controls the main web page and receives all requests made from this page. It receives the information regarding the type of action to be performed by the platform (simulate, generate a sensor image or deploying to a testbed), the sensor code and the platform type. After gathering this information, it sends them to the *Execution Manager*. This component is also responsible for receiving data from the *Execution Manager* and present it to the user. The Web2Compile interface is shown in Fig. 2.

The *Compile Manager* subsystem is responsible for the compiling process, based on sensor platform. The *Execution Manager* forwards the code and compiling details (such as platform, simulator) to the *Compile Manager* that will compile and generate the sensor images. Then there are two possible actions for this subsystem: (i) deliver the generated sensor image or (ii) simulate based on the code received.

The *Testbed Manager* subsystem manages the connection with external testbeds such as IoT-Lab. This subsystem is responsible for deploying the code in the testbeds and receiving the testbed outputs and send them to The *Execution Manager*.

The *Platform database* stores the sensor platform details, such as commands to compile the code, tools to be used to compile, such as NesC [15] used in TinyOS, and WSAN simulators to be used, such as TOSSIM [15] and Cooja [5].

The *Testbed database* stores the information regarding the testbeds, such as procedures for connecting and deploying the sensor images in the testbeds. Logging procedures and passwords are also stored in this database.

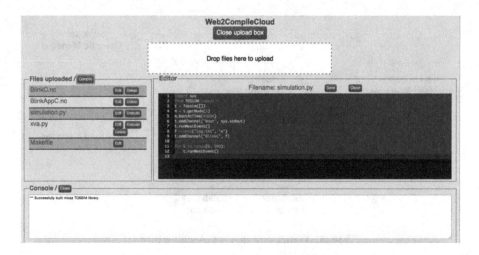

Fig. 2. Web2Compile-CoT interface

All subsystems and components were designed with a modular architecture. Such design approach allows changing, for instance, the *Compile Manager* by just replacing its internal components and databases, provided that the predefined communication APIs are respected. It also allows changing testbeds by just replacing the *Testbed Manager* subsystem as well as the Testbed database.

3.2   Web2Compile-CoT Operation

The client devices have the main function of uploading the code to the dedicated web server. In this first part of the process, as can be seen in Fig. 3, the client can choose among three options after performing the compilation of his application: (i) simulation only; (ii) deployment of the compiled code or (iii) load and run the compiled application on the IoT-lab environment.

After all the files (required to compilation) are uploaded to the compiler located on the web server, and after the required sensor images (compilations) are generated, the application will be ready to be deployed on the sensor hardware, and then it can run.

The operation sequence of Web2Compile-CoT is given as follows: from the web page loaded in his browser, the user can perform the selection of the code files according to the options provided by the Web2Compile-CoT.

When the user opts for simulation, the necessary files should be selected and subsequently, they must be uploaded to the compiler hosted on the server. At compile time, if all the selected files are correctly implemented (no compilation errors detected), there will be success in the compilation. In addition, these files should be available for download, later, by the web page itself, using a download indicator button. On the other hand, if there is no success in the compilation, the user is requested to review the implementation and correct the errors found by the compiler. After this, the user performs again the selection and upload of files to be compiled.

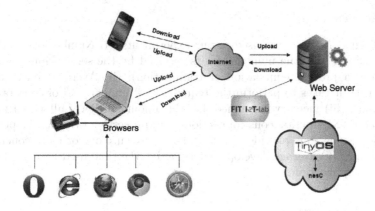

Fig. 3. Web2Compile-CoT operation

When the user opts for the deployment, the files required for the compilation and deployment should also be uploaded. In this case, the selected files will undergo the same process in the case of simulation. However, in this case, with the successful compilation, the image files will be generated (build). These generated files may be downloaded for the client computer, as well as the simulation. They may also be sent to the IoT-Lab for testing on real platforms. The only difference in this case is that the image generated from the compilation can be deployed on the sensor, given the correct hardware configuration on the computer.

4 Experiments

We conducted an evaluation to determine if the proposed WebIDE meets our stated objective presented in Sect. 1, and also to assess the benefits of using our WebIDE when compared to traditional methods to build WSN/CoT applications. The first set of experiments was performed for assessing our tool regarding its scalability. In other words, if the webIDE would still be usable if the number of simultaneous applications increased. The second set of experiments aimed at assessing if the tool is capable of helping students to perform development tasks in classroom. The second set of experiments divided the students of our university laboratory (Labnet [17]) into two groups: (i) a group using the Web2Compile-CoT and (ii) a group using a native installed TinyOS development environment. The students that participated in the experiments had intermediate knowledge of nesC programming for TinyOS.

This section is organized as follows: Sect. 4.1 presents the metrics used to evaluate the tool. Section 4.2 details the technologies used to implement Web2Compile-CoT. Section 4.3 describes the scalability tests. Finally, Sect. 4.4 describes the effectiveness tests.

4.1   Metrics

The following metrics were used in our experiments: (i) Number of simultaneous connections, i.e. the number of hits received by the server simultaneously to perform a process (simulation or compilation); (ii) Average time, i.e. the average time it takes to perform the requests of a number "X" of simultaneous connections; (iii) memory consumed, i.e. the amount of RAM allocated for the execution of "X" simultaneous connections, (iv) processing rate, i.e. the percentage of processing time provided by the CPU to execute one or more concurrent processes and (v) average development time, i.e. the time used by a student to develop an application.

4.2   Implementation

For the development of Web2Compile-CoT system we opted for the Python programming language and the web framework Bottle (bottlepy.org). The tests were performed from a server with Intel i5-2500 k processor, quad-core 3.3 Ghz and 8 GB of RAM.

In the currently developed prototype, the Web2Compile-CoT supports applications developed in nesC programming language [15] for the TinyOS operating system [4] and Contiki [5] operating system. To edit code within the platform, we used the ACE tool [16].

For performing the simulations of WSN/CoT applications, we used TOSSIM [15] and Cooja [5] simulators, two discrete event simulation tools developed, respectively, for the simulation of TinyOS and Contiki applications.

4.3   Scalability Experiments

The scalability experiments were performed in order to verify that the Web2compile-CoT maintained its performance, given an increased amount of simultaneous connections. We varied the number of simultaneous connections on values 1, 3, 5, 7 and 10, and each computer is connected to the server via a switch. For each variation, we performed the following experiments: (i) using only simulation on the Web2Compile-CoT server and (ii) deploying the code on the IoT-lab testbed. We have used the Blink Application, a simple application that blinks a led on a sensor as our default application.

We can see in Fig. 4 the results of the experiments to measure average execution time of simultaneous applications. In Fig. 4, we can observe that when the applications are being executed in the server, the average execution time increases linearly. Overall, the running times with 3, 5, 7 and 10 simultaneous connections had on average a rise of 0.5 s in relation to the first experiment. With this, one can observe that even with a number of simultaneous connections rising, the completion time of the simulation had no significant variation.

When the applications are being executed in the testbed (IoT-lab), the average execution time increases since the code must be uploaded to the server and after that to IoT-lab. The server will then compile the code and generate the

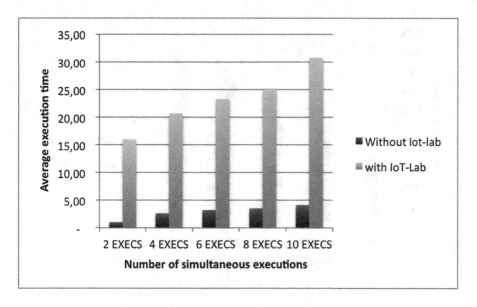

Fig. 4. Average execution time

sensor's image. This image will be uploaded to the testbed. In the testbed, the application will be executed and the result returned to Web2Compile-CoT. All this process increases the execution delay.

Regarding the percentage of CPU utilization over the same number of simultaneous connections, it was observed that CPU usage has increased linearly, as expected, according to the increase in simultaneous connections. It is noteworthy that all the threads were created on the same processor core, so the high utilization rate of the processor would be reduced when refactoring the tool to use parallel programming.

As a result, it was found that with only one connection, the processing rate reached 40% of the capacity of a core and due to the elevation of simultaneous connections, up to 10 connections, the processing rate was 100%, as can be seen in Fig. 5.

When we use the testbed, the amount o CPU utilization is much lower since all the processing goes into the testbed. We therefore conclude that using a testbed increases the possible number of simultaneous connections to be performed. Combining the results of this experiment and the previous one, we can conclude that for classrooms with more than 50 students it is better to use the testbed. Although the average execution time increases using the testbed, more students can execute experiments simultaneously.

Regarding memory consumption, it can be seen that with a single connection only, the RAM consumption reached 10 Mb for running the simulation, both in TOSSIM and Cooja. As the number of applications increases, the RAM consumption increased almost linearly, as expected. The amount of RAM consumed in 10 simultaneous executions reached 165 Mb. The same situation happened both using the testbed and without using it.

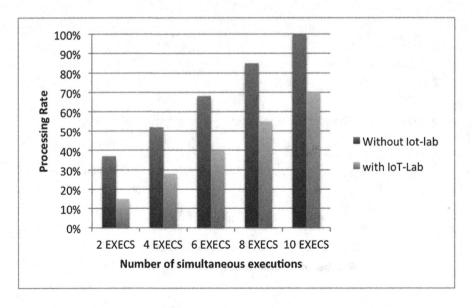

Fig. 5. Processing rate

4.4 Effectiveness Tests

The average development time was assessed through a set of experiments using as subjects 6 students from our laboratory (Labnet [17]). The subjects were assigned the task of developing a set of WSN applications. The subjects were divided into two teams: the first one used Web2Compile-CoT and the second a traditional WSN programming approach. Both teams had the same experience level in programming for TinyOS. The experiment started with the explanation of the applications for both teams. Each team developed four applications: the first four lessons of the official TinyOS tutorial [18]. All applications had the same complexity level regarding the sensing task, but different complexity regarding the specific processing algorithms. The experiment results (Fig. 6) show that the first team successfully completed the development of all applications in much shorter time than the second team. Therefore, the experiment demonstrates the significant reduction in the programming effort achieved with our tool. When compared to manual programming of WSN application, our approach offers advantages since it handles various specific features of WSNs, unburdening the student of: (i) learning low-level details about sensor platforms, (ii) avoiding the need to learn each one of the libraries available for the target platforms and (iii) debugging problems in the development environment installation.

As we can observe, the average time for development of an application using the traditional approach has four hours while the mean time using our approach was two hours and 30 min, demonstrating a significant reduction in classroom time using Web2Compile-CoT.

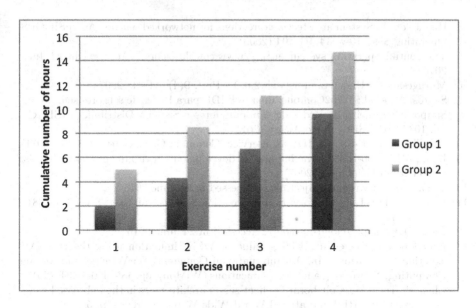

Fig. 6. Effectiveness result

5 Conclusion

This paper presented a proposal for fostering the development of WSN/CoT applications, aiming to encourage new developers and enthusiasts. In Web2Compile-CoT, it is strictly unnecessary to download and install any software regarding the development environment. Also, no complex environment configurations of WSN operating systems are demanded. It is also worth mentioning that our proposal avoids the need for performing the compilation of the code in local IDEs.

Regarding future work, we encourage the study of the following subjects: (i) implement the Remote Flashing, allowing the images (compiled programs) to be loaded on a sensor hardware connected to a USB port of a personal computer through the browser; (ii) integrate other tools provided by IoT-lab in Web2Compile-CoT, as well as other testbeds, and perform more scalability tests, and (iii) create an app for using Web2Compile-CoT, and publish it in Google's web store.

References

1. Aazam, M., et al.: Cloud of things: integrating internet of things and computing and the issues involved. In: International Bhurban Conference on Applied Sciences and Technology (IBCAST), pp. 414–419. IEEE (2014)
2. Culler, D., et al.: Guest editors' introduction: overview of sensor networks. IEEE Comput. **37**(8), 414–419 (2004)
3. Su, W., Alzaghal, M.: Channel propagation measurement and simulation of micaz mote. W. Trans. Comp. **7**(4), 259–264 (2008)

4. Hill, J., et al.: System architecture directions for networked sensors. ACM SIGOPS Operating Syst. Rev. **34**, 93–104 (2000)
5. The contiki operating system. http://www.contiki-os.org/. Accessed in 24 June 2015
6. Murugesan, S.: Understanding web 2.0. IT Prof. **9**(4), 34–41 (2007)
7. Santos, A., et al.: Web2Compile: uma web IDE para Redes de sensores sem fio. In: Simpósio Brasileiro de Redes de Computadores e Sistema Distribuídos (SBRC), pp. 1037–1044. SBC, Porto Alegre (2014)
8. Aho, T., et al.: Designing IDE as a service. Commun. Cloud Softw. **1**, 1–10 (2011)
9. Ryan, W.: Web-based java integrated development environment. BEng thesis, University of Edinburgh (2007)
10. eLua. http://www.eluaproject.net/. Accessed in 24 June 2015
11. Beimborn, D., et al.: Platform as a service (PaaS). Bus. Inf. Syst. Eng. **3**(6), 381–384 (2011)
12. Cloud IDE. http://cloud-ide.com/. Accessed in 24 June 2015
13. Papadopoulos, G., et al.: Adding value to WSN simulation using the IoT-LAB experimental platform. In: 9th International Conference on Wireless and Mobile Computing, Networking and Communications (WiMob), pp. 485–490. IEEE (2013)
14. Chen, P., Teng, W.: Collaborative client-server architectures in the web-based viewing scheme. In: 11th International World Wide Web Conference, p. 5 (2002)
15. David, G., et al.: Nesc 1.1 language reference manual. Technical report (2003). http://nescc.sourceforge.net/papers/nesc-ref.pdf
16. Ace: The High Performance Code Editor for the Web. http://ace.c9.io/. Accessed in 24 June 2015
17. Labnet. http://www.labnet.nce.ufrj.br/. Accessed in June 24 2015
18. TinyOS Tutorials. http://tinyos.stanford.edu/tinyos-wiki/index.php/TinyOS_Tutorials/. Accessed in 24 June 2015

Fuzzy Logic Based Energy Aware VM Consolidation

Mohammad Alaul Haque Monil[(⊠)] and Rashedur M. Rahman

Electrical and Computer Engineering Department, North South University,
Dhaka, Bangladesh
monil01@gmail.com, rashedur.rahman@northsouth.edu

Abstract. Global need of computing is growing day by day and as a result
cloud based services are getting more prominent for its pay-as-you-go modality.
However, cloud based datacenters consume considerable amount of energy
which draws negative attention. To sustain the growth of cloud computing,
energy consumption is now a major concern for cloud based datacenters. To
overcome this problem, cloud computing algorithm should be efficient enough to
keep energy consumption low and at the same time provide desired QoS. Virtual
machine consolidation is one such technique to ensure energy-QoS balance. In
this research, we explored Fuzzy logic and heuristic based virtual machine
consolidation approach to achieve energy-QoS balance. Fuzzy VM selection
method has been proposed to select VM from an overloaded host. Additionally,
we incorporated migration control in Fuzzy VM selection method. We have used
CloudSim toolkit to simulate our experiment and evaluate the performance of the
proposed algorithm on real-world work load traces of PlanetLab VMs. Simulation results demonstrate that the proposed method provides best performance in
all performance metrics while consuming least energy.

1 Introduction

Cloud computing services are getting more popular for its scalability, reliability and
pay-as-you-go model. Techno-giants have already started providing cloud services and
IT companies are now moving from traditional CAPEX model (buy the dedicated
hardware and depreciate it over a period of time) to the OPEX model (use a shared
cloud infrastructure and pay as one uses it). To cope up with the ever increasing need of
computing, cloud service providing companies are now using warehouse sized datacenters to meet user demand which incurs considerable amount of energy. At the
beginning of this cloud computing era, cloud service providers were focused mainly on
catering the computing demand that leads to expansion of cloud infrastructures; hence
energy consumption. For these reasons, energy consumption by data centers worldwide
has risen by 56 % from 2005 to 2010, and in 2010 is accounted to be between 1.1 %
and 1.5 % of the total electricity use. Moreover, carbon dioxide emissions of the ICT
industry are currently estimated to be 2 % of the global emissions which is equivalent
to the emissions of the aviation industry [4].

VM Consolidation is one of the techniques which draws researchers' attention and
is an active field of research in recent time. VM consolidation method makes the

© Springer International Publishing Switzerland 2015
G. Di Fatta et al. (Eds.): IDCS 2015, LNCS 9258, pp. 31–38, 2015.
DOI: 10.1007/978-3-319-23237-9_4

underutilized servers shut-down by increasing the utilization of active datacenters. As we know that inactive datacenter or datacenter in sleep mode causes minimal energy and in this way energy consumption can be reduced considerably. However, to achieve this outcome, we need to consolidate different VM in one server and migrate VMs from datacenter to datacenter which may lead to SLA violation. So, algorithms must be designed in such a way that not only reduces power consumption but also serves desired QoS (such as SLA).

2   Related Works

VM consolidation algorithm needs to be designed in such a way that there will be minimum energy consumption, minimum violation of SLA, efficient VM migration and minimum number active hosts in a given time. Considerable number of researches has been conducted for VM consolidation using various methods based on heuristics.

In [1, 2, 4], Beloglazov et al. proposed heuristic based approach to deduce thresholds thorough different statistical measures. VM Consolidation problem is divided into sub-problems and algorithms for each sub-problem had been designed. The sub-problems are: (i) Under load detection, (ii) Overload detection, (iii) VM selection and, (iv) VM placement. Heuristic based algorithms are designed for each sub-problems and designed in such a way that they can adapt and keep their threshold changing based on different scenario in different time so that they can still provide the functionality and consolidation decision in changed environment. This adaption process allows the system to be dynamic. These algorithms were implemented in CloudSim developed by Clouds lab in the University of Melbourne. References [5, 6] describe CloudSim which provides various functionalities of a cloud environment and facilitates cloud simulation. References [1, 2, 4] have also used CloudSim for simulation. The main components of CloudSim are datacenter, Virtual Machine (VM) and cloudlet. Cloudlet can be real data from real cloud. The simulator creates datacenter, Virtual Machine and cloudlet on the run based on the defined parameters. When the simulation starts, virtual machines are placed in the datacenter for processing. Sub problems (i–iv) are already developed in CloudSim. To develop further, one needs to create new class to develop new methods and test it. In [7, 8] we worked with basic VM selection algorithm and introduced migration control in the built in CloudSim VM selection methods. Farahnakian et al. [9] used the ant colony system to deduce a near-optimal VM placement solution based on the specified objective function. In [3] VM consolidation with migration control is introduced. Here VMs with steady usage are not migrated and not steady VMs are migrated to ensure better performance, the migrations are triggered and done by heuristic approaches. Main advantages of heuristics are that a static and acceptable performance could be achieved with very less amount of errors. Sheng et al. [11] designed a prediction method based on Bayes model to predict the mean load over a long-term time interval and also the mean load in consecutive future time intervals. Prevost et al. [10] introduced a framework combining load demand prediction and stochastic state transition models. They used neural network and autoregressive linear prediction algorithms to forecast loads in cloud data center applications.

3 Proposed Method

In this work we have designed Fuzzy VM Selection with migration control algorithm and VM placement and underload detection are adjusted. However, before going in detail, CloudSim overview of VM consolidation is introduced. The algorithm below portrays the basic VM consolidation approach designed in CloudSim.

Algorithm 1. VM consolidation in CloudSim

1. *Input number of hosts;*
2. *Interface with real cloud data;*
3. *VM created and assigned to hosts;*
4. *Cloudlet created and assigned to VMs;*
5. *for every specified time interval*
6.   *Execute Underload detection;*
7.   *Identify overloaded host through overload detection.*
8.   *VM is selected for migration from overloaded host.*
9.   *VM is placed in available datacenters.*
10.   *Preserve history and calculate QoS*
11. *end*
12. *Simulation ended and provide Energy consumption and other QoS value*

Algorithm 1 provides a basic flow of VM consolidation in CloudSim. At first the hosts are created, then the real cloud data is taken as input. Based on the real data, VMs and cloudlets are created. Then VMs are assigned to hosts and cloudlets are assigned to VMs. Based on dynamic consolidation technique, status is checked for every scheduled interval. For every scheduled interval, underload detection algorithm is executed and less utilized hosts are put into sleeping mode by transferring all VM to other active VMs. Then overload detection is executed, and overloaded hosts are identified. At later steps, VM is selected from the overloaded hosts to migrate. Then those VMs are placed in available hosts or if needed hosts are switched on from sleeping mode. After each iteration, a log is kept to calculate energy consumption and QoS. At the end of the simulation energy consumption and QoS is shown. In the next section our proposed methods are discussed.

3.1 Fuzzy VM Selection with Migration Control

Fuzzy technique is an attractive approach to handle uncertain, imprecise, or un-modeled data in solving control and intelligent decision-making problems. Different VM selection methods offer different advantages. Therefore, if we want to generate a method which will have the benefits of all selection methods, then we can combine them together and based on the merit of the metric a fuzzy output value will be generated and our objective will be fulfilled. A set of rules of inference can be devised to generate result. So, fuzzy logic is an ideal tool for this work. It will consider all the options and depending on those options a fuzzy value will be generated based on the predetermined rules of inference. To develop the fuzzy VM selection method, we have selected three distinguished methods as metric and each of them offers some advantages over others and different researches have already proven them. The following subsections will be focusing on the metrics we will be using as inputs to our fuzzy systems, member ship functions generated, inference rules and algorithms for computation.

(1) Minimum migration Time: Minimum Migration time policy selects the VM which can be migrated within minimum time limit [2, 4]. The migration time is limited by the memory the VM is using and the bandwidth and migration control is applied. At any moment t, the MMT with Migration Control policy finds VM x that will be selected for migration by the following formula:

$$x \in V_h | \forall y \in V_h, \frac{RAM(x)}{NET_h} \leq \frac{RAM(y)}{NET_h} \tag{1}$$

This policy gives us the lowest SLA from all the VM selection models. So this will be considered as one input of the fuzzy system.

(2) Correlation: This method works based on the idea that the higher the correlation between the resource usage by applications running on an oversubscribed server, the higher the probability of server being overloaded [4]. Basically this instructs that higher correlation of CPU usage of one VM with other VM should be migrated. Migration control is applied with maximum correlation method to identify the migratable VM.

Let there are n numbers of VMs and $X_1, X_2...X_n$ is the CPU usage of n VMs which are under consideration for migration. Let Y be the VM for which we want to determine the maximum correlation with i^{th} VM. The augmented matrix for the rest is denoted by X and the $(n-1)x1$ vectored of Y is expressed by y.

$$X = \begin{bmatrix} 1 & x_{1,1} & \cdots & \cdots & x_{1,n-1} \\ \vdots & \vdots & \vdots & \vdots & \vdots \\ \vdots & \vdots & \vdots & \vdots & \vdots \\ 1 & x_{n-1,1} & \cdots & \cdots & x_{n-1,n-1} \end{bmatrix} \quad y = \begin{bmatrix} y_1 \\ \vdots \\ \vdots \\ y_n \end{bmatrix} \tag{2}$$

A vector of predicted value is denoted by $\hat{y}$.

$$\hat{y} = Xbb = (X^T X)^{-1} X^T y \tag{3}$$

Having found the predicted value the correlation coefficient is:

$$R_{Y,X_1,...X_{n-1}}^2 = \frac{\sum_{i=1}^n (y_i - m_y)^2 (\hat{y}_i - m_{\hat{y}})^2}{\sum_{i=1}^n (y_i - m_y)^2 \sum_{i=1}^n (\hat{y}_i - m_{\hat{y}})^2} \tag{4}$$

This is how correlation can be calculated.

(3) Migration control metric for steady resource consuming VM: It has been proven that migration control provides better result in energy aware VM consolidation. Besides, this approach saves the unwanted traffic load [3]. Migration control can be done in various ways. We can stop migrating the high CPU using VMs or we can restrict steady resource consuming VM from migration. In this work we will take steady resource consumption as a non migration factor because when a VM consumes

almost constant resource, it means it will be the least possible VM to make this host overloaded. We have used standard deviation as a calculation of migration control.

Let, there are two VMs x and y in host h and V_h be the set of VMs. $CPU_u(x_t)$ is the CPU utilization of time t, which is current time. $CPU_u(x_{t-1})$, $CPU_u(x_{t-2})$ ..... $CPU_u(x_{t-n})$ are the CPU utilization of up to previous n number time frames when overload detection algorithm was activated. So migration control parameter can be given by 5. Here $CPU_{average}$ means average CPU utilization for last n cycles.

$$stdev = \sqrt{\frac{1}{n}\sum_{1}^{n}\left(CPU_i - CPU_{average}\right)^2} \tag{5}$$

(4) Fuzzy Membership function: A FIS (Fuzzy Inference System) is developed to provide fuzzy VM selection decision using three metrics we discussed above as input. Member ship function needs to be defined to develop the FIS. We are using total 4 linguistic variables including VM selection as output. We have used trapezoidal membership function. Range of these membership functions is chosen from the simulation from Real cloud data of PlanetLab. In order to do so, we have run the simulation and collected data of all these variables and proportioned to decide the range. Membership functions of the linguistic variables are given below:

- RAM: T(RAM) = {Low, Medium, High}
- Correlation: T(Correlation) = {Low, Medium, High}
- Standard Deviation: T(Stdev) = {Low, Medium, High}
- VM selection: T(Vmselection) = {Low, Medium, High, Very High}

(5) Fuzzy Inference Rule: Fuzzy inference rules are generated from the given linguistic variables. We have given equal weight on the variables to influence the VM selection value. If RAM is low it gets high priority as it makes the migration faster. If correlation is high then it gets high priority in migration as the higher the correlation is, the higher the probability of host being overloaded. Finally, if standard deviation is high then it will get priority in migration compared to its steady state counterparts.

(6) Fuzzy VM selection with migration control: Combination of Fuzzy VM selection method and migration control is given in 6 & 7. These equations indicate that a VM will be nominated for migration if it produces lower CPU usage value than the migration control threshold and posses highest fuzzy value among the lower migration control value group. If all VMs of an overloaded host produce more CPU usage value than the migration control threshold, then the highest fuzzy output producing VM will be migrated. Migration control is calculated by CPU usage of last n cycle. The equations are as follows:

$$x \in V_h | \forall y \in V_h, \quad Fuzzy\ Output(x) \geq Fuzzy\ Output(y)$$

Only if;

$$\frac{[CPU_u(x_t) + CPU_u(x_{t-1}) + CPU_u(x_{t-2}) + \ldots CPU_u(x_{t-n})]}{(n+1)} < CPU_{thresold} \tag{6}$$

If for every VM vm,

$$\frac{[CPU_u(vm_t) + CPU_u(vmx_{t-1}) + \ldots + CPU_u(vm_{t-n})]}{(n+1)} \geq CPU_{thresold}$$

Then;

$$x \in V_h | \forall y \in V_h, \quad Fuzzy\ Output(x) \geq Fuzzy\ Output(y) \tag{7}$$

4   Experimental Result

We have implemented our algorithms in CloudSim 3.0.3 to evaluate the performance of our proposed method. We have considered 800 heterogeneous physical nodes, half of which are HP ProLiant G4 and the rest are HP ProLiant G5 servers. Energy consumption is calculated based on the HP ProLiant G4 and HP ProLiant G5. CPU usage and power consumption are calculated based on the data provided in Table 1. These servers are assigned with 1860 MIPS (Million Instructions Per Second) and 2660 MIPS for each core of G4 and G5 servers. Network bandwidth is considered as 1 GB/s. The VMs which were created were single core. VM were assigned 4 types. High-CPU Medium Instance (2500 MIPS, 0.85 GB); Extra Large Instance (2000 MIPS, 3.75 GB); Small Instance (1000 MIPS, 1.7 GB); and Micro Instance (500 MIPS, 613 MB) [4]. We have used real world work load data provided as part of CoMon project, a monitoring infrastructure for PlanetLab. This data are collected from more than thousand VMS of from server located more than 500 different locations. These real world traces contain VM utilization files every 5 min. Data of 10 days of 2011 has been used in this experiment. Based on two metrics the performance of the proposed method is compared.

(1) Energy Consumption (kWh): Energy consumption is computed taking into account all hosts throughout the simulation time and by mapping CPU and energy consumption from the Table 1.
(2) SLAV: Service level agreement violation, SLAV, comes from the product of overload time fraction (OTF) and performance degradation due to migration (PDM), i.e. SLAV = OTF*PDM.

Table 1. Power Consumption for different level of utilization

Machine Type	Power consumption based on CPU utilization					
	0 %	20 %	40 %	60 %	80 %	100 %
HP G4 (Watt)	86	92.6	99	106	112	117
HP G5 (Watt)	93.7	101	110	121	129	135

In CloudSim, there are five built in Overload detection algorithms (IQR, LR, LRR, MAD and THR) and three built in VM selection (MC, MMT, RS) methods. So in combination there are 15 methods (IQR_MC, IQR_MMT, IQR_RS, LR_MC, LR_MMT, LR_RS, LRR_MC, LRR_MMT, LRR_RS, MAD_MC, MAD_MMT, MAD_RS, THR_MC, THR_MMT, THR_RS) which will be compared to our proposed MSMD_FS method based on aforementioned performance metrics. Based on the result for 10 days Fig. 1 Box graphs have been prepared to compare the results. Metric wise result is given below:

(1) Energy Consumption: Basic target of this research is to design a VM consol-idation algorithm so that the energy consumption is reduced. By comparing the pro-posed and existing methods in the first graph of Fig. 1, it is found that energy consumption is significantly reduced in Proposed (MMSD_FS) method. Minimum energy consumption by proposed method is 102 Kwh where the minimum of all other methods is 112 Kwh, 8.5 % reduction. If we consider average value, MMSD_FS consumed 136.5 Kwh and all other method consumed 169 Kwh on average resulting 19 % energy saving. So by this we can infer that the basic objective of this research is achieved by saving energy consumption.

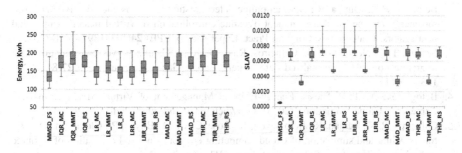

Fig. 1. Energy and SLAV is shown in these box graphs. MMSD_FS is the fuzzy VM selection method, which is the first one in the both chart and rest are the built in algorithms of CloudSim.

(2) SLA Violation (SLAV): SLA violation is one of the key indicators of QoS. SLA violation is calculated by keeping two scenarios into consideration, (1) if any VM got overloaded, and (2) the SLA violation incurred while migration. With a method having low SLA violation indicates ensuring users the desired QoS. From Fig. 1, it is clearly visible that SLA violation is considerably decreased. Minimum SLAV by proposed method is 0.0004 % whereas the minimum of all other method is 0.00279 %, resulting 84 % reduction. If we consider average value, MMSD_FS incurred 0.0005 % SLAV and all other methods incurred 0.00617 % on an average, resulting 91 % reduction in SLA violation.

From the performance metrics it can be inferred that the proposed method out-performs all other methods.

5 Conclusion

In this paper we have devised algorithm for fuzzy VM selection method and introduced migration control in the selection method. Fuzzy VM selection methods take intelligent decision to select a VM to be migrated from one host to other. After simulation and making comparison against existing methods, it has been found that the proposed method outperformed other previous methods in both perspectives, i.e., more energy saving and less SLA violation. Therefore, it can be inferred that the objective, energy-SLA trade off has been achieved in this work in an efficient manner. As a future work we have plan to improve the default VM placement and underload detection algorithm built in CloudSim to achieve more energy saving and less SLA violation.

References

1. Beloglazov, A., Abawajy, J., Buyya, R.: Energy-aware resource allocation heuristics for efficient management of data centers for Cloud computing. Future Gener. Comput. Syst. (FGCS) **28**(5), 755–768 (2011)
2. Beloglazov, A., Buyya, R.: Optimal online deterministic algorithms and adaptive heuristics for energy and performance efficient dynamic consolidation of virtual machines in Cloud data centers. Concurrency Comput. Pract. Experience (CCPE) **24**(13), 1397–1420 (2012)
3. Ferreto, T.C., Netto, M.A.S., Calheiros, R.N., De Rose, C.A.F.: Server consolidation with migration control for virtualized data centers. Future Gener. Comput. Syst. **27**(8), 1027–1034 (2011)
4. Beloglazov, A.: PhD Thesis: Energy-Efficient Management of Virtual Machines in Data Centers for Cloud Computing (2013). http://beloglazov.info/thesis.pdf
5. Calheiros, R.N., Ranjan, R., Beloglazov, A., Rose, C.A.F.D., Buyya, R.: CloudSim: a toolkit for modeling and simulation of Cloud computing environments and evaluation of resource provisioning algorithms. Softw. Pract. Exp. **41**(1), 23–50 (2011)
6. CloudSim link. http://code.google.com/p/CloudSim/
7. Monil, M.A.H., Qasim, R., Rahman, R.M.: Incorporating migration control in VM selection strategies to enhance performance. IJWA **6**, 135–151 (2014)
8. Monil, M.A.H., Qasim, R., Rahman, R.M.: Energy-aware VM consolidation approach using combination of heuristics and migration control. In: ICDIM 2014, pp. 74–79 (2014)
9. Farahnakian, F., Ashraf, A., Liljeberg, P., Pahikkala, T., Plosila, J., Porres, I., Tenhunen, H.: Energy-aware dynamic VM consolidation in cloud data centers using ant colony system. In: 2014 IEEE 7th International Conference on Cloud Computing (CLOUD), pp. 104–111 (2014)
10. Prevost, J., Nagothu, K., Kelley, B., Jamshidi, M.: Prediction of cloud data center networks loads using stochastic and neural models. In: Proceedings of the IEEE System of Systems Engineering (SoSE) Conference, pp. 276–281, 27-30 2011
11. Di, S., Kondo, D., Cirne, W.: Host load prediction in a Google compute cloud with a Bayesian model. In: Proceedings of the International Conference for High Performance Computing, Networking, Storage and Analysis (SC), Salt Lake City, UT, 10–16 November 2012

Autonomic and Cognitive Architectures for the Internet of Things

Claudio Savaglio$^{(\boxtimes)}$ and Giancarlo Fortino

DIMES, Università della Calabria, Via P. Bucci, cubo 41C,
87036 Rende (CS), Italy
csavaglio@dimes.unical.it, g.fortino@unical.it

Abstract. Internet of Things promises to be an innovative scenario in which the user experience will be enriched by new cyber-physical services and content, shared by multiple actors (things, places, people) with an higher frequency and quality of the current ones. The countless challenges and opportunities that the development of such an ecosystem entails require a marked intervention on the current Internet architectural frameworks and models, primarily as regards the management function. Pointing in this direction, the most relevant autonomic and cognitive architectures for the Internet of Things have been surveyed and compared.

Keywords: Internet of things · Autonomic computing · Cognitive computing · Management architectures

1 Introduction

The advent of Internet and subsequently of the Web represented the greatest technological revolution of the last decades. The next disruptive technology is expected to be provided by the full realization of a visionary scenario, defined in 1990 as the "Internet of Things" (IoT) [1]. In this vision men and machines will achieve an unprecedented level of interaction and integration in cyber-physical systems. Billions of networked devices, including conventional computers, smart objects, wireless sensors, actuators and RFID-based devices, will be scattered in the physical world and will be seamlessly cooperating in cyberspace. The transition from the current Internet toward a global cyber-physical network where the machines will be orders of magnitude more numerous than individuals is already in place. To cope with heterogeneous and complex cyber-physical systems, more advanced network architectures need to be devised and developed, especially in relation to the orchestration and the management functionalities, which are deeply different from the traditional ones adopted in the Internet.

The purpose of this work is to review the current trends in IoT management architectures, inspecting the underlying motivations and framing the current state-of-the-art of the most relevant autonomic and cognitive architectures.

© Springer International Publishing Switzerland 2015
G. Di Fatta et al. (Eds.): IDCS 2015, LNCS 9258, pp. 39–47, 2015.
DOI: 10.1007/978-3-319-23237-9_5

The rest of the paper is structured as follows. Section 2 provides an overview of the main concepts of Autonomic Computing and Cognitive Networks. Section 3 presents a survey of the main IoT Architectures that implement the autonomic/cognitive concepts, which are then compared in Sect. 4. Finally, Sect. 5 provides some conclusions.

2   Current Trends

The growth of the Internet and successively of the Web has brought innovation in almost any domain, ranging from economics to sociology and politics, from education and entertainment to the labor market. The transition from an academic network toward a world-wide commercial platform imposed to strengthen the original narrow waist model with several ad-hoc patches, seamlessly added, for security, mobility, multimedia, determinism, timing abstraction, quality of service, etc. These critical issues, so far individually addressed with tailor-made solutions, recur together and are magnified within the IoT scenario. In fact, the IoT is a loosely coupled, decentralized, dynamic system in which billions (even trillions) of everyday objects are endowed with smartness, in order to increase their own capacities, seamlessly communicate and cooperate despite their physical/functional heterogeneity. Such kind of entities, defined Smart Objects (SOs), represent the IoT building blocks [2] and they play a crucial role, becoming active participants in business, logistics, information and social processes. In order to face such an increasing complexity, viable solutions have been identified in those inspired by biological organisms, which represent the highest form of complex systems. In particular, recent research trends have laid in the spotlights two different but complementary paradigms, the autonomic computing and the cognitive network.

2.1   Autonomic Computing

Natural self-governing systems are defined "autonomic"when the definition of policies and rules are sufficient to guide the self-management process. For example, the human autonomic nervous system is able to free our consciousness from managing major and minor, inter-connected and complex, vital functions. In computer science, the attribute autonomic refers to computing systems that can manage themselves according to high-level objectives initially defined by the administrator [3]. From an architectural point of view, instead, autonomic systems may be considered as interactive collections of autonomic elements, each of which performs its objectives and interactions following their own policies and the system ones. Since autonomic elements have complex life-cycles, it is required that they expose autonomy, proactivity, and goal-directed interactivity with the environment: these are precisely the agent-oriented [4] architectural concepts. The depth analysis of history and of features of the Autonomic Computing falls outside the scope of the article; anyway, the four main aspects that characterize autonomic systems or elements are:

- self-configuration, which enables system and its components to automatically and seamlessly configure themselves following high-level policies, despite vendors' specifics, technological heterogeneity and low-level details;
- self-optimization, which guides system to continually seek opportunities for improving performance, without human intervention of tuning;
- self-protection, which automates system defense and prevents from system failures due to malicious attacks;
- self-healing, which consists in the automatic detection, diagnosis and repairing of system defections, both hardware and software.

The term "self-*" hence refers to a cognitive system or element which exposes all such features. In a complex scenario such as IoT, the design of systems that prescind from a constant human monitoring and the adoption of techniques that automatize the management of the nodes is more than ever necessary. For these reasons, the autonomic computing principles have inspired the design of numerous architectures and frameworks, as discussed in Sect. 3.

2.2 Cognitive Networks

Cognitive Networks [5] have been originally considered a self-* kind of systems since they autonomously make use of the information gained from the experience of each node to improve the overall network and user performance. In details, each node is involved in a loop, defined cognition loop, which oversees

- the perception of the current network conditions,
- the planning of actions according to both input and policies,
- the decision between the available solutions,
- the actuation of the plan and
- the learning from the consequence of the actions.

Context-awareness and self-awareness are essential requirements to realize the cognition loop, since it is required that every node should have knowledge about itself, its functionalities and its interfaces to the outside. Just like the autonomic systems, cognitive networks have been conceived to cope with the increasing network complexity but relying as little as possible on human intervention. Hence, in analogy with the autonomic system's architecture, cognitive networks aggregate cognitive agents, which are entities with reasoning capabilities that are able to cooperate, to act selfishly or to do both. Since the need of cognition is spread among the system components and layers, and it is not only limited to the management one, the cognitive networks have given rise to an independent line of research, which often exploits the Multi-Agent Systems (MAS) [4] as enabling paradigm. Examples of IoT cognitive frameworks are discussed in Sect. 3.

3 Autonomic and Cognitive IoT Architectures

The growing complexity of the IoT scenario and of its composing devices emphasizes the need of autonomic and cognitive approaches for the system design, especially for the management aspects, as argued in the previous Section. This perspective is often confirmed in the literature: agents are widely used as enabling cognitive technology and paradigm, while the IBM autonomic model represents the cornerstone for a significant research direction. However, at the best of our knowledge, there are few fully-realized architectures in which such principles find a concrete implementation. Among these, interesting contributions can be found in Cascadas, Focale, Inox, and I-Core.

Cascadas [6] (Component-ware for Autonomic Situation-aware Communications, and Dynamically Adaptable Services) proposes a general purpose toolkit in which the autonomic element (AE) model stands out: Cascadas AE is conceived around the biological notion of organ. Its key principles refer to situation awareness, semantic self organization, scalability and modularity, and are federated in a sound framework with the aim of providing adaptive, composite and situated communication intensive services. Each Cascadas AE is mainly structured in 5 parts: (i) a specific part, which contains plans, desires, achievable goals that are specific of each AE; (ii) a self-model, which represents the AE lifecycle as an automa and semantically defines the possible states and their associated transitions; every AE is aware of its own and of the other AEs' self-models, so it acts at the best of its possibilities and knowledge; (iii) a reasoning engine, which elaborates the external stimulus, interacts with the self-model and organizes appropriate reactions; (iv) a facilitator, which on the basis of the indications coming from the reasoning engine notifies context changes to the self-model; (v) a message handler, which exploits a shared communication interface and a conventional passing messages mechanism in order to link the AE with the other framework components. Accomplishing the aforementioned high-level reference model allows the generation of a fully interoperable and reactive AE, which is able to overcome data heterogeneity through a plugin-based formats conversion.

Focale [7] (Foundation, Observation, Comparison, Action, and Learning Environment) is an autonomic network-oriented architecture which seamlessly manages and integrates heterogeneous and distributed computing resources. One of the features that immediately characterize Focale is the presence of three levels of non-static control loops (namely, an inner loop, an adaptation loop and an outer loop), which allows the cohabitation of multiple policy languages and data formats, context awareness and uniform but dynamic orchestration functionalities. Managed resources, ranging from simple network element to complex systems, are represented as Autonomic Computing Elements (ACEs) and are connected by an enterprise service bus (ESB) that supports simple as well as semantic queries and communication interfaces. Within every ACEs, one could recognize the following components: (i) an Observe component, which combine information/data models and ontologies to translate vendor-specific data in a neutral form, solving the issue regarding the heterogeneity of programming models and data representation (ii) a Compare element, which determines the current state of the ACE and proactively dispose appropriate actions within the adaptive control loops until a desired state is reached (iii) a Context-aware/Policy Server component, which controls that ACEs actions follow the business goals and the established objects (iv) a Learning and Reasoning engine, exploiting ontologies, machine learning and a dynamic knowledge base to analyze the input data and plan the future actions, without the awareness of the other ACEs internal models.

Inox [8] is a strongly IoT-oriented platform, that poses in the spotlight the combination of interconnected smart objects, sensor networks, services becoming from networks of traditional computer unconventional devices. Concepts as autonomic managements, entity virtualization and federation, extended connectivity, scalability and adaptability are crucial, as results analyzing the Inox multi-layered architectures, structured as follows: (i) the hardware layer, which contains the physical entities like sensors, intelligent and dumb things, smart objects and servers, together with the devices that provide network interconnectivity through IP-based protocols, enhanced M2M mechanisms, ZigBee, 6LoWPAN, CoAP, etc. (ii) the platform layer, which cope the communication heterogeneity through common protocols and resource access API and cope the technological heterogeneity exploiting objects, networking and computational resources virtualization techniques; autonomic devices management and service orchestration functionalities are embedded at this level, aiming at a better interoperability, scalability, monitoring and discovery (iii) the service layer, containing the services themselves and the related API needed to access the other systems elements. A such structured architecture allows Inox to evolve from a conventional centralized and fixed computing/networking model towards a dynamic architecture, more suitable for the highly complex IoT context.

I-Core [9] is a cognitive management framework for the IoT which addresses the heterogeneity of objects and the need for resilience in very large scenarios. Most of the I-Core concepts have been implemented following the indications provided by the IoT-A (Internet of Thing- Architecture) [10], that is an organic collection of architectures, reference models and guidelines which provides a number of means (models, views, perspectives, best practices, etc.) that can be used to derive a concrete IoT architecture. The I-Core building blocks refer to four main concepts: virtualization, composition, cognition and proximity. Virtualization is the process that links every real world object (RWO) with a digital always-on alter ego, called virtual object (VO). VOs reflect RWOs status and capabilities, and can be dynamically created, destroyed or changed. Moreover, VOs can be aggregated in more sophisticated entities, called composite virtual objects (CVOs), that are cognitive mashup of semantically interoperable VOs (and their offered services) aiming at rendering services in accordance with both the application and user requirements. VOs and CVOs represent the cornerstone for the first two levels of the I-Core architecture, the VO Level and the CVO Level. At the third and last level, the Service one, mechanisms related to User Characterization, Situation Awareness (situation detection, recognition, classification) and Intent Recognition support the Service Request Analysis, providing the input parameters for the composition processes of CVO Level. Cognition spreads in all the three aforementioned architectural levels, under different forms (optimization techniques, learning mechanism, ontology, etc.). In detail, at VO Level cognition needs for VOs self-management and self-configuration in order to handle data flows, to optimize resources, to monitor relevant RWOs. At CVO Level, cognition needs for meeting the application requirements and the

VOs/CVOs capabilities, choosing between VOs/CVOs candidates, recognizing already faced scenarios (pattern recognition and machine learning techniques) and reuse or adapt already built solutions. Finally, at Service Level cognition is used as semantic reasoning in order to capture the application requirements, translate them into appropriate request service format and so guide the selection process at the lower levels. The proximity concept instead expresses the level of relatedness/usefulness between any IoT user/application and any object in order to achieve more and more automation and scalability in the cognitive selection of VOs/CVOs. Recently, I-Core has been integrated with another IoT platform, BUTLER [11], with the objective of increasing the interconnectivity between heterogeneous SOs and encouraging the creation of dynamic and on-demand IoT applications.

Table 1. Comparison of architectures

MC	Features	Cascadas	Focale	Inox	I-Core
MC1	Clean Slate or Evolutionary Approach	Clean Slate	Evolutionary	Evolutionary	Evolutionary
	General Purpose or Network Oriented	General Purpose	Network Oriented	General Purpose	General Purpose
	Management of Future Objects	yes	yes	yes	yes
MC2	Data Abstraction Techniques	plug-in	model-based translation	shared interfaces	XML and RDF
	Business/Policy Management	yes	yes	yes	yes
	Entity Virtualization	no	no	at Platform layer	VOs and CVOs
MC3	Context Awareness	yes	yes	yes	yes
	Dynamic KB	yes	yes	no	yes
	Control Loops	adaptative	multi-adaptative	adaptative	adaptative
	Ontology and Semantic	yes	yes	no	yes
	State Machine Mode	published	unpublished	no	no
	Self-X Properties*	SO, SA, SP, SH, SC	SA, SG	SM, SH, SO, SP, SA, SC	SH, SP, SO, ST
	Adaptability	reactive	proactive	reactive	reactive
MC4	System Programming Model	Agent-based	Component-based	Component-based	Agent-based
	Communication Paradigm	message passing	ECB bus	IP-based	message passing, publish-subscribe
	API Support	no	no	yes	yes

*SA=Self-Adaptation,   SC=Self-Configuration,   SG=Self-Governance,   SH=Self-Healing, SM=Self-Monitoring, SO= Self-Organization, SP=Self-Protection, ST=Self-Optimization

4   Comparison

In the previous Section four architectures have briefly been described, which share common features and differ in others. In order to compare them, the following set of macro criteria (MC) has been established, drawing inspiration from comparisons criteria shown in other works [12–14].

- MC1-Architectural Approach: this criterion deals with the high level architectural choices. In particular, each architecture may have a general purpose or may be network oriented, on the basis of the goals (services lifetime or specific tasks) and the composing elements (e.g. sensors, smart/dumb things, etc., or traditional network devices) that are involved. The design may follow a clean slate or an evolutionary approach: in the first case, conventional design choices are strongly reviewed or totally dropped in place of new and innovative ideas; in the latter, the current models and practices are maintained but updated with new technological trends. Finally, frameworks may be naturally prone to support element evolution, such as the rapid prototyping of SOs and services make hard to foresee what to expect.
- MC2-Abstraction Level: abstraction expedients are required in order to embed within the frameworks devices and services with heterogeneous hardware and software features, such as model, data formalism, etc. Moreover, also real world objects need to be integrated and cooperate in the context of the cyber-physical services. In this direction, virtualization techniques become crucial to provide technology independence and to support entities federation. At lower level, instead, common formalisms and shared standards need to be defined to abstract the heterogeneous data.
- MC3-Management Features: in order to achieve a fully realized IoT scenario, the management function should be as much as possible distributed among the single components as well as close to the autonomic and cognitive principles. In order to reach these goals it is common to use ontologies, knowledge bases, semantic matchers, static or adaptive control loops and other components. These expedients, together with policies and context awareness techniques, aim at minimizing the human operator interventions, making the system elements autonomic and proactive.
- MC4-Implementative Features: this criterion considers the paradigms and the strategy adopted in order to make the frameworks work. In fact, the programming model, the communication mechanisms, the presence of API support represent a non exhaustive but useful set of elements to compare the aforementioned architectures.

On the basis of these four MCs, Cascadas, Focale, Inox, I-Core have been compared as shown in Table 1. Two main considerations arise. First, I-Core can be considered the most complete and ready-to-use framework and probably the most suitable for a "cooperating smart-object based"IoT vision [15]. In fact, the virtualization and composition processes allow the creation of an open plug-and-play environment, while the cognitive management makes the framework sound under user, business and technological perspectives. Moreover, the adoption of well-known paradigms (software agents, message passing) and technologies (XML, RDF, conventional security mechanisms) should help and encourage the developers. The second consideration that arises from the analysis of Table 1 is that also Cascadas provides a satisfying set of features but it is not clear how much its clean slate approach, whereas unique and very interesting, may slow the development phase.

5 Conclusions

The dividing line between cyber and physical worlds is becoming more and more blurred and in a few years the Internet may be deeply different from the current one. Following the principles of autonomic computing and cognitive networks, some of the most interesting IoT architectures with a holistic approach to the management function, have been surveyed and compared. These computing paradigms can help to minimize the human intervention and to overcome technological and protocol heterogeneity. Moreover, they may enable an evolution from the current status of isolated "Intranet of Things" toward a fully integrated Internet of Things.

References

1. Mattern, F., Floerkemeier, C.: From the internet of computers to the internet of things. In: Sachs, K., Petrov, I., Guerrero, P. (eds.) Buchmann Festschrift. LNCS, vol. 6462, pp. 242–259. Springer, Heidelberg (2010)
2. Kortuem, G., Kawsar, F., Fitton, D., Sundramoorthy, V.: Smart objects as building blocks for the internet of things. IEEE Internet Comput. **14**(1), 44–51 (2010)
3. Kephart, J.O., Chess, D.M.: The vision of autonomic computing. Computer **36**(1), 41–50 (2003)
4. Zambonelli, F., Omicini, A.: Challenges and research directions in agent-oriented software engineering. Auton. Agent. Multi-Agent Syst. **9**(3), 253–283 (2004)
5. Fortuna, C., Mohorcic, M.: Trends in the development of communication networks: Cognitive networks. Comput. Netw. **53**(9), 1354–1376 (2009)
6. Manzalini, A., Zambonelli, F.: Towards autonomic and situation-aware communication services: the cascadas vision. In: IEEE Workshop on Distributed Intelligent Systems: Collective Intelligence and Its Applications, pp. 383–388. IEEE (2006)
7. Strassner, J., Agoulmine, N., Lehtihet, E.: Focale: A novel autonomic networking architecture (2006)
8. Clayman, S., Galis, A.: Inox: A managed service platform for inter-connected smart objects. In: Proceedings of the Workshop on IoT and Service Platforms, p. 2. ACM (2011)
9. Vlacheas, P., Giaffreda, R., Stavroulaki, V., Kelaidonis, D., Foteinos, V., Poulios, G., Demestichas, P., Somov, A., Biswas, A.R., Moessner, K.: Enabling smart cities through a cognitive management framework for the internet of things. IEEE Commun. Mag. **51**(6), 102–111 (2013)
10. IoT-A (2014). http://www.iot-a.eu/public/public-documents
11. Butler: I-core integration demo (2014). http://www.iot-week.eu
12. Tsagkaris, K., Nguengang, G., Galani, A.:Grida Ben Yahia, I., Ghader, M., Kaloxylos, A., Gruber, M., Kousaridas, A., Bouet, M., Georgoulas, S., et al.: A survey of autonomic networking architectures: towards a unified management framework. Int. J. Netw. Manag. **23**(6), 402–423 (2013)

13. Strassner, J., Kim, S.-S., Hong, J.W.-K.: The design of an autonomic communication element to manage future internet services. In: Hong, C.S., Tonouchi, T., Ma, Y., Chao, C.-S. (eds.) APNOMS 2009. LNCS, vol. 5787, pp. 122–132. Springer, Heidelberg (2009)
14. Fortino, G., Guerrieri, A., Russo, W., Savaglio, C.: Middlewares for smart objects and smart environments: Overview and comparison. In: Internet of Things Based on Smart Objects, pp. 1–27. Springer International Publishing (2014)
15. Fortino, G., Guerrieri, A., Russo, W.: Agent-oriented smart objects development. In: IEEE 16th International Conference on Computer Supported Cooperative Work in Design, CSCWD 2012, 23–25 May, 2012, Wuhan, China, pp. 907–912 (2012)

Sensor Networks

Sensor Web Enablement Applied
to an Earthquake Early Warning System

Ana María Zambrano$^{(\boxtimes)}$, Israel Pérez, Carlos E. Palau,
and Manuel Esteve

Universitat Politècnica de València, Valencia, Spain
anzamvi@posgrado.upv.es, cpalau@dcom.upv.es

Abstract. Earthquake early warning systems are of high interest due to their consequences and life losses they may cause. Sensor Web Enablement (SWE) and their related standards allow interoperability of sensors from different vendors and detect earthquakes in advance. For the proposed system we propose the use of the Sensor Observation Service and smartphones as gateways to transmit information from their embedded sensors like the accelerometer. The paper includes an architecture to integrate and process this information, with the possibility of incorporate other sensors out of the smartphones, like seismographs and the generated date in the SOS harmonization platform. The system has been tested in an emulated environment in order to train it and eliminate false positives, improving early warning existing systems of this nature.

Keywords: Sensor Web Enablement · Sensor Observation Service · Distributed system · Real time · Early warning system · Wireless sensor networks

1 Introduction

Wireless sensor networks, social networks and distributed systems are becoming the most important ingredients for the new computing era, the Internet of Things (IoT). IoT allows digital interconnection of everyday objects with the Internet, including those electronic ones as home appliances or cars which may be controlled by developed applications over a Smartphone (SP) or tablet, or any personal device, e.g. [1]. By 2017, there will be 8,6 billion handheld or personal mobile devices and there will be nearly 1,4 mobile devices per capita, which means over 10 billion mobile-connected devices including M2 M modules that will exceed the world's population at that time (7,6 billion) [2]. So, these multi-sensor and multi-network electronic devices have become a fundamental part of the bridge to the knowledge of the physical world, reaching any kind of (measurable) information, anytime, and anywhere.

While it is true that the quality of *MEMS* sensors, as well as of the ones embedded into SPs, is lower than specific sensors in their respective areas of work: take an accelerograph in seismology, or a magnetometer in navigation as an example, it is also important to take two important considerations into account. First, SP manufacturers are continuously expanding *Hw* and *Sw* features of SPs, making their measurements more reliable and accurate and, second, through data collection from a large number of SPs, known as mobile crowd-sensing (MCS), it is possible to obtain a huge low-cost,

© Springer International Publishing Switzerland 2015
G. Di Fatta et al. (Eds.): IDCS 2015, LNCS 9258, pp. 51–62, 2015.
DOI: 10.1007/978-3-319-23237-9_6

overlay networks that use individual sensing SPs capabilities where the average weight of the community (given a sufficient number of individuals) can be computed with a high degree of accuracy, e.g. [3]. Nowadays, community resources such as SPs are taken as an advantage in opportunistic-sensing applications [4] attempting to resolve global current problems in different areas like telecommunication, entertainment, seismology and more. And it is in one of these fields, that our research focuses. This research presents a real time and economic solution to a natural hazard: the earthquakes. The earth's movements should be regularly monitored: by means of an online service is possible to know all about a zone and their hazard just in seconds. And still more, with affordable sensors it is absolutely possible to monitor a whole area, learn their physical characteristics, and most importantly, detect seismic movements to raise early warnings in order to provide extra time for making better decisions. This is one of the key contributions of this work. However, the SP market is full of highly heterogeneous devices with different characteristics *Hw* and *Sw*. And if there were not a process of unification, this would lead to restriction of sensors, decreasing the number of devices on the network, and therefore creating less accuracy. The Open Geospatial Consortium (OGC) [5] solves this problem by defining the Sensor Web Enablement (SWE) framework [6] and specifically to its Sensor Observation Service (SOS) component, which defines a unified communication standard for sensors and sensor services achieving a higher level of compatibility. And it means lower costs and better quality sensor communications because we are using an only protocol instead of several proprietary ones, which involve serious problems in interoperability [7]. Much of this project focuses on coupling the type of communication to the system requirements: Standardization sensor data, quick access to data, real time communication, and immediate notifications. We use a paradigm of distributed systems SWE.

Seismic activity is increasing, and consequently the risk that these also attract; so much so that in April 2014 there was a world record number of large earthquakes (greater than 6,5) [8]. There are places more exposed to this type of natural disaster such as the countries which make up the "Pacific Ring of Fire", where at least 80 % of all earthquakes are produced [9]. Take the case of Ecuador, a country in which the validation of this proposed architecture is based, where only in 2013 it registered 2.420 seismic events (6 earthquakes per day) and around 10 % exceeded of them a magnitude of 4.

The rest of the paper is organized as follows: The previous and related works in the area with their respective contribution can be found in Sect. 2. Section 3 contains the proposed architecture structure and its justification. While in Sect. 4 the evaluation and results are cited, in the Sect. 5, the conclusions of our research are presented. Future work is also referred to in this section.

2 Motivation and Related Work

The use of SPs in the field of Earthquake Early Warning Systems *(EEWS)* is booming: [10] is a project that detects seismic events using *MEMS* accelerometers where, if the acceleration exceeds a threshold value, the information is transmitted to a server and presumes the intensity and the hypocenter. References [11, 12] are projects that use static devices composed of a fixed accelerometer and a personal computer providing good accuracy by means of P and S waves [13] as peak detection mechanism. Reference [14] is a system that uses SPs to measure the acceleration and then determines the arrival of an earthquake. Furthermore, in contrast to our proposal, which uses an accelerometer as the principal sensor, [14] includes a compass sensor for peaks validation. Reference [15] uses *MEMS* accelerometers, a seismological processing unit and 3 types of alarms. The effective warning time in average is 8,1 s to be detected and 12,4 s the time from the maximum vibrations. On the other hand, there are different *EEWS* using other types of communications. Reference [16] was put into operation from December 2000 to June 2001 in Taiwan. It proposed a Virtual Subnet Network for *EEWS* achieving to detect an event in 30 s with an average of 22 s after the origin time to cities at distance were greater than 145 km from the source. The proposed architecture achieves detect the maximum acceleration peak in 12 s surpassing the results of the projects mentioned above. (See Sect. 4). Reference [17] gathers data from SPs and implements a distributed decision-making process using virtual servers provided by the *Google App Engine* architecture [18]. References [19, 20] detect waves of a quake and report the event using *Google Cloud to Device Messaging* (C2DM).

All of them have been the motivation to achieve a different and innovative *EEWS*. We proposed a future perspective to exploit community resources as SPs together with a reliable and robust real time communication infrastructure, specially during the natural disaster. Contrary to [10], our seismic detection uses dynamic thresholds for distinguishing between a repetitive sudden movement by the user and an actual seismic event. Our architecture involves additional challenges as incorporating heterogeneous devices, thus gaining in scalability; new detection algorithms, mobility and suitability to the application environment demands unlike [11, 12]. In contrast to our work, [12] performs accurate validations without taking into account either the processing time or the computational cost, something that is implicit in its working process, due to SP usage. Furthermore [11, 12] are complemented by our work, widely covering the future work proposed by both. Reference [14] still has great limitations of usage and efficiency because an accurate orientation, due to issues with the compass, cannot be obtained if the device is in constant motion, and consequently forces the system to remain stationary. Should one day disaster happen and *Google* cease service, [17, 19, 20] would cease to work too. To be more realistic, should the *Google* go down for an hour, these projects would also be down for an hour without the least idea of what happened. So these are completely at the mercy of *Google*.

A Service oriented approach for sensor access and usage is used by several groups: [21, 22] use their proprietary standards and data repositories, each one with different functions, access and use of sensors. SWE and its SOS component have been successfully applied to indoor [23] and outdoor scenarios. References [24] presents an Internet based urban environment observation system that is able to monitor several environmental variables (temperature, humidity, seismic activity) in real time. In conclusion the SWE's approach offers a standard method for use sensor data to facilitate a rapid response to a disaster scenario. And this work takes advantage of this.

Finally, citing the post-event management, a project that is worth emphasizing is [25] which is a Europe-Union project with 1, 2 million euros. Reference [25] investigates current media as Facebook, Twitter or YouTube, and uses them in crisis management to promote collaboration of first-responders and citizens. Limitations such as marginalization of people who do not use social media, or the reliability of information like spreading of false information are its points to improve.

3 System Architecture

The accelerograph network developed in the paper us based on a three layer hierarchical architecture for *EEWS* as shown Fig. 1. On Layer-1, SPs are used as processing units and send samples to the Intermediate Server (IS), corresponding to Layer-2 as soon as SP detects a seismic-peak after overcoming a process which has been specifically designed. Each IS decide whether there was a seismic event or not, and immediately notifies their own users and, at the same time, communicates the incident to the Control Center (CC), the third layer. The data gathered from the sensors are inserted in a SOS (SWE) into the IS. The CC aggregates different applications that make decisions based on the information available in each SOS.

The three layers and the SOS will be integrated in a scalable manner (1 or more SPs, 1 or more ISs) until to complete the system in order to verify how these interact properly, cover the functionalities and conform to the requirements; and furthermore contribute in non-functional requirements as: agile and easy portability, simple maintenance, ensure the integrity, confidentiality and availability of information (security) in the architecture, reduce the cost in locating errors and indispensable, an economic huge sensor network.

3.1 Layer 1: Client Application and Acceleration Processing

The SP application must be simple, non-interfering with the user's daily activities and non-battery consuming, as well as a great help during and after a seismic catastrophe in

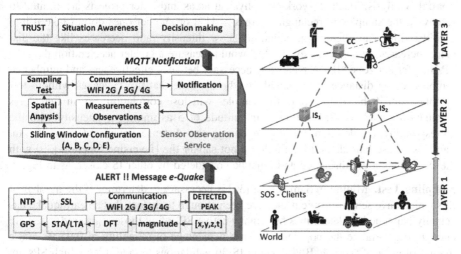

Fig. 1. Hierarchical 3-layered architecture: Layer 1: Smartphone application and acceleration processing; Layer 2: The intermediate server; Layer 3: The control center.

order to assist crisis managers to make better decisions. Figure 1 shows the designed and implemented algorithm to detect acceleration peaks representing the destructive power of an earthquake.

An accelerogram is defined as the union of seismic signal and noise *vs.* time. The Discrete Fourier Transform (DFT) [26] is used to change the time to frequency domain to apply low-pass filters to remove high frequencies corresponding to the noise. Later the Short Term Averaging/Long Term Averaging algorithm (STA/LTA) [27] is used because of its wide capabilities in detecting events in seismology, the low amount of computation, low energy consumption, contributing towards the overall success of the system. We keep a dynamic threshold in order to distinguish between user's periodical movements (running, jogging, or walking) and a real seismic peak. Samples which present a lower threshold than the calculated in each window are discarded and continue working. The application accesses the GPS sensor to get the user's current location, which is necessary for a validation on the IS and important to the SOS. In case the application should not be able to manage this sensor, the sample will not be sent to the IS. Then, in a hard real-time system it is necessary to maintain the same timeline throughout the architecture, for which, the protocol NTP is implemented in order to synchronize the whole network.

3.2   Layer 2: Intermediate Server

The whole process performed by the IS is required to ensure the global reliability of the system, with the following assumptions: (1) The samples of the first layer are independent of each other; (2) the higher number of samples analyzed more reliably; (3) the mathematical and statistical process support the data fusion; (4) ability to receive information from heterogeneous devices. Figure 2 presents an overview of the IS process, and described continue in greater detail:

Spatial Analysis. Each IS works by physical areas and other projects are limited to subdivide the samples in rectangular areas as [17] or another ones do not take it into consideration. The attenuation equations show intensity ratio decreases like the distance increases; in a seismic event, "A" would measure a greater acceleration than the SPs in a farther zone "B". A balance is necessary between effectiveness and number of samples. If the distance is too small, maybe the case that the IS leaves without test samples, and if this is too long, the samples will lose correlation. So, in Ecuador's attenuation equations [28]: setting a magnitude of 5 as minimum intensity with the corresponding acceleration for this intensity, the distance calculated was 35 km. Samples whose latitude and longitude do not satisfy the Haversine function [29] with the IS's location are discarded and must be considered by other IS closer, as in Fig. 2.

Sampling Test. Minimum Sample test [30] is necessary to determine if the number of SPs which have sent a seismic peak have been enough to deduce that an earthquake has actually happened. It determines how many active SPs of all those registered in ISs are enough to generalize the population with a percentage of reliability of 0,95 %, and a margin of error of 0,05 %. Both SP and IS do validations to determine which SPs are alive (active) and which are not. First, SPs send beacons and are constantly monitoring

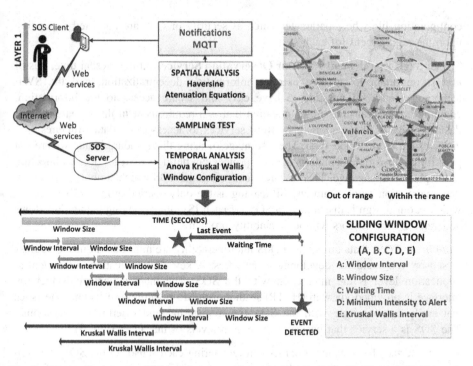

Fig. 2. Intermediate server: Sliding window configuration (A, B, C, D, E) (Kruskal Wallis) and temporal and spatial analysis.

the network for reconnections, and second, the IS validates the last connection's time and, after a fixed time period (30 min) changes the SP's state to inactive state.

Kruskal Wallis Test. Kruskal Wallis [31] is an analysis variance ANOVA test used to compare samples or group of samples that better fits the nature of the seismic data. A periodical sliding windows algorithm has been developed in order to couple the Kruskal Wallis to seismic data *vs*. time. Figure 2, shows the configuration (A, B, C, D, E), that will be tested to find the optimal one whose results demonstrate the best correlation measured by the Kruskal Wallis Probability (KWP), and the most important, the time in advance to an earthquake. The optimal configuration is (explained in Sect. 4) **(0.3, 1, 20, 5, 1):** The algorithm is performed three times in each window of size one second (B = 1), comparing whether the variability of the samples exceeds the KWP of 0,5 or not (A = 0.3, E = 1). Next, trying to eliminate the risk of notifying very close replicas to the user, it validates that the time between the last and the present event is at least 20 s (C = 20). And the minimum intensity to alert is 5 (D = 5).

Message Queue Telemetry Transport (MQTT). When the IS detects a seismic event, it sends an alarm to their users in coverage, and the CC at the same time using MQTT [32] as messaging protocol for real time notifications. MQTT has been designed for devices as SPs due to reduced available resources, low power usage and efficient distribution of information to one or many receivers and, in addition, offers privacy and security. MQTT is easy to implement because of it only requires to modify a configuration file where parameters such as security or QoS are modified depending upon the requirements of each system.

Sensor Web Enablement – Sensor Observation Service. At the present time, it is of utmost important to achieve extreme information decentralization, and the SWE technology makes it possible to have easy and secure access to the information, enabling a near real time communication that is a requirement in this research. SWE describes sensor observations and (web) services to access those data structures specially using World Wide Web. The advantage of using this standard is that we are not prescribing any implementation, so each project can build its own services architecture in the preferred language. This research focuses on the SOS which supports a common data registration model from any SP leaving as the only restriction in SOS's capacity; which in our design is distributed (a SOS for each IS) thus achieving gather data flows generated by the sensors without scalability problems.

Data in the SOS. Data quality and QoS interoperability are important issues to address in sensor web standards development activities. A key communication component at application level is the interaction with the SOS. The main advantage is that the interface is provided via web (HTTP) so that each SP, regardless of its characteristics can easily communicate with the SOS (i.e. registering and inserting observations). The SOS is a service that basically offers two levels of interfaces (Fig. 3):

- An interface for sensors: it consists in registering each sensor in the SOS and then sending measurements. The first step is performed by means of a *registerSensor* operation, which allows saving a new sensor. Once the sensor has been registered, it can start sending measurements at certain intervals, which depends either on the physical quantity being measured or the need of control required. The operation is called *insertObservation*. The SOS supports both fixed and mobile sensors. In the latter case, mobile sensors must send (besides measurements in the *insertObservation* operation) their current location. The operation is called *updateSensor*.
- An interface for external processes, through which any application can access historical data (even real-time data) regarding any registered sensor. Note that, as the SOS service centralizes all sensors, it is possible to search and apply simple spatio-temporal filters, e.g. "get all sensors that monitor temperature" or "get all sensors located in an area".

3.3 Layer 3: Control Center

The CC must behave as a good command and control post, delivering information about global risks to the emergency management centers (firefighter, police, ambulance and others), helping them to make proper decisions, as e.g. the Geographic Institute at the National Polytechnic School (IGEPN) [33] in Ecuador. The CC allows a system's extension from a pre-event to a post-event management schema. At a first stage, each SP helps the CC by sending multimedia information such as comments, pictures and videos helping in the process of achieving a global view of what is going on in a disaster in real time; and hence, in the second instance, CC helps the users make better post-event

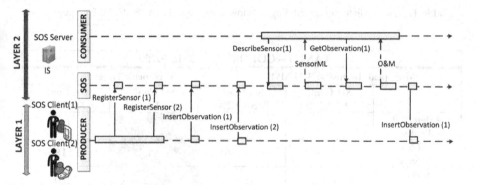

Fig. 3. Basic sequence diagram for the SOS service.

decisions by providing "tips" about closest aid-centers, safer and faster routes (the user on their own knowledge is totally unaware of the real situation of the disaster).

4 Performance Evaluation

For a more accurate and real validation, the IGEPN provided seismic-data of recent earthquakes into (or near) Ecuador: (1) 2013/02/09 - 09:14; Pasto-Colombia, 345 km north of Quito; lasted 30 s; Richter-Magnitude 7,4. In Quito-Ecuador, it was felt in around 5 provinces with an intensity of 4; (2) 2012/02/08 – 13:50; Esmeraldas-Ecuador; 288 km north of Quito; lasted 6 s; In Quito was felt with an intensity of 5,2; (3) 2011/10/29 – 10:54; Quito-Ecuador; Richter-Magnitude 4,3.

To determine the best configuration-parameters set (A, B, C, D, E) the validation process for each earthquake is accomplished and then comparing them taking account two considerations: First, the parameter C (Waiting Time), which corresponds to the time between two detected seismic-peaks, is set to 1 ($C = 1$), in order to compare which of them (configurations) detects a higher number of seismic peaks. Shown in Table 1. If it is too large, a peak (aftershock) cannot be detected, even if it is higher than the last one. Second, the parameter D (Minimum Intensity) is set to 2 ($D = 2$) to check that the algorithm is able to sense an earthquake even of very low intensity. However, in the optimal configuration, D is set to 5; according to Modified Mercalli Intensity Scale (MMI) [34], it has a very light potential damage, and is perceived as moderate. So, the analysis in each earthquake signal leads us to choose the best configuration, achieving a balance (0.3, 1, 20, 5, 1):

- It reduces the number of false positives because of the KWP average in 0,362. It also avoids that all data are recognized as a seismic peak, but nevertheless higher than other configurations.
- The Table 1 highlight the good correlation existing between window-samples, and there exists a good data correlation at the just at the instant when the maximum seismic peak occurs.

Table 1. Intermediate Server. Sliding window configuration (A, B, C, D, E) comparison.

PASTO – COLOMBIA 2013/02/09				
Max. peak Intensity: 3,57 MMI		Max. peak Time: 16:47		
	Set Conf. (1,1,1,2,2)	Set Conf. (0.5,1,1,2,1)	Set Conf. (0.3,1,1,2,1)	Set Conf. (0.5,0.5,1,2,1)
# Detected Peaks	8	10	11	10
MMI Min. Detected	2,1802	2,1186	2.0697	2,1186
KWP mean	0,18	0,21	0,37	0,20
Time Gained (sec)	1	2	2	2
ESMERALDAS - ECUADOR 2012/02/08				
Max. peak Intensity: 2,69 MMI		Max. peak Time: 50:53		
	Set Conf. (1,1,1,2,2)	Set Conf. (0.5,1,1,2,1)	Set Conf. (0.3,1,1,2,1)	Set Conf. (0.5,0.5,1,2,1)
# Detected Peaks	3	5	6	6
MMI Min. Detected	2,1803	2,1186	2,0496	2,0491
KWP mean	0,08	0,25	0,31	0,29
Time Gained (sec)	1	3	4	3
QUITO - ECUADOR 2011/10/29				
Max. peak Intensity: 4.57 MMI		Max. peak Time: 55:27		
	Set Conf. (1,1,1,2,2)	Set Conf. (0.5,1,1,2,1)	Set Conf. (0.3,1,1,2,1)	Set Conf. (0.5,0.5,1,2,1)
# Detected Peaks	3	5	6	6
MMI Min. Detected	2,1803	2,1186	2,0496	2,0491
KWP mean	0,16	0,32	0,54	0.28
Time Gained (sec)	1	3	4	3

- This configuration allows arise an early warning 12 s ahead the maximum seismic peak occurs, providing extra time, for even the epicenter zone, which is the best achievement obtained.
- The optimal configuration detects the higher number of seismic peaks into each signal. As e.g. in Pasto-Colombia earthquake reached 11 detected peaks.
- This configuration perceives a lower MMI, implying that would be possible to alert earthquakes whose damage are less, and more, it could become an extra information that *IGEPN* (or another CC) needs.

5 Conclusions and Future Work

It is impossible to know where and when a seismic event can happen, thus it is known that an earthquake is unpredictable at the epicenter. So, the best way to mitigate damages in infrastructure, assets and even human lives, is the early detection, where a real-time architecture and an efficient communication between actors becomes a requirement. Now, in this case, big part of the success corresponds to heterogeneous actors (smartphones), all of them forming the Layer-1 of our architecture. Therefore the key point is standardization the sensor data, and it is achieved by SWE and his component SOS which are used to gather sensor observations in a standard way, so they allow an easily integration in any terminal improving the communication in the whole design. A connection using *World Wide Web* allows a standardization of all this community sensors could communicate with their SOS (i.e. registering and inserting observations) in real time and secure way. Further, taking to account that the incorporation of a SOS, allows to have thousands of sensors each one with different advantages and limitations resulting in other words in efficiency and accuracy.

This provides a modular and scalable architecture design. The Layer-2 is a server, named Intermediate Server, with enough capacity to listen and process the SP's samples, detect a seismic event and, notify to all clients in the covered area through the information collected in SOS. This server implements temporal and spatial analysis not presented in another works promoting in the success of the proposal. The last layer, the Control Center can manage in a proper way the actual information in order to help the aids-centers to properly distribute their resources (human or monetary). And second, it can help the users to make better post decisions, being that, they are totally unaware of the real situation of the disaster.

The architecture was validated by means past actual data from Ecuador, which is a country in constant seismic risk. Our solution anticipates the maximum seismic-peak in 12 s in the seismic focus, however this time could be greater in further areas from the epicenter. As well the benefits provided could be greater depending on the earthquake's features (when, duration and location).

Given the limitations of validation, our first step would be improve the structure of the testing process and find agreements with centers that have new testing devices, like rooms with earthquake simulators to achieve better validation and improvement of the overall system. As further work, it would be interesting to more disaster scenarios, considering multiple sensors totally heterogeneous using the same design and coupling the detection process, into the two first layers, to de type of the natural disaster, such as: fires, volcanic eruptions, and many more.

References

1. Fortino, G., Giannantonio, R., Gravina, R., Kuryloski, P., Jafari, R.: Enabling effective programming and flexible management of efficient body sensor network applications. IEEE Trans. Human-Mach. Syst. **43**(1), 115–133 (2013)

2. Cisco Systems, Inc, Cisco Visual Netorking index: Global Mobile Data Traffic Forecast Update 2012-2017 (2013). http://www.cisco.com/en/US/solutions/collateral/ns341/ns525/ns537/ns705/ns827/white_paper_c11-520862.pdf. Accessed 14 March 2014
3. Fortino, G., Parisi, D., Pirrone, V., Di Fatta, G.: BodyCloud: a SaaS approach for community body sensor networks. Future Gener. Comput. Syst. **35**, 62–79 (2014)
4. Ganti, R.K., Ye, F., Lei, H.: Mobile crowdsensing: current state and future challenges. IEEE Commun. Mag. **49**(11), 32–39 (2011)
5. Open Geospatial Consortium, OGC Making Location Count. http://www.opengeospatial.org/ogc. Accessed 16 April 2015
6. Open Geospatial Consortium, Sensor Web Enablement (SWE). http://www.opengeospatial.org/ogc/markets-technologies/swe. Accessed 16 April 2015
7. Funk, A., Busemann, C., Kuka, C., Boll, S., Nicklas, D.: Open sensor platforms: the sensor web enablement framework and beyond. In: MMS, vol. 1, pp. 39-52, (2011)
8. Cadena SER, Ciencia y Tecnología. Record Mundial en Grandes Terremotos, April 2014. http://cadenaser.com/ser/2014/05/07/ciencia/1399417567_850215.html. Accessed 17 April 2015
9. USGS, Earthquake Hazard Program U.S. Geological Survey (2013). http://earthquake.usgs.gov/earthquakes/world/world_deaths.php. Accessed 14 January 2014
10. Uga, T., Nagaosa, T., Kawashima, D.: An emergency earthquake warning system using mobile terminals with a built-in accelerometer, de ITS Telecommunications (ITST), Taipei (2012)
11. Chandy, R., Rita, A., Skjellum, Ø., Chandy, K.M., Clayton, R.: QuakeCast: Distributed Seismic Early Warning, California (2011)
12. Cochran, E., Lawrence, J., Christensen, C., Jakka, R.: The quake-catcher network: citizen science expanding seismic horizons. Seismol. Res. Lett. **80**(1), 26–30 (2009)
13. Bormann, P., Engdahl, B., Kind, R.: Seismic Wave Propagation and Earth models, de New Manual of Seismological Observatory Practice 2 (NMSOP2), Potsdam, Germany, Deutsches GeoForschungsZentrum GFZ, pp. 1–105 (2012)
14. Dashti, S., Reilly, J., Bray, J., Bayen, A.M., Glaser, S.D., Mari, E.: iShake: Mobile phones as seismic sensors-user study findings. In: Conference Mobile and Ubiquitous Multimedia, vol. 28(10), pp. 43–52 (2011)
15. Peng, C., Zhu, X., Yang, J., Xue, B., Chen, Y.: Development of an integrated onsite earthquake early warning system and test deployment in Zhaotong, China. Comput. Geosci. **56**, 170–177 (2013)
16. Wu, Y.M., Teng, T.L.: A virtual subnetwork approach to earthquake early warning. Bull. Seismol. Soc. Am. **92**(5), 2008–2018 (2002)
17. Faulkner, M., Olson, M., Chandy, R., Krause, J., Chandy, K.M., Krause, A.: The next big one: Detecting earthquakes and other rare events from community-based sensors. Information Processing in Sensor Networks (IPSN), International Conference, vol. 10, pp. 13–24 (2011)
18. Google, Google Cloud Plataform (Official Site) (2014). http://cloud.google.com/. Accessed 17 April 2015
19. Finazzi, F., Fassò, A.: Earthquake monitoring using volunteer smartphone-based sensor networks, de METMA VII and GRASPA14, Torino (2014)
20. Soni, A., Sharma, A., Kumar, P., Verma, V., Sutar, S.: Early disaster warning & evacuation system on mobile phones using google street map. Int. J. Eng. Tech. Res. (IJETR) **2**(4), 9–11 (2014)
21. Nath, S.: Challenges in building a portal for sensors world-wide, pp. 3–4. ACM (2006)

22. Gupta, V., Poursohi, A., Udupi, P.: Sensor Network: An open data exchange for the web of things. In: Pervasive Computing and Communications Workshops PERCOM, Mannheim (2010)
23. Giménez, P., Molina, B., Calvo-Gallego, J., Esteve, M., Palau, C.E.: I3WSN: industrial intelligent wireless sensor networks for indoor environments. Comput. Ind. **65**, 187–199 (2014)
24. Giménez, P., Molina, B., Palau, C.E., Esteve, M.: SWE simulation and testing for the IoT. In: Proceedings of the 2013 IEEE International Conference on Systems, Man, and Cybernetics, Manchester (2013)
25. COSMIC, Contribution of Social Media in Crisis Management. http://www.cosmic-project. eu/. Accessed 16 June 2015
26. Sheng, X., Zhang, Y., Pham, D., Lambare, G.: Antileakage Fourier transform for seismic data regulation. Geophysics **70**(4), 87–95 (2005)
27. Sharma, B., Klumar, A., Murthy, V.M.: Evaluation of seismic events detection algorithms. J. Geol. Soc. India **75**(1), 533–538 (2010)
28. Beauval, C., Yepes, H., Bakun, W., Egred, J., Alvarado, A., Singaucho, J.C.: Historical earthquakes in the sierra of ecuador (1587–1996). Geophys. J. Int. **181**(3), 1613–1633 (2010)
29. Robusto, C.: The Cosine-Haversine formula. Am. Math. Monthly **60**(1), 38–40 (1957)
30. Cochran, W.G.: The Sampling Techniques. Wiley, New York (1963)
31. Kruskal, W.H., Waliis, W.A.: Use of ranks in one-criterion variance analysis. J. Am. Stat. Assoc. **47**(260), 583–621 (1952)
32. Hunkeler, U., Truong, H.L., Stanford-Clark, A.: MQTT-S – a publish/subscribe protocol for wireless sensor networks. In: Communication Systems Software and Middleware and Workshops COMSWARE, pp. 791–798 (2008)
33. Instituto Geofísico Escuela Politécnica Nacional, Informe Sísmico para el Ecuador 2013 (2014). http://www.igepn.edu.ec/index.php/informes-sismicos/anuales/231–50/file. Accessed 3 December 2014
34. Wood, H.O., Neumann, F.: Modified mercalli intensity scale. Bull. Seismol. Soc. Am. **21**(4), 277–283 (1931)

Towards Motion Characterization and Assessment Within a Wireless Body Area Network

Martin Seiffert[(✉)], Norman Dziengel, Marco Ziegert, Robert Kerz,
and Jochen Schiller

Department of Mathematics and Computer Science, Freie Universität Berlin,
Takustraße 9, 14195 Berlin, Germany
{seiffert,dziengel,ziegert,robsn,schiller}@inf.fu-berlin.de
http://www.inf.fu-berlin.de

Abstract. The combination of small wireless sensor nodes and inertial sensors such as accelerometers and gyroscopes provides a cheap to produce ubiquitous technology module for human motion analysis. We introduce a system architecture for in-network motion characterization and assessment with a wireless body area network based on motion fragments. We present a segmentation algorithm based on biomechanics to identify motion fragments with a strong relation to an intuitive description of a motion. The system architecture comprises a training phase to provide reference data for segmentation, characterization and assessment of a specific motion and a feedback phase wherein the system provides the assessment related to the conduction of the motion. For fine-grained applicability, the proposed system offers the possibility of providing a motion assessment on three different evaluation layers during the motion assessment process. We evaluate the system in a first practical approach based on a dumbbell exercise.

Keywords: Motion assessment · Motion fragment · Wireless body area network · Biomechanical segmentation · In-network processing

1 Introduction

How we move our body in daily activities has a significant influence on personal health and could be crucial if we want to reach outstanding goals, e.g. in sports. In order to improve our movements we need a personal expert who makes us aware of wrong moves at the right moment. Though the constant presence of a human expert does not seem feasible, such a function could be supported by a wearable wireless sensor system. The combination of small wireless sensor nodes and inertial sensors such as accelerometers and gyroscopes provides a cheap to produce ubiquitous technology module for human motion analysis [2]. Such sensor nodes can be built small enough so as not to interfere with daily life. Multiple nodes equipped with appropriate communication devices could form a

© Springer International Publishing Switzerland 2015
G. Di Fatta et al. (Eds.): IDCS 2015, LNCS 9258, pp. 63–74, 2015.
DOI: 10.1007/978-3-319-23237-9_7

wireless body area network (WBAN), which is able to sense human motion in its entirety. The development of systems which analyze the movement of the human body can be divided into three categories, dependent on the processing of the collected data: single sensor systems, centralized sensor networks and distributed sensor networks.

Single sensor systems with close-fitting application are already available in the form of the strong growing market of wearables. The functionality is usually limited to counting easily detected sizes (steps/heartbeat/pulse) or to the classification of different activities (sleeping/walking/running/biking). The data is analyzed either on the sensor node or on additional infrastructure such as a mobile phone. Single sensor systems measure the motion of only one extremity of the body and therefore lack a comprehensive body measurement. Centralized WBANs that use inertial sensors are already used for the off-line analysis of a human motion in the form of a classical motion tracking system. Several sensor nodes collect data from inertial sensors and send them to a base station. At the base station the data will be combined in a kinematic model and analyzed in a post-processing step by considering the model data such as joint angles [1]. In research more general concepts for developing centralized WBANs are considered, which move necessary calculations more and more into the sensor nodes [5]. Centralized systems achieve high accuracy but are tied to communicate with the central base station. This results in a lack of mobility. Distributed sensor networks are the most promising technology to support human motion directly because they will be able to sense human motion in its entirety and to compute all data within the network [12]. Thus they could provide direct feedback to a specific motion, independent of any infrastructure and with high accuracy, which enables the use in daily activities outside of a laboratory. Distributed WBANs are currently a subject of research. There are currently only a few approaches in the field of WBANs which handle all data within the network [11,12]. These approaches investigate e.g. classifying different activities within the sensor network, but make no statement about the quality of individual body movements or about improperly performed parts of the movement.

The characterization and assessment of how a movement is carried out within a WBAN would permit the qualitative evaluation of the movement and therefore a movement related feedback to the user. Such feedback could be related to incorrectly performed parts of the movement. In sports training, feedback regarding wrong body movements is essential for learning and improvement of motor skills and physical fitness. This also applies to the execution of physiotherapy movements. A WBAN that monitors the execution of physiotherapy movements and provides a motion related feedback will support patients in performing a valuable training on their own, in addition to the regular supervised training. Such technical support could contribute by optimizing the treatment in terms of time and the success. Furthermore, motion related feedback could be important for people typically working with heavy load (construction, transport or elderly care). Both employer and employee benefit from motion related warning systems. E.g. employers lower the risk of sick days because of work-related pain while the employee's health benefits directly from avoiding risky movements.

2   Requirements

As terms related to motion and movement are often used in a different manner, we define the terms we use in this work in Fig. 1. We use *motion* to mean a change in position of an object with respect to time [10]. Concerning the motion of the human body, motion represents the position, velocity and acceleration of a body part at a given time. If we reference motion in a time discrete frame we reference the frame of motion as a *motion segment*. If the motion segment was defined by a segmentation algorithm based on biomechanics we reference this motion segment as a *biomechanical motion segment* (e.g. extension or flexion of a body part). If a motion segment is identified as a part of a defined more complex motion we reference the motion segment as a *motion fragment* of this more complex motion (e.g. raise a dumbbell). Multiple sequential motion fragments together form the overall more complex motion which we reference as a *movement* (e.g. a dumbbell exercise).

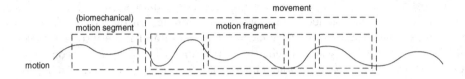

Fig. 1. Terminology

A WBAN which satisfies the introduced expectations has to fulfill the following requirements. In medicine and sports, biomechanical principles are fundamental in analyzing and assessing the human locomotor system [6]. A first step in the analysis of a complex movement is to establish motion fragments into which the movement can be divided for analysis. The motion fragments of the movement should be selected so that they have a biomechanically distinct role in the overall movement, which is different from that of preceding and succeeding motion fragments [7]. As a consequence, we recommend the segmentation of human movements based on biomechanics. The challenge is to identify these motion fragments reliably and with a high temporal correlation to motion parts of an intuitive partitioning of the movement. By *reliability* we mean that a repeated conduction of the same movement should result in the same sequences of motion fragments. By *temporal correlation* we mean that a motion fragment starts and ends at the same time within the movement as the corresponding motion part of the intuitive partitioning. Reliably identified motion fragments with a biomechanical function and easily identified fragment boundaries build the key feature for a comprehensible system. Only if the user can understand and follow the segmentation computed by the wearable system can he interpret a motion fragment related assessment.

Furthermore it should be possible to adapt the functionality of the WBAN to a specific motion or to a specific user. Methods of machine learning could be used to realize this individualization process. In order to characterize and assess human motions, a ground truth is needed to create a reference description of a correct motion. A supervised training of the WBAN could provide a reference model for the motion assessment. This will enable the WBAN to assess multiple previously trained motions.

3   System Architecture

The proposed approach considers a *training phase* and a *feedback phase*. While the training phase allows the customization of the system to a particular exercise conducted by a determined person within the feedback phase the system provides the assessment related to the conduction of the motion. During both phases the WBAN is attached to the body of the user. Once a motion is carried out by the user, sensor data are gathered and analyzed for a plurality of sensor nodes of the WBAN. The analysis comprises for each sensor node four major steps: *biomechanical segmentation, segment characterization, fragment identification* and *movement identification*.

Within the biomechanical segmentation process, the gathered sensor motion data is separated into motion segments on the basis of segmentation parameters, wherein each segment is biomechanically distinct from the preceding and succeeding motion segment. During segment characterization for each motion segment, features are extracted from the sensor data which characterize the motion segment. Fragment identification means the process of identifying a motion segment as a dedicated motion fragment of the conducted movement by consideration of the extracted features. In relation to the dedicated motion fragment, a corresponding symbol is assigned to each identified motion fragment. Out of the identified motion fragments, a symbol sequence is formed which identifies the complete movement conducted by the user at the sensor node.

3.1   Biomechanic Segmentation

As mentioned in Sect. 2, we propose a biomechanics based approach for motion segmentation. Biomechanics is divided into statics and dynamics. Statics is the study of objects at rest or in uniform motion. Dynamics is the study of objects being accelerated by the actions of forces. Most importantly, dynamics is divided into two branches: kinematics and kinetics. While kinetics is concerned with determining the causes of motion, kinematics describes the motion itself. Kinematics is usually measured in linear or angular terms [6]. While this could be easily done with the acceleration sensor as well as the gyroscope, it makes kinematics very interesting for describing motion within the WBAN. Most movements of the human body are made possible by the joints, but are also limited by them. The movements at the joints are mainly rotational [7,8]. Therefore, we propose to analyze the gyroscope data with respect to the rotational motion of the joints to retrieve a biomechanical segmentation of human motion. The rotational motion of the joints is characterized by the angular velocity ω measured by the gyroscope of a sensor mounted at the joint.

Concerning ω, three observations can be made. If ω equals zero while the prior and subsequent velocity differs in sign, the rotation switches direction, which intuitively implies a segment switch concerning a conducted angular motion. If ω approaches zero, a previous angular motion is completed. If ω moves away from zero, an angular motion is starting.

We use these observations to provide segmentation candidates for each of the axes of the gyroscope. To detect segmentation candidates for the start and the completion of angular motion, we monitor whether ω enters or leaves a defined corridor around zero. The size of this corridor is determined for each axis of the gyroscope as segmentation parameters during the training phase. To detect rotation switches, we use a Zero-Velocity Crossing (ZVC) approach which is already used in other work for motion segmentation but tends to over-segment with noise or as the number of DoFs increases [9]. To determine the most relevant axis concerning the conducted angular motion, the covered angles between the last segmentation point and the segmentation candidates are calculated and compared to each other. A segmentation candidate is refused if the covered angle of the corresponding axis is below the covered angle of one of the other axes. Furthermore, a segmentation candidate is refused if the covered angle of the corresponding axis is below a dedicated intensity threshold, which is determined as a segmentation parameter during the training phase. If a segmentation candidate is not refused, a segmentation point is detected. This indicates the end of a current segment and the start of a new segment at the segmentation point.

3.2   Training Phase

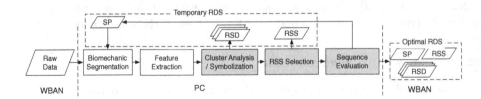

Fig. 2. Training phase with highlighted key components (grey)

During the training phase, the conduction of a movement is supervised by an expert to ensure correct execution. The data gathered by each sensor node is used for a detailed reference analysis of the individual motion, which provides reference data for segmentation, fragment identification, movement identification, and detailed biomechanical assessment of the motion. This reference data is provided separately for each sensor node of the WBAN and represents the motion of the part of the body the sensor node is attached to. The analyzing process during the training phase is depicted in Fig. 2.

During the training phase, a dedicated movement is carried out several times. For each iteration, the raw data passes the biomechanical segmentation as well as the feature extraction process. This results in a set of feature vectors, wherein each feature vector represents a biomechanical segment of the conducted movements. Next, a *cluster analysis* is applied to the set of feature vectors to build groups of motion segments which correspond to the same motion fragment. The cluster analyzing process implements the motion fragment identification step within the training phase. In this respect, the number of resulting partitions is related to the number of motion fragments of the movement. Based on the partition to which a feature vector is allocated, a symbol is assigned to the corresponding segment. The prototype of a partition serves as a reference symbol description (RSD). The RSDs are used later on for fragment identification within the feedback phase. For each movement, a symbol sequence is formed out of the identified motion fragments, which represents the particular movement conducted by the user at the sensor node. During the *RSS selection* process, out of the formed symbol sequences a symbol sequence is selected as reference symbol sequence (RSS) by comparing the symbol sequences by means of similarity. The symbol sequence with the highest similarity to all other symbol sequences is selected. The degree of similarity between two symbol sequences can be determined, e.g., using the edit distance or other distance metrics [14]. The analyzing process during the training phase is repeated several times. With each repetition of the analyzing process, the segmentation of the raw data into biomechanical segments is performed with different segmentation parameters (SP). Each repetition results in a temporary reference data set (RDS) comprising SP, RSD and RSS. During the *sequence evaluation* process, out of these RDSs the optimal RDS is selected as input for the feedback phase. The optimal RDS is selected in consideration of the similarity value of the particular RSS, calculated during the RSS selection process. In this respect the RDS which contains the RSS with the highest similarity value is selected.

3.3   Feedback Phase

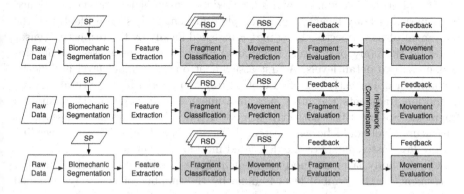

Fig. 3. Feedback phase with highlighted key components (grey)

During the feedback phase, the given RDS is used by each sensor node to identify and assess the trained movement. The corresponding analyzing process is presented in Fig. 3. At each sensor node, the raw data is segmented into separate biomechanical motion segments on the basis of the SP provided by the training phase. As soon as a biomechanical motion segment is built up, features are extracted from the raw data to identify the motion fragment within the following *fragment classification* process. Based on the RSDs provided by the training phase, the classification process assigns a symbol to the biomechanical motion segment.

Within the *movement prediction* process, the trained movement is detected from the resulting symbol sequence of consecutively identified motion fragments. Therefore, the symbol sequence is compared to the RSS provided by the training phase. This is done by calculating a similarity value, e.g. using the edit distance again. It is determined whether the trained movement is carried out by the user and which motion fragment is expected next. The movement is detected when the similarity value is above a dedicated threshold. This threshold determines how many motion fragments have to be identified in the correct order to detect the conducted motion as the trained movement.

For fine-grained applicability, our proposed system provides motion assessment on three different evaluation layers concerning the hierarchical structure of the human body: *fragment layer, body part layer* and *body layer.* Within these layers, an assessment is organized in two detail levels: *symbol level, feature level.*

At a first fragment layer an identified motion fragment is assessed by the *fragment evaluation* process. A first assessment on the symbol level takes place by comparing the symbol of the present motion fragment with that of the motion fragment that was to be expected from the RSS. If the assigned symbol does not match the expected symbol from the RSS, the movement was not carried out in the correct manner. If the assigned symbol matches the expected symbol from the RSS, a more detailed assessment of the conducted motion fragment on the feature level is possible. This can be done by comparing the values of individual features of a motion fragment to the values of these features in the RSD.

The additional assessment of a completed movement is done by the mentioned body part and body layer. After a complete movement has been identified, the movement of the respective body part is assessed locally by the respective sensor nodes on the body part layer. By analogy with the fragment assessment, this is done at two detail levels. A first assessment on the symbol level is done by the number of correctly classified motion fragments regarding the total number of motion fragments the body part movement is composed of. If all motion fragments are identified correctly, a more detailed local movement assessment on feature level could be aggregated. This could be done using the preceding feature level assessments of the dedicated motion fragments.

On the body layer the body movement is assessed in its entirety. The first assessment on the symbol level is done by the number of correctly classified motion fragments of all respective body parts, regarding the total number of motion fragments that all body part movements are composed of. If all motion fragments are identified correctly, a more detailed body movement assessment on feature level could be aggregated from the preceding feature level assessments of the dedicated body part movements.

The assessment of the body movement in its entirety becomes possible due to the exchange of assessments within the network realized by the *in-network communication* process. In relation to the application dependent resolution of the body movement assessment, the current body part assessments are communicated into the WBAN after a certain number of motion fragments have been evaluated.

The present approach thus allows to identify the trained movement out of a fluid motion of the user, to assess this movement based on data collected in a training phase, and thus to communicate a feedback to the user with respect to the quality of the movement. The fragment assessment as well as the body part assessment enables an instant feedback, locally by the processing sensor node, while the movement is still being carried out, such as a tactile or acoustical feedback. In addition, a feedback concerning the entire body motion can be signalled by any sensor node of the WBAN, e.g. by an LED with different colors depending on the results of the body movement assessment.

4 Practical Approach

For the evaluation of the basic functionality of the introduced system architecture we make the following configuration. Concerning the cluster analysis within the training phase we make use of k-means clustering [13]. We provide the number of wanted partitions equal to the number of segments of the dumbbell exercise as mentioned in Sect. 4.2. For fragment classification within the feedback phase we use a prototype classifier [15] that already provided good classification results in our previous work [12]. For fragment characterization within the feature extraction we provide three features, each representing the covered angle within a motion segment of one of the axes of the gyroscope. The degree of similarity between two symbol sequences is determined by applying the edit distance. A movement is detected by a sensor node, if the symbol sequence resulting from consecutively identified motion fragments matches at least 75 % of the RSS.

4.1 Sensor Platform

Driven by the needs of the application domain for distributed motion evaluation in WBANs, we make use of our specialized sensor board F4VI2 [3], shown in Fig. 4 (a), to evaluate human motion. The sensor board provides a very compact form factor of $35.5\,mm * 24.3\,mm$. According to the given application more available resources will allow us to cache longer chunks of data and process the data within short time slots. We target this on the F4VI2 by utilizing the Cortex-M4 microcontroller STM32F415RGT running at a maximum of 168 MHz, providing 1 Mb of Flash, 192 Kb of SRAM while including DSP support and a FPU unit. An optional SD-card is used to store network configurations, firmware images and reference data assigned to distributed event detection and evaluation. For wireless communication between sensor nodes we chose the 868 MHz transceiver TI CC1101 whose output power level is configurable to fit short-range environments like WBANs with several sensor nodes on one extremity. To sense linear

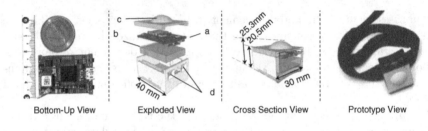

Bottom-Up View   Exploded View   Cross Section View   Prototype View

Fig. 4. Sensor platform F4VI2

and angular motion we use the MPU9150 [4] integrated nine degrees of freedom motion tracking device. We created a setup to integrate our board into a compact $40\,mm * 30\,mm * 25.3\,mm$ housing (Fig. 4, Exploded View) which makes use of a 400 mAh battery (b) to provide long-term applications and enhances the visibility of the LED beam angle with an integrated diffusor (c). The housing can be worn on the body by the use of an easy to attach Velcro® tape that can be edged through the housing as can be seen in (Prototype View). The user interface of the F4VI2 consists of two buttons as input (d), one RGB SMD-LED on the top and one Beeper for feedback. Furthermore an optional Bluetooth serial bridge and two PWM outputs that are capable of driving two vibration motors are available. The vibration motors enable the application to give feedback to the user on demand and can be integrated e.g. into the wristband.

4.2   Motion Model

For evaluation, we choose a combination of dumbbell curl and arnold press to strengthen the muscles of the forearm, the upper arm and the shoulder [16]. The motion sequence as illustrated in Fig. 5 comprises four segments. In the first segment (a), the barbell is lifted to the biceps and turned about 90° in clockwise direction. In the second segment b), the barbell is lifted above the head until the arm is stretched. At the same time, the barbell is turned in counter-clockwise direction about 180°. The third segment (c) regards the reverse movement to the movement in segment (b). The barbell is returned to the position in segment (b), with the barbell moving downwards and turning 180° in clockwise direction. The fourth segment (d) is the counterpart segment to segment (a). The barbell is returned to a neutral position and, by doing so, turned by 90° in counter-clockwise direction.

4.3   Experiments and Results

For characterization and assessment of the barbell exercise conducted by the user, we add one sensor node to the back of the hand (HAR), one sensor node to the forearm (UAR) and one sensor node to the upper arm (OAR) (see Fig. 5, Motion Model). We fluidly conduct 28 correctly executed movements (TYPE_C) of the barbell exercise described in Sect. 4.2. We use 50 % of these movements to

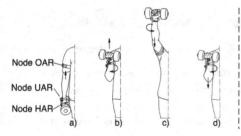

Fragment Error	TYPE_C		TYPE_F1		TYPE_F2	
0	9	64%	0	0%	0	0%
1	5	36%	5	36%	2	14%
2	0	0%	4	29%	7	50%
3	0	0%	2	14%	5	36%
Not Detected	0	0%	3	21%	0	0%

Node	Training		Feedback	
HAR	56	100%	55	98%
UAR	56	100%	55	98%
OAR	56	100%	53	95%

Fig. 5. Motion model (left), Movement assessment (right, top), Fragment reliability (right, bottom)

train the system and 50 % for movement evaluation. Furthermore, we perform 28 movements representing faulty executions of the dumbbell exercise. While conducting 14 executions, we skip turning the dumbbell in counter-clockwise direction as described for segment (b) of the dumbbell exercise (TYPE_F1). While conducting the other 14 executions, we skip turning the dumbbell as described for segment (a) and for segment (b) of the dumbbell exercise (TYPE_F2). All executions are performed by one person. For the movements of TYPE_C we provide a manual reference segmentation based on video data recorded while the movement was carried out and the motion model described in Sect. 4.2.

By using the movements of TYPE_C, we evaluate the motion fragment identification process in terms of reliability and temporal correlation to motion parts of an intuitive partitioning, as we claimed in Sect. 2.

Concerning the reliability of the identification process, we evaluate the sequence of motion fragments resulting from the conduction of the barbell exercise on any of the three sensor nodes assigned to the body (see Fig. 5, Fragment Reliability). On every sensor node, the conduction of 14 repetitions of the barbell exercise should result in a sequence of 56 correctly identified motion fragments. Within the training phase on all sensor nodes, all motion fragments are identified as expected. During the feedback phase on all sensor nodes, at least 95 % and in average 97 % of the motion fragments are identified as expected. These results confirm a high reliability of the motion identification process during the training as well as during the feedback phase.

In Fig. 6 we evaluate the temporal correlation of the segment points which separate sequential motion fragments to the segment points of the reference segmentation. Within the training phase for all sensor nodes, all reference segmentation points are identified by the biomechanical segmentation process. During the feedback phase 98 % of the segmentation points are identified. 81 % of these identified segmentation points are within a temporal distance of 0.3 s to the corresponding reference segmentation point. As each motion fragment of the barbell exercise covers 1.5 s on average, it could be stated that within the feedback phase the large majority of the identified motion fragments are deferred about max. 20 % of their length.

By use of the movements of TYPE_C, TYPE_F1 and TYPE_F2, we evaluate the proposed assessment process referring to the body layer. In this respect

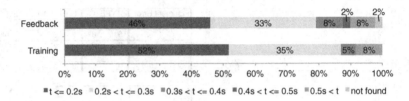

Fig. 6. Temporal correlation of segmentation points to the reference segmentation

we evaluate the assessment on the symbol level. If the trained movement is detected by a sensor node, the number of incorrectly conducted motion fragments is communicated into the WBAN for body level evaluation. On the body level, the total number of incorrectly conducted motion fragments is calculated (see Fig. 5, Movement Assessment). As expected, all wrongly conducted movements are assessed with one or more faulty motion fragments. While most of the correctly conducted movements are assessed with no fragment errors, five of the correctly conducted movements are represented with one fragment error. On average, the detected movements of TYPE_C, TYPE_F1 and TYPE_F2 are represented with 0.36, 1.73 and 2.21 fragment errors respectively. As the amount of the implemented error in TYPE_F2 is higher than in TYPE_F1 the assessment of the faulty executions meets the expectations. For a definite differentiation between the correct and the faulty movements, the evaluation of identified motion fragments on the feature level is necessary.

5   Conclusion and Future Work

We introduced a trainable system architecture for online motion characterization and assessment within a WBAN, based on motion fragments. We presented a biomechanics inspired segmentation algorithm to identify motion fragments as parts of an intuitive description of a movement. The system architecture provides a motion assessment on three different evaluation layers and two detail levels during the motion assessment process and thus a feedback to the user with respect to the quality of the entire body movement. In a first practical approach, we showed that we can identify motion fragments of a barbell exercise with high reliability. Our results confirm the functionality of the proposed system architecture and show that the system can assess movements in relation to the correct conduction and the faulty conduction of the movement on the body layer. In further experiments we will evaluate the system to additional motion models and with respect to more mobile environments as well as with respect to the other possible evaluation layer and detail levels.

The presented results motivate new applications of holistic and distributed motion assessment in the domains of sports and health care. In the future and with further improvements to our work we expect new applications giving real time feedback during the motion for high performance sport assessments or rehabilitation surveillance and training systems especially in prosthetic and orthotic application optimization.

Acknowledgments. This work was funded in part by the German Federal Ministry of Education and Research (BMBF, VIP-Project VIVE, Project-ID: 03V0139).

References

1. Felisberto, F., Costa, N., Fdez-Riverola, F., Pereira, A.: Unobstructive Body Area Networks (BAN) for efficient movement monitoring. Sensors **12**(9), 12473–12488 (2012)
2. Cuesta-Vargas, A.I., Galn-Mercant, A., Williams, J.M.: The use of inertial sensors system for human motion analysis. Phys. Ther. Rev. **15**(6), 462–473 (2010)
3. Ziegert, M., Dziengel, N., Seiffert, M., Pfeiffer, S.: A Developer and a reference board for distributed motion evaluation in wireless sensor networks. In: IEEE International Conference on Industrial Technology, pp. 2412–2419 (2015)
4. InvenSense Inc.: MPU-9150 Product Specification Revision 4.3 (2013)
5. Fortino, G., Giannantonio, R., Gravina, R., Kuryloski, P., Jafari, R.: Enabling effective programming and flexible management of efficient body sensor network applications. IEEE Trans. Hum.-Mach. Syst. **43**(1), 115–133 (2013)
6. Knudson, D.: Fundamentals of Biomechanics, 2nd edn. Springer, Heidelberg (2007)
7. Bartlett, R.: Introduction to Sports Biomechanics, 3rd edn. Taylor & Francis Ltd., London (2014)
8. Tözeren, A.: Human Body Dynamics. Springer, Heidelberg (2000)
9. Lin, F.-S., Kulic, D.: Segmenting human motion for automated rehabilitation exercise analysis. In: Annual International Conference of the IEEE Engineering in Medicine and Biology Society (EMBC), pp. 2881–2884 (2012)
10. Goel, V.K.: Fundamentals of Physics Xi. Tata McGraw-Hill Education, New Delhi (2007)
11. Ghasemzadeh, H., Ostadabbas, S., Guenterberg, E., Pantelopoulos, A.: Wireless medical-embedded systems: a review of signal-processing techniques for classification. IEEE Sens. J. **13**(2), 423–437 (2013)
12. Dziengel, N., Ziegert, M., Seiffert, M., Schiller, J., Wittenburg, G.: Integration of distributed event detection in wireless motion-based training devices. In: IEEE International Conference on Consumer Electronics (ICCE-Berlin), pp. 259–263 (2011)
13. Webb, A.R., Copsey, K.D., Cawley, G.: Statistical Pattern Recognition. Wiley, Malvern (2011)
14. Navarro, G.: A guided tour to approximate string matching. ACM Comput. Surv. (CSUR) **33**(1), 31–88 (2001)
15. Kalton, A., Langley, P., Wagstaff, K., Yoo, J.: Generalized clustering, supervised learning, and data assignment. In: Proceedings of the Seventh ACM SIGKDD International Conference on Knowledge Discovery and Data Mining, pp. 299–304 (2001)
16. Schwarzenegger, A., Dobbins, B.: The New Encyclopedia of Modern Bodybuilding. Simon & Schuster, New York (2012)

Data Driven Transmission Power Control
for Wireless Sensor Networks

Roshan Kotian$^{(\boxtimes)}$, Georgios Exarchakos, and Antonio Liotta

Technical University Eindhoven (TU/e), Department of Electrical Engineering,
5600 MB, Building 19 Flux, PO Box 513, Eindhoven, The Netherlands
{r.kotian,gexarchakos,A.Liotta}@tue.nl

Abstract. Transmission Power Control (TPC) is employed in the sensor nodes with the main objective of minimizing transmission power consumption. However, major drawbacks with well-known TPC are time consuming and energy inefficient initialization phase. Moreover, they employ Received Signal Strength Indicator (RSSI), Link Quality Indicator (LQI) metrics for initialization phase that are sensitive to environmental conditions and hence are not appropriate parameters to adjust the power. To overcome these shortcomings of existing TPC, we propose a novel TPC algorithm dubbed as Data-Driven Transmission Power Control (DA-TPC) that has shorter initialization phase and uses priority of data as the only metric to adjust the power level. The two main aims of this paper are to minimize power consumption during initialization phase and to show how by utilizing priority of data as a sole metric for power adaptation improves reliability and decreases not only latency but also overall energy consumption while transmitting data packets.

Keywords: WSN · Transmission power · Routing · Reliability · Latency

1 Introduction

Wireless Sensor Networks (WSN) with their distributed sensing, communication, and computing capabilities offer effective solution to monitor events of interest occurring in a remote area [4]. However, limited power supply and uncertainty in the propagation medium play a disruptive role in the normal operation of the sensor network [2]. Compared to all other components of a sensor node, transciever consumes maximum power. Therefore, TPC is used to prolong the battery life. Many TPC algorithms have been discussed in the past [8,10,14,16]. These algorithms rely on the variation of link quality metric such as Received Signal Strength Indicator (RSSI), Link Quality Indicator (LQI) to adapt the transmission power. Link quality variation depends on a location. If TPC relies on link variation alone, then it is tightly coupled to specific conditions prevailing at that location. As a result, TPC must undergo many trial and error phases before it is tweaked to provide accurate power change recommendations.

© Springer International Publishing Switzerland 2015
G. Di Fatta et al. (Eds.): IDCS 2015, LNCS 9258, pp. 75–87, 2015.
DOI: 10.1007/978-3-319-23237-9_8

This process is often too energy demanding and counters the very need of the TPC protocol. TPC such as MODTPC [14] recommends the power level that is just enough to maintain a communication link between pair of nodes. Due to the uncertainty in the propagation medium, this type of link often has the tendency to break. This results in triggering the TPC more often than required causing unstable network. In addition, the routing table created by the respective routing protocols at the lower layer has to be modified by sending control messages to maintain a desired network topology. This process consumes additional energy. In addition, existing TPC's have time-consuming initialization phase that increases the latency of the network.

To overcome these disadvantages we propose DA-TPC. Our algorithm establishes a strong link between a pair of nodes making it more robust to changing environmental conditions. DA-TPC introduces multiple routing layers working in parallel and on different transmission power ranges. Instead of using variation in link quality as a trigger to adjust the power level, priority of the data is used as the only metric to make a decision to boost the transmitting power.

As shown in Fig. 1 the application layer tags the data that it receives from the sensors with specific priority. Based on the tagged information appropriate power level and routing protocol is activated at the lower layers. For instance, the temperature of the room is classified as high priority data once it reaches an unusual level. If the temperature of the room is within an expected pre-defined level it is classified as a low priority data. In case of high priority data, DA-TPC boosts the transmission power to make sure that the critical (high priority) data reaches the destination with higher guarantee. DA-TPC targets the reliability of high priority data by boosting the transmission power to the maximum level available by the transciever. This also reduces path length and latency. In case of low priority data, reliability is improved by employing transmission power slightly better than the Critical Transmission Range (CTR). Achieving more stable links saves energy as there is no extra overhead in transmitting control messages by the routing protocol in case the link breaks due to CTR. Furthermore, by executing the initialization phase in all the nodes simultaneously the network becomes operational instantaneously.

The main objective of the paper is to provide a proof of concept of our idea and to evaluate its performance in terms of reliability, latency, and energy

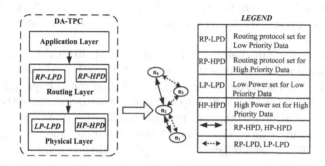

Fig. 1. Overview of DA-TPC

consumption of not only the initialization phase but also the power consumed transmitting data in the networks of various sizes.

The rest of the paper is organized as follows. In Sect. 2, we provide the related work. Section 3 provides the information about the design of DA-TPC. Section 4 talks about the experimental setup. Section 5 provides the information about performance metrics used to evaluate our algorithm. Section 6 gives the detailed analysis of the results obtained. In Sect. 7, we summarize and conclude the paper.

2 Related Work

The general working of the TPC algorithm discussed in the literature is elaborated in Fig. 2.

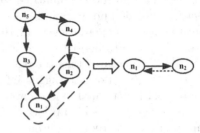

Fig. 2. Link quality model based TPC architecture

In Fig. 2 all of N; where N=$n_1,n_2,...,n_5$ nodes in the network performs initialization phase. In the subset of the network consisting a pair of nodes (n_1, n_2); n_1 broadcasts certain amount of beacon messages to the receiver node n_2 using different power levels supported by specific radio transceiver of the sensor node. Node n_2 then builds a model that reflects the correlation of the transmission power and the link quality. Based on the knowledge inferred from the model, node n_2 recommends specific power level to node n_1 (ACK phase) to use in case there is a variation in the link quality in course of time. This generic TPC design has the following drawbacks

1. Building a model on the receiver node that accurately correlates the transmission power with link quality consumes high power. This is because a significant amount of probe packets has to be sent from the sender node. Furthermore, initialization performed by all the nodes at different time slots delays the uptime of the network.
2. If the link quality falls below a certain predefined threshold specified in the TPC algorithm, the receiver node sends ACK packet to the sender node suggesting a change in the power level. Calibrating the link quality threshold level may differ from one location to another due to uniqueness of the location. Therefore, due to uncertainty in the propagation medium, the ACK phase might be executed more often and thereby consumes more energy. Hence, fine-tuning the threshold level is error prone, time consuming and energy inefficient.

3. Though RSSI can be used to assess the link quality proactively during actual data transfer between the nodes in a multihop fashion [9], adopting it as a network metric for the initialization phase is more error prone. This is especially the case when all the nodes simultaneously perform the initialization phase to reduce latency. This is because RSSI is the summation of the signal strength and the noise floor. The noise floor is the transmission signal from other adjacent pair of nodes that are not directly in communication. Therefore, utilization of the RSSI as a metric by the receiver nodes to calculate the power level to be adopted by the sender nodes is not appropriate.
4. As a part of an effort to maintain certain network topology, prominent routing protocols such as RPL, AODV and CTP transmits control messages quite often. These control messages along with frequent piggybacking of the messages from the TPC algorithm can drain the battery of the nodes sooner.
5. Frequent adjustment of the power level can destabilize the network [19]. If transmission power changes frequently, there is a potential risk of breaking previously well-connected network. As a result, routing protocols may take extra time and energy to readjust and find a new best route.

Our proposed DA-TPC algorithm eliminates the above-mentioned drawbacks of the generic TPC and provides higher reliability and lower latency in the networks of various sizes with 35 % to 96 % lower power consumption compared to other prominent TPC algorithms in discussion.

3   Design of DA-TPC

DA-TPC is implemented in the TelosB motes equipped with a CC2420 transceiver running Contiki OS. First, we provide the general architecture of our algorithm. Next, we describe the three phases and overall working of DA-TPC.

3.1   Overview of DA-TPC Modules

The uniqueness of DA-TPC lies in adapting the power level based on the priority of the data rather than changing it based on the variation of RSSI or LQI. DA-TPC has three main components as shown in Fig. 3. The purpose of the initialization phase is to discover the neighboring nodes and determine the optimal power level (refer Sect. 3.2) to use while relaying low priority data. The anomaly detection component at the application layer is responsible for checking the priority of the data, setting the appropriate power level, and calling the appropriate routing protocol. The purpose of the routing component is to multihop the data from the source to destination. DA-TPC has two routing tables - one for relaying low priority data and the other for relaying high priority data.

3.2   Initialization Phase

The main purpose of the initialization phase is to determine a power level to be used by the routing protocol to relay low priority data. The chosen power

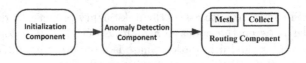

Fig. 3. General Architecture of TPC

is adequate enough to transmit data without corruption while maintaining the links and the energy as stable and energy efficient as possible. All the nodes in the network performs initialization phase, where each node advertises a probe packet. These packets contain the subset of power levels that was used to transmit it. The neighboring nodes that are within the range of above mentioned power levels receives a unique probe packets from a specific node and stores the corresponding power levels and their node id. Receiving nodes then use this power level to relay sensor data. A detailed list of the power levels used by the CC2420 transceiver is provided in the Table 1 [6].

Table 1. Power consumption and their communication range for CC2420 obtained from COOJA Simulator

Power Levels	3	7	11	15	19	23	27	31
Distance(m)	3	10	16	22	29	34	40	48
Output Power(mA)	8.5	9.9	11.2	12.5	13.9	15.2	16.5	17.4

One of the simplest methods to save energy of the nodes is to use only a subset of the power levels. A WSN deployment technician would know the minimum distance the nodes are placed from one another. Designing the algorithm based on this fact and knowing the communication range offered by each power level of respective transceiver, one can avoid broadcasting probe packets at every power level as it is done in ATPC [10]. For example, as a proof of concept, we used only 3 power levels (11, 15, and 19) out of 8 available levels provided by the CC2420 transceiver [6] to transmit low priority data. In addition, configuring the algorithm to use a subset of power levels based on the network topology is much easier than tweaking the RSSI threshold model that are widely used in existing TPC to adapt transmission power. The reason for this is that RSSI can change abruptly because of change in environmental conditions [3]. Moreover, the orientation of the node also has significant impact on RSSI [22]. As a result, configuring the link quality threshold model based TPC algorithms must undergo time-consuming trial and error phase before the network becomes operational.

Next, we provide a scenario and explain the working of initialization phase. During boot up, all nodes perform the initialization phase by broadcasting three probe packets every three seconds at power levels 11, 15, 19 respectively. In Fig. 4, Node D receives only one unique packet from all the nodes. Let us assume that the packet sent at power level 11 by the node A is received by node D and corresponding packets sent at level 15 and 19 are dropped by the node D. Since initialization phase is performed simultaneously by all the nodes, due to collision,

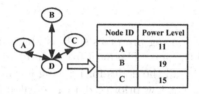

Fig. 4. Working of Initialization Phase of DA-TPC

the probe packet sent by node B at first two power levels might not be received by node D. However, the packet sent at level 19 is received by the node D which stores the information in memory. Similarly due to collision, node C s packet sent at level 15 alone is received by the node D. Finally, node D sets the maximum power level (19) from the list. The mesh routing algorithm in node A then uses this power level to relay a low priority data with any of the nodes based on the shortest path to the sink.

DA-TPC employs an initialization phase that does not maintain a comprehensive list of information from all the nodes and hence is more memory efficient. In Fig. 4, imagine node A is 15 m apart from the source node D and has a low priority data to send. The mesh routing algorithm of DA-TPC running in node D chooses node A has the first hop to its destination. As per working of the algorithm discussed above, Node D to communicate with node A uses power level 19 that has a communication range of 29 m (refer to Table 1). Not utilizing a minimum power (11) which is just enough to establish a link between pair of nodes D and A as done by various other TPC algorithms such as MODTPC, AODPTC [13] seems counter intuitive. However, by establishing a weak link with minimum power, we run into the risk of breaking the communication path. Therefore, maximum power level from the subset is chosen to keep the network stable as long as possible. After the sink completes its initialization phase, it uses the maximum power level (31) of CC2420 to advertise its presence as a sink at fixed interval rate shorter than the initialization phase using Collect routing protocol available in Contiki OS.

3.3 Anomaly Detection Phase

Anomaly detection component has two main tasks. First, it checks if the priority of the data is low or high. Second, it is a mapper function as shown in (1) that maps the priority of the data to specific power level and routing protocol to be used by the node to relay the low or high priority sensor data.

$$(P_{tx}, R) = f(P_r) \tag{1}$$

$P_r \epsilon \{P_l, P_h\}$ is the set of priorities that a sensor data is tagged with. Here, P_l and P_h represents a low and high priority. The set $P_{tx} \epsilon \{Max_{initpow}, Max_{transpow}\}$ represent the specific power levels selected. $Max_{initpow}$ and $Max_{transpow}$ are the subset of power levels determined at initialization phase and the maximum power level available in CC2420 transceiver respectively. The setR $\epsilon \{R_m, R_c\}$ contains routing protocols such as mesh (R_m) and Collect (R_c).

3.4   Routing Phase

Nodes use two standard routing protocols such as Mesh and Collect of Contiki OS to multihop data to the sink. The path from source to the destination node is dynamically selected by all the nodes for relaying low and high priority data. A multihop path to relay a low priority data is created by mesh the routing protocol and is initiated by the node that has a data to relay. A path to relay critical a data must be created beforehand to ensure high reliability. Therefore, the sink node initiates the creation of the high priority data path by advertising its presence every two seconds to all the nodes within its maximum power level (31) range. Having more than one routing protocol is a purposeful design choice. When a particular node has a high priority data, it must relay this with low delay. This would require a source node to reach the intermediate node much farther in the network so as to reduce the path length. This implies that the source node must choose a node other than the one that is has selected for relaying low priority data.

Adapting the topology on the fly to multihop a low or high priority data means clearing the previously constructed routing table frequently. Modifying a routing table causes delay in relaying sensor data. Above all, it incurs additional energy spending.

By having two different routing tables constructed by the two different routing protocols we have separate dedicated links readily available. This contributes to increase in a overall network reliability.

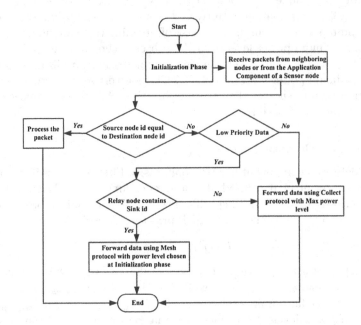

Fig. 5. Flow Chart of DA-TPC

3.5 DA-TPC Workflow

Figure 5 illustrates the entire workflow of DA-TPC. Once the initialization phase running in the nodes determines the power level to be utilized to relay low priority data, the anomaly detection component in the node checks the data priority (low or high) and maps it to a specific power level and a routing protocol (Mesh or Collect).

4   Experimental and Simulation Set Up

Our algorithm is evaluated for two networks comprising a set of 10 and 20 nodes as shown in Fig. 6. These networks are deployed and executed in the Cooja Simulator [17]. The nodes are randomly deployed. The minimum distance between a two adjacent nodes that can be connected directly is 10 m in both the networks. The low and high priority data are represented by a dashed and a solid lines respectively. The low priority data is sent every 6 and 12 s in two different networks for 30 min each. Similarly, a high priority data is sent randomly every 2 to 4 s in two different networks for 30 min as well. The following settings were kept constant for the entire experiments:

1. Both networks consists of only one source node represented as n_1 and one sink node represented as n_{10} and n_{20} respectively.
2. Both networks use the Unit Disk Graph Model (UDGM) to emulate a link failure [1].
3. The node start-up delay was set to a default simulator value of 1000 ms.
4. CSMA is used as the Medium Access Control (MAC) protocol and CXMAC, a version of X-MAC [5] is used as the Radio Duty Cycle (RDC)model with channel check rate set to 2 Hz.
5. We assume the wireless link to be a symmetrical.

5   Performance Evaluation Metrics

The performance of our algorithm is evaluated in terms of Packet Delivery Ratio (PDR), average end-to-end latency, per packet energy consumption while transmitting low and high priority data along a specific path in both the networks

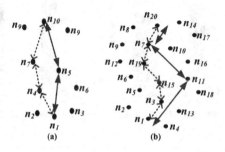

Fig. 6. Networks with 10 (Fig. 6a) and 20 (Fig. 6b) nodes showing multihop path taken by a data from the source to a sink

shown in Fig. 6. In addition, energy consumption of the initialization phase of DA-TPC is also compared with other prominent TPC algorithms.

PDR is defined as the successful transmission of data packets from the source node to a sink node [21]. It is calculated as shown in (2)

$$PDR = \frac{TotalPacketsReceived}{TotalPacketsSent} \tag{2}$$

Latency is defined as the time taken for the packets to reach the sink node from the source node [1]. It is calculated as shown in (3) and (4)

$$TotalLatency = \sum_{k=1}^{p} Receivedtime(k) - Senttime(k) \tag{3}$$

$$AverageLatency = \frac{TotalLatency}{TotalPacketsReceived} \tag{4}$$

Here, p is the total number of packets received successfully.

The total transmission energy spent by the nodes in communication on a specific path for both the networks is calculated as shown in (5) [21]

$$\sum_{i=1}^{N} \frac{E_i}{N} \tag{5}$$

Here E_i, is the energy spent during transmission of packets by node i. N is the total number of nodes in the mutlithop paths.

6   Results and Discussion

Network Reliability is measured in terms of PDR. From Fig. 7a we can see that by using DA-TPC, PDR above 98 % is achieved while transmitting low priority packets and 100 % PDR is achieved while transmitting high priority packets in

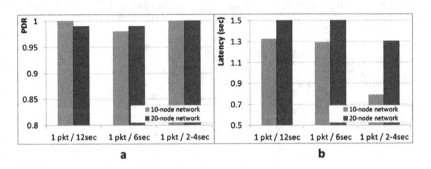

Fig. 7. Reliability and Latency of the networks. Fig. 7(a) and Fig. 7(b) presents PDR and Latency of 10 and 20 nodes network relaying packets at different time intervals

both the networks. The reason for this 2 % packet loss while sending low priority packet in both the networks is because, the relay nodes take some time to find the best path to destination and, as a result, some of the sensor data are lost due to packet timeouts. However, since the sink advertises itself more frequently and faster than the initialization phase, the path from the source to a sink through the relay node is built quicker.

Figure 7b provides the latency results under various scenarios. The average latency of a 10 nodes network while transmitting higher priority data is 40 % and 38 % lower compared to transmitting low priority data at 12 and 6 s intervals.

Similarly, the average latency of 20 nodes network while transmitting high priority data is 44 % and 28 % lower compared to its counterpart sent at the same intervals. In spite of doubling the size of the network from 10 to 20 nodes, the latency while transmitting higher priority data in the dense network is not increased significantly. As the density of the network increases, reducing the latency of the network while transmitting a crucial data is important. From Fig. 7b, it is evident that DA-TPC is capable of reducing latency, which is a desirable property for WSNs.

Apart from high reliability and reduced latency, saving the power of the nodes is also important. Figure 8a provides the information about the energy consumed to send one packet on a specific path in the two networks under scrutiny. The path chosen to route a packet from the source to a sink in 10 and 20 nodes networks is shown in the Sect. 4. The energy consumed to relay high priority packet in the 10-node network is 25 % lower compared to relaying a low priority data in the same network. The energy consumed transmitting a high priority data in 20 nodes network stands at 30 %. The reason for this is that packets take a fewer hops before they reach their destination. This shows that even by doubling the network size, the energy necessary to transmit high priority data remains low. This also confirms that multihop does not necessarily save energy [15].

Finally, we compare the energy drawn during the initialization phase between a pair of nodes having CC2420 transceivers in the best-case scenario using the equation as shown in (6)

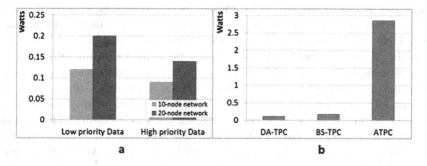

Fig. 8. Fig. 8(a) presents per path energy consumption consumed to send low and high priority data in 10 and 20 nodes network. Figure 8(b) presents energy consumption of initialization phase of various TPC's

$$\sum_{i=1}^{P} TP_{sn} + TP_{rn} \qquad (6)$$

Here TP_{sn}, TP_{rn} are the energy spent during transmission of probe packets by the source and the receiver nodes respectively.p is the total number of probe packets sent. Figure 8b provides the energy consumption details of DA-TPC and other popular TPC protocols. It is evident from Fig. 8b that DA-TPC consumes 35 % and 96 % less power than TPC-BS and ATPC respectively. The reason for higher power utilization in ATPC and TPC-BS is because they have a longer initialization phase and the receiving nodes acknowledge every probe packets sent by the source node. On the other hand, DA-TPC has a short initialization phase with receiving nodes not acknowledging the probe packets.

7 Conclusion and Future Work

In this paper, we introduced a new TPC algorithm, dubbed DA-TPC, that employs priority of the data as a metric to adapt the transmission power instead of relying on network metric such as LQI, RSSI. Uncertainty in the environment causes the variations in the link quality and thereby triggering TPC to change the power level frequently. Switching the power level often can destabilize the network. Furthermore, nodes using just enough power to communicate with one another can also increase the probability of breaking the network causing the underlying routing algorithm to send control messages. All these issues cause the delay and increases the energy consumption. By introducing data as a metric and changing the power only when the data is of high priority, we keep the network stable for a longer duration. Running DA-TPC in a sensor network of various sizes in COOJA simulator we find that reliability above 98 % can be achieved while transmitting both low and high priority data. The latency is reduced by 40 % and 38 % while transmitting high priority data at various time intervals in a 10-node network. Similarly, the latency in 20 nodes network while transmitting high priority data is 44 % and 28 % less compared to its counterpart sent at different time intervals. Energy consumption transmitting a high priority data is 25 % and 30 % less compared to relaying a low priority data in 10 and 20 nodes network. In addition, the energy consumption of the initialization phase in DA-TPC is 35 % and 96 % less compared other popular TPC's.

In the future, we would like to test the performance of our algorithm in larger network deployments with multiple source nodes and various other routing protocols [7,18]. In addition, having decentralized algorithm without the static sink makes it more scalable [12]. Predicting the sensor data quality and network condition before choosing appropriate routing path is necessary. This feature will enable DA-TPC to make a highly dynamic topology in a scalable manner [20].Therefore, our goal in the future work will be to design DA-TPC to be more cognitive in nature [11].

Acknowledgment. This work has been partially supported by ARTEMIS project DEMANES (Design, Monitoring and Operation of Adaptive Networked Embedded Systems, contract 295372). I also take this opportunity to thank my colleague Chetan Belagal for providing his valuable insights.

References

1. Ali, H.: A Performance Evaluation of RPL in Contiki. Ph.D. thesis, Blekinge Institute of Technology, Sweden (2012)
2. Baccour, N., Koubâa, A., Mottola, L., Zúñiga, M.A., Youssef, H., Boano, C.A., Alves, M.: Radio link quality estimation in wireless sensor networks. ACM Trans. Sens. Netw. **8**(4), 1–33 (2012)
3. Bannister, K., Giorgetti, G., Gupta, S.K.: Wireless sensor networking for hot applications: effects of temperature on signal strength, data collection and localization. In: Proceedings of the 5th Work. Embed. Networked Sensors (HotEmNets 2008) (2008)
4. Barrenetxea, G., Ingelrest, F., Schaefer, G., Vetterli, M.: Wireless sensor networks for environmental monitoring: the sensorscope experience. In: 2008 IEEE International Zurich Semin. Commun., pp. 98–101. IEEE, March 2008
5. Buettner, M., Yee, G.V., Anderson, E., Han, R.: X-MAC: a short preamble MAC protocol for duty-cycled wireless sensor networks. In: Procdings of the 4th International Conference on Embed. Networked Sens. Syst. - SenSys 2006, pp. 307–320. ACM Press, New York, October 2006
6. Chipcon: 2.4 GHz IEEE 802.15.4 / ZigBee-ready RF Transceiver. Technical report (2004). http://www.alldatasheet.com/datasheet-pdf/pdf/125399/ETC1/CC2420.html
7. Geelen, D., Van Kempen, G., Van Hoogstraten, F., Liotta, A.: A wireless mesh communication protocol for smart-metering. In: 2012 International Conference on Computing, Networking and Communications (ICNC), pp. 343–349. IEEE (2012)
8. Kim, J., Chang, S., Kwon, Y.: ODTPC: on-demand transmission power control for wireless sensor networks. In: 2008 International Conference on Inf. Netw. - ICOIN 2008, pp. 1–5. IEEE, Busan, January 2008
9. Kotian, R., Liotta, A.: Assessment of proactive transmission power control for wireless sensor networks. In: 9th International Conference on Body Area Networks, pp. 253–259 (2014)
10. Lin, S., Zhang, J., Zhou, G., Gu, L., Stankovic, J.A., He, T.: ATPC: adaptive transmission power control for wireless sensor networks. In: Proceedings of the 4th International Conference on Embed. networked Sens. Syst. - SenSys 2006, pp. 223–236. ACM Press, New York, October 2006
11. Liotta, A.: The cognitive net is coming. IEEE Spectrum **50**(8), 26–31 (2013)
12. Liotta, A., Knight, G., Pavlou, G.: On the performance and scalability of decentralised monitoring using mobile agents. In: Stadler, R., Stiller, B. (eds.) DSOM 1999. LNCS, vol. 1700, pp. 3–18. Springer, Heidelberg (1999)
13. Masood, M.M.Y., Ahmed, G., Khan, N.M.: A Kalman filter based adaptive on demand transmission power control (AODTPC) algorithm for wireless sensor networks. In: 2012 International Conference on Emerg. Technol., pp. 1–6, October 2012
14. Masood, M.M.Y., Ahmed, G., Khan, N.M.: Modified on demand transmission power control for wireless sensor networks. In: 2011 International Conference on Inf. Commun. Technol., pp. 1–6. IEEE, July 2011

15. Min, R., Chandrakasan, A.: Top five myths about the energy consumption of wireless communication. In: ACM SIGMOBILE Mob. Comput. Commun. Rev., vol. 7, p. 65. ACM, January 2002
16. Oh, S.H.: TPC-BS: Transmission power control based on binary search in the wireless sensor networks. In: 2012 IEEE Sensors Appl. Symposium Proceedings, pp. 1–6 (2012)
17. Osterlind, F., Dunkels, A., Eriksson, J., Finne, N., Voigt, T.: Cross-level sensor network simulation with COOJA. In: Proceedings of the 2006 31st IEEE Conference on Local Comput. Networks, pp. 641–648. IEEE, November 2006
18. Qadri, N.N., Liotta, A.: Analysis of pervasive mobile ad hoc routing protocols. In: Pervasive Computing, pp. 433–453. Springer, London (2010)
19. Santi, P.: Topology control in wireless ad hoc and sensor networks. ACM Comput. Surv. **37**(2), 164–194 (2005)
20. Sivavakeesar, S., Pavlou, G., Bohoris, C., Liotta, A.: Effective management through prediction-based clustering approach in the next-generation ad hoc networks. In: 2004 IEEE International Conference on Communications, vol. 7, pp. 4326–4330. IEEE (2004)
21. Teo, K.H., Abdullah, A., Subramaniam, S.K., Sinniah, G.R.: New reassembly buffer management system in 6LoWPAN. In: Proceedings of the Asia-Pacific Adv. Netw., vol. 36, pp. 57–64 (2013)
22. Wadhwa, M., Rali, V., Shetty, S.: The impact of antenna orientation on wireless sensor network performance. In: 2009 2nd IEEE International Conference on Comput. Sci. Inf. Technol., pp. 143–147. IEEE (2009)

Mining Regularities in Body Sensor Network Data

Syed Khairuzzaman Tanbeer[1], Mohammad Mehedi Hassan[2(✉)],
Majed Alrubaian[2], and Byeong-Soo Jeong[1]

[1] Department of Computer Engineering, Kyung Hee University,
Seoul, South Korea
{tanbeer,jeong}@khu.ac.kr
[2] College of Computer and Information Sciences, King Saud University,
Riyadh, Saudi Arabia
{mmhassan,malrubaian.c}@ksu.edu.sa

Abstract. The recent emergence of body sensor networks (BSNs) has made it easy to continuously collect and process various health-oriented data related to temporal, spatial and vital sign monitoring of patient. As such, discovering or mining interesting knowledge from the BSN data stream is becoming an important issue to promote and assist important decision making in healthcare. In this paper, we focus on mining the inherent regularity of different parameter readings obtained from different body sensors related to vital sign data of a patent for the purpose of following up health condition to prevent some kinds of chronic diseases. Specifically we design and develop an efficient and scalable regular pattern mining technique that can mine the complete set of periodically/regularly occurring patterns in BSN data stream based on a user-specified periodicity/regularity threshold for the data and the subject. Various experiments were carried on both real and synthetic data to validate the efficiency of the proposed regular pattern mining technique as compared to state-of-the-art approaches.

Keywords: Body sensor network · Regular pattern mining · Healthcare · Decision support

1 Introduction

Recent advances in the intelligent sensors, microelectronics, and wireless communication have enabled the development of body sensor networks (BSN) that is used to collect and process biological information of a patient, which can be used to extract knowledge about the health condition of patients [1]. Therefore, in recent years, activity recognition [2–4] has been one of the most focused research areas with the data generated by body sensor network. The main goal of activity recognition is to monitor the activities of daily living for providing better healthcare, social care and/or proactive assistance to users (e.g., elderly, cognitively impaired people, and/or patients). However, in some scenarios it might be helpful to provide better assistance, if we have knowledge about the behavior profiles of the parameters sensed by the body sensors. For example, identifying the periodical changes in blood pressure of a patient can be

© Springer International Publishing Switzerland 2015
G. Di Fatta et al. (Eds.): IDCS 2015, LNCS 9258, pp. 88–99, 2015.
DOI: 10.1007/978-3-319-23237-9_9

useful information for doctors to provide proper treatment to a particular patient. Additionally, prediction on the change of blood pressure of the patient can be helpful in pro-active healthcare. Thus, discovering patterns having temporal relationship among the readings obtained from the BSN can make a great difference in handling/providing care to the user. In other words, discovering shape of occurrence–i.e., whether the pattern occurs periodically, irregularly, or mostly in a specific time interval can be important criteria for analyzing BSN data.

Nevertheless, finding such interesting knowledge from BSN data by using pattern matching [5, 6] or activity recognition [7, 8, 20, 21] algorithms may not be suitable, mainly because of the involvement of large volume and variety of BSN data streams which include text as well as media data such as image, video having high data rate. Recently, data mining techniques are being utilized in discovering interesting knowledge from the BSN data [5, 6, 9, 11–14]. Ali et al. [9] has developed a software architecture to find routine behavior based on patient's activity pattern. It uses a frequent pattern mining [10] technique to obtain frequent activity patterns which enables the observation of the inherent structure present in a patient's daily activity. Gu et al. [5] exploited the notion of emerging patterns to identify the significant changes between the classes of data for a smooth and efficient recognition of daily living activity. A close look at all of these pattern mining approaches may reveal that their ultimate goal is still to identify or classify subject's activity.

In this paper, our approach is different in the sense that, we focus on identifying or mining the inherent regularity of different parameter readings obtained from different body sensors for the purpose of following up patient's health condition to prevent some kinds of chronic diseases. The pattern appearance behavior in transactional databases has been extensively studied by Tanbeer et al. in [15–17]. In [15] they introduced regular patterns, a new type of pattern that follows temporal occurrence regularity in a transactional database. This approach uses a regularity measure determined by the maximum occurrence interval of a pattern in a database and a regularity threshold to identify such patterns. This work also proposed a tree-based data structure, called RP-tree, to capture database information with two database scans. In case of BSN data stream scenario, however, the database is updated with a new block of data at regular time intervals (incremental). Thus, the two database-based RP-tree approach is not suitable in finding regularity in incremental sensor data. The IncRT in [17] also fails to address the above problem, as it fails to update the tree on transaction deletions.

Hence, to find regularity in BSN data, we propose a novel approach, called the SDR-tree (Sensor Data Regularity-tree), to capture the updated sensor data information in a compact manner. Once the SDR-tree is constructed, we use an efficient pattern growth-based mining technique [10] to mine the inherent regularities in patient readings. Study on both real and synthetic datasets shows that finding inherent regularities in continuously updated BSN data with SDR-tree is more efficient than that with the RP-tree.

The remaining part of the paper is presented as follows. We introduce the problem of finding pattern regularity on updated BSN in Sect. 2. Section 3 presents the structure and mining technique of our proposed SDR-tree. Section 4 reports the experimental results and finally, Sect. 5 concludes the paper.

2 Problem Definition

Similar to the problem definition in [17], we present the basic notations and definitions of the *regular* pattern mining in body sensor database.

Let $L = \{s_1, s_2, ..., s_n\}$ be a set of body sensors in a particular body sensor network. A set $X = \{s_j, ..., s_k\} \subseteq L$, where $j \leq k$ and $j, k \in [1, n]$, is called a *pattern* of sensors. A body sensor database, *SD*, over L, is defined to be a set of epochs $T = \{t_1, ..., t_m\}$, where each epoch $t = (tid, Y)$ is a tuple where *tid* represents the timeslot-id of sensor event occurrence (we assume that the time space is divided into equal sized slots) and Y is a pattern of event-detecting sensors that report events within the same time slot. If $X \subseteq Y$, it is said that t contains X or X occurs in t and such timeslot-*id* is denoted as $t_j^X j \in [1, m]$. Therefore, $T^X = \{t_j^X, ..., t_k^X\}$, $j, k \in [1, m]$ and $j \leq k$ is the set of all timeslot-*ids* where X occurs in *SD*.

Table 1. A sensor dataset (*SD*)

Id	Epoch	Id	Epoch	Id	Epoch
1	$S_4, S_1,$	4	S_1, S_2, S_5, S_3	7	S_5, S_3, S_4
2	S_3, S_2, S_1, S_5	5	S_1, S_5, S_2, S_6	8	S_4, S_5, S_6
3	S_6, S_1, S_5, S_2	6	S_4, S_2, S_3	9	S_2, S_3, S_4

Definition 1 (a period of X). Let t_{j+1}^X and $t_j^X j \in [1, (m-1)]$, be two consecutive timeslot-*ids* in T^X. The number of timeslots (or the time difference) between t_{j+1}^X and t_j^X is defined as a period of X, say p^X (i.e., $p^X = t_{j+1}^X - t_j^X j \in [1, (m-1)]$). For the simplicity of period computation, a '*null*' epoch with no sensor sensor is considered at the beginning of *SD*, i.e., $t_f = null$, where t_f represents the first epoch to be considered. Similarly, t_l, the last epoch to be considered, is the *m*-th epoch in *SD*, i.e., $t_l = t_m$. For instance, in the body sensor database in Table 1 the set of epochs where pattern "S_2, S_6" appears is $T^{S2,S6} = \{3, 5\}$. Therefore, the periods for "S_2, S_6" are 3 (= 3 - t_f), 2 (= 5 - 3), and 4 (= t_l - 5), where $t_f = 0$ and $t_l = 9$.

The above occurrence periods present relevant information about the appearance behavior of a pattern. As discussed in [17], a pattern will not be *regular* if, at any stage in database, it appears after sufficiently large period. The largest occurrence period of a pattern, therefore, can provide the upper limit of its periodic occurrence characteristic. Hence, the measure of the characteristic of a pattern of being *regular* in a *SD* (i.e., the *regularity* of that pattern) can be defined as follows.

Definition 2 (regularity of pattern X). Let for a T^X, P^X be the set of all periods of X i.e., $P^X = \{p_1^X, ..., p_r^X\}$, where r is the total number of periods of X in *SD*. Then, the *regularity* of X can be denoted as $reg(X) = Max(p_1^X, ..., p_r^X)$. For example, in the database of Table 1, $reg(S_2, S_6) = 4$ i.e., $Max(3, 2, 4)$.

Therefore, a pattern is called a *regular* pattern if its *regularity* is no more than a user-given maximum *regularity* threshold called *max_reg* λ, with $1 \leq \lambda \leq |SD|$. The *regularity* threshold can be set as the percentage of database size e.g., *max_reg* = 10 % of $|SD|$ may indicate $\lambda = 0.1 \times |SD|$. *Regular pattern mining problem*, given a λ and a *SD*, is to discover the complete set of *regular* patterns having *regularity* no more than λ in the SD. RP_{SD} refers to the complete set of all *regular* patterns in a *SD* for a given *max_reg*.

Let SD^+ and SD^- respectively denote the set of added and deleted transactions to and from *SD*. The updated database denoted as *USD*, is obtained from $SD \cup db^+$, or $SD \cup db^-$, or $SD \cup db^+ \cup db^-$. Given *SD*, $SD_i^{+/-}$ (*i* be the number of updates on *SD*) and a λ, *incremental regular pattern mining*, is to discover the RP_{USD}, *regular* pattern mining, is to find the RP_{SD} or RP_{USD} with the change of λ but keeping the database fixed.

3   SDR-Tree: Design, Construction and Mining

The proposed Sensor Data Regularity-Tree (SDR-tree), is designed to capture complete (updated) BSN data with a single scan of sensor network readings. It captures all information of each sensor epoch in a compact structure, that allows us avoid repeated scanning of the sensor database.

3.1   SDR-Tree Structure

Similar to a RP-tree, the SDR-tree has a root node and a set of sub-trees (children of the root). It also maintains a header table called sensor data table (SD-table) to capture information for each distinct sensor with relative regularity. A separate pointer from each sensor in the SD-table points to the first node in the SDR-tree that carries the sensor. Similar to an RP-tree, there are two types of nodes in an SDR-tree: the ordinary node and the tail-node. While both nodes maintain parent, children, and node traversal pointers, the tail-nodes additionally keep track of all epochs (in a tid-list) where it is the last node. Thus, N[t1, t2, ..., tn], represents a tail-node, where N is the name of sensor node and ti, is the timeslot-id of an epoch where N is the last sensor sensor (n be the total number of epochs from the root down to the node). It is important to note that, neither an ordinary node nor a tail-node in an SDR-tree does maintain support count value in it.

Unlike the R-table in an RP-tree, the SD-table in an SRD-tree consists of five fields in sequence (i, r, t_l, m, p): (i) sensor name (i), (ii) the *regularity* of i (r), (iii) the most recent *tid* where i occurred, (iv) a one-bit flag (m) to indicate any changes for i and (v) a pointer to the SDR-tree for i (p). The structure and the construction processes of the SD-table in an SDR-tree significantly differ from those of the R-table in an RP-tree. Each entry in the SD-table The *regularity* (r) and t_l for each sensor is calculated after constructing the SDR-tree and traversing it once - as explained in the next subsection. The m field is set only if the sensor data sensor is modified (i.e., appeared or deleted) in any epoch in the current database (e.g., either original *SD* or SD^+). The pointer p facilitates a fast traversal to the tree for sensor i.

3.2   SDR-Tree Construction

The construction of an SDR-tree is similar to that of the FP-tree [10] and RP-tree [12]. However, unlike the FP-tree and RP-tree, it uses (i) single database scan and

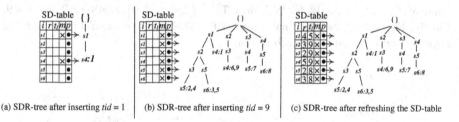

(a) SDR-tree after inserting *tid* = 1 | (b) SDR-tree after inserting *tid* = 9 | (c) SDR-tree after refreshing the SD-table

Fig. 1. Construction of an SDR-tree for the *SD* of Table 1

(ii) captures the complete database information in a compact fashion. Moreover, an SDR-tree can be constructed without prior knowledge of the *regularity* threshold. The single pass construction also allows the SDR-tree to arrange sensors according to any canonical order, determined by the user prior to the tree construction-such as lexicographic or alphabetical order, or according to some specific order on sensor properties (e.g., weights, values, or some constraints). Once the sensor order is determined (say, for *SD*), all sensors will follow this order in our SDR-tree for subsequent updated databases (e.g., $SD \cup db_1^+, SD \cup db_1^+ \cup db_2^+, \ldots$). With this setting (i.e., the canonical order), an SDR-tree holds the following property:

Property 1. Sensors in an SDR-tree are arranged in a fixed global (canonical) order.

Let us visit the following SDR-tree construction example for the SD in Table 1 in lexicographic order (in Fig. 1).The construction of SDR-tree starts with an empty *root* node. The first inserted epoch is. As shown in Fig. 1(a), the first epoch $\{S_4, S_1\}$ (i.e., *tid* = 1) is inserted in lexicographic order, and the *tid* information of the epoch is recorded in the tail node "S_4:1". This figure also shows the status of the SD-table which sets the *m*-field for both sensors (i.e., 'S_1' and 'S_4') indicating that these two sensors appeared in the current *SD*. To simplify the figures, we the node traversal pointers are not shown. After inserting all the epochs in a similar fashion, the final SDR-tree is given in Fig. 1(b).

As mentioned before, once the SDR-tree is constructed, we use the sensor pointers from the SD-table to traverse the tree and calculate the *regularity* (*r*) of each sensor in the SD-table. We call this process of updating the SD-table entries as refreshing the SD-table. To assist this process, we assign a temporary array for each sensor in the SD-table and accumulate the *tid*(s) in its *tail*-node(s) in the array by traversing the whole tree once. This process of accumulating *tid*(s) starts from the bottom-most sensor of the SD-table and ends with the top-most sensor.

Continuing with our running example, after visiting all the *tail*-nodes of the last sensor 'S_6' in the SD-table, the contents of the temporary arrays for sensors 'S_1', 'S_2', 'S_4', 'S_5', and 'S_6' (i.e., sensors from *tail*-nodes up to the *root*) are S_1:{3, 5}, S_2:{3, 5}, S_4:{3, 5, 8}, S_5:{3, 5, 8}, and S_6:{3, 5, 8}. We repeat the whole process for each sensor in the SD-table. Thus, the temporary array of every sensor will contain the complete list of its *tid*s, very when we finish the tree traversal for the top-most sensor in the SD-table.. For example, the set of epochs for sensor 'S_1' we get, $T^{S1} = \{1, 2, 3, 4, 5\}$. Then, it is trivial calculation to find the P^{S1} from T^{S1}, which gives $reg(S_1) = 4$ and t_l

value of 'S$_1$' = 5. Similarly, for 'S$_3$', since T^{S3} = {2, 4, 6, 7, 9}, reg(S$_3$) = 2, and t_l = 9. Finally, Fig. 2(c) shows the final status of the SDR-tree and the SD-table with the *regularity* and the last *tid* of each sensor.

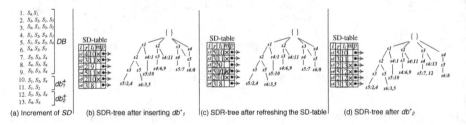

Fig. 2. The SDR-tree on increment of SD

The SDR-tree update mechanism discussed above is also effective on updating the tree on deletion of epoch(s). To keep the tree updated and ready-to-mine condition after each epoch (say *t*) deletion, we follow the following steps: First, we visit each tail nodes, remove the *tid* of *t* from its *tid*-list (if it contains that *tid*), and decrement *tids* in the list by one for the *tids* greater than tid of *t*. Second, if the tid-list contains only 0 (zero) or no *tid*, remove the path from the *tail*-node up to the root. Third, we refresh the SD-table to reflect the updated information. Since only *tail*-nodes in an SDR-tree keeps epoch information, adjusting only the *tid* values in *tid*-lists of *tail*-nodes guarantees complete update of the SDR-tree for epoch deletions from the database. It is tempting to assume that the SDR-tree may be memory inefficient, as it explicitly maintains tids in it. But, with a further observation we can argue that the memory efficiency is achieved by an SDR-tree through (i) keeping *tid*-information only at the tail-nodes and (ii) avoiding the support count field at each node. Moreover, various efficient frequent pattern mining tree structures in literature were designed maintaining the *tid* information in it [18].

The SD-table refreshing process terminates the SDR-tree construction, and makes the tree readily available for mining and/or for further updates. To reflect the next update for each sensor, all m-fields in the SD-table are reset before the update of the SDR-tree, or as the mining operation completes.

3.3   The SDR-Tree in Incremental Database

Let the *DB* in Table 1 is updated by two blocks of epochs (db_1^+ and db_2^+), each block may consist of one or more epochs, as shown in Fig. 2(a). This figure demonstrates the status of our SDR-tree after inserting the epoch in db_1^+. Since the SDR-tree always maintains a fixed global order, new epochs in db_1^+ (i.e., *tids* 10 and 11) can be inserted in the same order following its construction process discussed in the previous subsection. It is important to note that, m-field values for 'S$_1$', 'S$_2$', 'S$_4$', 'S$_5$', and 'S$_6$' in the SD-table are again set in Fig. 2(b), which specify the appearance of only these sensors in db_1^+. Later in this section, we explain how such information (i.e., status in m-field) in SD-table significantly reduces the mining cost during incremental mining. To obtain the updated *regularity* of each sensor, we need to refresh the SD-table once again. We save substantial amount effort in this process by refreshing the tree only for the sensors that got set value in the *m*-field (i.e., for sensors 'S_1', 'S_2', 'S_4', 'S_5', and 'S_6'). With the help of the contents in the temporary array, and the previous values in *r* and t_l fields, it is rather trivial to obtain the updated *regularity* of each of such sensor. For other sensors in the SD-table (e.g., 'S_3', and 'S_6'), we consider only the t_l value of each sensor by the *tid* of t_{cur} (i.e., $t_{cur} = 11$), and at the same time the updated *regularity* of the sensor is calculated using its previous *r* and t_l values. After refreshing the SD-table, the updated SDR-tree and corresponding SD-table for db_1^+ are presented in Fig. 2(c). Similar to Fig. 2(c), Fig. 2(d) illustrates the status of the SDR-tree and corresponding SD-table after the update for db_2^+.

The SDR-tree update mechanism discussed above is also effective on updating the tree on deletion of epoch(s). To keep the tree updated and ready-to-mine condition after each epoch (say *t*) deletion, we follow the following steps: First, we visit each tail nodes, remove the *tid* of *t* from its *tid*-list (if it contains that *tid*), and decrement *tid*s in the list by one for the *tid*s greater than *tid* of *t*. Second, if the *tid*-list contains only 0 (zero) or no *tid*, remove the path from the *tail*-node up to the root. Third, we refresh the SD-table to reflect the updated information. Since only *tail*-nodes in an SDR-tree keeps epoch information, adjusting only the tid values in *tid*-lists of *tail*-nodes guarantees complete update of the SDR-tree for epoch deletions from the database.

It may be considered that SD-table refreshing mechanism of SDR-tree may need more computation cost compared to scanning the database twice as in RP-tree. However, we believe that the cost of refreshing the SD-table by traversing the SDR-tree once is much less than that by scanning the database a second time, since reading epoch information from the memory-resident tree is much faster than scanning it from the database.

3.4   Mining an SDR-Tree

As mentioned before, once the SDR-tree is constructed, we can mine *regular* patterns from it in a pattern growth-based approach. We proceed to construct the conditional pattern-base PB_i for sensor *i*, starting from the bottom-most sensor in the SD-table, by projecting only the prefix sub-paths of nodes labeled *i* in the SDR-tree. During this projection, we only include *regular* sensors. Determination of whether an sensor is *regular* can be easily done by a simple look-up (an $O(1)$ operation) at the SD-table. There is no worry about possible omission or doubly counting of sensors. Since *i* is the last sensor in SD-table, each node labeled *i* in the SDR-tree must be a *tail*-node. Therefore, the *tid*-lists of all such *tail*-nodes are pushed-up to respective parent nodes in the SDR-tree and in PB_i. Thus, the parent node is converted to a *tail*-node, if it was an *ordinary* node; otherwise (i.e., if the parent is not a *tail*-node), the *tid*-list is merged with its previous *tid*-list. All nodes labeled *i* in the SDR-tree and the entry for *i* in SD-table are, thereafter, deleted. Similar to the SD-table refreshing technique, to compute the *regularity* and the last occurring epoch of each sensor *j* in the SD-table*i* (i.e., the SD-table for PB_i) we refresh the SD-table$_i$ during constructing the PB_i. Therefore, computing $reg(ij)$ from T^{ij} by generating P^{ij} is rather trivial calculation.

Figure 3(a) represents the status of the SDR-tree of Fig. 1(c) after creating the conditional pattern-base of 'S_6' (i.e., the bottom-most sensor in the SD-table) PB_{S6} for $\lambda = 3$. The entry of 'S_6' in the SD-table, and all nodes representing sensor 'S_6' (i.e., nodes "S_6:3,5" and "S_6:8" in Fig. 1(c)) in the SDR-tree are deleted. The *tid*-list of each of such node is pushed-up to respective parent node of 'S_5' in the example. The PB_{S6} is constructed by projecting prefix sub-paths of nodes "S_6:3,5" and "S_6:8". Figure 3(b) shows the structure of PB_{S6} after the projections of the prefix sub-paths. Note that, nodes of only the *regular* sensors in each sub-path are accumulated in the PB_{S6}. For example, nodes of sensors 'S_5' and 'S_2' for the node "S_6:3,5", and that of sensor 'S_5' for "S_6:8" together constructs the PB_{S6}. Figure 3(b) also shows the status of the SD-Table$_{S6}$ which we obtain by executing the refresh SD-table operation for the PB_{S6}.

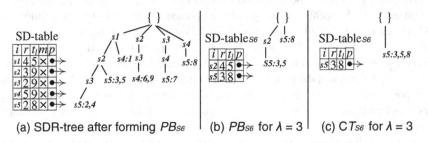

(a) SDR-tree after forming PB_{S6} | (b) PB_{S6} for $\lambda = 3$ | (c) CT_{S6} for $\lambda = 3$

Fig. 3. Conditional pattern-base and conditional tree construction with the SDR-tree of Fig. 1(c) for $\lambda = 3$

The conditional tree for i CT_i is, then, constructed from PB_i by removing the *irregular* sensor nodes respectively from SD-table$_i$ and PB_i. The *tid*-list of the deleted node is pushed-up to its parent node, as done before. The conditional tree for 'S_6' CT_{S6} can be created by removing sensor 'S_2' from the SD-Tables$_{S6}$ and node "S_2" from the PB_{S6}, since the *regularity* of 'S' in SD-Tables$_{S6}$ is greater than 3, the *regularity* threshold. The CT_{S6} is shown in Fig. 3(c). From the CT_i we create and store the set of *regular* patterns prefixing the sensor i. At the same time, we also store the last *tid* related to each pattern. From the CT_{S6} we generate pattern "S_5,S_6" with $reg(S_5,S_6) = 3$, and explicitly store the value of t_l of 'S_5' (i.e., 8). The whole process of conditional pattern-base and conditional tree constructions is repeated until the SD-table becomes empty. Before the update of the database, the m-field for each sensor in the SD-table is reset. Therefore, while mining after the next database increment (say, after inserting db_1^+) we mine only for the sensors m-fields of which in SD-table are found set. Since we store all *regular* patterns generated in previous mining operation with respective last *tid*, it is easy to update the *regularity* of other sensors in the SD-table considering t_{cur} = the last *tid* in db^+. Therefore, through the above mining process the complete set of *regular* patterns for a given *max_reg* can be generated from an SDR-tree constructed on a database. The technique is complete due to taking only *regular sensor* into consideration and performing the mining operation from bottom to top. Moreover, the SDR-tree, with its important feature of using previous mining information, offers an efficient technique in incremental *regular* pattern mining. The next section reports our experimental results.

Table 2. Dataset characteristics

Dataset	Size (MB)	#Trans	#Items	Max TL
T10I4D100K	3.93	100000	870	29
chess	0.34	3196	75	37
kosarak	30.50	990002	41270	2498

4 Experimental Results

We compare the performance of our SDR-tree with that of the RP-tree over several real (e.g., chess, kosarak) and synthetic (e.g., T10I4D100 K) datasets. There are primarily two reasons for choosing these commonly used datasets in frequent pattern mining experiments: the RP-tree is designed for transactional datasets, and they maintain similar characteristics to sensor epochs. These datasets are obtained from and UCI Machine Learning Repository (University of California – Irvine, CA). The characteristics of the datasets are shown in Table 2. For space constraint, we report the results on only a subset of the datasets. All programs were written in Microsoft Visual C ++ 6.0 and run with Windows XP on a 2.66 GHz machine with 1 GB of main memory.

4.1 Compactness of the SDR-Tree

In the first experiment, we report the results of compactness test for our SDR-tree on *chess*, *T10I4D100 K* and *kosarak* datasets in Fig. 4. For each of the datasets, we constructed the SDR-tree and measured the amount of memory it requires in each case to store the whole database content. *T10I4D100 K* and *kosarak* are reasonably large datasets with large number of transactions, and *chess*, on the other hand, is a small dataset with long transactions. The results depicts that even though the SDR-tree captures the full database information, its size can easily be handled with the currently available memory.

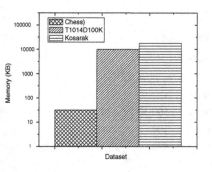

Fig. 4. Compactness of the SDR-tree

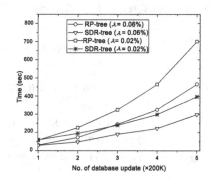

Fig. 5. Incremental mining on *kosarak*

4.2   Experiments on Incremental Mining

We show the results on the effectiveness of SDR-tree in incremental *regular* pattern mining on *chess* (with 3,196 transactions) and *kosarak* (with around 1 M transactions) datasets. To obtain an incremental setup for the datasets, we first divided *kosarak* into 5 consecutive slots of 200 K transactions in each, and *chess* into 3 consecutive slots of around 1 K transactions in each. Then we varied the number of incremental updates and tested the effect on runtime for both RP-tree and SDR-tree. We also varied the *max_reg* values at each update. The results are shown in Figs. 5 and 6 over *kosarak* and *chess* datasets, respectively.

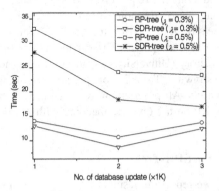

Fig. 6. Incremental mining on *chess*

For the RP-tree, at each update of database the whole process is executed from the scratch. However, in the case of our SDR-tree we just perform the SDR-tree update operation and corresponding mining at each update of database. Note that, Fig. 5 are opposite to those of Fig. 6. It reflects that, the overall runtime depends on the size of RP_{DB} as shown in Table 3 for two *max_reg* values for *chess*, and *kosarak*. This table also shows that for a fixed database, the number of regular pattern increases with the increase of *max_reg* in both datasets.

Table 3. No. of regular patterns

	Chess			Kosarak		
	$\lambda_1 = 0.2\ \%, \lambda_2 = 0.5\ \%$			$\lambda_1 = 0.1\ \%, \lambda_2 = 0.2\ \%$		
	$|UDB|$			$|UDB|$		
	1 K	2 K	3 K	100 K	500 K	1 M
λ_1	767	15	39	11	104	342
λ_2	3071	1023	559	38	472	1597

As shown in the graphs, for lower *max_reg* values and smaller database sizes both RP-tree and SDR-tree show similar performance. Our SDR-tree, in contrast, uses only a single scan to insert only the incremented portion of database in the already constructed

SDR-tree and then performs the mining operation. Therefore, the above experiments demonstrate that our SDR-tree significantly outperforms RP-tree in incremental *regular* pattern mining.

5   Conclusions

In this paper, we have introduced the concept of incremental *regular* pattern mining, a new interesting pattern mining problem, for body sensor data, and proposed a novel tree structure, called SDR-tee to efficiently capture the database content to facilitate a pattern growth-based mining technique. The experimental results demonstrate that the easy-maintenance feature of our SDR-tree provides the time and space efficiency in *regular* pattern mining upon update of database.

Acknowledgement. This project was funded by the National Plan for Science, Technology and Innovation (MAARIFAH), King Abdulaziz City for Science and Technology, Kingdom of Saudi Arabia, Award Number (12-INF2885-02).

References

1. Barroso, A., Benson, J., et al.: The DSYS25 sensor platform. In: Proceedings of the ACM Sensys 2004, Baltimore (2004)
2. Gaber, M.M., Gama, J., Krishnaswamy, S., Gomes, J.B., Stahl, F.: Data stream mining in ubiquitous environments: state-of-the-art and current directions. Wiley Interdisc. Rev. Data Min. Knowl. Discovery **4**(2), 116–138 (2014)
3. Bulling, A., Blanke, U., Schiele, B.: A tutorial on human activity recognition using body-worn inertial sensors. ACM Comput. Surv. (CSUR) **46**(3), 33 (2014)
4. Minnen, D., Starner, T., Essa, I., Isbell, C.: Discovering characteristic actions from on-body sensor data. In: Proceedings 10th IEEE International Symposium on Wearable Computers, pp. 11–18 (2006)
5. Gu, T., Wang, L., Wu, Z., Tao, X., Lu, J.: A pattern mining approach to sensor-based human activity recognition. IEEE Trans. Knowl. Data Eng. **23**(9), 1359–1372 (2011)
6. Hemalatha, C.S., Vaidehi, V.: Frequent bit pattern mining over tri-axial accelerometer data streams for recognizing human activities and detecting fall. Procedia Comput. Sci. **19**, 56–63 (2013)
7. Rashidi, P., Cook, D.J.: Mining sensor streams for discovering human activity patterns over time. In: Proceedings 2010 IEEE International Conference on Data Mining, pp. 431–440 (2010)
8. Lombriser, C., Bharatula, N.B., Roggen, D., Troster, G.: On-body activity recognition in a dynamic sensor network. In: Proceedings International Conference on Body Area Networks (BodyNets) (2007)
9. Ali, R., ElHelw, M., Atallah, L., Lo, B., Yang, G-Z.: pattern mining for routine behaviour discovery in pervasive healthcare environments. In: Proceedings of the 5th International Conference on Information Technology and Application in Biomedicine, China, pp. 241–244, 30-31 May 2008
10. Han, J., Pei, J., Yin, Y.: Mining frequent patterns without candidate generation. In: Proceedings ACM SIGMOD International Conference on Management of Data, pp. 1–12 (2000)

11. Suman, M.C., Prathyusha, K.: A body sensor network data repository with a different mining technique. Int. J. Eng. Sci. Adv. Technol. 2(1), 105–109 (2012)
12. Mooney, C.H., Roddick, J.F.: Sequential pattern mining–approaches and algorithms. ACM Comput. Surv. (CSUR) 45(2), 19 (2013)
13. Maqbool, F., Bashir, S., Baig, A.R.: E-MAP: efficiently mining asynchronous periodic patterns. Int. J. Comput. Sci. Netw. Secur. 6(8A), 174–179 (2006)
14. Amphawan, K., Lenca, P., Surarerks, A.: Mining top-k regular-frequent itemsets using database partitioning and support estimation. Expert Syst. Appl. 39(2), 1924–1936 (2012)
15. Tanbeer, S.K., Ahmed, C.F., Jeong, B.-S., Lee, Y.-K.: CP-tree: a tree structure for single-pass frequent pattern mining. In: Washio, T., Suzuki, E., Ting, K.M., Inokuchi, A. (eds.) PAKDD 2008. LNCS (LNAI), vol. 5012, pp. 1022–1027. Springer, Heidelberg (2008)
16. Tanbeer, S.K., Ahmed, C.F., Jeong, B.-S., Lee, Y.-K.: Mining Regular Patterns in Transactional Databases. IEICE Trans. Inf. Syst. E91-D(11), 2568–2577 (2008)
17. Tanbeer, S.K., Ahmed, C.F., Jeong, B.-S.: Mining regular patterns in incremental transactional databases. In: Proceedings 12th International Asia-Pacific Web Conference, pp. 375–377 (2010)
18. Chi, Y., Wang, H., Yu, P.S., Muntz, R.R.: Catch the moment: maintaining closed frequent itemsets over a data stream sliding window. Knowl. Inf. Syst. 10(3), 265–294 (2006)
19. Tanbeer, S.K., Ahmed, C.F., Jeong, B.-S.: Mining Regular Patterns in Data Streams. In: Kitagawa, H., Ishikawa, Y., Li, Q., Watanabe, C. (eds.) DASFAA 2010. LNCS, vol. 5981, pp. 399–413. Springer, Heidelberg (2010)
20. Fortino, G., Giannantonio, R., Gravina, R., Kuryloski, P., Jafari, R.: Enabling effective programming and flexible management of efficient body sensor network applications. IEEE T. Hum.-Mach. Syst. 43(1), 115–133 (2013)
21. Raveendranathan, N., Galzarano, S., Loseu, V., Gravina, R., Giannantonio, R., Sgroi, M., Jafari, R., Fortino, G.: From modeling to implementation of virtual sensors in body sensor networks. IEEE Sens. J. 12(3), 583–593 (2012)

Smart Cities and Smart Buildings

Task Execution in Distributed Smart Systems

Uwe Jänen[1]([✉]), Carsten Grenz[1], Sarah Edenhofer[1], Anthony Stein[1],
Jürgen Brehm[2], and Jörg Hähner[1]

[1] Lehrstuhl für Organic Computing, Institut für Informatik,
Universität Augsburg, 86135 Augsburg, Germany
uwe.jaenen@informatik.uni-augsburg.de
[2] Leibniz Universität Hannover, Institut für Systems Engineering,
Fachgebiet System- und Rechnerarchitektur, 30167 Hannover, Germany

Abstract. This paper presents a holistic approach to execute tasks in distributed smart systems. This is shown by the example of monitoring tasks in smart camera networks. The proposed approach is general and thus not limited to a specific scenario. A job-resource model is introduced to describe the smart system and the tasks, with as much order as necessary and as few rules as possible. Based on that model, a local algorithm is presented, which is developed to achieve optimization transparency. This means that the optimization on system-wide criteria will not be visible to the participants. To a task, the system-wide optimization is a virtual local single-step optimization. The algorithm is based on proactive quotation broadcasting to the local neighborhood. Additionally, it allows the parallel execution of tasks on resources and includes the optimization of multiple-task-to-resource assignments.

Keywords: Job-resource-model · Optimization transparency · Virtual local single-step optimization · Proactive quotation-based optimization · Multiple-task-to-resource assignment

1 Introduction

The scientific achievements of the past years enforced a rapid augmentation of computerized systems, so called *smart systems*. From the perspective of the authors, this smart trend is driven by standardization and modularization of system components, the increase of computing power and capabilities of individual system components and their interconnection. This trend makes new applications possible. The configuration space of individual systems and their possibilities for collaboration have increased significantly. Former passive systems now can actively service novel application scenarios. Example scenarios are smart home, smart desktop-grids and distributed smart camera networks. In a smart home a possible application may be to illuminate the kitchen by a defined luminous flux. Therefore, a smart electric stove with a lamp, a smart table lamp or a smart ceiling lamp can be used to fulfill this task. Another example is a smart desktop-grid with the task of executing a simulation. Therefore, different

© Springer International Publishing Switzerland 2015
G. Di Fatta et al. (Eds.): IDCS 2015, LNCS 9258, pp. 103–117, 2015.
DOI: 10.1007/978-3-319-23237-9_10

desktop configurations are available, like multi-core CPU and GPU. Within this work we focus on networks with pan-tilt-zoom capable smart cameras, because it is one of the most challenging scenarios. In a smart camera network, as illustrated in Fig. 1(a), the task could be to observe an event with different cameras. Figure 1(b) shows the system architecture of a smart camera. The new possibilities to fulfill a task, increase the configuration space rapidly. So, one question comes up: Which task has to be fulfilled by which smart system component? The first research subject is to create a model to handle this new possibility to fulfill tasks by different smart system components. The second research subject is the optimization of task-to-smart-system-component assignment in naturally distributed systems with only local algorithms. Both are explained in the following Sects. 1.1 and 1.2. In the remainder of this paper, we will present an approach to handle the first and second research subject. Therefore, a job-resource model will be introduced in Sect. 2. Based on this model, a heuristic approach for virtual local single-step optimization is presented in Sect. 3. This approach is capable for parallel execution of tasks on a smart component within a distributed system. The algorithm will be evaluated on optimization speed and the capability to solve generalized assignment problem benchmarks in Sect. 6.

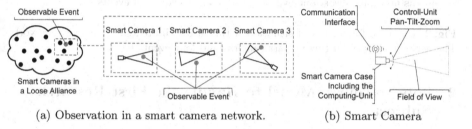

(a) Observation in a smart camera network.   (b) Smart Camera

Fig. 1. Distributed smart system exemplified as distributed smart camera network.

1.1 First Research Subject: Model Creation

In smart systems, different tools are available to satisfy different tasks. The model must be independent from the task, the optimization criterion and the smart system component. Generally, we have to decide whether we prefer centralized, local or hybrid algorithms in a natural distributed system. On one hand, this model must support user-objectives such as turn on the light in the kitchen or rather the observation of an event in a smart camera network. On the other hand, the system has to support system-wide objectives as well as the optimization to the resulting global criterion.

1.2 Second Research Subject: Optimization Transparency

In a distributed system using only local knowledge and local algorithms, it is hard to optimize on global criterion. This is illustrated in Fig. 2. Here, the scenario consists of three smart cameras (SC) and four events to observe. Initially in Fig. 2(a), only event 3 and event 4 are observed. The system objective is to observe as many events as possible. In Fig. 2(b) the obviously best alignment of the cameras field of view (FoV) is shown. The challenge is to optimize the configuration with local knowledge and local algorithms from the situation depicted in Fig. 2(a) as close as possible to the optimal state in Fig. 2(b). The system-wide optimization shall be transparent to the system. This means it will not be visible to the participants. In particular, we enforce a virtual, local single-step optimization (VLSO).

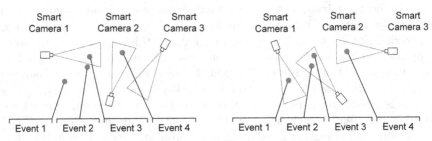

(a) Initial situation with three smart cameras and four observable events.

(b) Obviously best smart camera alignment to cover all events.

Fig. 2. Example for an initial situation within a distributed smart camera network. The network consists of three smart cameras and four events to observe.

2 Job-Ressource-Model to Handle the First Research Subject

To achieve universality and independence of explicit application scenarios, the model should contain as much order as necessary and as few rules as possible. A smart system consists of smart components. Based on the smart camera definition in [1], a smart component consists of a computing- and a communication-unit. In addition, it can be optionally extended e.g. by sensors, actuators etc. (Fig. 1(b)). A smart component can also consist of multiple other smart components. Each smart component has a *neighborhood RN* which is connected ad-hoc (e.g. wlan). Smart components have a *neighborhood relation* if they can communicate directly with each other. Two smart cameras are in a neighborhood if they are in the same broadcast domain (layer-2 broadcast in the OSI-model). Messages will not be forwarded beyond this neighborhood (routing). A smart system is used to fulfill different objectives, so called *micro-* and *macro-objectives*. How are they related to the smart components? Micro-objectives are individual objectives which result in a software instance i.e. a program in the main storage of a smart component, which can be executed, and the associated data. Macro-Objectives are superior system-objectives. As an example, we consider a smart camera network in which two glass break sensors detect events (A and B). This will automatically create two observation tasks. These micro-objectives are given to the smart camera network and are represented by software instances. Both instances compete for the smart cameras. Which instance aquires which camera has to be determined by the interaction of the software instances. This interaction is defined by the macro-objective of the system. The macro-objective could be the maximization of a system-wide observation success for example. We developed a *job-resource-model* based on this *objective-model*. A smart system component i will further be interpreted as a resource r_i from a set of resources R. A software instance, which pursues a micro-objective n and is bounded by the interaction rules of macro-objectives, is further called job a_n, an element of the set of all jobs A.

2.1 Resources

A resource r_i is the reduced representation of a smart component, which can be allocated by a job a_n to fulfill its micro-objective. A resource is defined by its ID i and the estimated success it will provide to a job's micro-objective running on it. The success of job a_n on resource r_i is denoted by P_i^n. If a resource i knows about a micro-objective, it broadcasts information about it proactively to its neighborhood RN_i. This proactive information broadcast is also called the resource-to-resource-interaction (R2R-interaction). A non-existing resource (neutral element) will be denoted by $r_\varnothing$.

2.2 Jobs

A job a_n is a representation of an individual objective, respectively a software instance. This software instance consists of a management part and an execution part. The management part is responsible for a self-organized allocation of a resource. The execution part is e.g. a thread for person detection in single images. A job *is on* a resource, if a software-instance is located on the corresponding smart component. A job *allocates* a resource, if the execution part of the software instance is running on the smart component. A job, which is on a resource, has full access to the data on that resource. Jobs can interact by *sending messages* and allocating a resource by *displacing an other job*. This job-to-job-interaction (J2J-interaction) is defined by the rules of the macro-objectives. The non-existing job, respectively the idle job on a resource, is denoted by $a_\varnothing$. The idle job is the only job which can allocate an idle resource and will do this automatically. The job-to-resource-interaction (or J2R-interaction) then is defined as follows: a job can allocate a resource and exchanges information, if the job is on the resource. After defining the job-resource-model we can focus on the macro-objectives which are congruent to the second research subject in the following section.

3 Proactive Quotation-Based Scheduling to Handle the Second Research Subject

In the previous section, we introduced an objective-model and derived a job-resource-model from it. The objective-model distinguishes between micro- and macro-objectives. The micro-objectives are individual objectives and macro-objectives are objectives regarding the whole system. The only admitted way to enforce macro-objectives in the presented job-resource-model, is to affect the J2J-interaction. That means the information which has to be exchanged between jobs and the rules, when a job is allowed to displace another job. So, we need a local algorithm which is capable to optimize system wide. Such an algorithm shall avoid long negotiation chains within the whole system. To enlight the challenge, we present a scene with three smart cameras in Fig. 3. SC1 and SC2 are observing the events 1 and 2. SC3 is idle. At time stamp T' a glass break sensor detects an additional event 3. The micro-objective to observe this event by a smart camera is represented by a job. On the right of Fig. 3, the related gantt charts to each resource and each job are depicted. Each bar represents the duration for how long the event can be observed. The predicted success P_i^n for executing job a_n on resource r_i is denoted at the end of each bar. The macro-objective is to increase the system wide observation success:

$$P_{sys} = \sum_{a_n} P_i^n \cdot [a_n \text{ allocates } r_i] \tag{1}$$

with Iverson brackets as $[statement] = 1$ if $statement == true$ and $[statement] = 0$ if $statement == false$. It is obviously the best solution that SC1 adjusts its FoV to observe event 3 at time stamp T'. Then, SC2 switches its FoV on event 1 and, additionally, SC3 turns on event 2. The challenge is to avoid long negotiation chains such as job 3 asks job 1 to handover the resource SC1. Then, job 1 has to ask its neighborhood to change on another smart camera and so on. In general, this simple approach will result in a tree search. As already said, we try to achieve a transparent optimization with local algorithms in distributed smart systems. In particular, we want to achieve a virtual, local single-step optimization (VLSO): From a job's point of view, it shall seem to be a local optimization, which only needs one step to complete. Such an algorithm can be found in [3] and it is called *Proactive Quotation-Based Scheduling (PQB)*. This algorithm will be shortly introduced in the following subsection. Afterwards, we will extend the PQB algorithm to handle a parallel execution of several micro-objectives on single resources.

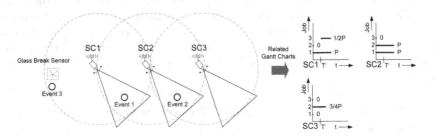

Fig. 3. Network with three smart cameras and two events. At time stamp T' an additional event occurs.

3.1 Single Micro-Objective to Single Resource Association

The main idea is: Each job a_n allocating a resource r_i locally broadcasts a *quotation* Q_i^n, which has to be fulfilled by another job to displace the offering job. This is illustrated in Fig. 4, following the example in Fig. 3. The resources proactively share the possible success of each job they know about with the neighborhood (Fig. 4(a)). One has to consider that this information will not be forwarded. Additionally, each job allocating a resource will send its quotation (Fig. 4(b)). At time stamp T' job a_3 is created. The resources again proactively broadcast the possible success (Fig. 4(c)). Job a_3 knows about the conditions to displace job a_1 because of the former quotation exchange (Fig. 4(b)). Then, job a_1 will displace job a_2. In the last step job a_2 will displace the idle job on resource r_3 (Fig. 4(d)). This illustration leads to the question: What was that quotation which causes job a_3 to displace job a_1 and temporarily decrease the local and system-wide observation success? The PQB-Scheduling algorithm is based on a *local mapping* of possible system-wide success improvement on a virtual local improvement of each job. In the following, a quotation Q_i^n is called *sales quotation*, because a virtual price has to be paid by a job a_x to receive the resource r_i from job a_n. In this context, success is equivalent to virtual money. A sales quotation solely implies that, if job a_n releases its resource r_i, the beneficiary job a_x has to compensate the loss:

$$Q_i^n = P_i^n \tag{2}$$

If job a_n can migrate to an alternative resource $r_{i'}$, the quotation has to be reduced by the predicted success on that resource. To create a low priced quotation for the resource, the job avoids to the resource with the maximum success:

$$Q_i^n = P_i^n - \max_{i'}\{P_{i'}^n\} \tag{3}$$

If job a_n has to ransom the alternative resource $r_{i'}$ from an offering job $a_{n'}$, the possible success on resource $r_{i'}$ has to be reduced by these costs. The quotation to be broadcasted by job a_n on resource r_i are given by:

$$Q_i^n = P_i^n - \max_{i'}\{P_{i'}^n - Q_{i'}^{n'}\} \tag{4}$$

A job a_n that receives the quotation, has to decide if its current success is greater than the possible success on resource $r_{i'}$. The possible success is given by the success $P_{i'}^n$ subtracted by the costs $Q_{i'}^{n'}$.

$$P_{i',red}^n = P_{i'}^n - Q_{i'}^{n'} \tag{5}$$

This approach by itself is not capable to achieve the solution we aimed for (see Fig. 2(b)), because grouping multiple micro-objectives on one resource is not supported. In the following, we extend the PQB-Scheduling algorithm to cope with this challenge.

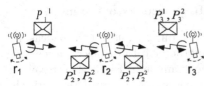

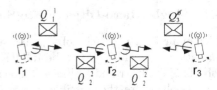

(a) Exchange of the possible job successes within the resource neighborhoods RN_i by proactively R2R-Interaction.

(b) Exchange of quotations within the resource neighborhoods RN_i by J2J-interaction.

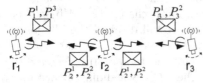

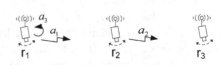

(c) At time stamp T' job a_3 occurs. Job a_3 knows about the conditions to displace job a_1 because of the former quotation exchange.

(d) Job a_3 displaces a_1. Afterward job a_1 displaces a_2 and subsequently job a_2 displaces the idle job $a_\emptyset$ on r_3.

Fig. 4. Message exchange within the proactive quotation-based scheduling.

3.2 Multiple Micro-Objective to Single Resource Assignment

The calculation of a system-wide optimal grouping of micro-objectives is a hard problem. There are two general challenges and two problems to adapt the PQB-Scheduling algorithm to this scenario.

General Problem 1: The success of multiple micro-objectives executed on a single resource is the sum of the single micro-objective success within that group. The first problem is the dependency of a single micro-objective success on the group composition. Simply explained: If job a_1 and job a_2 share a resource r_1, usually $P_1^{a_1 \subseteq \{a_1, a_2\}} \neq P_1^{a_1}$. This is caused by the sharing of resources. In example Fig. 2(b), smart camera 2 is for instance not capable to adjust the focus on event 2 and 3 in the same quality as observing only event 2 or event 3.

General Problem 2: The next challenge is to create the groups using only local knowledge and local algorithms. Two oppositional approaches are conceivable. In the first approach, the jobs form groups by themselves. The second approach is to build all possible combinations and only the micro-objective within a group with the highest success will be actively executed. At first sight, the dynamic grouping is preferable, because the amount of software-instance increases linearly with the number of micro-objectives. The amount of all possible combinations increases exponentially. Unfortunately, the dynamic grouping is hard with the local knowledge and local algorithms restrictions we choose. An example to show this issue is depicted in Fig. 5. In Fig. 5(a), the system view of SC1 is depicted. SC1 is not informed about SC3 and event 5 as shown in Fig. 5(c). So, with this different knowledge, the optimal camera alignment differs. With the knowledge

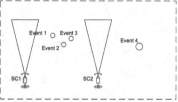

(a) System knowledge from the point of view of SC1.

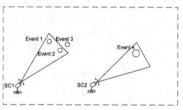

(b) Best camera alignment from the point of view of SC1.

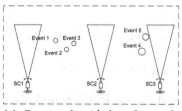

(c) System knowledge from the point of view of SC2.

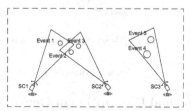

(d) Best camera alignment from the point of view of SC2.

Fig. 5. Dynamic grouping on runtime with local knowledge and local algorithms is not possible.

of SC1, the events 1 and 2 should be grouped. With the knowledge of SC2, event 2 and 3 as well as event 4 and 5 should be grouped.

PQB-Scheduling Problem 1: When calculating a quotation in the PQB-Scheduling approach, the splitting of a group has to be considered. In Fig. 6(a) an example is depicted. SC3 is observing event 1 and 2. SC1 and SC2 are not capable to observe both. The best solution will be that event 1 is observed by SC1, event 2 by SC2 and event 3 by SC3. So, the calculated quotation must consider the separation of event 1 and 2. Otherwise, the job that is responsible for observing event 3 is not able to buy SC3. This will increase the search space exponentially.

PQB-Scheduling Problem 2: When calculating a quotation in the PQB-Scheduling approach, the part of a group that remains on the resource has to be taken into account. Figure 6(b) shows an example. The SC2 is observing event 1 and 2. The best solution will be that event 1 is observed by SC1 and event 2 and 3 by SC2. So, the calculated quotation must consider the separation of event 1 and 2 and, additionally, that job a_1 observing event 2 stays on SC2. Otherwise, the job responsible for observing event 3 is not able to buy SC2. The received quotation has to be adopted by the receiving group. Unfortunately, this term cannot be calculated. The quotation is calculated under the constraint that no parts of the group remain on the resource. Theoretically an alternative more suitable quotation can exist.

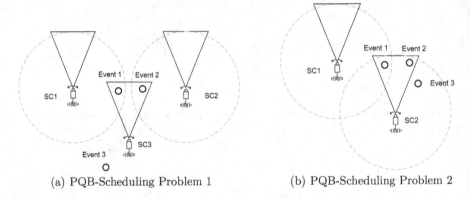

(a) PQB-Scheduling Problem 1   (b) PQB-Scheduling Problem 2

Fig. 6. Example scenarios for PQB-Scheduling Problem 1 and 2

Formal Description of General Problem 1 and 2 And PQB-Scheduling Problem 1 and 2: Assuming a group g is allocating resource i. If group g leaves the resource r_i, the displacing job has to compensate the loss of group g. That equals to Eq. 2.

$$Q_i^g = P_i^g \tag{6}$$

If sub-groups g_{sub} of g are able to split up on several other resources $r_{i'}$, this success on the alternative resources $P_{i'}^{g_{sub}}$ has to be subtracted from Q_i^g.

$$Q_i^g = P_i^g - \max_{i', g_{sub}} \{ \sum_{i'} (P_{i'}^{g_{sub}}) \} \tag{7}$$

Here, the groups offering the alternative resources i' are donated with g'. It must be remarked that some parts g'_{sub} of the displaced groups g' can be integrated into the sub-groups g_{sub}.

$$Q_i^g = P_i^g - \max_{i', g_{sub}, g'_{sub}} \{ \sum_{i'} (P_{i'}^{g_{sub} \subseteq \{g_{sub} \cup g'_{sub}\}}) \} \tag{8}$$

The price $Q_{i'}^{g'}$ has to be paid to displace a group g' on resource i'. Again, the following has to be noted: if a sub-group of g' can be integrated, the price has also to be adopted to $Q_{i'}^{g' \setminus g'_{sub},\ g'_{sub} \cup g_{sub}}$.

$$Q_i^g = P_i^g - \max_{i', g_{sub}, g'_{sub}} \{ \sum_{i'} (P_{i'}^{g_{sub} \subseteq \{g_{sub} \cup g'_{sub}\}} - Q_{i'}^{g' \setminus g'_{sub},\ g'_{sub} \cup g_{sub}}) \} \tag{9}$$

Equation 9 states a hard combinatorial problem. Additionally, as mentioned in PQB-Scheduling Problem 2, the term $Q_{i'}^{g' \setminus g'_{sub},\ g'_{sub} \cup g_{sub}}$ can not be calculated exactly on the base of $Q_{i'}^{g'}$, but it can be estimated. On first sight, the problems seem to be solved with these equations. But they only represent the problems in a formal way. The term $\max_{i', g_{sub}, g'_{sub}}$ represents the computationally intensive part. For calculating a quotation, this part represents how to spread the micro-objectives on neighboring resources $\{i', ..., I'\}$.

All these equations contain groups g. But so far it is not clear where these groups came from.

4   Heuristic Approach for Parallel Execution of Multiple Micro-Objectives on Resources

We have developed a heuristic solution that solves all these problems in one stroke. The algorithm is based on a hybrid version of 'dynamic grouping of micro-objectives' and the 'parallel consideration of all combinations'. For clarity, throughout the explanations of the following heuristic approach, we will refer to the example depicted in Fig. 7. It shows a smart camera network initially consisting of three smart cameras (SC1 - SC3). As depicted, only SC1 is able to observe event 1-4 simultaneously. SC2 can only observe event 3 and 4, as well as SC3 can only observe event 1 and 2. Initially, job $a_{1,2,3,4}$ is executed on resource r_1. Resources r_2 and r_3 are idle. At time stamp T', event 5 occurs which can only be observed by SC1.

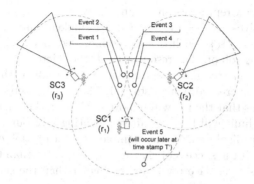

Fig. 7. Initial situation. Reference example for the heuristic approach.

First Step: On each resource, one job is created representing all micro-objectives which are executable on that resource: a_{all}. In the illustrated example, these will be $a_{1,2,3,4}$ for r_1, $a_{3,4}$ for r_2 and $a_{1,2}$ for r_3.

Second Step: Each job $a_{n,...,N}$ searches for an alternative resource (initially only a_{all}) and creates an *optimization matrix*. In the left table of Table 1, the optimization matrix of job $a_{1,2}$, which is on resource r_2, is depicted. The micro-objectives $m,...,M$ are the ones currently allocating the resources in the neighborhood $r_i,...,r_I$. This is denoted by an 'X' within the table. The row 'displaced' will be needed later.

Third Step: The micro-objectives $n,...,N$ will be randomly assigned to the resources $r_i,...,r_I$. The micro-objectives $m,...,M$ can only remain on the resource or change to $r_\varnothing$. This assignment is also random. Unallowed assignments are marked with a '-' in the optimization matrix. If one of the micro-objectives $n,...,N$ is already executed on a resource, the corresponding 'X' has to be deleted and it has to be marked in the line 'displaced'. Every row in the matrix with a micro-objective of $n,...,N$ represents a possible group of micro-objectives on that resource. Only these rows will be considered for the calculation of the matrix success. In the right table of Table 1, this is shown for job $a_{1,2}$ on resource r_2. This local solution will be rated. The success of that group and the costs to buy the resource has to be calculated: $P_{i'}^{g_{sub} \subseteq \{g_{sub} \cup g'_{sub}\}} - Q_{i'}^{g' \backslash g'_{sub}, \; g'_{sub} \cup g_{sub}}$. In the example, this will be $P_3^{1,2} - Q_3^{a_\varnothing}$. For any displaced job, an extra charge of the success of that objective within the group on that resource has to be paid, $P_i^{a_n \subseteq g}$. In the example, this will be $P_1^{1 \subseteq \{1,2,3,4\}}$ and $P_1^{2 \subseteq \{1,2,3,4\}}$. The third step is repeated multiple times to find the matrix with the highest success. This exploration needs a heuristic. We used stochastic tunneling (ST) [10]. In the ST heuristic a change in the optimization-matrix will occur with a certain probability which depends on the current success compared to the former success of that matrix.

Fourth Step: This step starts, when the former step has terminated. If the success of the matrix calculated in the former step is greater than 0, the following will happen: Each row represents an assignment of micro-objectives to a resource. If the micro-objectives $n, ..., N$ are assigned to a single resource $r_{i'}$, (not including any element of $\{m, ..., M\}$ which is not also included in $\{n, ..., N\}$) this job will displace the offering job on that resource $r_{i'}$. If the micro-objectives $n, ..., N$ are associated to different resources, corresponding to each of these associations, a time-limited job is created, which starts in the second step of this algorithm. Time-limited means that the job will remove itself from the system when a timer expires. The time-limit will be reset after allocating a resource and will not be decreased until it is displaced. In the example, this means, job $a_{1,2}$ may displace $a_\varnothing$ on resource r_3, if the success of that matrix is greater than 0. Keep in mind, the extra charge (see displace row) may be higher than the success, so job $a_{1,2}$ will not displace $a_\varnothing$ on resource r_3.

An additional advantage of this heuristic is, it also can be used to calculate a quotation. Only the listed resources do not include the resource allocated by the job itself. Below on the left of Table 2, the optimal optimization-matrix for calculating the quotation by job $a_{1,2,3,4}$ allocating resource r_1 is depicted.

Now assuming the time stamp T' and event 5 occurs. On the right of Table 2, the optimization matrix of job a_5 is depicted. Someone might mention that the micro-objectives 1 to 4 on the right of Table 2 are assigned to the idle resource

Table 1. Left: Optimization matrix in the second step. Right: Optimization matrix in the third step.

	micro-objectives n...N		micro-objectives m...M					micro-objectives n...N		micro-objectives m...M			
resources	1	2	1	2	3	4	resources	1	2	1	2	3	4
r_1			X	X	X	X	r_1			(X)	(X)	(X)	X
r_2							r_2			-	-	-	-
r_3							r_3	X	X	-	-	-	-
$r_\varnothing$							$r_\varnothing$						X
displaced							displaced			X	X		

Table 2. Left: Optimization matrix to calculate the quotation by job $a_{1,2,3,4}$ on resource r_1. Right: Optimization matrix to illustrate how job a_5 takes over r_1.

	micro-objectives n...N				micro-objectives m...M	
resources	1	2	3	4	∅	∅
r_2			X	X		
r_3	X	X				
$r_\varnothing$						
displaced						

	...	micro-objectives m...M			
resources	5	1	2	3	4
r_1	X				
r_2		-	-	-	-
r_3		-	-	-	-
$r_\varnothing$		X	X	X	X
displaced					

$r_\varnothing$. It has to be considered that a_5 is not responsible for job $a_{1,2,3,4}$. To job a_5 it seems to be a virtual single-step optimization. $a_{1,2,3,4}$ takes care of the fallback resources by itself by calculating the quotation.

5   Related Work

In this section, the related work is discussed. First, the job-resource model is considered. The name of the model is influenced by scheduling theories [2]. The scheduling theory focuses on the amount of tasks and machines, their type and their arrival rate to classify the scheduling problem. The presented job-resource model is more general and focused on distributed smart systems. A job can be considered as a software agent, respectively intelligent agent, in multi-agent systems as described in [11]. The approach of using software agents in the execution of tasks is well established. In Monari et al. [5], an agent-based multi-sensor process for each object to be tracked in a smart camera network is created. An agent is focused on the execution of computer vision like data association and fusion. They used a well defined system architecture called NEST, which is still a research field [6]. Ukita et al. [9] also used agents. In their approach, the smart system components are the agents (so called active vision agents). Our focus is on the definition of a model that is as accurate as necessary and as less restrictive as possible. It is more general and defines interaction possibilities to achieve micro- and macro-objectives.

The second research objective of an optimization transparency and a system-wide optimization have not been considered in that way before. Most approaches used in the field of distributed smart camera networks make use of auction based algorithms like [7], which can be understood as a distributed greedy search. Also, some algorithms using negotiation chains were developed, for instance in [8]. The handling of these chains needs more maintaining than the proactive quotation-based approach we used. The heuristic expanding of this approach [3] enabled the parallel execution of tasks on smart components, which is a necessity to be able to track multiple persons by the same smart camera.

6   Evaluation

We presented an algorithm, which is capable to optimize the execution of multiple micro-objectives on resources. The optimization is transparent to a job and is especially a local single-step optimization from its point of view. Caused by the proactive quotation broadcasting, the optimization is done directly and it is avoiding negotiation chains. To show this, we evaluated the algorithm using the MASON[1] simulation toolbox. We set up a resource network as depicted in Fig. 8(a). Each resource is only capable to communicate with its direct neighbor resource. A message needs 3 simulation steps to be transferred from resource to resource. The graph in Fig. 8 shows the average system success at each simulation step, measured during the evaluation of 10 repeats. During the initialization phase step 10 to step ~20, the optimization converges up to a success of 7000. At simulation step 50, the events 8 and 9 occur. The system needs only 10 steps to reach the maximum success and to reconfigure the whole network. Keeping in mind that the message exchange takes 3 steps.

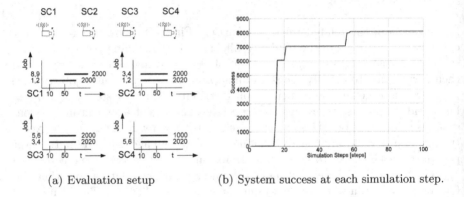

(a) Evaluation setup

(b) System success at each simulation step.

Fig. 8. Simulation setup with resulting graph.

In the following, we want to demonstrate the capability to solve a complex problem, like the generalized assignment problem (GAP) [4] using only local algorithms. Therefore, we used a benchmark set[2]. The term $\max_{i',g_{sub},g'_{sub}}$ in Eq. 9 represents the computationally intensive part. This is handled by using stochastic tunneling (ST) in the third step of the heuristic PQB approach. We compare the results of stochastic tunneling implemented as central approach to the introduced local PQB heuristic. A single run of the central ST contains 500 explorations to find the best assignment. These runs were repeated 200 times within a single simulation. Each simulation (central ST and local PQB) was repeated 10 times. The results of the 200th step are depicted in Table 3. It is obvious that the ST heuristic is not the best approach to solve GAP. The evaluation also showed that the local

---

[1] http://cs.gmu.edu/~eclab/projects/mason/.
[2] http://people.brunel.ac.uk/~mastjjb/jeb/orlib/gapinfo.html.

PQB approach is able to reach similarly good results as a centralized approach with a percentual deviation of 5.37 % and 8.31 %.

Table 3. Comparison of central ST vs. local PQB

Benchmark set	Optimal solution	Ø central ST	Ø local PQB	Deviation
c515-1	336	285.0 (stdev:5.88)	269.7 (stdev:11.55)	5.37 %
c515-2	327	283.9 (stdev:5.37)	260.3 (stdev:17.69)	8.31 %

7   Conclusion and Future Work

In this paper, we described a holistic approach for task execution in distributed systems. Therefore, a job-resource model was introduced. This model pursues individual objectives (micro-objectives), which might be created by a user, as well as system-wide objectives (macro-objectives) considering e.g. load-balancing issues. The optimization of macro-objectives is transparent to a job. More precisely, to a job it appears as a so-called virtual local single-step optimization (VLSO). This is achieved by means of the presented technique called proactive quotation broadcasting (PQB). In the presented algorithm, micro-objectives are able to share resources. The challenge of grouping objectives on resources, and an approach to overcome it, was explained. Experimental results revealed the capabilities of the PQB algorithm, i.e. its fast reaction to disturbances and its ability for an optimal objective-to-resource assignment.

Future research activities will focus on using alternative heuristics for the third step of the algorithm, e.g. evolutionary strategies, instead of stochastic tunneling.

References

1. Bramberger, M., Doblander, A., Maier, A., Rinner, B., Schwabach, H.: Distributed embedded smart cameras for surveillance applications. Computer **39**(2), 68–75 (2006)
2. Conway, R.W., Maxwell, W.L., Miller, L.W.: Theory of scheduling (1967)
3. Jaenen, U., Spiegelberg, H., Sommer, L., von Mammen, S., Brehm, J., Haehner, J.: Object tracking as job-scheduling problem. In: 2013 Seventh International Conference on Distributed Smart Cameras (ICDSC), pp. 1–7, October 2013
4. Martello, S., Toth, P.: Knapsack Problems: Algorithms and Computer Implementations. Wiley, New York (1990)
5. Monari, E., Maerker, J., Kroschel, K.: A robust and efficient approach for human tracking in multi-camera systems. In: Sixth IEEE International Conference on Advanced Video and Signal Based Surveillance, pp. 134–139, September 2009
6. Mossgraber, J., Reinert, F., Vagts, H.: An architecture for a task-oriented surveillance system: A service- and event-based approach. In: 2010 Fifth International Conference on Systems (ICONS), pp. 146–151, April 2010

7. Rinner, B., Dieber, B., Esterle, L., Lewis, P., Yao, X.: Resource-aware configuration in smart camera networks. In: IEEE Computer Society Conference on Computer Vision and Pattern Recognition Workshops, pp. 58–65, June 2012
8. Starzyk, W., Qureshi, F.Z.: A negotiation protocol with conditional offers for camera handoffs. In: Proceedings of the International Conference on Distributed Smart Cameras, ICDSC 2014, pp. 17:1–17:7. ACM, New York (2014)
9. Ukita, N.: Real-time cooperative multi-target tracking by dense communication among active vision agents. In: IEEE/WIC/ACM International Conference on Intelligent Agent Technology, pp. 664–671, September 2005
10. Wenzel, W., Hamacher, K.: A stochastic tunneling approach for global minimization. Phys. Rev. Lett. **82**(15), 3003–3007 (1999)
11. Wooldridge, M.: An Introduction to Multiagent Systems, 2nd edn. Wiley, Chichester (2009)

Inferring Appliance Load Profiles
from Measurements

Geir Horn[1]([✉]), Salvatore Venticinque[2], and Alba Amato[2]

[1] University of Oslo, Oslo, Norway
geir.horn@mn.uio.no
[2] Second University of Naples, Caserta, Italy
{salvatore.venticinque,alba.amato}@unina2.it

Abstract. Good demand side management in smart grids does not only depend on the amount of energy consumed by various appliances, but also on the temporal characteristics of the consumption, *i.e.* the load profile of the appliances. Representative load profiles can be used for predicting future energy consumption. However, a load profile is hard to characterise as it often depends on the operational conditions of the appliance when the measurements were taken. For instance the load profile of a washing machine will depend on the amount of cloths and the inlet water temperature. This paper presents a methodology for empirically obtaining the load profile from an ensemble of event driven traces of a stochastically varying mode of an appliance.

Keywords: Smart grid · Demand side management · Appliance load profiles

1 Introduction

Load forecasting has always been important for planning and operational decision conducted by utility companies [7]. It is relevant and at the same time difficult to predict the evolution of the load demand because it depends on human activity and it changes over time with cycles that are daily, weekly, seasonal. However, load forecasting is essential for effective planning and power plant management at the energy supplier's side, and similarly for customers to avoid running devices when energy prices are higher [13]. With the introduction of renewable energy sources, demand side management [10] becomes essential as optimal utilisation of green energy is affected by the lack of alignment between production and consumption over the day [1].

A micro-grid is commonly confined to a smart home or an office building, and embeds local generation and storage of renewable energy, and a number of power consuming devices. There are now several initiatives aiming to foster

The research leading to these results has received funding from the European Union Seventh Framework Programme (FP7/2007-2013) under grant number 608806 CoSSMic.

G. Di Fatta et al. (Eds.): IDCS 2015, LNCS 9258, pp. 118–130, 2015.
DOI: 10.1007/978-3-319-23237-9_11

a higher rate of self-consumption from decentralised renewable energy production by extending the micro-grid to neighbourhoods involving multiple renewable energy production sites, *e.g.* photo-voltaic (PV) panels, as well as a range of consuming devices. Maximising the use of renewable energy requires shifting loads to find a good match between consumption and production in the neighborhood during the day.

This is a complex task, and there is consequently a need for innovative autonomic systems for the management and control of power micro-grids on users' behalf. This will allow households to optimise consumption and power sales to the network by a collaborative strategy within a neighborhood. Short-term load forecasting is essential to help estimating demand and to make decisions about task scheduling.

This paper discusses how energy profiles corresponding to different working modes of a device can be measured, learned, and modeled. Sampling is discussed in Sect. 4, and mode identification in Sect. 5. Section 6 presents a novel technique for representing program profiles of a consuming appliance, and improving the profile by statistical learning from continuous device measurements.

2   Related Work

Modern home automation systems offer to customers continuous information and power measurements of individual devices [16] in terms of households aggregated consumption or a continuous measurement series for each appliance. However, unknown factors, such as the randomness of the human consumer behaviour, make it difficult to develop a theoretical device model. Instead, it is necessary to monitor and measure real load profiles belonging to single appliances in order to learn and model the appliance load. An important issue is to find a methodology for detecting the various modes in a continuous measurement series, recognising loads in real-time. The main challenges in recognising appliance activity are mainly due to the following [15]:

- Appliances with similar current draw: The system should be able to discriminate between two appliances with similar or same energy consumption;
- Appliances with multiple settings (modes): Some appliances can be either tuned according to user needs or have different phases with different associated consumption, e.g. standby mode or washing cycles. The system should either understand the various appliance settings or recognise appliances based on additional data independent from the chosen setting;
- Long appliance cycles: The system should be able to cope with appliances with long working cycle, which may result in long profiling periods.

The principal benefits for a human consumer are the possibility to monitor power consumption for informal feedback purposes, coordinating and controlling of appliances, or for load learning and forecasting. All of these factors are essential for demand side management of energy consumption [10]. Here we focus on the sampling of measurement series for each appliance, and the application of modelling techniques and a statistical inference to learn and represent the load profile. Several studies have proposed methodologies for modelling the loads and detecting the various modes in continuous measurement series. A large variety of statistical and artificial intelligence techniques have been developed for short-term load forecasting. As stated in [7], some typical approaches are:

The Similar-load approach is based on searching historical data about loads to identify similar characteristics to predict the next load. The forecast can be a linear combination or regression procedure that can include several similar loads. Barker *et al.* presented a methodology for modelling common electrical loads [4]. The authors derived their methodology empirically by collecting data from a large variety of loads and showing the significant commonalities between them.

Regression is the one of most widely used statistical techniques. For electric load forecasting regression methods are usually used to model the relationship of load consumption and other factors such as weather, day type, and customer class. Rothe *et al.* proposed a multi-parameter regression method for forecasting [14].

Time series methods are based on the premises that the data have an internal structure, such as autocorrelation, trend, or seasonal variation. These methods identify a pattern in the historical data and use that pattern to extrapolate future values. Past results can, in fact, be very reliable predictor for a short period into the future. Time series forecasting methods detect and explore such a structure. Classical time series methods like Auto Regressive Moving Average (ARMA), Auto Regressive Integrated Moving Average (ARIMA), Auto Regressive Moving Average with eXogenous variables (ARMAX), and Auto Regressive Integrated Moving Average with eXogenous variables (ARIMAX) are the most used appproaches [11].

Artificial Intelligence Techniques that have been used for load forecasting include expert systems, fuzzy, genetic algorithms, artificial neural network (ANN), etc. [3] presents an overview of papers on load forecasting based on AI techniques.

There are already many studies on load inference and forecasting. However, we are forced to focus on methodologies that are easy to implement using an Arduino microcontroller. Hence it is necessary to consider both physical limitations in terms of memory and the limited processing capacity of the microcontroller. For this reason we have excluded Artificial Intelligence techniques and and Similar-load approaches that are based on a need to train the system on historical data to identify similar characteristics to predict the next load. Nevertheless, Artificial Neural Network (ANN) based solutions have gained great popularity because of their simplicity and robustness. However, using ANN methodology alone is insufficient. Numerous articles have concluded that a hybrid method, which is a combination of different approaches, might be necessary to obtain an optimal prediction, and many different hybrid methods were explored in [2]. As future work, we propose to compare our method against a hybrid method based on a combination of ANN and statistical based solutions.

3   The CoSSMic Multi-Agent System

CoSSMic is an on-going European project that aims at fostering an effective utilisation of green energy produced by photo-voltaic (PV) panels distributed in a neighborhood. The CoSSMic approach exploits a multi-agent system (MAS) to optimise the schedule of consuming tasks to maximise the neighborhood's self-consumption of the PV energy.

Each household is a micro-grid composed of consuming appliances, PV panels, and possibly energy storages. Devices are handled by software agents, which takes care of negotiating energy to be consumed according to the preferences and constraints of the consumers. In particular, consumer agents know the planned usage profile of their care-of devices, and these agents learn the energy consumption profile using monitoring information from the device. These energy profiles are then attached to the bids in the negotiation for produced PV energy in the neighborhood. Producer agents use a prediction model to estimate the energy availability by their managed PV panels or energy storage. These agents receive bids from consumer agents and try to schedule the incoming requests to optimise the allocation of the production to the energy requests. Such a decentralised protocol does not exploit the full knowledge about the global energy availability and hence the produced schedule may not be optimal, however it addresses the complexity of distributed computation of the global schedule at the neighborhood level.

In fact, more micro-grids of the same neighborhood can connect to the P2P overlay, extending the energy market to entire districts. This provides a greater number of consuming tasks and decentralised green energy sources, which increases the flexibility for improving the overall self-consumption.

XMPP is used as transport protocol for exchanging messages within a single micro-grid using a local server. The same protocol is used to enable the communication between agents of different neighborhoods by server-to-server channels, which allow for extending the local energy market to all the agents belonging to the connected micro-grids of the same district.

4   Sampling Methodology

A profile describes the predicted evolution of a given parameter over a given time period. Efficient task scheduling can only be based on the load profiles, i.e., the temporal power consumption of the devices. Profiles are represented as time series, i.e. series of time and energy value pairs, and are used for various purposes. Each device has one or more profiles describing its energy consumption, production, or charging characteristics, depending on the kind of device. As an example dishwashers and washing machines typically have different operation modes, and in that case there is one device profile for each mode. Fundamentally there are two ways to sample the values of a time series:

Time regular sampling is when the samples are taken at regular intervals. The samples are equidistant in time, i.e. $t_k - t_{k-1} = t_{k+1} - t_k = \Delta t$, where Δt is the sampling rate identical for all k sample intervals.

Event driven sampling is when samples are obtained at irregular intervals based on the occurrence of some event. In this case the time distance between two samples is varying.

Time regular sampling is the normal way of converting a continuous signal to discrete values, as Shannon's sampling theorem [6] guarantees that the continuous signal can be reconstructed from its sampled signal if the sampling rate is twice the highest frequency present in the continuous signal. Thus, one should first determine the highest frequency of the continuous load, and then fix Δt accordingly.

There are, in many cases, stochastic variation in an appliance's energy consumption profile between repeated runs of the same mode. An obvious example is a particular programme of a washing machine whose energy consumption profile will depend on the inlet water temperature during the run, and on the amount of cloths in the machine. Under regular sampling, one can therefore expect a distribution $\mathcal{L}(t_k)$ of values in the sample value set $\mathbb{L}(t_k)$ obtained for time t_k. The *average load profile* can be represented as the time series $(t_k, E\{\mathcal{L}(t_k)\})$. Confidence intervals for this load profile can be given as sample Chebyshev bounds [8], and tighter confidence intervals can be obtained if there are reasonable reasons to assume that the empirical sample distribution $\mathcal{L}(t_k)$ is a representative of a known probability density function. One would typically base demand side management [10] in smart energy systems on the upper limit of the confidence interval for the load profile in order quantify the probability that the variation in the energy consumption exceeds the load profile of the appliance mode.

Most electricity meters will, however, integrate the energy consumption and record a sample whenever the sampled appliance has consumed a certain amount of energy, say, one kWh. This is event driven sampling, and the stochastic variation expected between runs of a particular mode of an appliance will be reflected in the recorded *time stamps* of the sampled series. In an ensemble of runs, one could consequently expect that each sample has a unique time stamp if the time resolution is high enough. In practice, the discrete time scale will have a maximal resolution given by the time resolution of the electricity meters used, and some samples could end up with the same time stamp.

The above method of deriving statistically the average load profile and its confidence bounds does consequently not apply for event driven sampling, and our alternative proposal will be presented in Sect. 6.

5   Detecting Modes of Appliances

Dynamic profiling is needed to predict the energy consumption because it may change run by run and according to the current working mode. In the initialisation phase a default profile could be provided, but a learning approach is necessary to improve dynamically the characterisation of each working mode. Initial device profiles can be provided, e.g., by measuring beforehand their consumption. During the trial, the device profile can be measured using smart plug with metering capability for each run during the different settings.

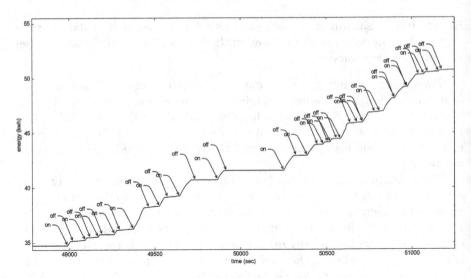

Fig. 1. The cumulative energy consumption of an appliance as provided by the energy meter with the identification of the start and stop periods of the working modes.

In Fig. 1 an excerpt of a time series of energy samples is shown. It has been extracted from monitoring information about a trial of the CoSSMic project. For the proposed example the cumulative consumed energy time-series has been collected using a PG&E Landys+Gyr smart meter.

It is straightforward to observe that the detection of the different runs and the identification of different working modes from this time-series of energy samples is itself a challenging task, at least if we aim at using an automatic and unsupervised approach. However in the CoSSMic project such task is leveraged by the user, who plans the utilisation of smart appliances by a friendly graphical interface defining the working mode. Moreover the system will be aware about the starting time because it is switching on the device at the best scheduled start time that satisfies the user's constraints.

The time series of in Fig. 1 includes different runs of a washing machine, but we have no information about the working programs and their start time. The first issue we addressed is the identification of the different runs. Another problem is that the consumed energy is sampled with a dynamic rate, that depends on the amount of energy consumed.

For breaking long measurements into individual runs we used a supervised technique. In particular a silence threshold for the specific appliance has been tuned empirically in order to identify the end of each run. The detection of a start event is triggered by a minimal energy increment between two samples. Also in this case the energy threshold has been estimated manually. It depends on the noise measured by the meter and on the specific device. Each interval of the time series between the start and stop events shown in Fig. 1, by the *on* and *off* arrows, has been normalised by computing the delay of each sample after the first sample and computing the energy increment from the identified start time.

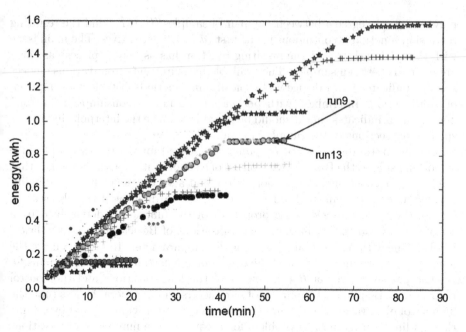

Fig. 2. The various working modes identified from the continuous consumption measurement. Two runs are obviously from the same mode and these will be used to build the profile for that mode.

In Fig. 2 some identified runs are shown. In a first phase they are clustered according to their duration. In a second step all the traces of the same cluster are grouped according the total consumed energy.

6   Representing Statistically the Load Profile

6.1   Minimum Variance Regression

Event driven sampling, as introduced in Sect. 4, of a mode of an appliance basically produces a set of points where the ordinate values represents cumulative energy consumption, and the abscissa values are the times these values were observed.

Every new run of particular mode of a device adds new samples to the *observation set* of the ensemble of runs. The *load profile* for a given mode of an appliance should represent the mean value of the cumulative energy consumption at a given time based the scattered observation set. It is therefore natural to think of the load profile as a *regression function, i.e.* the conditional expectation of the energy consumption given the time samples. In general, a regression function is a *model* of the relation between the independent time variable and the dependent energy consumption, $L(t|\theta)$, where θ is a vector of model parameters.

It is normally not possible to know a good model for the regression function *a priori*. One model free solution would be to use *smoothing splines* that are polynomials of degree d between any pair of samples $\langle t_k, t_{k+1} \rangle$ and the resulting regression function is continuous in the first $(d+1)/2$ derivatives. The main issue with this approach is that the resulting function has as many "pieces" as there are intervals between samples. The available measurements from various devices seem to indicate that a device will typically have periods of little consumption, or "off" periods intermixed with periods of continuous consumption or "on" periods. This indicates that it should be possible to make the interpolating curves span larger sections of the sample interval.

Our suggestion is to use *basis splines* (B-splines) for the regression [9]. Like smoothing splines the B-spline will consist of a set of continuous polynomials that are joined to a continuous regression function at a set of *knots* whose cardinality may be much less than, and independent of, the cardinality of the observation set. Furthermore, the geometric properties of the function is determined by a set of *control points*. B-splines are generalisations of Bézier curves as the latter is a B-spline with no internal knots. The design parameters to be chosen are the number of control points, C, and the degree of the partial spline polynomials, d.

The parameter vector $\boldsymbol{\theta}$ will consist of the knot positions and the control points of the B-spline. The number of parameters will in general be less than the number of observation points, and the parameter vector will be found by solving the non-linear programming problem for n equal to the number of observations

$$\min_{\boldsymbol{\theta}} \frac{1}{n-1} \sum_{k=1}^{n} \left[L\left(t_k\right) - L\left(t_k | \boldsymbol{\theta}\right) \right]^2 \tag{1}$$

As $L(t|\boldsymbol{\theta})$ is the conditional expectation, the objective function in (1) is easily recognised as the *unbiased sample variance* of the observations. The resulting load profile will consequently be a minimum variance regression to the available observations.

6.2   Making the Observations Bijective

The sampling is a surjective map from the set of sample times $\{t_1, \ldots, t_k, \ldots t_n\}$ to the set of observed cumulative energy consumptions; *i.e.* for each energy sample recorded there is a corresponding time. The issue is that this mapping is not necessarily *injective*, meaning that there could be many different energy samples corresponding to the same time t_k. The reason for this is the finite time resolution of the meter making it not too unlikely that two different runs of the same appliance mode will reach a consumption event at exactly the same measured time, but with a different cumulative energy consumption recorded.

The mapping function is made bijective by randomly perturbing the sample time of observations with equal measured time. If the least time interval between two samples supported by the meter is δT, *e.g.* one second, one millisecond, one nanosecond; then a random quantity from the open interval $\langle -\delta T/2, +\delta T/2 \rangle$ will be added to the original sample time. Because the interval is open, the problem coinciding times will not be recreated by perturbing two samples to the half same interval. However, it is necessary to ensure that the random quantities added to all samples at a given time t_k are different. This results in Algorithm 1, which is linear in the number of observations as a result of the scan necessary to do the partitioning of the observation set in Line 1.

Algorithm 1. Making observations bijective

---

    input : A set of surjective observations $\mathbb{O} = \{(t_k, E_k)\}$
    output: A set of bijective observations $\mathbb{O}_b$ where no time stamps equal

1   Partition $\mathbb{O}$ into subsets $\mathbb{O}_i$ such that all time stamps in each subset are equal
2   $\mathbb{O}_b \leftarrow \emptyset$
3   **foreach** $\mathbb{O}_i$ **do**
4   **if** $|\mathbb{O}_i| > 1$ **then**
5         $\mathrm{d} \leftarrow \{\text{random}\,(-\delta T/2, +\delta T/2)\}$
6   **while** $|\mathrm{d}| \neq |\mathbb{O}_i|$ **do**
7            $\mathrm{d} \leftarrow \mathrm{d} \bigcup \{\text{random}\,(-\delta T/2, +\delta T/2)\}$
8   **foreach** $(t_k, E_k) \in \mathbb{O}_i$ *and* $\delta \in \mathrm{d}$ **do**
9            $\mathbb{O}_b \leftarrow \mathbb{O}_b \bigcup \{(t_k + \delta, E_k)\}$
10   **else**
11        $\mathbb{O}_b \leftarrow \mathbb{O}_b \bigcup \mathbb{O}_i$

6.3   A Heuristic for the Knots

The knots are represented by the vector of time points, $\boldsymbol{k}$, where the different parts of the spline curve join. In order to satisfy the boundary conditions a non-periodic B-spline of degree d will have the first d knots at the least time coordinate in the observation set, and then again d knots at the maximum time coordinate. The number of *internal knots* is taken as $C - d$ where C is the number of control points. A spline is *uniform* if all the internal knots are equally spaced, however variable knots will in general give a better regression. The goodness of the fit of the least-squares regression depends on the knots, and as commented by de Boor [5, p.239]: *"(...) finding a (locally) best approximation (...) is expensive. (...) an approximation with two or three times as many well chosen knots is much cheaper to obtain and, usually, just as effective."* We therefore propose the heuristic of Algorithm 2 to place the knots where there is high variability of the sample data.

6.4   Finding the Control Points

Given control points $C = [c_1, \ldots, c_C]$ the regression curve is the B-spline given as

$$\ell\,(t|d, \boldsymbol{k}, C) = \sum_{i=1}^{C} c_i B_{i,d}\,(t|\boldsymbol{k}) \tag{2}$$

where the spline basis polynomials are given recursively as

Algorithm 2. Variable knot heuristic

---

input : A set of bijective observations $\mathbb{O} = \{(t_k, E_k)\}$
Interpolation polynomial degree d
Number of control points C
output: A vector of knot times $\boldsymbol{k}$

1 $\boldsymbol{t} = [t_1, \ldots, t_{|\mathbb{O}|}]^T$ `// Sorted time samples in` $\mathbb{O}$

2 $k_1 = k_2 = \cdots = k_d = t_1$ `// Set boundary knots`

3 $i = d + 1$ `// Next knot index`

4 $m = \left\lceil \dfrac{|\mathbb{O}|}{C - d} \right\rceil$ `// Number of samples per knot`

5 $s = 1$ `// Start of an observation sequence`

6 **repeat**

7   **if** $\mod(m, 2) \neq 0$ **then**   `// Odd number of samples in sequence`

8           $k_i = t_{s+(m-1)/2}$ `// Median sample time of sequence`

9   **else**   `// Even number of samples in sequence`

10           $k_i = \left(t_{s+m/2-1} + t_{s+m/2}\right)/2$

11       $i = i + 1$

12       $s = s + m$

13 **until** $s > |\mathbb{O}| - m$

14 **if** $\mod(|\mathbb{O}| - s + 1, 2) \neq 0$ **then**   `// Odd number of samples remaining`

15       $k_i = t_{(s+|\mathbb{O}|+1)/2}$ `// Median sample time`

16 **else**   `// Even number of samples remaining`

17       $k_i = \left(t_{(s+|\mathbb{O}|+1)/2-1} + t_{(s+|\mathbb{O}|+1)/2}\right)/2$

18 **for** $j = 1$ **to** d **do**   `// Set boundary knots`

19       $k_{i+j} = t_{|\mathbb{O}|}$

$$B_{i,0}(t|\mathbf{k}) = \begin{cases} 1 & \text{if } k_i \leq t < k_{i+1} \\ 0 & \text{otherwise} \end{cases} \tag{3}$$

$$B_{i,j}(t|\mathbf{k}) = \frac{t - k_i}{k_{i+j} - k_i} B_{i,j-1}(t|\mathbf{k}) + \frac{k_{i+j+1} - t}{k_{i+j+1} - k_{i+1}} B_{i+1,j-1}(t|\mathbf{k}) \tag{4}$$

It should be noted that the control points $\boldsymbol{c}_i$ are points (t_i, E_i) and $\boldsymbol{\ell}$ is consequently a *vector valued* function. The load profile function is therefore the second value in this vector, $L(t|\boldsymbol{\theta}) = \boldsymbol{\ell}(t|d, \boldsymbol{k}, \boldsymbol{C})_2$.

Since (2) is *linear* in the control points, the control points can be located by solving a *linear least squares regression* problem in both the time and the energy dimension. Let $\boldsymbol{c}_t = \boldsymbol{C}_1^T$ be the first row of the control points, *i.e.* the vector of the abscissa or time values, and $\boldsymbol{c}_E = \boldsymbol{C}_2^T$ be the vector of the ordinate or energy values. Let $\boldsymbol{t}$ be the vector of sorted time samples, as in Algorithm 2, and $\boldsymbol{e}$ the vector of the corresponding energy samples. Define the matrix of spline basis polynomial values evaluated at the observed event times as

$$B\left(t|k\right) = \begin{bmatrix} B_{1,d}\left(t_1|k\right) & \dots & B_{C,d}\left(t_1|k\right) \\ \vdots & \ddots & \vdots \\ B_{1,d}\left(t_n|k\right) & \dots & B_{C,d}\left(t_n|k\right) \end{bmatrix} \tag{5}$$

Evaluated at the time stamps of the observations t, (2) can now be written in matrix form as $\ell\left(t|d, k, C\right) = B\left(t|k\right)C^T$. Given that the number of observations n, in general, is much larger than the number of control points, (1) corresponds to finding the c_E that minimises $\|e - B\left(t|k\right)c_E\|^2$. Similarly, to find the abscissa of the control points one needs to find the c_t that minimises $\|t - B\left(t|k\right)c_t\|^2$. It is beyond scope of this paper to discuss numerical methods to solve stably and efficiently these two standard least squares problems. The interested reader may consult [12] for a comprehensive treatment.

It should be noted that the regression function obtained by first finding the knots by the heuristic of Algorithm 2 followed by solving the least square problems of this section still yields a minimal variance regression function. The knot placement only gives a partial specialisation of the parameter vector θ of (1), and so the resulting load profile is conditioned on the knots k. Without this specialisation the regression problem becomes less tractable for practical applications.

6.5   Confidence Interval for the Load

The vector of regression errors follows directly from the minimisation problem as $e - B\left(t|k\right)c_E$. Its sample average is $[e - B\left(t|k\right)c_E]^T 1/n$ where 1 is a vector with all elements equal to unity. Its unbiased variance estimate is $\|e - B\left(t|k\right)c_E\|^2/(n-1)$. Both quantities are readily available after solving the minimisation problems, and one can then use sample Chebyshev bounds [8] to establish a confidence interval around the load profile.

This process is illustrated in Fig. 3, which shows the 62 observations of the same *mode* indicated as *run9* and *run13* in Fig. 2. The 95 % Chebychev confidence interval using sample mean and variance is about ±0.092 kWh for these time series. It evident that scheduling the load based on the upper bound seems a safe choice.

6.6   New Measurements

Once the appliance has executed a run of a particular mode, one can add the new set of observations to the past observation for this mode, and gradually build more confidence in the regression function. Once the new set of observations has been amalgamated the past observations, one must run Algorithm 1 and Algorithm 2 again, and expand the matrix (5) with one row before solving the two minimisation problems again to find the coordinates of the control points. By perturbing new observations as they are emplaced in the observation set, Algorithm 1 can be made linear only to the number of new measurements to insert.

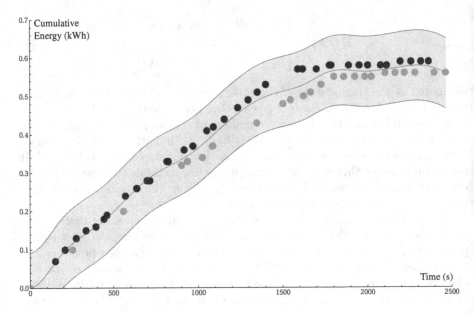

Fig. 3. The two runs 9 and 13 of the same mode with the conditional mean load as a B-spline curve of degree $d = 3$ with 15 control points and its 95 % Chebychev bound based on the sample mean and variance.

7   Conclusion

Load profiles are used for prediction based demand side management in smart grids and the scheduling of tasks in micro-grids where a set of appliances from a neighbourhood of users will be scheduled according to the periods of the day with the largest production of renewable energy and thereby reducing the need for energy storage. Energy consumption is stochastic by nature, and it is important that the load profiles are able to learn statistically as measurements from new runs of an appliance mode become available.

This paper has highlighted the issues of event driven sampling of the energy consumption, and proposed a minimum variance B-spline regression function as a representation of the mean load profile and provided the necessary algorithms to compute this load profile from the available measurements.

References

1. Amato, A., Di Martino, B., Scialdone, M., Venticinque, S., Hallsteinsen, S., Jiang, S.: A distributed system for smart energy negotiation. In: Fortino, G., Di Fatta, G., Li, W., Ochoa, S., Cuzzocrea, A., Pathan, M. (eds.) IDCS 2014. LNCS, vol. 8729, pp. 422–434. Springer, Heidelberg (2014)
2. Asar, A., Hassnain, S., Khattack, A.: A multi-agent approach to short term load forecasting problem. Int. J. Intell. Control Syst. **10**(1), 52–59 (2005)

3. Bansal, R.C., Pandey, J.C.: Load forecasting using artificial intelligence techniques: a literature survey. Int. J. Comput. Appl. Technol. **22**(2/3), 109–119 (2005)
4. Barker, S.K., Kalra, S., Irwin, D.E., Shenoy, P.J.: Empirical characterization and modeling of electrical loads in smart homes. In: International Green Computing Conference, IGCC 2013, Arlington, VA, USA, 27–29 June 2013, Proceedings. pp. 1–10 (2013)
5. de Boor, C.: A Practical Guide to Splines, Applied Mathematical Sciences, vol. 27. Springer, New York (1978)
6. Claude, E., Shannon, C.E.: Communication in the presence of noise. Proc. Inst. Radio Eng. **37**(1), 10–21 (1949)
7. Feinberg, E., Genethliou, D.: Load forecasting. In: Chow, J., Wu, F., Momoh, J. (eds.) Applied Mathematics for Restructured Electric Power Systems. Power Electronics and Power Systems, pp. 269–285. Springer, US (2012)
8. Saw, J.G., Yang, M.C.K., Mo, T.C.: Chebyshev inequality with estimated mean and variance. Am. Stat. **38**(2), 130 (1984)
9. Höllig, K., Hörner, J.: Approximation and Modeling with B-Splines. Society for Industrial and Applied Mathematics, Philadelphia (2014)
10. Gelazanskas, L., Gamage, K.A.A.: Demand side management in smart grid: a review and proposals for future direction. Sustain. Cities Soc. **11**, 22–30 (2014)
11. Mahmoud, A., Ortmeyer, T., Reardon, R.E.: Load forecasting bibliography phase ii. Power Apparatus Syst. IEEE Trans. PAS **100**(7), 3217–3220 (1981)
12. Björck, Å.: Numerical Methods for Least Squares Problems. Other Titles in Applied Mathematics, Society for Industrial and Applied Mathematics (SIAM) (1996)
13. Rathmair, M., Haase, J.: Simulator for smart load management in home appliances. In: SIMUL 2012 : The Fourth International Conference on Advances in System Simulation, pp. 1–6 (2012)
14. Rothe, M., Wadhwani, D.A., Wadhwani, D.: Short term load forecasting using multi parameter regression. Int. J. Comput. Sci. Inf. Secur. **6**(2), 303–306 (2009). arxiv.org/abs/0912.1015
15. Ruzzelli, A., Nicolas, C., Schoofs, A., O'Hare, G.: Real-time recognition and profiling of appliances through a single electricity sensor. In: Proceedings of the 7th Annual IEEE Communications Society Conference on Sensor Mesh and Ad Hoc Communications and Networks (SECON), pp. 1–9, June 2010
16. Wood, G., Newborough, M.: Energy-use information transfer for intelligent homes: Enabling energy conservation with central and local displays. Energy Build. **39**(4), 495–503 (2007)

Intra Smart Grid Management Frameworks for Control and Energy Saving in Buildings

Antonio Guerrieri[1]([✉]), Jordi Serra[2], David Pubill[2], Christos Verikoukis[2], and Giancarlo Fortino[1]

[1] Dipartimento di Ingegneria Informatica, Modellistica, Elettronica e Sistemistica, Università della Calabria, 87036 Cosenza, Rende, Italy
aguerrieri@deis.unical.it, g.fortino@unical.it
[2] Centre Tecnològic de Telecomunicacions de Catalunya (CTTC), Castelldefels, 08860 Barcelona, Spain
{jserra,dpubill,cveri}@cttc.es

Abstract. In the context of Smart Grids and Internet of Things (IoT) Systems, distributed monitoring and actuation through Wireless Sensor and Actuator Networks (WSANs) is fundamental to control the energy usage in buildings. Moreover, the realization of algorithms for the optimization of the energy consumption is of paramount importance. This paper presents a loosely coupled integration between a flexible management framework for WSANs, namely the IGMF (Intra-Grid Management Framework), and a Dynamic Energy Scheduler with local control on sensors and actuators, namely the ITESS (IoTLAB Energy Scheduling System). The integrated system allows the users to manage whole buildings applying Dynamic Energy Schedulers for different environments.

Keywords: Smart grid · Internet of things · Wireless sensor and actuator networks · Building management · Energy scheduler

1 Introduction

New technologies are creating novel opportunities in the monitoring and in the maintenance of buildings [1,2]. In this context, the continuous monitoring of buildings can lead to the realization of important services (e.g. energy utilization optimization) that can be merged with the so called "intra-grid" network [3] that controls and regulates the energy consumption in the part of the Smart Grid [4] that is located within the buildings. One of the best methods to monitor and control buildings is through the utilization of Wireless Sensor and Actuator Networks (WSANs) [5] that allow any arrangement of sensors/actuators inside a building. WSANs offer a more flexible solution to audit buildings and control equipment with respect to traditional systems, which require retrofitting the whole building and therefore are difficult to implement in existing structures. Solutions based on WSANs for the building monitoring and control can be installed in existing structures with minimal efforts. This enables an effective

© Springer International Publishing Switzerland 2015
G. Di Fatta et al. (Eds.): IDCS 2015, LNCS 9258, pp. 131–142, 2015.
DOI: 10.1007/978-3-319-23237-9_12

distributed monitoring of building structure condition, and building space and energy (electricity, gas, water) usage while facilitating the design of techniques for intelligent actuation of devices in buildings. In order to transparently and easily use WSANs, several frameworks have to date been implemented [6]. One of these is the IGMF (Intra-Grid Management Framework) [6] that is a domain-specific framework designed for the flexible and efficient management of WSANs deployed in buildings. The IGMF allows an effective management of (large) sets of cooperating networked WSAN nodes, a flexible node group organization to capture the floor plan of the buildings, tecniques for intelligent and distributed sensing and actuation, heterogeneous WSANs integration, system programming at low- and high-levels, quick deployment and update of applications to the WSAN through message exchange.

Through the use of WSANs in buildings, important considerations about the energy spent can be done. The optimization of the energy consumption in buildings is of paramount importance in the future smart grid. The rationale behind this optimization is twofold. On the one hand, the energy demand is growing at a faster pace than the grid capacity which has provoked blackouts as well as environmental concerns [7]. This leads the utilities to incentivize a more rational and efficient energy consumption. To do so, they implemented smart pricing tariffs which are based on a variable energy price [8]. On the other hand, from the user side, the optimization of the energy consumption in buildings leads to important savings, especially under the smart pricing tariff paradigm. Several works in literature have to date tackled the problem of energy profiling/energy optimization in buildings [9]. Within the context of smart pricing, energy scheduling is the state-of-the-art methodology to address this problem from an analytical point of view [8]. Regarding the power-shiftable loads, heating, ventilation and air conditioning (HVAC) modules are considered as the most energy demanding appliances in home buildings [10,11]. According to studies, they represent the 43 % of residential energy consumption in the U.S. and the 61 % in U.K. and Canada. The significant energy consumption of the HVAC systems, along with their direct influence on the user's well-being, highlight the necessity for effective HVAC management algorithms that reduce the power consumption in the buildings, taking into account the end-user's comfort. In [12] IoTLAB Energy Scheduling System (ITESS) has been presented. Such system comprehends two HVAC energy scheduling methods in an IoT framework, where the users are able to interact remotely with the HVAC control system. In particular, the users may retrieve information about the temperature and the energy consumption at various spots of the building under control, while they are also able to remotely configure the desired temperature of comfort in given places.

This paper proposes the integration of the IGMF with the ITESS. Such integration leads to a whole system that allows the users to manage buildings applying Dynamic Energy Schedulers for different rooms. Thereby, IGMF permits a more flexible and scalable deployment of the HVAC energy scheduling approach.

The rest of the paper is organized as follows: Sect. 2 introduces some related work about the integrations of systems; Sect. 3 presents the IGMF, the ITESS, and the characteristics that their integration can have; Sect. 4 shows an example of loosly coupled integration applied to the systems introduced in the previous Section. Finally, in Sect. 5 some conclusions are drawn.

2 Related Work

The integration of heterogeneous systems is a notable issue, widely addressed both in academia and industry. Different integration solutions have been developed leading to different levels of coupling, that is the degree of direct knowledge that one element (or even, one system) has of another one. On the basis of the direct knowledge degree, in literature the integrated systems are usually divided into:

- **Loosely Coupled Systems**, in which multiple components can cooperate and interoperate regardless of hardware, software, incompatible technologies and other functional features. Moreover, to work properly they do not need to be dependent on each other.
- **Tightly Coupled Systems**, in which hardware and software are not only linked together, but are also inter-dependent, so that the slightest variation from the original status of one of the composing elements implies adverse effects;

These approaches may be applied at different levels [13]:

- at physical level, a tightly coupling implies a direct link between the components while a loosely coupling usually relies on physical intermediary devices;
- at communication level, tightly coupled systems usually exploits a synchronous communication style while loosely coupled systems an asynchronous one;
- at management level, the tightly coupling approach usually exploits a centralized control of process logic. On the contrary, the loosely coupling exploits a distributed control;
- at service level, services are discovered and bound statically in tightly coupled systems, while in loosely coupled systems it is done dynamically.

It is worth noting that both the approaches are not good or bad per-se, because everything depends on the benefits to be obtained after the integration process.

Such paper will mainly focus on loosely coupled architectures. Loose coupling occurs when the interconnected systems elements are highly inter-operable but at the same time minimally inter-dependent. In this case, the integrated system testing, maintenance and recovery costs are reduced, while system flexibility, modularity, robustness and agility increase. To realize a loose coupling, virtualization-based and gateway-based solutions are commonly exploited at different levels of the system architecture. Virtualization allows the creation of a digital artefact of a single device or of a whole system, with the aim of hiding the underlying complexity and reducing at same time the overall interdependency. Gateway-based solutions, instead, aim at increasing the interoperability, establishing shared standards and protocols to facilitate the integration of heterogeneous components/systems. Both these approaches realize loose coupling mainly by exploiting the Software Agent and the Web Service paradigms. In literature have been proposed several examples of loosely coupled integration. iCore [14] is a cognitive management framework for the IoT, in which every real world object (RWO) is virtualized into a digital always-on alter ego, called virtual object (VO), reflecting RWOs status and capabilities. The interactions between RWOs and related VOs happen through gateways, using the REST interface over various wireless or wired access technologies. The ITEA3 project [15] provides a network and services infrastructure for autonomic cooperating smart objects, with the goal of simplifying the development and the deployment of the distributed applications. Similarly to iCore, in ITEA3 heterogeneous components are concretely connected through gateways which exploit a REST interface. Vital framework [16] aims at federating heterogeneous IoT architectures and platforms in the context of the Smart Cities, loosely coupling them by means of different PPIs (Platform Provider Interfaces), which are specified and implemented as a set of RESTful web services and represent a uniform way for accessing the services and data sources regardless of the underlying platforms or providers. Butler [17] and Santander [18] frameworks present a unified, open and horizontal platform to provide services in the context of the Smart Cities. They both exploit a gateway, (defined SmartObject Gateway for Butler, SmartSantanderGateway for Santander) which relies on the REST paradigm and allows the interconnection of different networks to achieve access and communication among embedded devices, servers and mobile terminals.

3   The IGMF / IoTLAB Energy Scheduling System Integration

This section introduces the IGMF, the ITESS, and their system integration.

3.1   The IGMF

The IGMF (Intra-Grid Management Framework) [6] is a domain-specific framework based on WSANs that allows both a proactive monitoring of spaces and a flexible control of devices. The IGMF has the aim to overcome the limits of the frameworks already presented in literature by providing: (i) an effective management of (large) sets of cooperating networked WSAN nodes; (ii) flexible node group organization to capture the floor plan of the buildings; (iii) techniques for intelligent and distributed sensing and actuation; (iv) heterogeneous WSANs integration; (v) system programming at low- and high-levels; (vi) quick deployment and update of applications to the WSAN through message exchange. Figure 1 shows a component layered based representation of the IGMF. It is worth to be noted that the layers are divided in BS-Side (basestation-side) and Node-Side depending on the place where they are deployed. BS-Side and Node-Side communicate through the IGMF Communication Protocol. The Node-Side components are:

- the *Hardware Sensor Platform* which allows the interaction with platform specific sensors/actuators and radios;
- the *WSAN Management* which allows the communication according to the IGMF Communication Protocol;
- the *Sensing and Actuation Management* which provides a platform-independent access to all the sensors/actuators in the node;
- the *Node Management* which coordinates all the components for the task execution;
- the *Local Group Management* which enables the nodes to manage their groups. A node can be configured according to its group membership;
- the *In-node Signal Processing* which allows the nodes to calculate synthetic data on the samples collected from sensors;
- the *Multi Request Scheduling* which manages periodic requests for sensing/actuation.

The BS-Side layers are:

- the *Heterogeneous Platform Support* which allows the upper layers of the BS-side part to communicate with different platforms;
- the *WSAN Management* which allows the communication with the BS and the other nodes according to the IGMF Communication Protocol;
- the *Group Management* which manages the organizations of the nodes in the WSAN in groups. Groups are designed to represent physical or logical characteristics of the nodes;
- the *Request Scheduling* which allows high-level applications to use the WSAN.

On top of the Request Scheduling Layer an *IGMF Manager & GUI*, an IGMF manager providing a graphical interface that permits the local control of the IGMF WSAN, has been implemented. It allows to manage nodes and groups, to schedule requests for sensing/actuation, to visualize the nodes on the floor plan of a building, and to print charts of data from sensors.

3.2   The ITESS

In this section a description of the IoTLAB Energy Scheduling System (ITESS) is provided. Figure 2 presents a block diagram of the overall architecture. It consists of the following elements:

(i) A set of HVAC modules.
(ii) A set of actuators that control the HVAC modules.
(iii) A WSN, which sends measurements of temperature and energy consumption to a gateway.
(iv) A gateway (GW) that incorporates the proposed energy scheduling methods and connects the local network to the Internet. That is, it contains a web server and a database to store data received at the GW from the WSN or the internet.

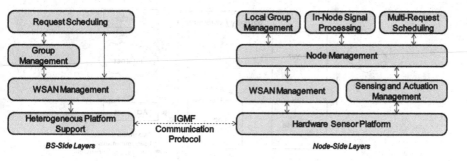

Fig. 1. The IGMF architecture.

(v) An embedded IP device (e.g., tablet or smartphone) with an interface to interact with the HVAC energy scheduler. It also displays both the temperature and the energy consumption in the building measured by the WSN.

The functionality and flow of information of the proposed architecture is explained as follows. The temperature is measured at several locations by means of the WSN. Then, the measurements are periodically sent to the gateway, where the energy scheduling algorithm is implemented. This algorithm selects the combination of the active HVAC modules that minimize the energy cost for given comfort constraints and energy price during a particular time period. These decisions are sent, through shell commands, to programmable surge protectors (actuators), which actuate on the HVAC modules. The HVAC modules modify the room temperature according to the decisions taken by the energy scheduler. In [12], two energy schedulers are proposed: the Dynamic Energy Scheduler with Comfort Constraints (DES-CC) and the Dynamic Energy Scheduler with Comfort Constraints Relaxation (DES-CCR), see [12] for further details.

Moreover, the gateway hosts a database to store the measurements of temperature and energy consumption. These measurements can be accessed by a remote Internet user. More specifically, they are displayed at the user's IP device, as the gateway implements a web server which manages the communication between the remote user and the local database. This is illustrated in more detail in Fig. 2, where the connections between the most relevant blocks are shown. Furthermore, users are allowed to interact with the energy scheduler through their IP devices, by setting the upper and lower bounds of the temperature of comfort.

To get more insights, let us shed light on the temporal behavior of the energy schedulers and the role of the temperature constraints on it. Note that the energy scheduler works in a time interval basis. At the end of each time interval ("current time" in Fig. 3), the energy scheduler must make a new decision. That is, it must decide which HVAC modules will be active during the next time interval. In order to make this decision, the energy scheduler should predict which would be the temperature provoked by each configuration of HVACs. As there are K HVAC modules and we assume that they are either turned on or off, this corresponds to predict 2^K curves of temperature, as it is illustrated in Fig. 3. These predicted temperatures are denoted by $Tp_i^j(n)$, where $1 \leqslant i \leqslant M$ denotes the i-th node and $1 \leqslant j \leqslant 2^K$ is the j-th combination of HVACs turned on or off. Finally, on one

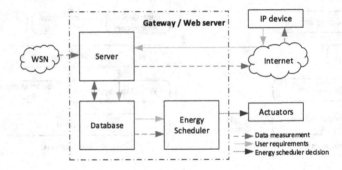

Fig. 2. Block diagram of the energy scheduler with comfort constraints system.

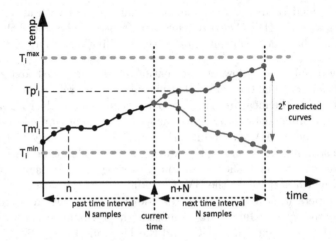

Fig. 3. Prediction of temperature, a fundamental step of the energy scheduler to assess comfort in the future time interval.

hand, the DES-CC selects the configuration of HVACs that minimizes the energy consumption cost within the bounds of comfort, i.e., $T_i^{\min} \leqslant Tp_i^j(n) \leqslant T_i^{\max}$, while the DES-CCR selects the HVAC configuration that optimizes the tradeoff between being closer to the comfort temperatures $T_{u,i}$ and saving energy. This selection is executed by the actuators that control the HVAC modules. It is worth to remark that the higher the number of sensors, the more accurate is the temperature measurement and thus the comfort assessment, though the overall computational cost increases. Also, the temperature dynamics do not change very fast, thereby the sampling rate can be rather slow, in practice it has been observed that 30 seconds is enough for a proper behavior of the system. Last but not least, the higher the time window for taking decision the least accurate the predictions. The interested reader is referred to [12] for further details.

3.3 IGMF / ITESS

The IGMF and the ITESS are two complementary systems that can present several advantages when used together. In particular, they both use WSANs to sample the real world but, while ITESS is configured to use only wireless nodes that sample temperature, the IGMF provides (and can complete the ITESS with) a flexible framework that can be used both to collect data from heterogeneous sensor nodes and to wirelessly control actuators. On the other side, the ITESS can complete the IGMF with mechanisms to control ethernet actuators. Moreover, the ITESS provides a remote interface to control its system that can be used to control the integrated IGMF/ITESS. Finally, the IGMF can have access to the energy schedulers from the ITESS so applying its own energy schedulers.

In particular, the integrated system main features will comprehend:

- the management of a range of cooperating networked wireless nodes in the different parts of the structure;
- the capture of the morphology of any building so to correlate sensed data to a specific portion of the building;
- the adaptive management of sensing and actuation techniques;
- the management of network communication to allow different duty cycles for different wireless nodes;
- the low and high level programmability of the network;
- the fast deployment of concurrent applications at runtime;
- the energy consumption optimization of HVAC systems taking into account the user's comfort constraints and smart pricing tariffs in smart grids;
- the integration with Internet of Things (IoT). Remote users can oversee the energy consumption and the temperature of the building under control;
- remote users can interact with the HVAC control system by setting the desired temperature of comfort.

4   A Loosely Coupled Integration Between the IGMF and the ITESS

A loosely coupled integration between the IGMF and the ITESS and based on Web Services has been designed. In particular, Fig. 4 shows a high level view of the IGMF and the ITESS where:

- the *IGMF Wireless Sensor and Actuator Network* layer represents all the WSAN nodes on which the IGMF is deployed;
- the *IGMF* layer represents the framework presented in Sect. 3.1;
- the *IGMF Manager & GUI* layer represents the access point to use the IGMF compliant WSAN;
- the *ITESS Gateway* is the one described in Sect. 3.2, i.e. it contains the energy scheduler, the server and the database that permit the interaction with external systems;
- *ITESS WSAN* is the WSAN taking temperature measurements;
- *ITESS Ethernet Actuators* are a set of actuators that control the HVAC modules.

Both the *IGMF Manager & GUI* and the *ITESS Gateway* expose a REST interface and stream sensor data. The following subsections will show the main designed high level functions that both the IGMF and the ITESS expose.

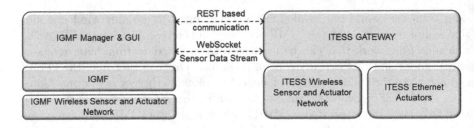

Fig. 4. Loosely Coupled Integration design between IGMF and ITESS.

4.1 IGMF Exposed Functions

The main designed high level functions that have been exposed by the IGMF to be integrated with the ITESS are shown in this section (see Fig. 5). In particular, this functions have been partially introduced in [3]. In the functions the concept of *group* has been highlighted. Every node belongs to one or more groups. A group is a set of nodes sharing logical (e.g. a sensor on its board) or physical (e.g. the place where a node is placed) characteristics. Using group composition/intersection flexible set of nodes can be addressed all at once. This possibility is important in a complex environment such as the building one.

It is worth to be noted that most of the functions (except 4, 5, 9) return an acknowledgment if the message has been successfully sent to the WSAN. The functions are explained in the following:

1. Creates a new group starting from a list of groups and a set theory operator to combine them;
2. Modifies a group according to a ModifyMethod (add/remove/update) and to a list of groups and a set theory operator to combine them;
3. Removes the group received;
4. Returns all the groups already created by the IGMF;
5. Returns all the nodes in a specific group;
6. Schedules a specific sensing task, configured according to the passed Sensor-Params, on a group;
7. Schedules a specific actuation task, configured according to the passed Actu-atorParams, on a group;
8. Unschedule the received request;
9. Returns all the requests already running in the IGMF;
10. Resets the nodes belonging to the passed group;
11. Provides a login operation for the loosely coupled system.

It must be noted that the commands 1–10 can only be invoked by the coupled system (that owns specific rights).

4.2 ITESS Exposed Functions

In this section a list of high level functions, provided by ITESS, are presented. They allow the interaction of IGMF with ITESS. In Fig. 6 the complete list of

```
1)  GroupAck addGroup(GroupList, Operator)
2)  GroupAck modGroup(Group, ModifyMethod, GroupList, Operator)
3)  GroupAck delGroup(Group)
4)  GroupList getGroups()
5)  NodeList getNodes(Group)
6)  RequestAck scheduleSensorRequest(Group, SensorParams)
7)  RequestAck scheduleActuatorRequest(Group, ActuatorParams)
8)  RequestAck unscheduleRequest(Request)
9)  RequestList getRequests()
10) ResetAck resetNode(Group)
11) LoginAck login(User)
```

Fig. 5. The IGMF exposed functions.

```
1)  [EnergySchedulerAck,EnergySchedulerID]=setEnergyScheduler(GroupList, EnergySchedulerParams)
2)  EnergySchedulerList getEnergyScheduler()
3)  EnergySchedulerAck modEnergyScheduler(EnergySchedulerID, EnergySchedulerParams)
4)  EnergySchedulerAck delEnergyScheduler(EnergySchedulerID)
5)  IoTPlotID=newIoTPlot(data,FigParams)
6)  IoTPlotAck=delIoTPlot(IoTPlotID)
7)  LoginAck=login(User)
```

Fig. 6. The ITESS exposed functions.

the functions that permit the interaction is shown. In the following, the functions are explained in more detail.

1. Permits to define a new energy scheduler with comfort constraints for the set of nodes defined by "GroupList". The variable, "EnergySchedulerParams" contains the parameters that characterize the energy scheduler, such as the temperature of comfort bounds, the energy cost definition or the energy scheduling interval.
2. Obtains a list of the energy schedulers that are currently active.
3. Modifies the parameters of the energy scheduler (specified by the "EnergySchedulerID" identifier).
4. Deletes, i.e. it stops, the activity of the energy scheduler (specified by the "EnergySchedulerID" identifier).
5. Creates a new IoT plot service. This will permit to plot the data measured by a group of WSAN nodes (managed within IGMF) into the device of a remote user (connected through ITESS).
6. Removes the plot associated to IoTPlotID.
7. Permits to login in a user. This allows him or her to use the previous described functions.

5   Conclusion

This paper has introduced a loosely coupled integration of the IGMF and the ITESS. The loosely coupled integration allows the systems to cooperate and interoperate without hardware or software dependencies. In particular, the systems have been integrated through sets of functions that have been exposed through REST interfaces.

Future work will be devoted to the real implementation of the presented loosely coupled integration and on the definition of a tightly coupled integration between the IGMF and the ITESS.

Acknowledgments. This work has been partially supported by E2SG project, funded by ENIAC Joint Undertaking under grant agreement n. 296131 and from the national program/funding authority of Italy.

This work was partially supported by the Catalan Government under grant 2014-SGR-1551.

References

1. Snoonian, D.: Control systems: smart buildings. IEEE Spectr. **40**(8), 18–23 (2003)
2. Ceriotti, M., Mottola, L., Picco, G., Murphy, A., Guna, S., Corra, M., Pozzi, M., Zonta, D., Zanon, P.: Monitoring heritage buildings with wireless sensor networks: the Torre Aquila deployment. In: International Conference on Information Processing in Sensor Networks, IPSN 2009, pp. 277–288, April 2009
3. Guerrieri, A., Geretti, L., Fortino, G., Abramo, A.: A service-oriented gateway for remote monitoring of building sensor networks. In: Proceedings of the 2013 IEEE 18th International Workshop on Computer Aided Modeling and Design of Communication Links and Networks (CAMAD), pp. 139–143, September 2013
4. Liotta, A., Geelen, D., van Kempen, G., van Hoogstraten, F.: A survey on networks for smart-metering systems. Int. J. Pervasive Comput. Commun. **8**(1), 23–52 (2012)
5. Stankovic, J.: When sensor and actuator cover the world. ETRI J. **30**(5), 627–633 (2008)
6. Fortino, G., Guerrieri, A., O'Hare, G., Ruzzelli, A.: A flexible building management framework based on wireless sensor and actuator networks. J. Netw. Comput. Appl. **35**, 1934–1952 (2012)
7. Lu, G., De, D., Song, W.: Smartgridlab: a laboratory-based smart grid testbed. In: IEEE International Conference on Smart Grid Communications, pp. 143–148 (2010)
8. Mohsenian-Rad, A.H., Wong, V., Jatskevich, J., Schober, R., Leon-Garcia, A.: Autonomous demand-side management based on game-theoretic energy consumption scheduling for the future smart grid. IEEE Trans. Smart Grid **1**(3), 320–331 (2010)
9. Diakaki, C., Grigoroudis, E., Kolokotsa, D.: Towards a multi-objective optimization approach for improving energy efficiency in buildings. Energy Build. **40**(9), 1747–1754 (2008)
10. Wood, G., Newborough, M.: Dynamic energy-consumption indicators for domestic appliances: environment, behaviour and design. Energy Build. **35**(8), 821–841 (2003)
11. Avci, M., Erkoc, M., Asfour, S.: Residential HVAC load control strategy in real-time electricity pricing environment. In: 2012 IEEE Energytech, pp. 1–6, May 2012
12. Serra, J., Pubill, D., Antonopoulos, A., Verikoukis, C.: Smart HVAC Control in IoT: energy consumption minimization with user comfort constraints. Sci. World J. **2014**, 1–11 (2014)
13. Krafzig, D., Banke, K., Slama, D.: Enterprise SOA: service-oriented architecture best practices. Prentice Hall Professional, Upper Saddle River (2005)

14. Vlacheas, P., Giaffreda, R., Stavroulaki, V., Kelaidonis, D., Foteinos, V., Poulios, G., Demestichas, P., Somov, A., Biswas, A.R., Moessner, K.: Enabling smart cities through a cognitive management framework for the internet of things. IEEE Commun. Mag. **51**(6), 102–111 (2013)
15. An, S., Park, S., Oh, H., Yang, J., Park, H., Choi, J.: Lightweight web-based communication interface design for web of objects. In: 2013 15th International Conference on Advanced Communication Technology (ICACT), pp. 535–539. IEEE (2013)
16. Petrolo, R., Loscrì, V., Mitton, N.: Towards a smart city based on cloud of things. In: Proceedings of the 2014 ACM International Workshop on Wireless and MobileTechnologies for Smart Cities, pp. 61–66. ACM (2014)
17. Butler (2011). http://www.iot-butler.eu/download/publications
18. Sanchez, L., Muñoz, L., Galache, J.A., Sotres, P., Santana, J.R., Gutierrez, V., Ramdhany, R., Gluhak, A., Krco, S., Theodoridis, E., et al.: Smartsantander: Iot experimentation over a smart city testbed. Comput. Netw. **61**, 217–238 (2014)

Urban Crowd Steering: An Overview

Claudio Borean[1], Roberta Giannantonio[1], Marco Mamei[2], Dario Mana[1],
Andrea Sassi[2], and Franco Zambonelli[2]([✉])

[1] Telecom Italia Lab, Turin, Italy
{Claudio.Borean,Roberta.Giannantonio,Dario.Mana}@telecomitala.it
[2] DISMI, University of Modena and Reggio Emilia, Modena, Italy
{Marco.Mamei,Andrea.Sassi,Franco.Zambonelli}@unimore.it

Abstract. Smart phones and environmental sensors make it possible to
dynamically monitor the positions and patterns of movements of people
in urban areas and public spaces, identify or predict possible dangerous
situations (e.g., overcrowded areas) or simply recognize the profitability
of a different patterns of distribution and collective movements. In this
overview paper, we focus on the problem of using such technologies also
to steer the movement of people. In particular, this paper has the goal of
motivating the general problem of crowd steering, identifying the technologies that can be put to play to enforce crowd steering strategies, and
presenting the possible strategies that can be adopted to steer people
movements, other than the key research challenges.

1 Introduction

The diffusion of smart phones, environmental sensors, and various classes of
cameras, make it possible to monitor at very fine-grained levels of details a variety
of social and urban phenomena. These technologies are being already widely used
to understand the dynamics of cities [6], there included the understanding of the
pedestrian mobility patterns [12,19,24]. Also, they have been used for urban
planning, e.g., to design walkaways and the structure of museums etc., other
than to simulate pedestrian and crowd movements with high levels of details
based on real data.

However, smart phones also introduce the possibility of feed backing users
with information about the current crowd conditions in a town, and possibly to
suggest them directions in order to better move in the city, i.e., to avoid crowd or
simply to get alerted about specific conditions. Closing the feedback loop make
a big shift from simply "sensing crowd" to "actuating crowd", i.e., steering the
behavior of people so as to serve both their individual needs and the global needs
of the city [13,30].

The technologies that can be put at work to enforce steering goes beyond the
simple app on smart phones, but can include advanced wearable systems and
interfaces (such as vibration and sound) [26], and also technologies to collectively
suggest all people in a specific location (e.g., in a room) how to move, such
as public sound announcements or public displays [9,22]. In addition, societal

G. Di Fatta et al. (Eds.): IDCS 2015, LNCS 9258, pp. 143–154, 2015.
DOI: 10.1007/978-3-319-23237-9_13

or economic incentives can be put at work to encourage people to follow the suggestions [16, 17].

Clearly, given the availability of crowd steering technologies, there must be some strategy to identify which suggestions to give. The main problem here is to have strategies to serve individual needs co-exists with possibly conflicting strategies to serve the global needs of the environment in which users situates.

This paper has the goal of overviewing some of the many issues related to crowd steering in urban spaces. In particular, the article:

- Motivates the need for crowd steering in urban spaces, to serve both individual and global needs (Sect. 2);
- Introduces the key technologies that can be put already at work to support crowd steering, and those that promise to be available soon (Sect. 3);
- Classifies and presents some of the more promising strategies that can be devised to support crowd steering at both individual and global level (Sect. 4);
- Surveys some of the key related works in the area (Sect. 5);

Section 6 concludes and outlines some open challenges in crowd steering.

2 Crowd Steering: Motivations

The problem of steering the movements of people can arise as a mean to help individuals or groups in achieving their own mobility objectives at the best, or as a mean for the institution that manage an environment to achieve some sort of overall distribution property within it (e.g., at urban scale or at the level of exhibition or museum), or both.

2.1 Steering to Support Individual Needs

We have all experienced the situation of moving in crowdy and unfamiliar places. In several cases, this can have become an uncomfortable experience, and we have desired some solutions to orient ourselves in a more informed way, and move by avoiding the crowd while reaching in any case the places we wanted to reach.

Most navigation systems in vehicles (e.g., Waze and Google Transit) already include solutions to suggest routes based on the detected traffic conditions, so as to avoid queues and minimize travel time. However, when it comes to pedestrians, none of the existing pedestrian navigation system consider the actual density of people in streets and walkways, and none of them exploit knowledge about current crowd conditions to suggest directions.

There are several reasons why individual people moving in an environment may wish to be altered on where to move, and such motivation slightly differs from those typically motivating vehicles. In particular:

- When moving in environments such as museum or big exhibitions or city fairs, pedestrians (unlike car drivers) are not simply willing to reach a specific point. They rather wish to visit a number of different places (e.g., museum rooms), but may have no clue on what could be the best order in which to visit them.

- As it happens to drivers, it may also happens that pedestrians can be slowed down in their speed by extreme crowd conditions, for which it is good to receive advice on how to avoid crowd. However, for pedestrians, avoiding crowd may be useful also for simply better enjoying a place (as it happens in museum).
- In some cases, pedestrians may wish to receive suggestions on how to move within an environment so as to avoid peculiar situations, such as moving across unsafe neighborhoods or extremely polluted streets.

All the above considerations are particularly critical for groups of people sharing similar interests or goals, and willing to share a mobility path across an environment. Examples of such groups may include groups of tourists, and groups of teachers herding young children around.

As a final consideration, the need of dynamically forming groups in which individuals can join and leave while the group walks across a path (as in walking school buses [29]), necessarily requires some form of steering to facilitate the dynamic shaping of the group.

2.2   Steering to Support Institutional Goals

Shifting the attention from the level of individual needs to a more global – institutional – level, steering the movements of people can be used by the administrator of some public spaces likely to host crowdy events (e.g., a large museum, an exhibition, a fair, a stadium, a large park) to promote a better or safer exploitation of the space. More specifically, the goals of an institutional crowd steering strategy may include:

- Load balancing, to ensure a fair exploitation of the available space and distribute people evenly. For instance, load balancing may aim at avoiding that people during an exhibition concentrate in specific areas with no apparent reasons (or simply because that area is easier to be reached), an approach we have experienced at the Vienna City Marathon [22]. In addition, load balancing may be aimed at ensuring that all areas of an exhibition receive a similar amount of visitors (e.g., consider the case in which exhibitors pay to be present and would not tolerate being penalized for being at an unfortunate location).
- Planning for evacuation, to ensure that the distribution of people facilitates a quick evacuation from the area. Such an issue may be particularly safety-critical for dangerous situations but – independently of safety issues – it may also be important to ensure no one is penalized with this regard. For instance, at some airport (such as Heathrow) the waiting time at different security gates is advertised via public displays, implicitly enforcing a local balancing crowd distribution strategy, in that displays implicitly invite people to move towards the less crowded gates.
- Enforcing other specific strategies, such as favoring the movements of specific classes of persons, or wishing to attract people towards specific location at a specific time. For instance, crowd-sensing campaigns (e.g., exploiting people as

sensors by having them report about or photograph some events in some specific locations [15,23]) may require dynamically mobilizing people according to some specific sensing goal.

Of course, whatever the goals to be achieved, any institutional strategy for crowd steering has to account for the fact that a percentage of people can decide to ignore the suggestions, and follow their own mobility paths in autonomy. Clearly, depending on the adopted strategies and technologies, this will somehow affect the effectiveness of the crowd steering strategy.

3   Crowd Steering Technologies

Crowd steering is enabled by a number of recently emerged ICT technologies and – most importantly – by their low cost and massive spread.

3.1   Detecting People Location and Density

The first, necessary, ingredient of any crowd steering approach in an area is the capability of detecting the location and density of people in portions of that area. With this regard, the number of technologies available is increasing in terms of number and accuracy.

For outdoor scenarios, smart phones currently have a high degree of penetration and high accuracy in localization (thanks to the concurrent exploitation of GPS, cellular telephony signal, and WiFi triangulation).

For indoor scenarios, the dense deployment of WiFi access point makes it possible to achieve high-levels of accuracy via WiFi triangulation even indoor [18]. In addition, novel low-cost technologies based on beacons [31] (small bluetooth-enable boxes to be detected by a smart phone, and that enable the smart phone to effectively estimate its distance from it) can very effective to achieve accurate indoor localization. It is also worth mentioning that cameras and artificial visions can be used as well to analyze the presence of people in a room or corridor and their density.

3.2   Smart Phones and Mobile Apps

Smart phones, other than a very important tool to localize people (as discussed in the previous subsection), are a very important mean via which to enforce crowd steering strategies. In fact, the primary mean by which we can expect a crowd steering strategy to inform individuals about a suggested route, is via some mobile app on a smart phone.

We do not exclude that in the near future different personal appliances will emerge as the primary mean via which to receive crowd steering suggestions. Given that the big hype for smart glasses is over, smart watches – if at all successful – will be definitely a suitable tool to adopt. It is also worth outlining that smart watches, other than being suitable for suggesting directions with traditional GUI (e.g., showing a map and, using the compass, a direction on it), will enable exploring alternate means for suggestion (e.g., vibrations or sounds).

3.3   Digital Signages and Public Displays

Public digital signals are already widely adopted in vehicular traffic to dynamically provide (near) real-time traffic information, and increasingly often to suggest routes to vehicles. However, we are assisting also to the application of digital
signals and public displays to suggest directions to people, and to enforce specific
crowd steering policies [10] (as it in the already mentioned examples of displays
signaling the length of queues at Heathrow airport).

   In the future, with the increasingly dense deployment of interactive wall-
mounted displays, it will be possible to exploit such displays to provide real-time
information on the density of crowd at different location. Also, it will be possible
to use displays to suggest passing-by people where to go, typically with the goal
of enforcing some kind of global-goal strategy. Clearly, exploiting public displays
to enforce private-goals strategies would raise notably privacy concerns, in that
it would disclose possibly sensible information about individuals' intentions and
goals [11].

3.4   Morphable Architectures

A last technology, possibly a bit more futuristic, by which it will be possible in
the future to steer the movement of people according to some strategy include
morphable architectures: places in which it is possible to dynamically change
the topology of space (i.e., making walls and door appear and reappear, as it
happens during the nights in the scenario of "The Maze Runner" [8]) so as to
force specific patterns of movements in the crowd.

   To some extent, dynamic signage can already obtain similar effects (e.g., by
making a one-way sign appears at the beginning of a street). However, recent
conceptual experiments (e.g., the Slothbot moving wall, http://arch-os.com/
projects/slothbot/) shows that the concept could be applied for crowd steering
as well.

4   Strategies

In the previous section, we have presented the enabling technologies for crowd
steering, i.e., to collect information about the distribution of people in an environment (and possibly about their own mobility intentions) and to actuate steering actions. In this section, we discuss possible "crowd steering strategies" to
analyze location and mobility data and decide which steering actions to actuate.

   To create an effective taxonomy of possible strategies, we identify three
(nearly) orthogonal axis along which strategies might vary: (i) strategies with
aims to achieve a local goal vs. strategies that aims for some global goals, (ii)
strategies using local information vs. strategies that exploit some global information, and (iii) strategies giving personalized recommendations to individual
users vs. strategies that multicasting recommendations to groups of users.

   As it often happens with taxonomies, there are not crisp boundaries among
the categories and the taxonomy space is a continuum of possibilities.

Local VS. Global Goal. The goal of steering strategies is to "arrange" people in the environment in order satisfy specific criteria. A local goal is simply about sidestepping a local condition (e.g., an overcrowded room). A global goal is about achieving a global distribution of people in the environment. More specifically:

- Local goal strategies aim at recommending users about the next step to take. For example, a local goal could be *"avoid neighbor crowded rooms"*. The system would recommend the user not to visit a neighbor crowded room. This kind of strategies can be useful to better navigate across an environment sidestepping blocked or crowded areas.
- Global goal strategies aim at giving recommendations to influence the long term behavior of users. These strategies can be formulated with a user-centered perspective (e.g., *"minimize the time to visit the environment"*), or an environment-centered perspective (e.g., *"balance the crowd in the environment"*).

Local VS. Global Information. The information available to the steering component might be local (i.e., the component provides recommendation on the basis of nearby crowd conditions), or global (i.e., the steering component oversee the whole environment).

- Local information strategies give recommendations by taking into account the user local neighborhood only. For example, a local information strategy can recommend user to visit the least crowded neighbor room.
- Global information strategies give recommendations on the basis of the knowledge of the whole people distribution across the environment.

Personalized Unicast VS. Multicast. The steering component might provide personalized recommendations to individual users (e.g., via their smartphone), or general recommendations to a whole group of people (e.g., via public displays).

- Strategies adopting a personalized unicast approach can give recommendations via the users' smartphones. Using data from the smartphone (e.g., user location and planned itinerary) such strategies are able to highly personalize the steering recommendation.
- Strategies adopting a multicast approach can typically give recommendation via displays deployed in the environment. Recommendation can take into account approximate users location (as represented by the display own location) and other information, but it cannot be specifically tailored to individual users, as all users would see the same steering advice.

Figure 1 illustrates the taxonomy. Specifically, we describe exemplary systems that would fit in each area of the taxonomy space:

- *Recommend Detours* and *Greedy Steering*. In these strategies the system recommends a next step (detour) on the basis of the crowd conditions in the user local neighborhood. In *Recommend detours*, the system can interact with users individually proposing detours compatible with the user planned trip.

In *Greedy steering*, the system cannot give personalized advices so it tends to greedily steer users where most convenient at the moment. In our simulation set up we tested a strategy of this latter kind termed Hot Potato (HP). It is finally worth noting that the repeated execution of local goal strategies, often induce global "emergent" behaviors. On the one hand, these emergent behaviors can represent a global version of the local strategy. On the other hand, such behaviors are often hard to predict and control [14].

- *Gray Areas.* These strategies are very uncommon. In fact, once global information is available, it is rather natural to pursue global goals rather than local ones. Global information is often an overkill for local goals.
- *Emergent Planning* and *Swarm Intelligent Mechanisms.* These strategies try to exploit some kind of collective (i.e., swarm intelligence) mechanism to achieve a global goal on the basis of local information only. In *emergent planning* personalized recommendations can be given to individual users, accordingly the problem is to coordinate individual movements toward the achievement of the global goal. In *swarm intelligent Mechanisms* control over individuals is much more coarse and self-organizing algorithms could be used [14,22].
- *Navigator* and *Traffic Control.* These strategies exploit global information to achieve a global steering goal. *Navigator* strategies guide individual users across the environment on the basis of all the information available. In our simulation set up we tested a strategy of this king termed Best Path (BP). *Traffic control* strategies try to achieve a similar goal but without addressing individual users. These are like of coordinating traffic lights in a city to steer the traffic.

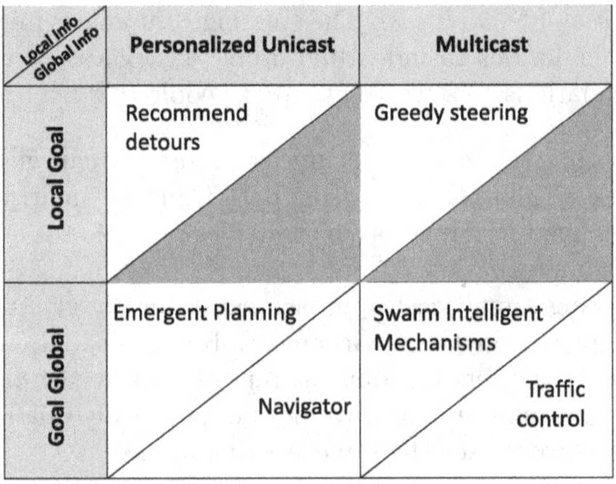

Fig. 1. Taxonomy of steering strategies

An example of a *local info - global goal* strategy, suitable both for personal and unicast and multicast recommendation, is what can be called the Hot Potato one. Simply, the hot potato strategy recommends the agent to visit the less crowded stand among its adjacent ones that belong to the agent's planned itinerary.

As an example of a *global info - global goal* strategy, suitable for unicast recommendations, is what can be called the Shortest Path one. This shortest path strategy takes into account the distance between a user and all the stands in its itinerary, and the crowding level at the stand and on the path to reach it. The two measures are linearly combined together by using two weighting parameters that complement to 1. They balance the influence of each component according to their respective standard deviations to the means computed with all the stands to visit. The ratio between the standard deviation of the mean distance and the mean crowding from the user's location to all the stands determines the value of the weighting parameter for the distance component. Its complement to 1 determines the weight for the crowding component in the linear combination.

5   Related Work

The study of mechanisms and strategies for crowd steering is quite a recent research area.

In the past decade, most of the studies on crowd steering have focussed on analyzing and simulating mobility patterns and behaviours in an environment, and at shaping the environment (e.g., changing size of corridors and moving doors so as to affect paths [1,14]) so as to enforce specific behaviours. In most of the cases, the key goals was to avoid overcrowded situations, prevent the formation of waves of people moving in opposite directions, and more in general ensure safety of public environments and roads.

It is worth emphasizing that this kinds of studies involve an accurate modeling and simulation of pedestrians 'behaviors', and indeed a large amount of recent work deals with the issue of defining realistic models for such simulations [20,21,27]. Such simulation approaches, though, have rather different goals than our. In fact, they are mostly aimed at identifying how the behaviour of individuals in an environment (either modeled via mobility rules or by replicating the mobility schemes of real mobility data) can possibly lead to the emergence of peculiar (or dangerous) crowd phenomena. Being our studies simply focussed at identifying strategies to avoid overcrowding, we are more focussed on modeling at a coarse-grained level the movement of people across zones of an environment, and thus with no need for realizing realistic fine-grained model at the levels of individual mobility.

In the area of collective robotics [4], a large amount of work has been devoted to the problem of engineering (i.e., defining strategies and algorithms) to orchestrate the movements of (typically) a large number of robots. The kinds of collective movements that such approaches aims at orchestrating depends on the specific missions the robot swarms is deployed for. However, many classes of exploratory tasks (e.g., mapping an environment or monitoring it) involves a fair distribution of the swarm over the environment as its composing robots move. Accordingly, some of the strategies that can be devised to this purpose resembles the strategies we have identified for crowd steering [3,5,25]. Yet, robots misses an individual goal, and move only with a global cooperative goal in mind.

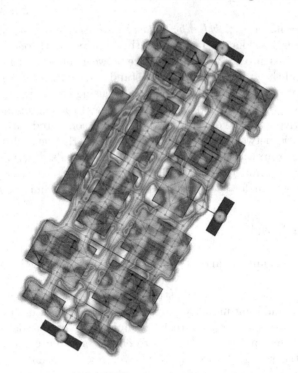

Fig. 2. The "heat map" of a simulated environment, showing the density of simulated users in an environment.

The problem of dynamic load balancing [2] – extensively studied over the past 20 years in the area of parallel and distributed high-performance computing – somehow relates to the study of crowd steering. Dynamic load balancing concerns re-allocating at run-time the processes composing the parallel computation so as to fairly balance the computational load on the processors, and eventually speed up the overall computation. In load balancing, some of the strategies upon which to base the decisions on which processes to move on which processors can somehow resemble the strategies we have discussed for crowd steering [7,28], and so can be the goal of balancing the overall distribution of processes. However, the approach are fundamentally different: in load balancing, movements of the processes is a mean and can be strictly enforced on processes; in crowd steering, movement are also the goals of the individuals and, in most of the cases, the strategies cannot be strictly enforced on all individuals.

6   Conclusions and Future Work

Smart phones, pervasive sensing, and interactive displays can be effectively put at work in public spaces to suggest pedestrians how to move based on current crowd conditions, on their specific mobility needs, or on other contingencies. The paper has shown that, beside technologies, there exists a number of reasons to enforce crowd steering, and that a number of possible strategies can be devised to follow in steering.

However, before the adoption of crowd steering can be widespread and effective at large scale, a number of open research challenges still needs to be face:

– There is need to extensively experiment with different crowd steering strategies, to understand how global goals can co-exists with individual ones, and to understand the impact of different amount of information (from local to global) on the effectiveness of crowd steering strategies;
– Concerning technologies, there is need to understand the actual impact of the different technologies, in terms of efficacy and acceptance by users, which can be done only on real deployment;

By our side, we are currently performing experiments in a simulated environment (see Fig. 2) to assess the trade-off between global vs. local information in load balancing strategies. Also, we intend to deploy a crowd steering system based on interactive displays in a controlled (indoor) environment.

Acknowledgements. Work supported by the Telecom Itala, Swarm Joint Open Lab.

References

1. Abdelghany, A., Abdelghany, K., Mahmassani, H., Alhalabi, W.: Modeling framework for optimal evacuation of large-scale crowded pedestrian facilities. Eur. J. Oper. Res. **237**(3), 1105–1118 (2014)
2. Alakeel, A.M.: A guide to dynamic load balancing in distributed computer systems. Int. J. Comput. Sci. Inf. Secur. **10**(6), 153–160 (2010)
3. Beal, J.: Superdiffusive dispersion and mixing of swarms with reactive levy walks. In: 7th IEEE International Conference on Self-Adaptive and Self-Organizing Systems, SASO 2013, pp. 141–148. Philadelphia, PA, USA, 9–13 September 2013
4. Brambilla, M., Ferrante, E., Birattari, M., Dorigo, M.: Swarm robotics: a review from the swarm engineering perspective. Swarm Intell. **7**(1), 1–41 (2013)
5. Capodieci, N., Hart, E., Cabri, G.: Artificial immune system driven evolution in swarm chemistry. In: Proceedings of the 2014 IEEE Eighth International Conference on Self-Adaptive and Self-Organizing Systems, pp. 40–49. IEEE, Piscataway, NJ, December 2014
6. Chourabi, H., Nam, T., Walker, S., Gil-Garcia, J.R., Mellouli, S., Nahon, K., Pardo, T., Scholl, H.J.: Understanding smart cities: An integrative framework. In: IEEE Hawaii International Conference on System Sciences, Maui (HI), USA (2012)
7. Corradi, A., Leonardi, L., Zambonelli, F.: Diffusive load-balancing policies for dynamic applications. IEEE Concurrency **7**(1), 22–31 (1999)
8. Dasher, J.: The Maze Runners. Delacorte Press, New York (2009)
9. Davies, N., Langheinrich, M., José, R., Schmidt, A.: Open display networks: a communications medium for the 21st century. IEEE Comput. **45**(5), 58–64 (2012)
10. Davies, N., Clinch, S., Alt, F.: Pervasive Displays: Understanding the Future of Digital Signage. Synthesis Lectures on Mobile and Pervasive Computing. Morgan & Claypool Publishers, New York (2014). http://dx.doi.org/10.2200/S00558ED1V01Y201312MPC011

11. Davies, N., Langheinrich, M., Clinch, S., Elhart, I., Friday, A., Kubitza, T., Surajbali, B.: Personalisation and privacy in future pervasive display networks. In: CHI Conference on Human Factors in Computing Systems, CHI 2014, pp. 2357–2366. Toronto, ON, Canada, 26 April– 01 May 2014

12. Ferrari, L., Mamei, M.: Classification of whereabouts patterns from large-scale mobility data. In: WOA (2010)

13. Helbing, D., Brockmann, D., Chadefaux, T., Donnay, K., Blanke, U., Woolley-Meza, O., Moussaid, M., Johansson, A., Krause, J., Schutte, S., Perc, M.: How to save human lives with complexity science. CoRR abs/1402.7011 (2014). http://arxiv.org/abs/1402.7011

14. Helbing, D., Buzna, L., Johansson, A., Werner, T.: Self-organized pedestrian crowd dynamics: experiments, simulations, and design solutions. Transp. Sci. **39**(1), 1–24 (2005)

15. Kanhere, S.: Participatory sensing: crowdsourcing data from mobile smartphones in urban spaces. In: IEEE International Conference on Mobile Data Management. Bengaluru, India (2012)

16. Koutsopoulos, I.: Optimal incentive-driven design of participatory sensing systems. In: 2013 Proceedings of IEEE INFOCOM, pp. 1402–1410. IEEE (2013)

17. Lee, J.S., Hoh, B.: Dynamic pricing incentive for participatory sensing. Pervasive Mob. Comput. **6**(6), 693–708 (2010)

18. Liu, H., Yang, J., Sidhom, S., Wang, Y., Chen, Y., Ye, F.: Accurate wifi based localization for smartphones using peer assistance. IEEE Trans. Mob. Comput. **13**(10), 2199–2214 (2014)

19. Liu, L., Biderman, A., Ratti, C.: Urban mobility landscape: Real time monitoring of urban mobility patterns. In: Proceedings of the 11th International Conference on Computers in Urban Planning and Urban Management, pp. 1–16 (2009)

20. Moussad, M., Helbing, D., Theraulaz, G.: How simple rules determine pedestrian behavior and crowd disasters. In: Proceedings of the National Academy of Sciences, **108**(17), 6884–6888 (2011)

21. Moussad, M., Perozo, N., Garnier, S., Helbing, D., Theraulaz, G.: The walking behaviour of pedestrian social groups and its impact on crowd dynamics. PLoS ONE 5, e10047, April 2010

22. Pianini, D., Viroli, M., Zambonelli, F., Ferscha, A.: HPC from a self-organisation perspective: the case of crowd steering at the urban scale. In: International Conference on High Performance Computing & Simulation, HPCS 2014, pp. 460–467. Bologna, Italy, 21–25 July 2014

23. Rana, R., C., Chou, Kanhere, S., Bulusu, N., Hu, W.: Ear-phone: an end-to-end participatory urban noise mapping system. In: International Conference on Information Processing in Sensor Network, Stockholm, Sweden (2010)

24. Roggen, D., Wirz, M., Tröster, G., Helbing, D.: Recognition of crowd behavior from mobile sensors with pattern analysis and graph clustering methods. Netw. Heterogen. Media **6**(3), 521–544 (2011)

25. Shen, W., Salemi, B., Will, P.: Hormone-inspired adaptive communication and distributed control for conro self-reconfigurable robots. IEEE Trans. Rob. Autom. **18**(5), 1–12 (2002)

26. Spagnolli, A., Chittaro, L., Gamberini, L. (eds.): PERSUASIVE 2014. Information Systems and Applications, incl. Internet/Web, and HCI, vol. 8462. Springer, Switzerland (2014)

27. Wijermans, N., Jorna, R., Jager, W., van Vliet, T., Adang, O.: Cross: modelling crowd behaviour with social-cognitive agents. J. Artif. Soc. Soc. Simul. **4**, 1 (2013)

28. Willebeek-LeMair, M.H., Reeves, A.P.: Strategies for dynamic load balancing on highly parallel computers. IEEE Trans. Parallel Distrib. Syst. 4(9), 979–993 (1993)
29. Winstanley, C., Davies, N., Harding, M., Norgate, S.: Supporting walking school buses. In: Proceedings of the 2014 ACM International Joint Conference on Pervasive and Ubiquitous Computing: Adjunct Publication. pp. 291–294. UbiComp 2014 Adjunct, ACM, New York, NY, USA (2014). http://doi.acm.org/10.1145/2638728.2638791
30. Zambonelli, F.: Toward sociotechnical urban superorganisms. IEEE Comput. 45(8), 76–78 (2012)
31. Zhu, J., Zeng, K., Kim, K.H., Mohapatra, P.: Improving crowd-sourced wi-fi localization systems using bluetooth beacons. In: 2012 9th Annual IEEE Communications Society Conference on Sensor, Mesh and Ad Hoc Communications and Networks (SECON), pp. 290–298, June 2012

Distributed Computing

Towards a Self-Adaptive Middleware for Building Reliable Publish/Subscribe Systems

Sisi Duan[1]([⊠]), Jingtao Sun[2], and Sean Peisert[1]

[1] University of California, Davis, 1 Shields Ave, Davis, CA 95616, USA
{sduan,speisert}@ucdavis.edu
[2] National Institute of Informatics, The Graduate University for Advanced Studies,
2-1-2 Hitotsubashi, Chiyoda-ku, Tokyo, Japan
sun@nii.ac.jp

Abstract. Traditional publish/subscribe (pub/sub) systems may fail or cause longer message latency and higher computing resource usage in the presence of changes in the execution environment. We present the design and implementation of Mimosa Pudica, an adaptive and reliable middleware for adapting various changes in pub/sub systems. At the heart of Mimosa Pudica are two design ideas. First, the brokers can elect leaders to manage the network topology in a distributed manner. Second, software components can be relocated among brokers according to the user's pre-defined rules. Through these two mechanisms, brokers can be connected in a self-adaptive manner to cope with failures and guarantee delivery of messages. In addition, brokers can effectively utilize their computing resources. Our experimental results of a large-scale pub/sub system show that in the presence of environmental changes, each self-adaptive process generates as few as 30 ms extra latency.

1 Introduction

Today's large-scale publish/subscribe (pub/sub) systems require dynamically applicability to be adaptive to various changes in systems and applications. For instance, in the presence of environmental changes, message loss and broker/link failures are desired to be handled. In addition, for many applications, the software components of an application may need to be migrated from one node to another, so as to be adaptive to limited computing resources and high loading at a node. However, most existing approaches propose solutions in the software layer while the pub/sub system structure itself is not able to be adaptive to frequent changes. We propose Mimosa Pudica, a middleware that is dynamically adaptive to various changes from both pub/sub systems and applications on top. Base on the middleware, we build a reliable pub/sub system and also improve the overall efficiency in system resource usage.

An amount of past research efforts have been devoted to developing reliable pub/sub systems. Most of them guarantee that messages will eventually be delivered. In order to guarantee message order in the presence of failures, previous efforts have relied heavily on the topology, either through redundant nodes or

© Springer International Publishing Switzerland 2015
G. Di Fatta et al. (Eds.): IDCS 2015, LNCS 9258, pp. 157–168, 2015.
DOI: 10.1007/978-3-319-23237-9_14

links. However, redundant nodes have a high cost in replication, and redundant links usually require brokers to store large amount of redundant information, which limits the scalability of a system and may even render brokers unusable.

In this paper, we propose a design of a self-adaptive and reliable pub/sub system that scales more efficiently by not requiring redundant nodes or storage. At the core of our system is Mimosa Pudica, a middleware that is adaptive to various changes. We employ two novel design ideas. First, brokers of pub/sub systems can elect leaders through our leader election algorithm to manage the rest of brokers in a distributed manner. Second, the leader can automatically relocate the software components between brokers to achieve dynamic adaptation of the pub/sub system, according to the user's pre-defined rules. Based on such a design, brokers can be dynamically added or deleted to handle failures. Furthermore, software components can be distributed to effectively utilize computing resources and to prevent from node failures.

We use distributed *destination databases* that can be accessed by the brokers to store routing information of brokers and all the pre-defined adaptation rules. In the presence of environmental changes, the brokers access the destination database to obtain a broker group information. After a leader election among the group, the leader compiles the adaptation rules and notify brokers the results. Different groups of brokers run independently in a distributed manner to adaptively manage topology and migrate software components. Through such a mechanism, the system can cope with failures and better utilize broker resources. In addition, due to the flexibility of our design, the software components of an application can be reused and the rules can be free assembled and reused for regular and repeated changes.

Our paper makes the following key contributions:

- We designed and implemented a middleware Mimosa Pudica. In the presence of environmental changes, the system self-adaptively manages the topology and relocates software components between brokers in a distributed manner.
- We implemented a reliable, crash-tolerant pub/sub system based on Mimosa Pudica. Our solution can be built on top of any existing topology. In addition, no redundancy of messages, brokers, or storage, is required.
- Our evaluation results show that each adaptation process only imposes a temporary of 30 ms to 50 ms extra latency to the event delivery, which proves the efficiency of our approach.

2   Related Work

Building reliable pub/sub systems have been widely studied [2,3,6-9,18]. Periodic subscription [6], where subscribers actively re-issue their events [2], works well in preventing message loss. The use of redundant paths [2,3,7,9] or redundant links [8] handles broker/link failures. As long as all the brokers in at least one path are correct, messages can be reliably delivered. However, it may consume high bandwidth and storage at brokers and become very inefficient in the absence of failures. P2S [3] on the other hand, demonstrates a framework of using existing fault-tolerant libraries in pub/sub systems. It directly adapts Paxos [11], a classic crash-tolerant replicated state machine approach. However, the current framework employs a centralized set of replicated brokers and must be carefully designed in scalable systems.

There are four types of self-adaptation mechanisms. The first type [13,14] is policy-based. Most of them focus on how to define the context. The second type dynamically changes coordination between programs run on different computers [17]. It enables client-side objects to automatically select and invoke server-side objects according to the requirements and system architectures. However, this type only modifies the relationships between distributed programs instead of the computers executing them. The third type is genetic programming [10]. Most approaches focused only on target applications or systems such that they have no space to execute and evaluate large number of generated programs. The forth type is aspect-oriented programming (AOP) [15]. Unlike our work, existing adaptations do not support the migration of programs because reflective and AOP approaches are primitive to modify programs running on a single computer.

3 Approach

In this section we present background for our pub/sub system. We begin by introducing the preliminaries and then describe the design of *destination database*, the key component for data storage. Last, we show leader election, which is used to select a leader such that adaptation can be managed by brokers.

3.1 Preliminaries

We assume asynchronous model, where messages can be delayed, duplicated, dropped, or delivered out of order and brokers may crash and subsequently recover. For any n brokers between any pair of publisher and subscriber, up to $\lfloor \frac{n-1}{2} \rfloor$ crash failures are tolerated. In other words, in order to handle f broker failures, there are at least $2f + 1$ brokers on the path.

We aim to achieve the *in-order delivery*, where all the messages from a publisher to a set of corresponding subscribers are delivered in the same sequential order. Liveness guarantees that if a message is delivered to a subscriber, all the subscribers to the same topic eventually receive the same message. Liveness is ensured under *partial synchrony* [5]. That is, synchrony holds only after some unknown global stabilization time, but the bounds on communication and processing delays may be unknown.

3.2 Destination Database

We use a *destination database* that can be accessed by all the brokers. The destination database maintains all the routing information of the brokers and a set of pre-defined rules for adaptation purposes. When a broker communicates with the destination database and requests for group communication, the destination database replies with the identities of a group of brokers on the path based on the broker identity, the message information, and the corresponding publisher and subscriber information. It serves a simple purpose of storage, i.e., it does not manage the configurations of brokers or make any adaptation decisions. Instead, and all the adaptation decisions are made in a distributed manner by brokers.

In order to avoid single point of failure, we propose a two layer structure of distributing destination databases. The first layer contains replicated servers that stores metadata and the second layer contains several databases, each of which stores information of a set of brokers and a whole set of rules. The broker information can be replicated at different databases to prevent loss of data when certain database fails. When a broker requests for group information, it simply accesses the closest second layer database. The database replies directly if it has the information of all brokers on the path. Otherwise, it sends a request to the first layer database, obtains metadata, accesses the corresponding database(s) to get the information of the brokers, and sends a reply to the broker.

3.3   Leader Election

Leader election selects a leader among a set of brokers. A leader collects the information of environmental changes, makes decisions according to the adaptation rules as described in Sect. 4, and notifies all the brokers the adaptation decisions. We now describe the leader election process and illustrate it in Algorithm 1.

Algorithm 1. Leader Election Algorithm

1: **Initialization:**	18: $group \leftarrow B_k \cdots B_p$ {Group Info}
2: $B_i, B_j \cdots$ {Brokers}	19: ElectLeader($v, group$)
3: DD {Destination Database}	20: **on event** ElectLeader($v, group$)
4: Δ {Timer}	21: $B_q \leftarrow$ Leader($group$)
5: $v \leftarrow 0$ {View Number}	22: **send** [LEADER, B_q, v] **to** $group$
6: Leader() {Elect Leader}	23: $starttimer(\Delta)$ {Monitor}
7: $timeout()$ {Timeout}	24: **on event** [LEADER, B_q, v]
8: $starttimer()$ {Start Timer}	25: $count \leftarrow count + 1$
9: $canceltimer()$ {Cancel Timer}	26: **if** $count \leftarrow f$ **and** $i \leftarrow q$
10: $F()$ {Adaptation Results}	27: $action \leftarrow$ F(rules) {Actions}
11: **Broker** B_i**:**	28: **send** [NL, $B_q, v, action$] **to** $group$
12: **on event** adaptation	29: **on event** [NL, $B_q, v, action$]
13: **send** [LE, o, B_i, B_j, nd] **to** DD	30: $canceltimer(\Delta)$
14: **on event** $timeout(\Delta)$	31: **Destination Database:**
15: $v \leftarrow v + 1$ {Re-Elect Leader}	32: **on event** [LE, o, B_i, B_j, nd]
16: ElectLeader($v, group$)	33: $group \leftarrow B_k \cdots B_p$ {Group}
17: **on event** [GI, $B_k \cdots B_p$]	34: **send** [GI, $B_k \cdots B_p$] **to** group

---

When a broker B_i (or publisher/subscriber in corner cases) requests for leader election, B_i sends a message [LE, o, B_i, B_j, nd] to the destination database, where o represents the type of adaptation request, B_j is the broker to be added/deleted, and nd contains the corresponding information. For instance, if B_i detects B_j to be faulty, the message is $[LE, 1, B_i, B_j, M(src, dst)]$, where 1 represents broker deletion, $M(src, dst)$ is the message B_i is currently forwarding from src to dst. The destination database then sends a message $[GI, B_k \cdots B_p]$ to the brokers B_k to B_p between src and dst. After receiving the group information, the brokers start leader election. The leader election proceeds with views. All the brokers follow the same criteria when electing a new leader, as shown below. When the new leader receives at least $f + 1$ matching [LEADER] messages (including its own message), it sends a message to all the brokers to confirm its leadership and notifies brokers the adaptation results.

(1) Broker B_q is elected such that a) B_q is on the path; b) B_q is not suspected to be faulty; c) B_q has not been elected in previous views; and d) B_q is the closest to the publisher on the path.

(2) When a broker votes for a new leader, it starts a timer. If it has not received the [NL] message before its timer expires, it suspects the current leader to be faulty, increases v by 1 and votes for another new leader.

4 Design

This section describes the design of our Mimosa Pudica middleware system. We first present our system requirements and then describe the system architecture in details. We also show four adaptation rules and examples of applying the them to build our reliable pub/sub system.

4.1 Requirements

Existing middleware systems typically assume that formal descriptions focus on actions [16] and it is essential to identify which actions are controlled by the environment, which actions are controlled by the machine, and which actions of the environment are shared with the machine. Our Mimosa Pudica middleware focuses on where the software components should be migrated to and achieve the entire system's adaptability by relocating software components. Mimosa Pudica meets the following requirements.

Fault Tolerance. Our middleware is designed to tolerate fail-stop broker/link failures (i.e., crashes) in a timely manner such that faulty brokers are removed and can be later recovered.

Self-Adaptation. Distributed pub/sub systems essentially lack a global view due to the decoupling of publishers and subscribers. Our system coordinate software components between brokers in order to support their applications in a self-adaptive manner for higher efficiency in resource usage.

Separation of Concerns. All the software components of an application should be defined independently with our adaptation mechanism. This is because the applications where adaptive rules are defined inside software components can not be reused. Both the software components and adaptive rules are desired to be reused for better resource usage.

Service Availability. Our system guarantees that service should always be available with limited resources, whereas most existing approaches explicitly or implicitly assume that their targets of the systems have enriched resources.

General-Purpose. Our adaptation mechanism is designed to be a practical middleware that also supports general-purpose applications in the system.

4.2 System Architecture

Our proposed approach dynamically adds/deletes brokers and deploys software components of an application from one broker to one or multiple brokers, according to the predefined rules. As a result, our distributed pub/sub system is self-adaptive to various changes.

At the core of our system is a middleware system between OS and applications, as shown in Fig. 1. This architecture consists of two important parts: an adaptation manager and a runtime system. The adaptation manager manages the runtime system. It controls the behavior of components, selects rules from destination database, and determines where and when to migrate the software components. The runtime system is responsible for managing, executing, and migrating software components, as well as enabling them to invoke methods at other software components. In order to use these methods during migration, the software components are first serialized and then migrate themselves from one server to another. When the software components arrive at their destinations, servers can communicate with each other for naming inspection.

Adaptation Manager. In order to be self-adaptive to the changes of environmental properties, the deployment of components is managed by the adaptation manager. They are fully distributed and no centralized management server is required. In the presence of environmental changes, brokers follow several steps to be self-adaptive, as shown below.

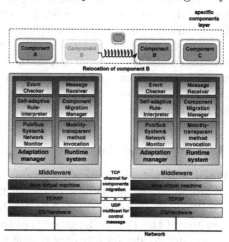

Step 1: When a broker detects the environmental changes, it first send messages to the destination database to obtain the group information. The brokers select a leader according to leader election algorithm as shown in Algorithm 1.

Step 2: The leader invokes the adaptation rules, compiles them, and notifies brokers the adaptation results,

Fig. 1. Mimosa Pudica middleware system architecture.

e.g., which broker should be added/deleted, or which one or part of the software components should be migrated to other brokers.

Step 3: Depending on the adaptation rules and results, as described in Sect. 4.3, brokers activate different software components. When a broker is deleted, neighbors of the broker are connected or new broker is added. The monitors of the brokers that are connected notify their software components. The brokers can then build the connection. On the other hand, when the software components are migrated to the destination broker, the monitor of destination broker notifies its software components. The methods of the migrated software component are then invoked by destination software components through reflection mechanism.

The adaptation manager contains three sub-modules: event checker, rule interpreter, and system and network monitor. The event checker identifies the type of event messages received by components runtime system and passes the event number to rule interpreter. The rule interpreter then searches rule from the destination database and executes it. Lastly, the system and network monitor dynamically monitors the state of brokers, e.g., threads count, CPU usage, used heap memory and the loaded class count, etc. Meanwhile, it also regularly monitors the changes of the component runtime system.

Component Runtime System. The component runtime system has three modules: message receiver, component migration manager, and mobility-transparent method invocation. The message receiver, which has at most one message receiver thread, is responsible for receiving messages. The component migration manager receives command from adaptation manager. Each component has a particular life-cycle state. e.g., create, terminate, migrate, and duplicate. When the component state is changed, adaptation manager notifies the component migration manager the adaptation decision. The decision contains the components that should be moved, the components that should be cloned and moved, and the destination of migration. With this module, runtime systems at different servers can exchange messages through TCP channels by using Object Input/Output Stream. When a component is transferred over the network, both the code and the state of the component are transmitted into a bit stream and then transferred to the destination. At the destination side, the mobility-transparent method invocation module dynamically invokes the components through the class name and method name. The incomplete tasks will be run after migration.

4.3 Adaptation Rules

When external environment changes, software components can be managed according to the predefined rules. To facilitate the definition of rules we use the Ponder language developed by the Imperial College [4]. Specifically, we use a subset of the Ponder language, i.e. the Ponder obligation rules. We list four rules using Ponder for topology management and software components mobility. We also include a few use cases of applying the rules in our pub/sub system. For simplicity, we illustrate the cases using a simple topology as shown in Fig. 2,

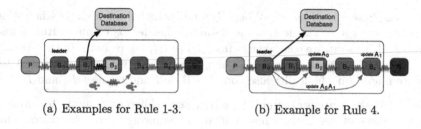

(a) Examples for Rule 1-3.   (b) Example for Rule 4.

Fig. 2. Examples of applying rules.

where messages are sent and forwarded from publisher P to subscriber S through 5 brokers. In addition to the four rules, system developers can add new rules to destination database to meet different system requirements.

Rule 1 (Delete Brokers). Dynamically delete a number of brokers. By using this rule, system can reduce the number of the brokers and handle failures.

```
type oblig deleteBrokerRules(target database, Broker<T> broker){
subject     AdaptationManager;
on          deleteBrokerRequest();
do          database.deleteBroker(broker);}
```

In the Presence of Failures. As illustrated in Fig. 2(a), broker B_2 crashes and its previous broker B_1 detects it. The leader B_0 compiles Rule 1 and deletes B_2. It notifies both B_1 and B_3. Broker B_1 and B_3 simply make a connection.

Rule 2 (Add Brokers). Dynamically add a number of brokers. The new broker only manages the routing information of its neighbors and is not required to know the state of other brokers. By using this rule, pub/sub system can better handle failures and improve system load balancing.

```
type oblig addBrokerRules(target database, Broker<T> broker){
subject     AdaptationManager;
on          addBrokerRequest();
do          database.addBroker(broker);}
```

Too Few Brokers on a Path. In the above example in Fig. 2(a), the leader B_0 can add a new broker B_5 to replace B_2. In this case, B_5 simply makes a connection with both B_1 and B_3 without knowing the identities of other brokers. Broker B_1, B_3, and B_5 then update their routing tables.

Rule 3 (Failure Judgment). Before the presence of broker failures, software components can be migrated to correct brokers to continue running. This rule works in systems where brokers are equipped with failure detectors or monitors. In this way, our system does not have to terminate the system operations.

```
type oblig failureJudgmentRules(target database, Broker<T> broker){
subject     AdaptationManager;
on          migrateBrokerRequest(Monitor, max_input_rate,; min_output_rate);
do          database.goBroker(broker);
when        max_input_rate <= min_output_rate;}
```

Before the Presence of Failures. When B_2 predicts its failure, it starts adaptation and sends message to the destination database. Leader B_0 compiles Rule 3 and migrates all the software components from B_2 to B_1, B_3, or both. In this specific case, broker B_1 and B_3 should also be connected for message delivery. After software migration, the leader also complies Rule 1 and connect B_1 and B_3.

Rule 4 (Task Transfer). Publishers may send different requests to brokers. However, some of the brokers may fail to communicate with subscribers. This rule can compress the parts of software component of brokers and transfer to one or several brokers. By using this rule, our system can effectively reduce the number of network transmission.

> **type oblig** taskTransferRules(**target** database, Broker<List<T>>brokers){
> **subject**   AdaptationManager;
> **on**   transferBrokerRequest(Compression brokers, local_ip_info, remote_ip_info);
> **do**   database.goBroker(brokers);
> **when**   brokers.getBrokersID() <= **User Defined;**}

Broadcast to Several Brokers. As shown in Fig. 2(b), if B_0 receives an update command and is required to update two of the applications A_0 and A_1, B_0 will compress the two update commands and migrate to all the brokers that run at least one application, e.g., B_2 runs A_0 and B_4 runs A_1, B_0 migrates the update components to both B_2 and B_4. After receiving the update command, broker B_2 and B_4 retrieve the corresponding command and update A_0 and A_1 respectively.

Conflict Resolution. Adaptations may have conflicts with each other, even when each of them is appropriately composed. In our current implementation, all the rules are executed by the leader. Therefore, when there are conflicts between groups of brokers (e.g. overlapping brokers), the leaders of different groups first analyze whether there are conflicts between the rules of their visiting components. Once conflicts are found, the executing sequences are decided according to their arrival sequences. In other words, an adaptation request will be executed until all the conflicting requests that arrive earlier are executed. In the future, we will further develop the system such that each broker can simultaneously execute their rules by adding priorities or privileges to rule format [12].

5   Evaluation

In this section we evaluate the performance by assessing the adaptation latency in the presence of broker failures and software components migration. First, our approach handles broker failures by connecting neighboring brokers and introducing new brokers while no known previous work use similar approach. Second, the migration of software components prevents from failures and is shown to be very efficient. We carry out experiments on Deterlab [1], utilizing up to 30 machines. Each machine is equipped with a 3 GHz Xeon processor and 2 GB of RAM. They run Linux 2.6.12 and are connected through a 100 Mbps switched LAN. We use up to 24 publishers and subscribers. Publishers run concurrently with an average workload of 1,250 events per second.

Implementation. Each component is implemented as a general-purpose and programmable entity. Defined as a collection of Java objects and packaged in the standard JAR file format, components can be migrated and duplicated between servers. Our middleware is built on the Java Virtual Machine (JVM) and can be abstracted away between different operating systems. The current implementation uses the Java object serialization package to marshal and duplicate components. The package dose not support the capture of stack frames of threads. Instead, when a component is duplicated, the runtime system issues events to invoke the specified methods. The methods are executed before the component is duplicated or migrated and active threads are suspended.

Adaptation Latency. We assess the adaptation delay of (1) adding/deleting brokers, as shown in Rule 1 and 2 in Sect. 4.3, and (2) migrating software components, as shown in Rule 3 and 4. We mainly evaluate two settings in the presence of broker failures: simple topology and bottleneck server crashes. Different sizes of random non-cyclic broker topologies are generated for each experiment. Simple topology simply evaluates failures in a single path where there is no side effect in the presence of broker failures. In comparison, the goal of the case where bottleneck broker crashes is to assess the latency when multiple paths request for adaptation in the presence of failures.

Add/Delete Brokers. We periodically inject random broker failures every 50 publications and assess end-to-end latencies. It can be observed in Fig. 3 that the average latency is 8 ms to 12 ms. When there are failures, subscribers experience a temporary 65 ms to 85 ms peak latency. The long latency resumes to normal after a few publications.

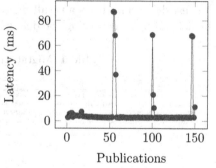

Fig. 3. End-to-end latency in the presence of broker failures.

We break down the peak latency into four phases: (1) timeout, where brokers use timers to detect the failures of their subsequent brokers; (2) vote for leader election, where brokers to obtain group information from destination database; (3) leader election, where brokers elect a new leader; and (4) adaptation, where the leader makes adaptation. We use instant acknowledgment (*ack*) messages for brokers to detect the failures, where if a broker has not received *ack* message before its timer expires after forwarding a message, it suspects its subsequent broker to be faulty.

As observed in Fig. 4, the value of the timer is set to 30 ms, which is also the bottleneck of the overall delay. Indeed, if a smaller timer is used, the overall latency can be greatly reduced but it also increases the false negatives since slow brokers are detected to be faulty. The second phase generates 8 ms average latency for simple topology and 15 ms latency for complicated topology. This is due to the fact that paths with overlapping broker(s) are given access sequentially by destination database to avoid conflicts. In this particular experiment, the

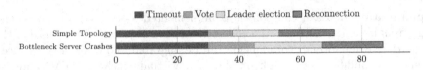

Fig. 4. Adaptation delay in details.

bottleneck server is the only overlapping server that crashes. Therefore, they run leader election concurrently, which generates 15 ms latency for simple topology and 22 ms in complicated topology. The adaptation phase causes $18 - 20$ ms latency for both settings since leaders compile the rules independently.

Migrate Software Components. We assess the delay of software components migration. We run four applications, each of which corresponds to one pre-defined rule, to evaluate the performance. Each software component has a life-cycle, as shown in Table 1. When the requirements change, its life-cycle will be changed to another state. Our experiment results show that the four applications generate 161 ms, 201 ms, 189 ms, and 184 ms latencies respectively. The temporary delays of the four cases are small because we only migrate the source code and the state of the components. Among all the applications, "app.RemoteSearch" generates the longest delay. This is because all the corresponding threads and processes need to be deleted when executing the delete rule.

Table 1. Migration of software components.

Runtime_ID	Rule	Component_ID	Component_Name	Life_cycle	Component_Time	Delay(ms)
1361870810568000150126163349959	/Rules/AddRule	dc36fae696d04cd18ff1eab7429606f1	app.Chat	creation	5:32 PM	161
1361870810568000150126163349959	/Rules/DeleteRule	b89ebe96181540259ce8e09a4e858485	app.RemoteSearch	creation	5:35 PM	201
1361870810568000150126163349959	/Rules/FaiJudgmentRule	2ea7663f79fa479a8a974222caf353dc	app.FileTransfer	creation	5:37 PM	189
1361870810568000150126163349959	/Rules/UpdateRule	5c55518e36404973b6a62dc665b32c6c	app.Update	creation	5:40 PM	184
...	...	...	...	...	...	...

To summarize, the adaptation of adding/deleting brokers cause around $65 - 70$ ms delay for simple topology and $80 - 85$ ms delay for complicated topology. The adaptation for migrating software components generate $160 - 200$ ms delay. A smaller value of the timers can reduce the overall latency but can also increase the false negatives. Also, when more than one overlapping brokers of multiple paths fail, the overall adaptation delay can also be increased.

6   Conclusion and Future Work

We present a self-adaptive middleware for building reliable pub/sub systems. Our approach does not require redundant brokers, network links, or storage at brokers in order to tolerate crash faulty brokers. It fits naturally in any existing topology. In addition, our approach self-adaptively manages the topology and software components among brokers and can be easily managed to serve different purposes. We have shown how our Mimosa Pudica middleware manages the adaptive rules in the presence of environmental changes. Our evaluation results show that our adaptation approach imposes a temporal period of slightly longer latency in the presence of environmental changes. In the future, we will further develop the system to address Byzantine failures and to add privileges for the adaptation rules and resolve the possible conflicts and divergences.

References

1. Benzel, T.: The science of cyber security experimentation: the DETER project. In: ACSAC (2011)
2. Chand, R., Felber, P.: Xnet: a reliable content-based publish/subscribe system. In: SRDS pp. 264–273 (2004)
3. Chang, T., Duan, S., Meling, H., Peisert, S., Zhang, H.: P2S: a fault-tolerant publish/subscribe infrastructure. In: DEBS, pp. 189–197 (2014)
4. Damianou, N., Dulay, N., Lupu, E.C., Sloman, M.: The ponder policy specification language. In: Sloman, M., Lobo, J., Lupu, E.C. (eds.) POLICY 2001. LNCS, vol. 1995, pp. 18–38. Springer, Heidelberg (2001)
5. Dwork, C., Lynch, N., Stockmeyer, L.: Consensus in the presence of partial synchrony. JACM **35**(2), 288–323 (1988)
6. Jerzak, Z., Fetzer, C.: State in publish/subscribe. In: DEBS, pp. 1–12 (2009)
7. Kazemzadeh, R.S., Jacobsen, H.-A.: Reliable and highly available distributed publish/subscribe service. In: SRDS, pp. 41–50 (2009)
8. Kazemzadeh, R.S., Jacobsen, H.-A.: Partition-tolerant distributed publish/subscribe systems. In: SRDS, pp. 101–110 (2011)
9. Sherafat Kazemzadeh, R., Jacobsen, H.-A.: Opportunistic multipath forwarding in content-based publish/subscribe overlays. In: Narasimhan, P., Triantafillou, P. (eds.) Middleware 2012. LNCS, vol. 7662, pp. 249–270. Springer, Heidelberg (2012)
10. Koza, J.R.: Genetic Programming: On the Programming of Computers by Means of Natural Selection. MIT Press, Cambridge (1992)
11. Lamport, L.: The part-time parliament. ACM Trans. Comput. Syst. **16**(2), 133–169 (1998)
12. Lupu, E., Sloman, M.: Conflicts in policy-based distributed systems management. IEEE Trans. Softw. Eng. **25**(6), 852–869 (1999)
13. Sun, J., Satoh, I.: Dynamic deployment of software components for self-adaptive distributed systems. In: Fortino, G., Di Fatta, G., Li, W., Ochoa, S., Cuzzocrea, A., Pathan, M. (eds.) IDCS 2014. LNCS, vol. 8729, pp. 194–203. Springer, Heidelberg (2014)
14. Hiroki, T., et al.: A rule-based framework for managing context-aware services based on heterogeneous and distributed web services. In: SNPD, pp. 1–6 (2014)
15. McKinley, P.K., Sadjadi, S.M., Kasten, E.P., et al.: Cheng: composing adaptive software. IEEE Comput. **37**(7), 56–64 (2004)
16. Zave, P., Jackson, M.: Four dark corners of requirements engineering. In: TOSEM, pp. 1–30 (1997)
17. Zhang, J., Cheng, B.H.: Model-based development of dynamically adaptive software. In: ICSE, pp. 371–380 (2006)
18. Zhang, K., Muthusamy, V., Jacobsen, H.: Total order in content-based publish/subscribe systems. In: ICDCS (2012)

Review of Replication Techniques
for Distributed Systems

Ahmad Shukri Mohd Noor[1]($\boxtimes$), Nur Farhah Mat Zian[1], Mustafa Mat Deris[2],
and Tutut Herawan[3]

[1] School of Informatics and Applied Mathematics, Universiti Malaysia Terengganu,
Kuala Terengganu, Terengganu, Malaysia
ashukri@umt.edu.my, farhah.matzian@outlook.com
[2] Faculty of Information and Technology Multimedia,
University Tun Hussein Onn Malaysia, Batu Pahat, Johor, Malaysia
mmustafa@uthm.edu.my
[3] Department of Information System, University of Malaya,
Pantai Valley, 50603 Kuala Lumpur, Malaysia
tutut@um.edu.my

Abstract. Distributed systems primarily provide the access to data
intensive computation through a wide range of interfaces. Due to the
advances of the systems, the scales and complexity of the system have
increased, causing faults are likely bound to happen leading into diverse
faults and failure conditions. Therefore, fault tolerance has become a
crucial property for distributed system in order to preserve its function
correctly and available in the presence of faults. Replication techniques
particularly concentrates on two fault tolerance manners; masking the
failures on the fly as well as reconfiguring the systems in response. This
paper presents a brief reviews on different replication techniques, such as
Grid Configuration (GC), Box-Shaped Grid (BSG) and Neighbor Replication on Grid (NRG) by comparing and formalizing its communication
costs and availabilities analysis based on k-out-of-n model. Each of these
techniques presents their own merits and demerits which form the subject matter of this review.

Keywords: Distributed systems · Fault tolerance · High availability ·
Replication techniques · Communication cost · Availability analysis

1 Introduction

Distributed systems consist of a determinate set of sites that are connected
to each other via communication links on various hardware hosts at different
physical locations where remotely located users sharing the data to produce
some invaluable results. The increase in complexity of distributed systems causes
most application unable to survive infrastructure outages in the event of failure.
A fault, a defect that come about the lowest level of abstraction may cause

© Springer International Publishing Switzerland 2015
G. Di Fatta et al. (Eds.): IDCS 2015, LNCS 9258, pp. 169–176, 2015.
DOI: 10.1007/978-3-319-23237-9_15

an internal data state, error which may later lead to failure, the external visible deviation from the system correctness behavior [1]. However, fault does not inevitably result in an error as well as an error in failure. Fault tolerance is an added property to ensure the availability and reliability of a distributed systems. There are two ways to implements fault tolerance in distributed systems. The first one is reconfiguring the service to utilize the components that replaced the failed one and the second one is by using the masking approach that is placing redundant components that able to operate under partial failures providing enough functionality to the users.

1.1 Replication Definition

Replication is a process of maintaining different copies of replicated data or objects as well as the synchronization of updating the data in its replica. The data is not automatically overwritten whenever any changes occurred in the original data that resulted in immediate lost at any historical state. Replication is divided to two types of solution that is synchronous or asynchronous solutions. The asynchronous solution manages the data by immediately capture any changes on the primary replica and will be timely propagated to its replica. This solution presents a low cost as well as flexible solution nevertheless have to deal with network bandwidth and data lost. Synchronous solution on the other hand based on quorum in updating its replicas at the same time and will roll back if one fails. It breaks into several schemes that are full replication (all-data-to-all-sites) and partial replication (all-data-to-some-sites). This solution offers high availability of data, auto fail-over and minimal data loss. However, the drawbacks of this solution are one has to deal with network efficiency, less flexible, scalability issues and cost.

Replication has been successfully implemented for distributed systems by allowing data to remain distribute and systems able to operate in the presence of fault. Considering a large number of different replication techniques available, choosing the best approach under different levels of faulty systems with different systems performance requirements is not an easy task. In this paper, we will present a brief review some of the replication techniques that has been implemented by addressing its own merits and demerits. The performance of each technique is analyze based on the communication costs and availability using k-out-of-n model. This comparison is focusing only on existing synchronous replication. The remainder of this paper is organized as follows. Section 2 will discuss briefly on the k-out-of-n model and Sect. 3 will review each of the replication techniques by presenting its communication costs and availability analysis. The conclusion of our work will be presented in Sect. 4.

2 System Availability Evaluation Using K-out-of-n Model

In this study, the k-out-of-n model is used to estimate the operation availability. This model refers to the independent nodes that have some identical data or services [12]. In other words, this configuration will not affect the remaining nodes and all nodes have the same failure distribution. The assumption of k-out-of-n model could be evaluated using the binomial distribution or as below:

1. The data item and its copies are in one of the two states: accessible or inaccessible.
2. The states of the copies are changed independently.
3. If at least k of its n copies is accessible, then the data item is available for an operation.

Thus, the k-out-of-n model can be formulated as:

$$\Sigma_{i=k}^{n}\binom{n}{i}p^{i}(1-p)^{n-1}, k \geq 1 \tag{1}$$

where the notation is given as:

- n: the total number of components in the systems
- k: the minimum number of components required for the system to success
- p: the availability of each data item.

3 Replication Techniques

3.1 Grid Configuration (GC) Protocol

This protocol is introduced by Maekawa [5] where all quorums are of equals size in order to obtain a distributed mutual exclusion algorithm which later extended by Cheung et al. [6] for replicated data objects. This protocol introduced n copies of data objects are logically organized in the form of a $\sqrt{n} \times \sqrt{n}$ as depicted in Fig. 1. Read quorum consists of a copy from each column in the grid will be acquire in order to perform read on the data items. While to perform the write operation, write quorum consists of all copies in one column and a copy from each of the remaining columns will be needed. This protocol introduced the read and write operation in the size of O ($\sqrt{n}$).

Fig. 1. Grid Configuration with 25 copies of data object

The communication cost for read operation of GC protocol, $C_{GC,R}$ can be formalized as:

$$C_{GC,R} = \sqrt{n} \tag{2}$$

Meanwhile, the communication cost for write operation of GC protocol, $C_{GC,W}$ can be formalized as:

$$C_{GC,W} = 2\sqrt{n} - 1 \tag{3}$$

In the case of quorum techniques, read quorums can be constructed as long as a copy from each column is available. Under this technique, as given in [3], read availability of GC protocol, $A_{GC,R}$ is:

$$A_{GC,R} = [1 - (1 - p)^{\sqrt{n}}]^{\sqrt{n}} \tag{4}$$

On the other hand, write availability of GC technique $A_{GC,W}$ can be write as:

$$A_{GC,W} = [1 - (1 - p)^{\sqrt{n}}]^{\sqrt{n}} - [1 - (1 - p)^{\sqrt{n}} - p^{\sqrt{n}}]^{\sqrt{n}} \tag{5}$$

The drawbacks of this technique is this structure degrades the communication cost and the availability of data as the number of copies for both read and write quorum is big as well as prone to failure of the entire row and column in the grid.

3.2   Box-Shaped Grid (BSG) Protocol

Box-Shaped Grid (BSG) was introduced by Deris, M.M et al. [7]. In this technique, all copies are logically organized in a box-shape structure with four planes. The box-shaped structure is classified as a perfect square if the number of copies in each plane is equal. From Fig. 2, BSG model consists of four planes (1, 2, 3, 4) and small circles symbolizing a copy of data object with location denoted in A, B, C, D, ... , and X. By assuming that each plane has a length (column), l and width (row) w, then l = w. Therefore, the number of copies in the structure can be calculated as $l = \frac{[1+\sqrt{(l+n)}]}{2}$.

Read transactions on a data object are executed by obtaining a read quorum that comprises of any hypotenuse copies, the pair of copies that located at hypotenuse edge. From the Fig. 2, hypotenuse copies are {X, A}, {V, C}, {G, R} or {I, P}. While for write transactions, a write quorum is formed from any planes that contain hypotenuse copies and all copies which are vertices where one of which is a hypotenuse copy. For an instance, if the hypotenuse copies, {I, P} are required to perform a read transaction, then the possible copies for write quorum are {I, P, V, R, X} that adequate enough to perform write operations. The size of a read quorum in BSG is hypotenuse copies, i.e., 2. Thus, the cost of a read operation, $C_{BSG,R} = 2$, and the cost of write operation C_BSG, w can be represented as $C_{BSG,W}$ = hypotenuse copies + (all copies of vertices in a plane - hypotenuse copy in the same plane) = 2 + (4 - 1) = 5.

If the copy that initiate the write transaction is not a vertex-replica, then communication cost becomes 6. For BSG protocol, a read quorum can be constructed from any hypotenuse copies in the system. Thus, the read availability $A_{BSG,R}$ for a perfect square box where it has 4 hypotenuse copies is:

$$A_{BSG,R} = 1 - (1 - p^2)^4 \tag{6}$$

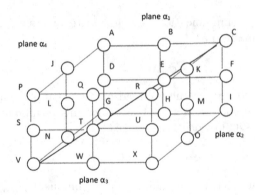

Fig. 2. A BSG organization with 24 copies of a data items

On the other hand, a write quorum can be constructed as: Let $\alpha_1, \alpha_2, \alpha_3, \alpha_4$ be a set of planes in the BSG protocol. Each of which consists of $l \times l$ copies. Let {V,C} be the hypotenuse copies, then write availability that consists of {V,C}, $W_{V, C}$, can be represented as:
Probability { V is available } * [ϕ available] + Probability { C is available } * [φ available] − Probability { C and V are available } * [(ϕ and φ) are available] where,

$\phi = \Omega(\alpha_1) + \Omega(\alpha_2) - \Omega(\alpha_1 \cap \alpha_2)$
$\varphi = \Omega(\alpha_3) + \Omega(\alpha_4) - \Omega(\alpha_3 \cap \alpha_4)$,
and $\Omega(\alpha_1)$ = probability of plane α_1 available.

Without loss of generality, we assume that copy B $\in\alpha_1$ is a primary replica. The probability of α_1 is available, $\Omega(\alpha_1)$, can be presented as:
Probability { all copies of vertices from α_1 and primary copy are available } + Probability { (all copies of vertices and primary copy + 1 copy) from α_1 are available } + ... + Probability { all copies from α_1 are available }
and by calculating $\Omega(\alpha_1 \cap \alpha_2)$ using Venn Diagram and substituting into previous probability, then

$$\varphi = p^4(1 + p - p^2) \tag{7}$$

$$\phi = p^4(2 - p^2) \tag{8}$$

Since the probability {V is available} = probability {C is available} = p, then, by substituting Eqs. (7) and (8) into first probability, W_i is:

$$p_\varphi + p_\phi - p^2(\phi * \varphi) \tag{9}$$

By the same token, for the write availability that consist of other hypotenuse copies, $W_i = W_j = W_k = W_l$, where i $\in$ R.To compute the write availability, $A_{BSG,W}$, it is analogous to the read availability. Let $W_i = \beta$, i $\in$R, then $A_{BSG,W}$ is:

$$A_{BSG,W} = 1 - (1 - \beta)^4 \tag{10}$$

For this technique, the hypotenuse of the copies will not be accessible if one of the copies of each pair is not available, therefore, resulted in failure at the

Table 1. Comparison of the read and write communication costs for the three protocols

	Number of copies in the system		
Protocol(X)	13	25	64
GC (R)	7	9	15
GC (W)	5	5	5
BSG (R)	2	2	2
BSG (W)	5	5	5
NRG (R)	3	3	3
NRG (W)	3	3	3

write quorum for executing write transaction. It also required both read and write quorum to intersect in order to access the read quorum hypotenuse. This resulted in the inability to update write quorum to the latest data object which affected the consistency of the data (Table 1).

3.3   Neighbor Replication on Grid (NRG)

Neighbor Replication of Grid has been introduced by N. Ahmad [3] by applying neighboring techniques in a two-dimensional grid structure. All the sites in this mechanism are logically organized in the form of n × n structure, by having a master data item stored in each site. The number of data replication from each site, d ≤ 5, that is the number of the sites neighbor sums up with a data from the site itself as in Fig. 3.

For simplicity, the read quorum equals to the write quorum is chosen in this analysis. Thus, the communication cost for read and write operations equals to total number of votes, v over 2, that is:

$$C_{NRG,R} = C_{NRG,W} = \lceil v_x / 2 \rceil$$

As an instance, let say the primary site has four neighbors and assuming that each site has voted once. Thus, $C_{NRG,R} = C_{NRG,W} = \lceil \frac{5}{2} \rceil = 3$.

Let p_i denotes the availability of a data item at site i. For any assignment B and quorum q for the data x, define ϕ (B_x, q) to be the probability that at least q sites in $S(B_x)$ are available. Then

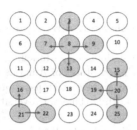

Fig. 3. Data Replication of 25 nodes in NRG

$\phi\,(B_{x,q}) = \Pr\{$ at least q sites in $S(B_x)$ are available$\}$

$$\sum G \in Q(B_{x,q}(\prod_{j \in G} \prod j \in S(B_x) - G(1 - p^j))$$ (11)

Thus, the availability of read, $A_{NR}G$, $_R$ and write operations $A_{NR}G$, $_W$ for the data item x for NRG, are $\phi(B_{x,r})$ and $\phi(B_{x,w})$ respectively.

The complexity of maintaining copies at different sites gave a challenged for NRG to handle its locking information especially in the current structure of distributed computing (Table 2).

Table 2. The read and write availabilities of each protocol when n = 13 and $0.1 \leq p \leq 0.9$

Read (R) and Write (W) availability (A_{XR})									
Protocol (X)	0.1	0.2	0.3	0.4	0.5	0.6	0.7	0.8	0.9
GC (R)	0.014	0.124	0.333	0.57	0.773	0.902	0.968	0.994	0.999
GC (W)	2E-6	1E-4	0.14	0.65	0.186	0.392	0.646	0.873	0.986
BSG (R)	0.039	0.151	0.314	0.502	0.684	0.832	0.932	0.983	0.999
BSG (W)	1E-4	0.004	0.030	0.112	0.319	0.614	0.875	0.986	1.00
NRG (R)	0.009	0.058	0.163	0.317	0.500	0.683	0.837	0.942	0.991
NRG (W)	0.009	0.058	0.163	0.317	0.500	0.683	0.837	0.942	0.991

4 Conclusion

This paper briefly discussed existing replication techniques in distributed computing by addressing its communication cost and availabilities analysis based on k-out-of-n model and the importance of replication in the distributed computing. Each technique have been appropriately analyzed and presented under different headings by reviewing its concepts, communication costs, and availability analysis as well as providing illustration for each model.

References

1. Helal, A.A., Heddaya, A.A., Bhargava, B.B.: Replication Techniques in Distributed Systems. Kluwer Academic Publishers, United States of America (1996)
2. Kuo, W., Zuo, M.J.: Optimal Reliability Modelling: Principles and Applications. John Wiley and Sons Inc, United States of America (2003)
3. Noraziah, A.: Managing Replication and Transactions using Neighbor Replication on data grid Database design. Ph.D. Thesis. Universiti Malaysia Terengganu (2007)
4. Deris, M.M., Mamat, A., Seng, P.C., Saman, M.Y.: Three dimensional grid structure of efficient access of replicated data. Intll J. Interconnection Netw. World Sci. **2**(3), 317–329 (2001)

5. Maekawa, M.: A vn algorithm for mutual exclusion in decentralized systems. ACM Trans. Comput. Sys. **3**(2), 145–159 (1992)
6. Cheung, S.Y., Ammar, M.H., Ahmad, M.: The grid protocol: a high performance schema for maintaining replicated data. IEEE Trans. Knowl. Data Eng. **4**(6), 582–592 (1992)
7. Deris, M.M., Abawajy, J.H., Mamat, A.: An efficient replicated data access approach for large-scale distributed systems. Future Gener. Comput. Sys. **24**, 1–9 (2008)
8. Noraziah, A., Mat, D.M., Saman, M.Y.M., Norhayati, R., Rabiei, M., Shuhadah, W.N.W.: Managing transactions on grid-neighbour replication in distributed systems. Int. J. Comput. Math. **86**(9), 1624–1633 (2009)
9. Bansal, S., Sharma, S., Trivedi, I.: A detailed review of fault tolerance techniques in distributed system. Int. J. Internet Distrib. Comput. Sys. **1**(1), 33 (2012)
10. Shen, H.H., Chen, S.M., Shen, M.M. and Zheng, W.M.: Research on data replica distribution technique for server cluster. In: IEEE Proceedings of the 4th International Conference on Peformance Computing, pp. 966–968, Beijing (2000)
11. Natanzon, A., Bachmat, E.: Dynamic synchronous asynchronous replication. ACM Trans. Storage **9**(3), 1–19 (2013). Article 8
12. Noor, A.S.M.: Neighbour replica affirmative adaptive failure detection and autonomous recovery. Ph.D. Thesis. Universiti Tun Hussein Onn Malaysia (2012)
13. Noor, A.S.M., Zian, N.F.M., Saman, M.Y.: Survey on replication techniques for distributed system. Sci. Int. Lahore **26**(4), 1523–1526 (2014)
14. Renesse, R.V., Guerraoui, R.: Replication Techniques for Availability. Theory and Practice. LNCS, pp. 19–40. Springer, Heidelberg (2010)
15. Deris, M.M., Evans, D.J., Saman, M.Y., Noraziah, A.: Binary vote assignment on a grid for efficient access of replicated data. Int. J. Comput. Math. **80**(12), 1489–1498 (2003)

Connectivity Recovery in Epidemic Membership Protocols

Pasu Poonpakdee[(⊠)] and Giuseppe Di Fatta

School of Systems Engineering, University of Reading, Whiteknights,
Reading, Berkshire RG6 6AY, UK
{p.poonpakdee,g.difatta}@reading.ac.uk

Abstract. Epidemic protocols are a bio-inspired communication and computation paradigm for extreme-scale network system based on randomized communication. The protocols rely on a membership service to build decentralized and random overlay topologies. In a weakly connected overlay topology, a naive mechanism of membership protocols can break the connectivity, thus impairing the accuracy of the application. This work investigates the factors in membership protocols that cause the loss of global connectivity and introduces the first topology connectivity recovery mechanism. The mechanism is integrated into the Expander Membership Protocol, which is then evaluated against other membership protocols. The analysis shows that the proposed connectivity recovery mechanism is effective in preserving topology connectivity and also helps to improve the application performance in terms of convergence speed.

Keywords: Topology connectivity · Expander graphs · Epidemic protocols · Extreme-scale computing · Decentralized algorithms

1 Introduction

In extreme-scale networked systems, the decentralized computation of aggregation functions is an interesting and challenging task. Due to problems such as communication bottlenecks and fault intolerance, centralized paradigms are not desirable solutions. Epidemic, or Gossip-based, protocols are fully decentralized and fault tolerant, which are particularly suitable for information dissemination and global aggregation tasks.

Applications based on epidemic protocols for large and extreme-scale networked systems are emerging in many fields, including Peer-to-Peer (P2P) overlay networks [1], distributed computing [2], mobile ad hoc networks (MANET) [3], wireless sensor networks (WSN) [4] and exascale high performance computing [5,6].

Epidemic protocols use a randomised communication paradigm, which is the foundation for their robustness and scalability. In order to perform randomised communication, a peer sampling service is required, which is considered a fundamental network service. Obviously, maintaining global knowledge, i.e. a complete

© Springer International Publishing Switzerland 2015
G. Di Fatta et al. (Eds.): IDCS 2015, LNCS 9258, pp. 177–189, 2015.
DOI: 10.1007/978-3-319-23237-9_16

list of nodes, is not a feasible approach in very large and extreme-scale distributed systems. A Membership Protocol is typically employed to provide this service.

Scalable and fault tolerant membership protocols can be implemented with an epidemic approach. The aim of membership protocols is to provide a node selection service that returns a random node with uniform probability, similar to a random selection from the global view of the system [7]. Instead of maintaining a complete list of nodes at each node, a membership protocol builds a local partial view (cache) of the system. The local view is continuously and randomly changed: the local partial membership information at each nodes is disseminated and mixed by exchanging messages with random peers.

Several membership protocols ([8–11]) have been proposed, which have been designed for generating random overlay topologies.

In particular, the *Expander Membership Protocol* (EMP) [11] is inspired by the expansion property of a graph, which is a fundamental mathematical concept [12]. EMP is based on a push-pull scheme that introduces a bias in the random node selection in order to maximise the expansion property of the overlay topology. To this aim EMP employs a push-forwarding procedure (a random walk) to search and select an ideal communication peer (quasi-random gossiping) for the exchange of information.

Topology connectivity is a fundamental property of the overlay graphs that is required to guarantee the accuracy of epidemic protocols and their applications. To the best of our knowledge, many approaches have focused on mechanisms aimed at preserving the topology connectivity in strongly connected graphs, while none has been dedicated at recovering the connectivity when lost. In fact, this is an important problem for applications deployed in real-world distributed systems, where overlay graphs may be weakly connected and the global connectivity be lost in spite of the best effort in trying to preserve it.

In this work, the first mechanism that addresses the connectivity problem in weakly connected graphs is introduced. The novel mechanism, the *Interleaving Management Procedure* (IMP), is integrated into EMP in order to recover from the degradation of the overlay topology from a single connected component to multiple connected components. The enhanced version of EMP will be referred to as EMP+.

The rest of the paper is organized as follows. In Sect. 2, details of the connectivity problem in epidemic membership protocols are given. Section 3 presents a brief description of EMP and the message interleaving event. Section 4 introduces a novel procedure that addresses the message interleaving problem to avoid and to recover from the loss of topology connectivity. Section 5 presents the integration of this procedure into EMP. Simulations and experimental results are presented in Sect. 6. Finally, Sect. 7 draws some conclusions and provides the direction of future work.

2   Connectivity Problems

Graph connectivity is a fundamental concept of graph theory which is also applied to overlay topology in Epidemic Protocols. For example, epidemic aggregation protocols are employed to compute local estimations of a global aggregation function: such estimations can converge to the true target value if and only if the global topology connectivity is preserved.

There are several reasons that may cause the degradation of overlay topologies, e.g. external causes may be node churn and node failures [11]. Surprisingly, in a weakly connected overlay topology, the internal mechanisms of a membership protocol can also turn the overlay topology from a single connected component into multiple connected components. This section briefly reviews some membership protocols and identifies their components that may introduce such connectivity problems.

The Node Cache Protocol [8] is a simple membership protocol that adopts a symmetric push-pull mechanism to exchange and shuffle local membership information (node cache). At each node, the protocol contains a local cache Q of node identifiers, where $|Q| = q_{max}$ is the maximum local cache size of each node (this parameter is applied to all membership protocols used in this work). At each cycle, the local cache is sent with a push message to a node randomly selected from the local cache. When a push message is received, the local cache is sent in a reply (pull message) to the remote node originating the push message. The local cache is merged with the remote cache and the remote node ID (refreshing mechanism). The local cache is finally trimmed to q_{max} entries by randomly eliminating the number of entries exceeding q_{max}. In the Node Cache Protocol, the trimming operation is the component that may cause connectivity problems, because the removed entries could be the single link between two connected components in an overlay topology with weak connectivity.

Cyclon [9] is a membership protocol that is an enhanced version of a basic node cache shuffling. The mechanism of Cyclon is similar to the Node Cache Protocol, which also adopts a push-pull mechanism. In Cyclon, cache entries are assigned an attribute age to track their lifetime. At each cycle, a number of entries randomly selected from the local cache are sent (push message) to the node corresponding to the oldest entry in the local cache. When the push message is received, the node replies with a pull message containing entries a number of randomly selected entries from its local cache. The received entries are used to replace the donated entries at both ends. Connectivity problems in Cyclon may arise when there is message interleaving between independent pairs of push-pull exchanges involving the same node. Message interleaving has been identified as a potential threat to the accuracy of those epidemic aggregation protocols [8] that would require atomic push-pull operations. Similarly, in Cyclon message interleaving introduces the risk of removing critical cache entries, as the atomicity of the push-pull operation for cache exchange is not guaranteed.

Eddy [10] is arguably the most complex membership protocol. In order to provide a better random distribution of node samples in the system, Eddy tries to minimize temporal and spatial dependencies between local caches. The mechanism in Eddy can be separated into two independent processes: gossiping and refreshing. Gossiping is based on a symmetric push-pull operation: when the entries in the local cache are chosen for an exchange, they are also removed from the local cache. Refreshing adopts entry lifetime and push-forwarding mechanism. A limited lifetime is assigned to each entry which is removed when expires. Expired entries are replaced with fresh entries by forwarding the entry to a random node within two hops. The refreshing process of Eddy is effective, however it introduces a significant communication overhead and an entry removal mechanism that can cause connectivity problems.

3   The Expander Membership Protocol

The Expander Membership Protocol (EMP) ([11]) directly employs the concept of expansion in graphs. Expander graphs are sparse graphs with strong connectivity properties. In general, a graph is an expander if any vertex subset (not too large) has a relatively large set of one-hop distant neighbours.

The typical cache shuffling mechanism in membership protocols is used to generate a continuous series of random overlay topologies that are sparse and have a strong connectivity. This task is particularly easy when the initial graph is already an expander, e.g. a random regular graph. The speed of transformation from an initial topology to an expander can be used as an indicator to evaluate the performance of membership protocols, which also affects the convergence speed of the application. EMP is inspired by these considerations and built on the concept of vertex expansion. The protocol adopts a symmetric push-pull mechanism and a push-forwarding mechanism. EMP adopts a random walk in order to search for a better communication partner (quasi-random gossiping).

4   Message Interleaving

Applications in real-world distributed systems have to cope with asynchronous communication and network latency. As a result of that, in epidemic protocols there is a possibility that some node is receiving a pull message while it is waiting for a pull message. In weakly connected overlay topologies, this message interleaving can harm the global connectivity of the system.

To describe the effect of message interleaving, it is useful to compare two scenarios with and without message interleaving. The first scenario (Fig. 1(a)) considers three nodes (i, j and k), which are exchanging their membership information without interleaving. First node i sends a push message to node j; then node i receives a pull message from node j. Eventually node k sends a push message to node i and, finally, node i sends a pull message to node k. In this scenario, the two independent push-pull operations happen in the expected sequence without message interleaving. Let Q_i be the local cache at node i, the sequence of events at node i are as follows:

1. Node i sends a push message (Q_i) to node j.
2. Node i receives a pull message (Q_i' and Q_j') from node j.
3. Node i updates the local cache $Q_i \leftarrow Q_i'$.
4. Node i receives a push message (Q_k) from node k.
5. Node i merges Q_i' and Q_k and generates two partitions Q_i'' and Q_k'.

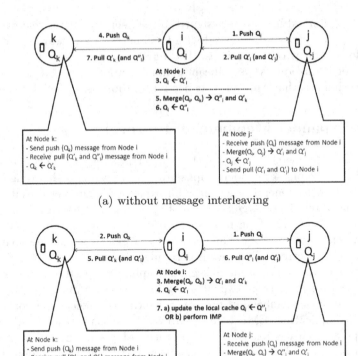

(a) without message interleaving

(b) with message interleaving

Fig. 1. The scenarios of message transmission with and without message interleaving

6. Node i updates the local cache $Q_i' \leftarrow Q_i''$.
7. Node i sends a pull message (Q_k' and Q_i'') to node k.

The second scenario (Fig. 1(b)) is similar to the first scenario, except that this time the two push-pull operations are overlapped and message interleaving happens. Node i sends a push message to node j. Before node i receives a pull message from node j, it receives a push message from node k. The sequence of events at node i are as follows:

1. Node i sends a push message (Q_i) to node j.
2. Node i receives a push message (Q_k) from node k.
3. Node i merges Q_i and Q_k and generates two partitions Q_i' and Q_k'.
4. Node i updates the local cache $Q_i \leftarrow Q_i'$.
5. Node i sends a pull message (Q_i' and Q_k') to node k.
6. Node i receives a pull message (Q_i'' and Q_j') from node j.
7. (a) Node i updates the local cache $Q_i \leftarrow Q_i''$.
   (b) **OR** Node i detects message interleaving and performs IMP.

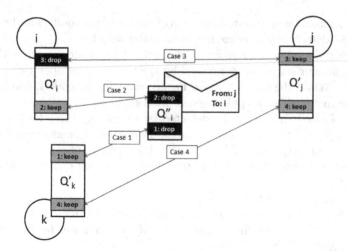

Fig. 2. The snapshot of cache configuration when node i detects a message interleaving event

After step 6, as a result of message interleaving, the three local caches have been updated (Q'_i, Q'_k, Q'_j) and an additional buffer (Q'') has been received at node i. In step 7, if node i would perform the simple update operation of 7(a), as in the case without message interleaving, there would be a risk of removing critical links, thus exposing the system to potential connectivity problems. Alternatively, node i can actually detect the message interleaving event and a more complex operation, the Interleaving Management Procedure (IMP) of 7(b), has to be performed to process the incoming pull message.

Figure 2 is a snapshot of the cache configuration after step 6, when node i detects the message interleaving event. The problem in this configuration is that some duplicated cache entries have been generated by the two merging operations. The total number of cache entries in the system is bounded by $N * q_{max}$, where N is the number of nodes. When a cache entry duplicate is generated, another cache entry needs to be discarded in order to accommodate the duplicate, introducing the risk that a critical link is removed from the system. Duplicated entries also negatively affect the node outdegree distribution in the system. Duplicated entries must be detected and eliminated when possible.

The next section describes the procedure used to detect and discard duplicated cache entries.

4.1   Detection of Cache Entry Duplicates

The aim of this procedure is to identify and eliminate the duplicated entries generated by the message interleaving event. Let us assume that the initial local caches $(Q_i, Q_j$ and $Q_k)$ of the three nodes in the last scenario do not share any entry, i.e. $Q_i \cap Q_j = \varnothing$, $Q_i \cap Q_k = \varnothing$ and $Q_j \cap Q_k = \varnothing$.

The duplicates have been generated because the push-pull operation between i and j has not been performed atomically: the merge and partition operation on Q_i and Q_j has generated Q'_j and Q''_i, while node i has changed its local cache.

Figure 2 shows the duplicated portions of the four cache buffers in the scenario when node i detects the interleaving event (after step 6).

In order to identify and remove duplicated entries, node i requires the information of the four partitions generated by the two merging operations: Q'_i, Q'_k, Q''_i and Q'_j. While the first three are locally available to node i, the buffer Q'_j needs to be included in the pull message from node j.

The duplicated entries can be detected by comparing these four buffers, for a total of $\binom{4}{2} = 6$ possible combinations. Two combinations cannot generate duplicates, as $Q'_i \cap Q'_k = \varnothing$, $Q'_j \cap Q''_i = \varnothing$. Four groups of potential duplicates can be identified and are shown in Fig. 2: (1) $Q''_i \cap Q'_k$, (2) $Q'_i \cap Q''_i$, (3) $Q'_i \cap Q'_j$, (4) $Q'_k \cap Q'_j$.

In the figure some buffer subsets have been indicated as 'drop' and others as 'keep': node i can identify and drop the duplicates of three cases. However, in case 4 node i cannot take any action to identify and remove the duplicates, nor can node j and node k.

This analysis has inspired a mechanism to detect message interleaving and perform a procedure to remove most, but not all, duplicates. This procedure will reduce the likelihood of connectivity problems, but will not eliminate the risk completely (case 4). For this reason a mechanism for connectivity recovery is still required.

The procedure to remove duplicated cache entries, the one for connectivity recovery and their integration in EMP are described in the next section.

5   The Enhanced Expander Membership Protocol

In the previous section it was shown how the number of potential duplicated cache entries can be reduced, thus minimising the negative effect in the degree distribution of the overlay topology and, more importantly reducing the risk of connectivity problems. However, the latter issue cannot be eliminated completely. This problem may not be likely in graphs with strong connectivity. However, in weakly connected overlay topologies, such as ring of communities [11], discarding even a few critical cache entries may result in the loss of global connectivity.

For this reason, an enhancement of EMP, EMP+, is introduced in this section, which is the integration of IMP into EMP. The goal of EMP+ is maintaining a global connectivity, while still supporting a good convergence speed of the applications.

The proposed method for solving the connectivity problem adopts a reserve cache, which is used to store the entries that are removed during the merging operation. To avoid that the size of the reserve cache may grow indefinitely, a maximum reserve cache size (r_{max}) is enforced. When the size of the reserve cache has reached the maximum, some entries must be discarded.

It is also necessary to store the entries donated with a pull message and a history cache is introduced for this purpose (line 16). In this cache, entries are associated with a maximum lifetime and when it expires the entry is removed to avoid that the cache may grow indefinitely.

Table 1. Notation adopted in the EMP+ pseudocode

i	a node in the network, $i \in V$, where V is the set of nodes
Q_i	main cache at node i, $|Q_i| \leq q_{max}$
R_i	reserve cache at node i
H_i	history cache at node i
h_{max}	maximum number of hops in the random walk
r_{max}	maximum reserve cache size
$m_{\rightarrow}$	push message with payload:
	- s, node originating the push
	- Q_s, main cache at s
	- d, current best destination node
	- v_d , current minimum overlap
	- h, hop count
$m_{\leftarrow}$	pull message with payload:
	- d, node originating the pull
	- Q, set of donated cache entries
	- Q_d, main cache at node d

The notation adopted in the following pseudocode is summarised in Table 1.

Algorithm 1 shows the pseudocode of EMP+, which is based on the pseudocode of EMP [11]. Here, the novel components of the protocol EMP+ are highlighted and discussed.

The main difference between EMP and EMP+ is the utilization of the reserve and history caches. Lines 10 and 11 describe how entries from the reserve cache are used during the merge operation to generate the two disjoint partitions Q_1 and Q_2. Lines from 28 to 34 describe the procedure to process incoming pull messages with and without message interleaving. If there is no message interleaving, the local cache can be immediately updated with the content of the message. When message interleaving occurs, the procedure IMP is performed.

Algorithm 2 shows the pseudocode of the Interleaving Management Procedure, which performs the removal of the duplicated entries. Lines from 2 to 7 show how the duplicates from the cases 1, 2 and 3 are detected and discarded. IMP is the only procedure in EMP+ that inserts entries into the reserve cache as shows in line 10. The reserve cache must contain unique entries for the same node ID at any time.

5   Experimental Analysis

The goal of this experimental analysis is to evaluate the proposed protocol EMP+ and to compare it against other membership protocols. The analysis is based on simulations, which are used to verify the global connectivity of the overlay topology and to measure the performance of an application when different membership protocols are used.

Algorithm 1. EMP+

1: **procedure** SENDPUSHMESSAGE
2:    remove expired entries from H_i
3:    $j \leftarrow$ get the oldest node from Q_i
4:    send a *push* message to j :$m_\rightarrow(s = i, Q_s = Q_i, d = null, v_d = \infty, h = 0)$

5:
6: **procedure** RECEIVEPUSHMESSAGE(message $m_\rightarrow$)
7:    compute total cache size $v = |Q_i \cup m_\rightarrow.Q_s \cup R_i|$
8:    **if** $(v + 1 \geq 2 * q_{max})$ or $(m_\rightarrow.h > h_{max})$ **then**
9:       $Q_m \leftarrow Q_i \cup m_\rightarrow.Q_s$
10:       **while** $(|Q_m| + 1 < 2 * q_{max})$ and $(|R_i| > 0)$ **do**
11:          insert entry from R_i into Q_m
12:       **while** $(|Q_m| + 1 < 2 * q_{max})$ **do**
13:          insert random entry into Q_m
14:       randomly partition Q_m into Q_1 and $Q_2 (|Q_1 \cup \{m_\rightarrow.s\}| = |Q_2| = q_{max})$
15:       update local main cache: $Q_i \leftarrow Q_1 \cup \{m_\rightarrow.s\}$
16:       add the donated cache entries to the history cache: $H_i \leftarrow H_i \cup Q_2$
17:       send a *pull* message to $m_\rightarrow.s$:$m_\leftarrow(d = i, Q = Q_2, Q_d = Q_i)$
18:    **else if** $(m_\rightarrow.h < h_{max})$ **then**
19:       **if** $v < m_\rightarrow.v_d$ **then**
20:          set $m_\rightarrow.d = i$ and $m_\rightarrow.v_d = v$
21:       select random node j from Q_i
22:       $m_\rightarrow.h + +$
23:       send $m_\rightarrow$ to j
24:    **else if** $(m_\rightarrow.h == h_{max})$ **then**
25:       $m_\rightarrow.h + +$
26:       send $m_\rightarrow$ to $m_\rightarrow.d$

27:
28: **procedure** RECEIVEPULLMESSAGE(message $m_\leftarrow$)
29:    **if** message interleaving == false **then**
30:       update local main cache: $Q_i \leftarrow m_\leftarrow.Q$
31:    **else**
32:       perform $IMP(m_\leftarrow)$
33:    **while** $|R_i| > r_{max}$ **do**
34:       remove the oldest entry in R_i

When membership protocols are executed over a random overlay topology, all of them seem to provide an optimal peer sampling service with respect to the convergence speed of a global aggregation. However, when the overlay topology is not random, membership protocols may induce different results on the application performance. This may happen, for example, when the overlay topology is initialised or when high node churn is present. Rather than studying optimal initialization procedure for the overlay topology, in this work we evaluate the performance of different membership protocols when the overlay topology has weak connectivity.

In past related work, the initial overlay topology is often chosen as a random regular graph. This is an arbitrary and unrealistic choice, which makes the overlay topology very robust to the loss of connectivity. On the contrary, the simulations carried out for this work, have used initial overlay topologies with weak connectivity in order to show the effect of membership protocols in the degradation of the topology. A ring of communities [11] is an artificial topology with poor expansion property and a good load balance: it has been used as initial overlay topology in the simulations.

The experimental tests have been carried out in PeerSim [13], a Java-based network simulation based on discrete events. The simulations have adopted an

---

Algorithm 2. IMP

1: **procedure** IMP(message $m_\leftarrow$)
2:     $D_1 \leftarrow m_\leftarrow.Q \cap H_i$, detect and remove the duplication from case 1
3:     $m_\leftarrow.Q \leftarrow m_\leftarrow.Q \setminus D_1$
4:     $D_2 \leftarrow m_\leftarrow.Q \cap Q_i$, detect and remove the duplication from case 2
5:     $m_\leftarrow.Q \leftarrow m_\leftarrow.Q \setminus D_2$
6:     $D_3 \leftarrow Q_i \cap m_\leftarrow.Q_d$, detect and remove the duplication from case 3
7:     $Q_i \leftarrow Q_i \setminus D_3$
8:     $T \leftarrow Q_i \cup m_\leftarrow.Q$, create a temporary cache
9:     **while** $|T| > q_{max}$ **do**
10:         remove the oldest entry in T and add it to R_i
11:     **while** $|T| < q_{max}$ and $|R_i| > 0$ **do**
12:         remove the oldest entry in R_i and add it to T
13:     **while** $|T| < q_{max}$ **do**
14:         select a random entry from the duplications and add it to T
15:     update local main cache: $Q_i \leftarrow T$

---

asynchronous network model with a uniform distribution of network latency. The simulations have been run with the following membership protocols, where their settings have been chosen for best performance according to the literature and to a preliminary analysis.

- The Node Cache Protocol [8] ($q_{max} = 30$).
- Cyclon [9] ($q_{max} = 30$ and shuffle length = 15).
- Eddy [10] (shuffle length = 15 and refresh rate = 10 cycles).
- EMP [11] ($q_{max} = 30$ and $h_{max} = 5$).
- EMP+ ($q_{max} = 30$, $h_{max} = 5$, $r_{max} = 100$ and history lifetime = 2 cycles).

The initial local cache in all membership protocols was populated with 30 entries according to the same initial overlay topology. The initial ring of communities topology is generated with 10 random connected communities of 1000 nodes: there are only two links between each pair of communities which make them to have weak inter-community connectivity.

5.1   Global Connectivity

In the first set of simulations, each protocols was run for 100 cycles starting from the initial ring of communities topology. The aim of the simulations is to collect information about the number of connected components in the topology to detect any loss of global connectivity. Each simulation was repeated 20 times with a different seed of the random number generator.

Figure 3 shows the maximum number of connected components over the 20 trials. It shows that all the membership protocols have lost global connectivity in at least one trial and at some point in time. For all protocols but EMP+ a connectivity problem is irreversible. The Node Cache Protocol produced the highest number of connected components. Between cycle 5 and cycle 10, the number of connected components for EMP is unstable because of the effect of message interleaving. Like EMP, EMP+ also has a loss of connectivity, though only temporarily. EMP+ is the only membership protocol that adopts IMP to be able to recover the global connectivity when lost.

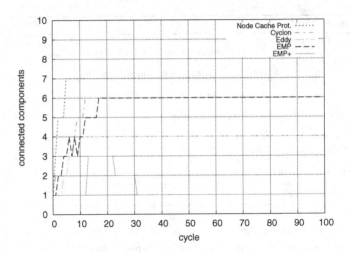

Fig. 3. The number of connected components in the overlay topology: maximum over 20 trials. (network size: 10000 nodes)

The results of our analysis have shown that IMP is often effective in recovering the global connectivity of the overlay topology. However, it does not provide guarantees because of the practical limitations imposed to the size of the history and reserve caches.

6.2 Application Accuracy

The second set of simulations is related to the accuracy of an application that makes use of the service provided by the membership protocol. The specific application used is an epidemic aggregation protocol, which computes the estimate of the global average of a set of distributed values. The epidemic aggregation protocol SPSP [8] was adopted to perform the global aggregation. All other settings are the same as in the previous set of simulations.

The local values of the aggregation protocol are initialized with a peak distribution: all nodes have initial value of 0, but one node that has a peak value equal to network size. After some cycles, the local estimates are expected to converge to the target value of the global average of 1.

The application performance is measured by the symmetrical mean absolute percentage error (sMAPE) [14], which is a statistical measure of accuracy based on the percentage errors. The performance index sMAPE is defined as:

$$sMAPE = \frac{200}{n} \times \sum_{t=1}^{n} \frac{|F_t - X|}{F_t + X},$$

where X is the target value, F_t is the forecast value (estimate) at each node and n is number of nodes. The index sMAPE is limited between 200 % and -200 %. Values closer to zero indicate better accuracy. This index is useful to avoid the problem of large errors when the real values are close to zero and there is a large different between the real value and the forecast.

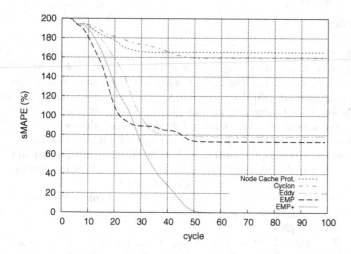

Fig. 4. The sMAPE in the overlay topology: average over 20 trials (network size: 10000 nodes)

Figure 4 shows the application performance when different membership protocols are used. At the beginning every protocol has an index of 200 %, which means that none of the nodes has reached the target values of the aggregation. A loss of connectivity hinders the application to reach a sufficient accuracy and to converge to the target value. The results show that EMP+ is the only membership protocol that helps the application to achieve the ideal target value (sMAPE=0 %) after about 50 cycles. EMP+ can maintain the global connectivity of the overlay topology and can also provide a good speed of convergence.

7   Conclusions

This work has investigated the effect of message interleaving on the global connectivity of the overlay topology generated by epidemic membership protocols. The internal mechanisms in membership protocols continuously transform the overlay topology by randomly rewiring the edges. This transformation is quite robust when applied to a random graph with good expansion properties. However, if the transformation is applied to an overlay topology with a weak connectivity, some edge rewiring can cause an irreversible loss of global connectivity.

The main contribution of this work is to introduce the first connectivity recovery mechanism. This mechanism has been embedded in EMP+, an enhanced version of Expander Membership Protocol (EMP). The key to achieve this goal is the Interleaving Management Procedure (IMP). The experimental analysis based on simulations has shown that EMP+ is effective in preserving and recovering the global connectivity of the overlay topology and can also provide a good speed of convergence at the application layer.

Future work will focus on the effect of node churn to the performance of epidemic membership protocols in very large and dynamic networks.

References

1. Bansod, N., Malgi, A., Choi, B.K., Mayo, J.: Muon: epidemic based mutual anonymity in unstructured p2p networks. Comput. Netw. **52**(5), 915–934 (2008)
2. Sheng, Di., Wang, C-L., Hu, D.H.: Gossip-based dynamic load balancing in an autonomous desktop grid. In Proceedings of the 10th International Conference on High-Performance Computing in Asia-Pacific Region, pp. 85–92 (2009)
3. Ma, Y., Jamalipour, A.: An epidemic P2P content search mechanism for intermittently connected mobile ad hoc networks. In: IEEE GLOBECOM, pp. 1–6 (2009)
4. Galzarano, S., Savaglio, C., Liotta, A., Fortino, G.: Gossiping-based aodv for wireless sensor networks. In: IEEE International Conference on in Systems, Man and Cybernetics (SMC 2013), pp. 26–31, October 2013
5. Strakov, H., Niederbrucker, G., Gansterer, W.N.: Fault tolerance properties of gossip-based distributed orthogonal iteration methods. Proc. Int. Conf. Comput. Sci. **18**, 189–198 (2013)
6. Soltero, P., Bridges, P., Arnold, D., Lang, M.: A gossip-based approach to exascale system services. In: Proceedings of the 3rd International Workshop on Runtime and Operating Systems for Supercomputers, Services (ROSS 2013), ACM (2013)
7. Jelasity, M., Voulgaris, S., Guerraoui, R., Kermarrec, A.M., van Steen, M.: Gossip-based peer sampling. ACM Trans. Comput. Syst. **25**(3), 8 (2007)
8. Blasa, F., Cafiero, S., Fortino, G., Di Fatta, G.: Symmetric push-sum protocol for decentralised aggregation. In: Proceeidngs of the International Conference on Advances in P2P Systems, pp. 27–32 (2011)
9. Voulgaris, S., Gavidia, D., van Steen, M.: Cyclon: inexpensive membership management for unstructured p2p overlays. J. Netw. Syst. Manage. **13**(2), 197–217 (2005)
10. Ogston, E., Jarvis, S.A.: Peer-to-peer aggregation techniques dissected. Int. J. Parallel Emerg. Distrib. Syst. **25**(1), 51–71 (2010)
11. Poonpakdee, P., Di Fatta, G.: Expander graph quality optimisation in randomised communication. In: IEEE International Conference on Data Mining Workshop (ICDMW 2014), pp. 597–604, December 2014
12. Hoory, S., Linial, N., Wigderson, A.: Expander graphs and their applications. Bull. Am. Math. Soc. **43**(4), 439–561 (2006)
13. Montresor, A., Jelasity, M.: PeerSim: A scalable P2P simulator. In: Proceedings of the 9th International Conference on Peer-to-Peer (P2P 2009), pp. 99–100, September 2009
14. Makridakis, S., Hibon, M.: The M3-competition: results, conclusions and implications. Int. J. Forecast. **16**, 451–476 (2000)

Parallel Computing

Optimisation Techniques for Parallel K-Means on MapReduce

Sami Al Ghamdi[✉], Giuseppe Di Fatta, and Frederic Stahl

School of Systems Engineering, University of Reading,
Whiteknights, RG6 6AY, Reading, UK
s.a.m.alghamdi@pgr.reading.ac.uk,
{g.difatta, f.t.stahl}@reading.ac.uk

Abstract. The K-Means algorithm is one the most efficient and widely used algorithms for clustering data. However, K-Means performance tends to get slower as data grows larger in size. Moreover, the rapid increase in the size of data has motivated the scientific and industrial communities to develop novel technologies that meet the needs of storing, managing, and analysing large-scale datasets known as *Big Data*. This paper describes the implementation of parallel K-Means on the MapReduce framework, which is a distributed framework best known for its reliability in processing large-scale datasets. Moreover, a detailed analysis of the effect of distance computations on the performance of K-Means on MapReduce is introduced. Finally, two optimisation techniques are suggested to accelerate K-Means on MapReduce by reducing distance computations per iteration to achieve the same deterministic results.

Keywords: K-Means · Parallel K-Means · Clustering · Mapreduce

1 Introduction

Clustering is the process of partitioning data points in a given dataset into groups (clusters), where data points in one group are more similar than data points in other groups. cluster analysis plays an important role in the Big Data problem. For example, it has been used to analyse gene expression data, and in image segmentation to locate objects' borders in an image.

K-Means [1] is one of the most popular and widely used clustering algorithms. K-means has been extensively studied and improved to cope with the rapid and exponential increase in the size of datasets. One obvious solution is to parallelise K-Means. K-Means have been parallelised based on different environments such as Message Passing Interface (MPI) [2] and MapReduce [3].

For a given number of iterations, the computational complexity of K-Means is dominated by the distance computations required to determine the nearest centre for each data point. These operations consume most of the algorithm's run-time because, in each iteration, the distance from each data point to each centre has to be calculated. Various optimisation approaches have been introduced to tackle this issue. Elkan [4] applied the triangle inequality property to eliminate unnecessary distance computations on high dimensional datasets. An optimisation technique based on multidimensional

© Springer International Publishing Switzerland 2015
G. Di Fatta et al. (Eds.): IDCS 2015, LNCS 9258, pp. 193–200, 2015.
DOI: 10.1007/978-3-319-23237-9_17

trees (KD-Trees) [5] was proposed by Pelleg and Moore [6] to accelerate K-Means. Judd et al. [7] presented a parallel K-Means formulation for MPI and used two approaches to prune unnecessary distance calculations. Pettinger and Di Fatta [8, 9] proposed a parallel KD-Tree K-Means algorithm for MPI, which overcomes the load imbalance problem generated by KD-Trees in distributed computing systems. Different approaches have been proposed to improve K-Means efficiency on MapReduce by reducing the number of iterations. However, we intend to accelerate K-Means on MapReduce by reducing distance computations per iteration.

This paper describes the implementation of K-Means on MapReduce with a mapper-combiner-reducer approach and how the iterative procedure is accomplished on MapReduce. In Addition, it presents some preliminary results relative to the effect of distance calculations on the performance of K-Means on MapReduce. Finally, two approaches are suggested to improve the efficiency of K-Means on MapReduce.

The rest of the paper is organised as follows: Sect. 2 briefly introduces K-Means and MapReduce, and presents a detailed description of Parallel K-Means on MapReduce. Section 3 reports the experimental results. Section 4 presents the work in progress. Finally, Sect. 5 concludes the paper.

2 Parallel K-Means on MapReduce

2.1 K-Means

Given a set X of n data points in a d-dimensional space $\mathbb{R}^d$, and an integer k that represents the number of clusters, K-Means partitions X into k clusters by assigning each $x_i \in X$ to its nearest cluster centre, or centroid, $c_j \in C$, where C is the set of k centroids. Given a set of initial centroids, data points are assigned to clusters and cluster centroids are recalculated: this process is repeated until the algorithm converges or meets an early termination criterion. The goal of K-Means is to minimise the objective function known as the Sum of Squared Error $(SSE) = \sum_{j=1}^{k} \sum_{i=1}^{n_j} ||x_i - c_j||^2$, where x is the ith data point in the jth cluster and n_j is the number of data points in the jth cluster. The time complexity for K-Means is $O(nkd)$ per iteration.

2.2 MapReduce

MapReduce [3] is a programming paradigm that is designed to, efficiently and reliably, store and process large-scale datasets on large clusters of commodity machines.

In this paradigm, the input data is partitioned and stored as blocks (or input-splits) on a distributed file system such as Google File System (GFS) [10], or Hadoop Distributed File System (HDFS) [11]. The main phases in the MapRede are *Map*, *Shuffle*, and *Reduce*. In addition, there is an optional optimisation phase called *Combine*. The MapReduce phases are explained as follows:

In the *Map* phase, the user implements a *map* function that takes as an input the records inside each input-split in the form of key1-value1 pairs. Each map function processes one pair at a time. Once processed, a new set of intermediate key2-value2 pairs is outputted by the mapper. Next, the output is spilled to the disk of the local file system of the computing machine. In the *Shuffle* phase the mappers' output is sorted, grouped by key (key2) and shuffled to reducers. Once the mappers' outputs are transferred across the network, the *Reduce* phase proceeds where reducers receive the input as key2-list(value2) pairs. Each reducer processes the list of values associated to each unique key2. Then, each reducer produces results as key3-value3 pairs, which are written to the distributed file system. The *Combine* phase is an optional optimisation on MapReduce. Combiners minimise the amount of intermediate data transferred from mappers to reducers across the network by performing a local aggregation over the intermediate data.

2.3 Parallel K-Means on MapReduce Implementation

Parallel K-Means on MapReduce (PKMMR) has been discussed in several papers (e.g., [12, 13]). However, in this paper we explain, in details, how *counters* are used to control the iterative procedure. Moreover, we show the percentage of the average time consumed by distance computations. PKMMR with a combiner consists of: *Mapper, Combiner, Reducer* user program called *Driver* that controls the iterative process. In the following sections, a data point is denoted as *dp*, a cluster identifier as *c_id*, the combiner's partial sum and partial count as *p_sum* and *p_count*.

Driver Algorithm. The Driver is a process that controls the execution of each K-Means iterations in MapReduce and determines its convergence or other early termination criteria. The pseudocode is described in Algorithm-1. The Driver controls the iterative process through a user defined counter called *global_counter* (line 2). The global_counter is used as a termination condition in the while loop. The counter is incremented in the Reducer if the algorithm does not converge or an early termination condition is not met, otherwise, the counter is set to zero and the while loop terminates. Besides configuring, setting, and submitting the MapReduce job, the Driver also merges multiple reducers' outputs into one file that contains all updated centroids.

Algorithm-1: *Driver*

1: Select k initial cluster centroids randomly;
2: global_counter := 1 //initialised and modified in Reducer (Algorithm-4)
3: **while** global_counter > 0 or a termination condition is not met **do**
4:     Configure and setup a MapReduce job;
5:     Send initial set of centroids to computing nodes,
6:     Run the MapReduce job;
7:     **if** number of reducers > 1 **then**
8:        Merge reducers output into one file
9:     **end if**
10:     global_counter := Counter(*global_counter*).getValue();
11: **end while**

Mapper Algorithm. Each Mapper processes an individual input-split received from HDFS. Each Mapper contains three methods, *setup*, *map* and *cleanup*. While the map method is invoked for each key-value pair in the input-split, setup and cleanup methods are executed only once in each run of the Mapper. As shown in Algorithm-2, setup loads the centroids to c_list. The map method takes as input the offset of the dp and the dp as key-value pairs, respectively. In lines 4−10, where the most expensive operation in the algorithm occurs, the loop iterates over the c_list and assigns the dp to its closest centroid. Finally, the mapper outputs the c_id and an object consists of the dp and integer 1. Because it is not guaranteed that Hadoop is going to run the Combiner, Mapper and Reducer must be implemented such that they produce the same results with and without a Combiner. For this reason, an integer 1 is sent with the dp (line 11) to represent p_count in case the combiner is not executed.

Algorithm-2: *Mapper*

Method   *setup ( )*
  1:   Load centroids to c_list;

Method   *map (key, value)*
  1:   Extract dp vector from value;
  2:   c_id := -1;
  3:   min_distance := ∞;
  4:   **for** i := 0 to c_list.size -1 **do**
  5:       distance := EuclideanDistance(c_list[i], dp)
  6:       **if** distance < min_distance **then**
  7:           min_distance := distance;
  8:           c_id := i;
  9:       **end if**
10: **end for**
11: output (c_id, (dp, 1));

Algorithm-3: *Combiner*

Method   *setup ( )*
  1:   Load centroids to c_list;

Method   *reduce(c_id, list<values>)*
  1:   p_count := 0, p_sum := 0;
  2:   **for** value **in** values **do**
  3:       Extract dp vector from value;
  4:       p_sum := p_sum + the vector sum of dps in d-dimensions;
  5:       p_count := p_count + 1;
  6:   **end for**
  7:   output(c_id, (p_sum, p_count))

Combiner Algorithm. As shown in Algorithm-3, the Combiner receives from the Mapper (key, list(values)) pairs, where key is the c_id, and list(values) is the list of dps assigned to this c_id along with the integer 1. In lines 2−6, the Combiner performs local aggregation where it calculates the p_sum, and p_count of dps in the list(values) for each c_id. Next, in line 7, it outputs key-value pairs where key is the c_id, and value is an object composed of the p_sum and p_count.

Reducer Algorithm. After the execution of the Combiner, the Reducer receives (key, list(values)) pairs, where key is the c_id and each value is composed of p_sum and p_count. In lines 2−6 of Algorithm-4, instead of iterating over all the dps that belong to a certain c_id, p_sum and p_count are accumulated and stored in total_sum and total_count, respectively. Next, the new centroid is calculated and added to new_c_list. In lines 9−11, a convergence criterion is tested. If the test holds, then the global_counter is incremented by one, otherwise, the global_counter's value does not change (stays zero) and the algorithm is terminated by the Driver.

Algorithm-4: *Reducer*

Method   *setup ( )*

1: Load centroids to c_list; //holds current centroids
2: global_counter = 0;
3: Initialise new_c_list; //holds updated centroids

Method   *reduce(c_id, list<values>)*

1: total_sum, total_count, new_centroid, old_centroid = 0;
2: **for** value **in** values **do**
3:      Extract dp vector from value;
4:      total_sum := total_sum + value.get_p_sum();
5:      total_count := total_count + value.get_p_count();
6: **end for**
7: new_centroid := total_sum / total_count;
8: add new_centroid to new_c_list
9: **if** new_centroid has changed or a threshold is not reached **then**
10:      Increment global_counter by 1
11: **end if**
12: output(c_id, dp)

Method   *cleanup( )*

1: Write new centroids in new_c_list to HDFS;

---

3   Experimental Results

To evaluate PKMMR, we run the algorithm on a Hadoop [14] 2.2.0 cluster of 1 master node and 16 worker nodes. The master node has 2 AMD CPUs running at 3.1 GHz with 8 cores each, and 8 × 8 GB DDR3 RAM, and 6 × 3 TB Near Line SAS disks running at 7200 rpm. Each worker node has 1 Intel CPU running at 3.1 GHz with 4 cores, and 4 × 4 GB DDR3 RAM, and a 1 × 1 TB SATA disk running at 7200 rpm.

The datasets used in the experiments are artificially generated where data points are randomly distributed. Additionally, initial cluster centroids are randomly picked from the dataset [1]. The number of iterations is fixed in all experiments at 10.

To show the effect of distance calculations on the performance of PKMMR, we run the algorithm with different number of data points n, dimensions d and clusters k. The percentage of the average time consumed by distance calculations in each iteration is represented by the grey area in each bar in the Figs. 1-(a), (b), and (c). The white dotted area represents the percentage of the average time consumed by other MapReduce operations per iteration including job configuration and distribution, map tasks (excluding distance calculations) and reduce tasks.

In each run, we compute the average run-time for one iteration by dividing the total run-time over the number of iterations. Then, the average run-time consumed by distance calculations per iteration is computed.

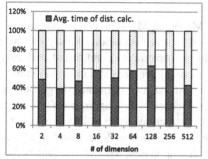

(a) Avg. time consumption with variable number of d. n=1000000, k=128.

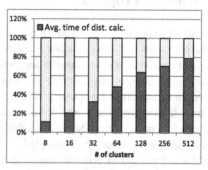

(b) Avg. time consumption with variable number of k. n=1000000, d=128.

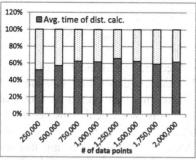

(c) Avg. time consumption with variable number of n. d=128, k=128.

Fig. 1. Percentage of the average consumed time by distance calculations per iteration with variable number of d, k and n.

We run PKMMR with a varied number of d, while n is fixed at 1,000,000, and k is fixed at 128. Figure 1-(a) shows that 39 % ($d = 4$) to 63 % ($d = 128$) of the average iteration time is consumed by distance calculations.

PKMMR is also run with a variable number of k, while n is set to 1,000,000 and d is set to 128. In Fig. 1-(b), it can be clearly seen the tremendous increase in the percentage of consumed time by distance calculations per iteration from 11 % ($k = 8$) to 79 % ($k = 512$). In this experiment, distance calculations become a performance bottleneck as the number of clusters increases, which is more likely to occur while processing large-scale datasets.

Figure 1-(c) illustrates the percentage of the average time of distance calculations when running PKMMR with variable number of n, while $d = 128$ and $k = 128$. As it can be observed, distance calculations consume most of the iteration time. About 65 % of the iteration time is spent on distance calculations when $n = 1,250,000$. Therefore, reducing the number of required distance calculations will most likely accelerates the iteration run-time and, consequently, improves the overall run-time of PKMMR.

4   Work in Progress

We intend to accelerate the performance of K-Means on MapReduce by applying two methods to reduce the distance computations in each iteration. Firstly, triangle inequality optimisation techniques are going to be implemented and tested with high dimensional datasets. However, such techniques usually require extra information to be stored and transferred from one iteration to the next. As a consequence, large I/O and communication overheads may hinder the effectiveness of this approach if not taken into careful consideration. Secondly, efficient data structures, such as KD-trees or other space-partitioning data structures [15], will be adapted to MapReduce and used with K-Means. Two issues will be investigated in this approach. First, inefficient performance with high dimensional datasets that has been reported in [6]. Second, load imbalance that was addressed in [8, 9].

5   Conclusions

In this paper we have described the implementation of parallel K-Means on the MapReduce framework. Additionally, a detailed explanation of the steps to control the iterative procedure in MapReduce has been presented. Moreover, a detailed analysis of the average time consumed by distance calculations per iteration has been discussed. From the preliminary results, it can be clearly seen that most of the iteration time is consumed by distance calculations. Hence, reducing this time might contribute in accelerating K-Means on the MapReduce framework. Two approaches are under investigations, which are, respectively, based on the triangle inequality property and space-partitioning data structures.

References

1. Lloyd, S.: Least Squares Quantization in PCM. IEEE Trans. Inf. Theor. **28**(2), 129–137 (1982)
2. Dhillon, I.S., Modha, D.S.: A data-clustering algorithm on distributed memory multiprocessors. In: Zaki, M.J., Ho, C.-T. (eds.) KDD 1999. LNCS (LNAI), vol. 1759, pp. 245–260. Springer, Heidelberg (2000)
3. Dean, J., Ghemawat, S.: MapReduce: simplified data processing on large clusters. In: Proceedings of the 6th Conference on Symposium on Operating Systems Design & Implementation, **6**, p. 10. Berkeley, CA, USA (2004)
4. Elkan, C.: Using the triangle inequality to accelerate k-means. In: presented at the International Conference on Machine Learning - ICML, pp. 147–153 (2003)
5. Bentley, J.: Multidimensional binary search trees used for associative searching. Commun. ACM **18**(9), 509–517 (1975)
6. Pelleg, D., Moore, A.: Accelerating exact K-means algorithms with geometric reasoning. In: Proceedings of the Fifth ACM SIGKDD International Conference on Knowledge Discovery and Data Mining, pp. 277–281, New York, NY, USA (1999)
7. Judd, D., Mckinley, P.K., Jain, A.K.: Large-scale parallel data clustering. IEEE Trans. Pattern Anal. Mach. Intell. **20**, 871–876 (1998)
8. Pettinger, D., Di Fatta, G.: Scalability of efficient parallel K-means. In: 2009 5th IEEE International Conference on E-Science Workshops, pp. 96–101 (2009)
9. Di Fatta, G., Pettinger, D.: Dynamic load balancing in parallel KD-tree K-means. In: IEEE International Conference on Scalable Computing and Communications, pp. 2478–2485 (2010)
10. Ghemawat, S., Gobioff, H., Leung, S.-T.: The google file system. In: Proceedings of the 19th ACM Symposium on Operating Systems Principles, pp. 29–43. New York, NY, USA (2003)
11. Shvachko, K., Kuang, H., Radia, S., Chansler, R.: The hadoop distributed file system. In: Proceedings of the 2010 IEEE 26th Symposium on Mass Storage Systems and Technologies (MSST), pp. 1–10. Washington, DC, USA (2010)
12. Zhao, W., Ma, H., He, Q.: Parallel K-means clustering based on mapreduce. In: Jaatun, M. G., Zhao, G., Rong, C. (eds.) Cloud Computing. LNCS, vol. 5931, pp. 674–679. Springer, Heidelberg (2009)
13. White, B., Yeh, T., Lin, J., Davis, L.: Web-scale computer vision using mapreduce for multimedia data mining. In: Proceedings of the Tenth International Workshop on Multimedia Data Mining, pp. 9:1–9:10. New York, NY, USA (2010)
14. Apache Hadoop. http://hadoop.apache.org/. Accessed on 03 January 2015
15. Pettinger, D., Di Fatta, G.: Space partitioning for scalable K-means. In: IEEE The Ninth International Conference on Machine Learning and Applications (ICMLA 2010), pp. 319-324. Washington DC, USA, 12–14 December 2010

Epidemic Fault Tolerance
for Extreme-Scale Parallel Computing

Amogh Katti$^{(\boxtimes)}$ and Giuseppe Di Fatta

School of Systems Engineering, University of Reading,
Whiteknights, Reading, Berkshire RG6 6AY, UK
{a.p.katti,g.difatta}@reading.ac.uk

Abstract. Process failure rate in the next generation of high performance computing systems is expected to be very high. MPI Forum is working on providing semantics and support for fault tolerance. Run-Through Stabilization, User-Level Failure Mitigation and Process Recovery proposals are the resulting endeavors. Run-Through Stabilization/User Level Failure Mitigation proposals require a fault tolerant failure detection and consensus algorithm to inform the application of failures so that it can employ Algorithm Based Fault Tolerance for quicker recovery and continued execution. This paper discusses the proposals in short, the failure detectors available in the literature and their unsuitability for realizing fault tolerance in MPI. It then outlines an inherently fault-tolerant and scalable Epidemic (or Gossip-based) approach for failure detection and consensus. Some simulations and an initial experimental analysis are presented, which indicate that this is a promising research direction.

Keywords: Fault tolerance · Message Passing Interface (MPI) · Failure detection · Epidemic protocols · Gossip-based protocols

1 Introduction

Future High Performance Computing (HPC) systems will be prone to frequent failures. The System Mean Time Between Failures (SMTBF) for these systems is estimated to be approximately equal to an hour or even less [19] in contrast to the SMTBF of five to six hours observed for current HPC systems [21].

Checkpoint/Restart is a generic fault tolerance technique, wherein the application state is restored from the last saved checkpoint during recovery, that can be used with all kinds of High End Computing (HEC) applications and hence it is the prominent fault tolerance technique in use; it is the only technique available in most of the commercial HEC deployments. However, the technique is deemed to be ineffective for extreme-scale systems due to the high recovery time associated with it [6, 17].

Application specific techniques like Algorithm Based Fault Tolerance (ABFT) [11] are recommended for extreme-scale systems [7] for their efficiency in terms of resource and energy utilization and high performance. ABFT is a technique wherein the fault tolerance logic is embedded in the algorithm by the application developer to deal with the loss of application state at failure. This reduces recovery time thereby increasing

© Springer International Publishing Switzerland 2015
G. Di Fatta et al. (Eds.): IDCS 2015, LNCS 9258, pp. 201–208, 2015.
DOI: 10.1007/978-3-319-23237-9_18

efficiency. Applications typically use data encoding, algorithm redesign, diskless checkpointing, etc. ABFT techniques for recovery when failures occur.

Failure detection and notification support from the underlying programming library is required for applications to employ ABFT. Therefore the Message Passing Interface's (MPI) [13], the dominant parallel programming interface, Fault Tolerance Working Group (FTWG) is working on providing failure detection and notification and recovery services to applications to enable ABFT. Run-Through Stabilization (RTS) / User-Level Failure Mitigation (ULFM) proposal in combination with Process Recovery proposal provide the fault tolerance semantics and interfaces to serve these purposes.

In this paper a promising research direction for this problem is presented. The proposed approach is based on Epidemic (or Gossip-based) protocols to implement a failure detector for extreme-scale parallel computing.

Uniform Gossip is an inherently fault tolerant and highly scalable communication scheme. It is aptly suitable for information dissemination and data aggregation in large scale, distributed and fault prone networked systems [3, 8]. Recently, they have also been adopted in high performance computing tasks [18, 20].

The paper is organized as follows. FTWG's endeavors to make MPI fault tolerant are discussed in Sect. 2. Failure detectors available in the HPC literature are discussed in Sect. 3. Section 4 proposes a completely distributed Gossip-based and hence inherently fault tolerant failure detection and consensus approach. Simulations and an initial analysis are presented in Sect. 5. The paper concludes in Sect. 6 with a discussion of the future work to comprehensively realize scalable fault tolerance in extreme-scale parallel computing.

2 Fault Tolerance in MPI

MPI's FTWG proposed RTS proposal to define semantics and interfaces to allow an application execute uninterrupted despite the occurrence of faults. ULFM proposal replaces the RTS proposal. Process Recovery proposal allows failed processes to re-join. Only fail-stop (crash) process failures are considered by these proposals. When a process crashes it stops communicating with rest of the processes. The three proposals are briefly discussed in this section.

According to the RTS proposal [9], an implementation is expected to inform an application of all process failures and let it run using the fault-free processes. RTS expects an eventually perfect failure detector [5] that is both strongly accurate and strongly complete. Strong accuracy means that a process must not be reported failed before it actually fails and strong completeness means that every failed process must be known to every fault-free process. The proposal weakens the completeness requirement to allow the processes to return different failed processes by the end of failure detection.

The RTS proposal has been suspended because of the implementation complexity of the failure detection and notification mechanisms involved [2]. User-Level Failure Mitigation (ULFM) proposal [1] supersedes the RTS proposal. Under the ULFM proposal, no operation hangs in the presence of failures but completes by returning an error. Asynchronous failure notification is not necessary. The proposal demands a weakly complete failure detector to achieve global consistency on the set of failed processes whenever necessary.

Process Recovery proposal [15] complements the RTS/ULFM proposal. It provides semantics and interfaces to facilitate recovery of a process that failed previously. Draft specification for the proposal is under development.

3   Failure Detectors

MPI requires failure detection and notification services to enable ABFT. Both centralized and completely distributed failure detectors are available in the HPC literature. Coordinator based and completely distributed Gossip-based failure detectors for fail-stop failures are discussed in this section.

3.1   Coordinator Based Failure Detectors

A two-phase fault-aware consensus algorithm over a static tree communication topology to construct a weekly complete failure detector was provided in [12]. A fault tolerant algorithm, in [4], provided an improvement to support strict completeness using an iterative formulation of the three-phase commit over a dynamic tree communication topology. Both the approaches are discussed in this section.

Over a Static Tree Topology. This approach assumes that processes locally know failed processes and participate in the consensus algorithm to consistently construct the global list of failed processes. A two-phase algorithm over a fault-aware tree topology constructs the global list of failed processes using reliable gather at the coordinator during the first phase and reliable broadcast to the participant processes during the broadcast phase. Participant failures are handles by routing around the failed processes to find the nearest parent and child process during the gather and broadcast operations respectively. Termination detection algorithm is used when the coordinator fails during the broadcast phase. Processes query the immediate children of the coordinator to get the global list of failed processes. If the coordinator fails during the gather phase or just before the broadcast phase, the algorithm aborts without constructing the global list of failed processes. Processes that fail during the algorithm will be detected during the next invocation of the algorithm.

Over a Dynamic Tree Topology. This approach also assumes that processes locally know failed processes and then participate in the consensus algorithm. A three-phase algorithm over a fault-tolerant dynamic tree topology constructs the global list of failed processes making sure that every process returns the same list of failed processes and thus implements a strongly complete failure detector. First phase constructs the list of failed processes and sends it to every participant and makes sure that every process has the same list of failed processes by the end of the phase, second phase informs to the participants that all the processes have the same failed process list by now and third phase commands the participants to terminate the algorithm. Every phase starts with a message from the coordinator and finishes when the coordinator receives acknowledgement from all the participants for the current phase. If any participant fails during a phase, a new instance of the broadcast starts by reconstructing the tree with the current alive processes. Coordinator failure is handled by electing a new coordinator.

3.2 Completely Distributed Failure Detectors

Coordinator based failure detection and consensus algorithms do not scale to large number of processes. Completely distributed failure detection can be accomplished as a side effect of Gossiping. Gossip-based failure detectors in the distributed computing systems literature considered for HPC are discussed in this section.

Gossip-based failure detectors can be either passive "heartbeat" failure detector or active "ping" failure detector. A process in "heartbeat" failure detection passively waits for Gossip messages whereas in "ping" failure detection a process actively pings other processes.

"Heartbeat" Failure Detector. In [16] a Gossip-based failure detection algorithm using liveness analysis is given. A process in the system periodically announces that it is alive by sending a Gossip message to another random process in the system. This liveness information disseminates throughout the network and ultimately every process will have information about every other process in the system. A process is suspected to have failed if its liveness information is old. When a majority of processes suspect a process it is detected to have failed. When all fault free processes have detected a faulty process consensus on its failure is reached.

"Ping" Failure Detector. A failure detection algorithm using distributed diagnosis considering network partitioning is given in [10]. A process randomly selects another process and pings it to find its status. If it does not receive a response from the process, it asks a random sample of the processes in the system to ping the process as well. The process is detected to have failed if none of the selected processes receives a response.

4 Failure Detector Maintaining Global Knowledge

Completely distributed Gossip-based heartbeat failure detection and consensus algorithms are based on passive and slow liveness analysis and consume very high memory and network bandwidth. There is need for fault tolerant yet scalable communication schemes. In this section a novel scalable Gossip-based and inherently fault tolerant ping type failure detector for fail-stop failures using a matrix to store global view of all the processes in the system is proposed.

The algorithm detects fail-stop failures and the failures are assumed to be permanent. A synchronous model of the system is assumed with bounded message delay. Failures during the algorithm are assumed to stop at some point to allow the algorithm to complete with successful consensus detection. Figure 1 shows pseudocode for the algorithm.

```
At each process p
  Require: Fault Matrix F_p[r,c] where 0≤r,c<n
      F_p[r,c] - system view of processes
  Initialisation:
      1. for (r=0, r<n, r++)            //start with all alive processes
      2.     for (c=0, c<n, c++)
      3.         F_p[r,c]=0
      4.     end for
      5. end for
  At each cycle:
      6. q = getRandomProcess()
      7. send a PING message to a random process, say q, with F_p
      8. for (c=0, c<n, c++)                    //consensus check on c
      9.     cnt = 0
      10.    for (r=0, r<n, r++)
      11.        if (F_p[r,c] || F_p[p,r]) then
      12.            cnt++
      13.        end if
      14.    end for
      15.    if (cnt==n) then
      16.        consensus_reached(c)
      17.    end if
      18. end for
  At event: received a message from j with F_j
      19. if(message == PING) then           //reply to the PING
      20.    send a REPLY message to j with F_p
      21. end if
      22. for (r=0, r<n, r++)           //merge the detections
      23.    for (c=0, c<n, c++)
      24.        F_p[r,c]= F_p[r,c]|| F_j[r,c]       //propagate failure detections
      25.        F_p[p,c]= F_p[p,c]|| F_j[j,c]       //indirect failure detections
      26.    end for
      27. end for
  At event: timeout without receiving REPLY from q
      28. F_p[p,q]=1                         //direct failure detection
```

Fig. 1. Pseudocode of the Gossip-based failure detection and consensus

A process p maintains a fault matrix F_p to store the system view of all the processes in the system. $F_p[r, c]$ is the view at process p of the status of process c as detected by process r. A value of 1 indicates failure and a 0 indicates alive.

Every process in the system is assumed to be alive by every process at the beginning and hence the fault matrix is initialized with all 0's (lines 1-5).

During a cycle of Gossip, of length T_{gossip} time units, process p pings a random process to check its status. It also handles reception of Gossip message and ping timeout events. A random process q is selected and a ping message is sent to it with the local fault matrix F_p (lines 6-7). When a ping message is received, an asynchronous reply is sent with the local fault matrix (lines 19-21). When the ping message times out without receiving a reply message from q, it is detected to have failed and 1 is stored at $F_p[p, q]$ (line 28). On receiving a Gossip message from j, the local and the remote fault matrices, F_p and F_j, are merged. Thus process p performs indirect failure detection through j and propagates the failures known to j (lines 22-27).

Consensus on the failure of each process is checked during every Gossip cycle. Consensus is reached when all the fault-free processes have recognized the failed process (lines 8-18).

5 Simulations and Results

The algorithm was implemented in Java and the simulations were carried out on PeerSim [14], a scalable network simulator based on discrete events. The latency and bandwidth were set to nominal values as only the number of Gossip cycles required to reach consensus were measured. Failures were simulated by restraining a process from participating in communications.

The algorithm's scalability and fault tolerance properties were tested. Failures were injected into randomly chosen processes. In the first experiment a single failure was injected at the beginning of the simulation. In the second experiment failures were injected during the simulation to test the fault tolerance property of the algorithm. Because processes reach consensus on the injected failure(s) at different cycles, the cycle number of the last process reaching consensus is considered and recorded.

Figure 2 shows the relationship between the number of Gossip cycles (average over multiple simulations) and system size to reach consensus when a single failure is injected at the beginning of the simulation. Consensus is reached in logarithmic number of Gossip cycles.

Figure 3 shows the transition towards consensus in terms of the relative number of processes which have detected the failure at each cycle. A typical epidemic information spreading can be observed.

The consensus algorithm is completely fault tolerant and it can also detect failures that happen during its execution. Figure 4 shows the results of simulations where failures were injected in randomly chosen processes and at random time within the first 10 cycles. The number of Gossip cycles needed to achieve consensus is still logarithm in terms of the system size from the Gossip cycle at which the last failure was injected.

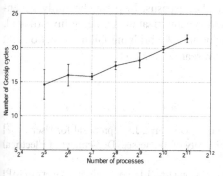

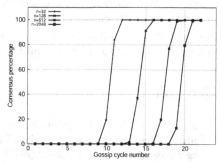

Fig. 2. Number of cycles to achieve consensus with a single failure

Fig. 3. Transition towards consensus with a single failure

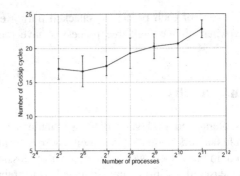

Fig. 4. Number of cycles to consensus with 4 failures injected during the simulations

6   Conclusion and Future Work

MPI's Fault Tolerance Working Group is working on including fault tolerance support into the standard to enable high performance computing systems to continue execution despite faults. Algorithm Based Fault Tolerance is the fault tolerance technique sought of and it requires failure detection and notification services.

Failure detection and consensus methods that use a coordinator do not scale to large number of processes. To overcome these limitations, this work has introduced a Gossip-based approach to provide scalable and fault tolerant failure detection and consensus. Each process builds and propagates a global view of the system. Failures are locally detected with direct timeout events based on Gossip messages and with indirect propagation of failures known to other processes. The experimental analysis based on simulations have shown that consensus on failures is reached in a logarithmic number of Gossip cycles w.r.t. the system size.

However, the proposed approach does not scale well in terms of memory requirements because each process has to maintain not only its own view of the system but also the views of all other processes. It also consumes a lot of network bandwidth due to transfer of this global view with each Gossip message.

Future work includes the design of memory and network bandwidth efficient methods for fault tolerant failure detection and consensus. In particular, fully decentralised algorithms for consensus detection and synchronization are being investigated. Supporting process re-spawning in the algorithm thereby bridging failure detection and process recovery is also an interesting future research direction.

References

1. Bland, W., Bosilca, G., Bouteiller, A., Herault, T., Dongarra, J.: A proposal for User-Level Failure Mitigation in the MPI-3 standard. University of Tennessee, Department of Electrical Engineering and Computer Science (2012)
2. Bland, W., Bouteiller, A., Herault, T., Bosilca, G., Dongarra, J.J.: Post-failure recovery of MPI communication capability: Design and rationale. Int. J. High Perform. Comput. Appl. (2013)

3. Blasa, F., Cafiero, S., Fortino, G., Di Fatta, G.: Symmetric push-sum protocol for decentralised aggregation (2011)
4. Buntinas, D.: Scalable distributed consensus to support MPI fault tolerance. In: 26th IEEE International Conference on Parallel & Distributed Processing Symposium (IPDPS), May 2012, pp. 1240–1249 (2012)
5. Chandra, T.D., Toueg, S.: Unreliable failure detectors for reliable distributed systems. J. ACM (JACM) 43(2), 225–267 (1996)
6. Daly, J.T., Lead, R.: Application resilience for truculent systems. In: Workshop on Fault Tolerance for Extreme-Scale Computing, Albuquerque, NM – 19–20 March 2009, ANL/MCS-TM-312 (2009)
7. Daly, J., Harrod, B., Hoang, T., Nowell, L., Adolf, B., Borkar, S., Wu, J.: Inter-Agency Workshop on HPC resilience at extreme scale. In: National Security Agency Advanced Computing Systems, February 2012 (2012)
8. Di Fatta, G., Blasa, F., Cafiero, S., Fortino, G.: Fault tolerant decentralised K-Means clustering for asynchronous large-scale networks. J. Parallel Distrib. Comput. 73(3), 317–329 (2013)
9. Fault Tolerance Working Group. Run-though stabilization interfaces and semantics. In: svn. mpi-forum. org/trac/mpi-forum-web/wiki/ft/run through stabilization (2012)
10. Gupta, I., Chandra, T.D., Goldszmidt, G.S.: On scalable and efficient distributed failure detectors. In: Proceedings of the Twentieth Annual ACM Symposium on Principles of Distributed Computing, August 2001, pp. 170–179. ACM (2001)
11. Huang, K.H., Abraham, J.A.: Algorithm-based fault tolerance for matrix operations. IEEE Trans. Comput. 100(6), 518–528 (1984)
12. Hursey, J., Naughton, T., Vallee, G., Graham, R.L.: A log-scaling fault tolerant agreement algorithm for a fault tolerant MPI. In: Cotronis, Y., Danalis, A., Nikolopoulos, D.S., Dongarra, J. (eds.) EuroMPI 2011. LNCS, vol. 6960, pp. 255–263. Springer, Heidelberg (2011)
13. Message Passing Interface Forum: MPI: A Message Passing Interface. In: Proceedings of Supercomputing 1993, pp. 878–883. IEEE Computer Society Press (1993)
14. Montresor, A., Jelasity, M.: PeerSim: A scalable P2P simulator. In: IEEE Ninth International Conference on Peer-to-Peer Computing, P2P 2009, pp. 99–100. IEEE (2009)
15. Process Recovery Proposal. https://svn.mpi-forum.org/trac/mpi-forum-web/wiki/ft/process_recovery_2. Accessed: 14 May 2015
16. Ranganathan, S., George, A.D., Todd, R.W., Chidester, M.C.: Gossip-style failure detection and distributed consensus for scalable heterogeneous clusters. Cluster Comput. 4(3), 197–209 (2001)
17. Schroeder, B., Gibson, G.A.: Understanding failures in petascale computers. In: Journal of Physics: Conference Series, vol. 78(1), p. 012022. IOP Publishing, July 2007
18. Soltero, P., Bridges, P., Arnold, D., Lang, M.: A Gossip-based approach to exascale system services. In: Proceedings of the 3rd International Workshop on Runtime and Operating Systems for Supercomputers, p. 3. ACM, June 2013
19. Song, H., Leangsuksun, C., Nassar, R., Gottumukkala, N.R., Scott, S.: Availability modeling and analysis on high performance cluster computing systems. In: The First International Conference on Availability, Reliability and Security, ARES 2006, April 2006, p.8. IEEE (2006)
20. Straková, H., Niederbrucker, G., Gansterer, W.N.: Fault tolerance properties of gossip-based distributed orthogonal iteration methods. Procedia Comput. Sci. 18, 189–198 (2013)
21. Taerat, N., Nakisinehaboon, N., Chandler, C., Elliot, J., Leangsuksun, C., Ostrouchov, G., Scott, S.L.: Using log information to perform statistical analysis on failures encountered by large-scale HPC deployments. In: Proceedings of the 2008 High Availability and Performance Computing Workshop, vol. 4, pp. 29–43 (2008)

A GPU-Based Statistical Framework for Moving Object Segmentation: Implementation, Analysis and Applications

Alfredo Cuzzocrea[1,2(✉)], Enzo Mumolo[1], Alessandro Moro[3], and Kazunori Umeda[3]

[1] DIA Department, University of Trieste, Trieste, Italy
alfredo.cuzzocrea@dia.units.it
[2] ICAR-CNR, Rende, Italy
[3] Chuo University, Tokyo, Japan

Abstract. This paper describes a real-time implementation of a recently proposed background maintenance algorithm and reports the relative performances. Experimental results on dynamic scenes taken from a fixed camera show that the proposed parallel algorithm produces background images with an improved quality with respect to classical pixel-wise algorithms, obtaining a speedup of more than 35 times compared to CPU implementation. It is worth noting that we used both the GeForce 9 series (actually a 9800 GPU) available from the year 2008 and the GeForce 200 series (actually a 295 GPU) available from the year 2009. Finally, we show that this parallel implementation allows us to use it in real-time moving object detection application.

1 Introduction

In computer vision systems, a background model is a representation of the background image and it is based on its associated statistics. Background models are widely used for foreground objects segmentation, which is a fundamental task in many computer vision problems including moving object detection, shadow detection and removal, and image classification problems. As the visual scene changes with time, these models are continuously updated to include the required background modifications; the development of model updating algorithms is called Background Maintenance Problem.

As described in [3,18], there are many problems that the background mainenance algorithms should solve, mainly related to the reaction of the background to both sudden or gradual changes in the visual scene, such as the sudden or gradual environmental light changes. Moreover, the moving object detection process can generate ghost images if the background image reconstruction is not fast enough. Other problems may be caused by shadows, because foreground objects often generate cast shadows which appear different from the modeled background.

Hence high quality background management algorithms are generally quite compex. In fact, there is a trade-off between the accuracy of the background

© Springer International Publishing Switzerland 2015
G. Di Fatta et al. (Eds.): IDCS 2015, LNCS 9258, pp. 209–220, 2015.
DOI: 10.1007/978-3-319-23237-9_19

image and the computing time the algorithms require. Of course the complexity of the computation of these methods is the big obstacle for real-time applications.

For this reason, many authors implemented background management algorithms on a Graphic Processing Unit (GPU). GPU's have a high number of parallel processors and implement the stream processor paradigm, a form of Single Instruction, Multiple Data (SIMD) parallel processing. Under this paradigm, the same series of operations (kernel function) are independently applied onto each element in a set of data (stream) in an unspecified order and in batches of an (a priori) undetermined number of elements. This type of processing is particularly suited when each input pixel is independently processed.

In this paper we describe the GPU implementation of the background maintenance algorithm described in [4]. The algorithm is indeed pixel-wise, as almost all the processing are performed independently on each pixel and, as such, it is well suited to GPU implementation and high speed-ups can be expected. It is worth remarking that an important characteristic of real time computation of background maintenance algorithms is important at least for detecting moving objects from high definition images. It is worth recalling that the trend of digital cameras concerns increasing image resolution and increasing frame rate. In fact, with high resolution images it is possible to perform zoom of a particular region of the image, such as a door or an entrance (as shown in Fig. 1, right panel). Moreover, high frame rate allows to capture elements moving at high speed, such as fast running persons or high speed cars. Both these features are very important in video surveillance. Another application of the proposed algorithm is when the scene is crowded: the background is quite completely hidden for a long period of time and need to be reconstructed in real-time. In Fig. 1 we report two examples of typical images used in the experimental measurements described in Sect. 6.

This paper is organized as follows. Section 2 deals with some previously published work on GPU implementation of other Computer Vison algorithms. The related speed-up figures are reported. In Sect. 3 a review of the previously

Fig. 1. Example of complex scenes that requires highly accurate background maintenance.

published ([4]) the pixel-wise algorithms for background maintenance is reported, and in Sect. 4 the parallelization of the previously proposed algorithm is presented. In Sect. 6 its performances in term of computational efficiency, speedup and quality are outlined and discussed. Finally in Sect. 7 some final remarks are proposed.

2   Related Work

Graphic Processing Units or GPUs are highly parallel processors, initially thought for graphic processing and rapidly evolved to general purpose processing, or GPGPU. Image processing and Computer graphic remain however the fields where the GPU can give the greatest benefits, as long as the algorithms are mostly pixel-wise. Clearly using the GPU for algorithmic processing, frees the CPU for other tasks.

Many GPU implementations of background methods have been published in the previous years. The work of [11] presents a foreground-background segmentation based on a color similarity test in a small pixel neighborhood, integrated into a Bayesian estimation framework, where iterative MRF-based model is applied. Using images of size 640x480 pixels on an NVIDIA GeForce 6800GT graphics card with AGP 8x, the following run-times are reported, depending on the number of MRF-iterations. The time needed for uploading the input images to the GPU and downloading the final segmentation is not included. The run-time varies from 2.51 ms to 4.84 ms for 0 and 10 iterations, correspondingly. In [15], a background model with low latency is constructed to detect moving objects in video sequences. Subsequent frames are stacked on top of each other using associated registration information that must be obtained in a preprocessing step. Their GPU implementation is running on a test system equipped with Nvidia GeForce 8800 GTX model, featuring 768 MB of video ram. The time required to construct the mean and median approximation backgrounds of length 48 on a combined GPU and CPU implementation is 16 and 151 ms, respectively. The authors in [20] describe a GPU-based implementation of motion detection from a moving platform. A step compensating for camera motion is required prior to estimating of the background model. Due to inevitable registration errors, the background model is estimated according to a sliding window of frames. The background model is based on an RGB texture histogram and a search for the bin with the largest number of samples. The resulting GPU-based implementation can build the background model and detect motion regions at around 18 fps on 320videos. Finally, the work of [13] proposes an approach that incorporates a pixel-based online learning method to adapt to temporal background changes, together with a graph cuts method to propagate per-pixel evaluation results over nearby pixels. The speed of their method is measured on a Lenovo T60 laptop with Intel Centrino T2500 CPU and ATI Mobility Radeon X1400 GPU. For image sequences with 320x240 resolutions, they achieve 16 fps.

In [16] Pham et al. describe a GPU implementation of an improved version of the Extended Gaussian mixture background model. Pham et al. show in this paper that their GPU implementation gained a speed-up of at least 10 with respect to a CPU implementation. Pham et al. used Core 2 2.6 GHz CPU and a GeForse 9600GT GPU.

In [14], the authors implemented a background maintenance algorithm based on an adaptive mixture of Gaussians (AGMM). Using an NVIDIA GPU with the CUDA [1] they achieved 18 acceleration compared with an implementation on an Intel multicore CPU using multithreading. In the same paper, an implementation on IBMs Cell Broadband Engine Architecture (CBEA) achieved 3 the acceleration compared with the same Intel multicore CPU benchmark.

3   The Baseline Method in a Nutshell

The block diagram of the resulting algorithm is shown in Fig. 2.

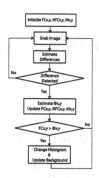

Fig. 2. Block diagram of the proposed algorithm.

The difference between background and foreground is computed to establish which pixels of the image would be updated. The difference vector Δ is calculated as follows:

$$\Delta = \left[\left| I_{x,y}^R - B_{x,y}^R \right|, \left| I_{x,y}^G - B_{x,y}^G \right|, \left| I_{x,y}^B - B_{x,y}^B \right| \right]^T$$

where (x, y) is the pixel position, I^c the intensity of the current image for the channel c, $c = (Red, Green, Blue)$, B^c the intensity of the background image and $\tau = [\tau^R, \tau^G, \tau^B]^T$ is a vector of thresholds used to detect changes in each channel.

For each image I^c, at each frame t, the color distribution for each pixel (x, y) is calculated using histogram analysis:

$$H(t+1, I^c) = \begin{cases} H(t, I^c) + 2 \cdot \delta \left[p(x, y) - I^c \right] & \text{if } \Delta \geq \tau \\ H(t, I^c) + \delta \left[p(x, y) - I^c \right] & \text{otherwise} \end{cases} \quad (1)$$

At each frame t, the numbers of Found Changes (FC) and Not Found Changes (NFC) are updated as shown in (2) and (3), where U is a parameter that have to be assigned in order to control the update rate of the background model. A typical value of U is equal to 100 frames.

$$FC_{x,y}(t+1) = \begin{cases} FC_{x,y}(t) + 1 & \text{if } \Delta \geq \tau \\ 0 & \text{if } \Delta \ngeq \tau \wedge NFC_{x,y}(t) = U \end{cases} \quad (2)$$

$$NFC_{x,y}(t+1) = \begin{cases} NFC_{x,y}(t) + 1 & \text{if } \Delta \not\geq \tau \\ 0 & otherwise \end{cases} \tag{3}$$

FC and NFC are used to trigger the background updating phase, which is performed if the number of Changes Found for the pixel (x, y) is greater than a given threshold. In the EHB algorithm, this threshold is constant for all the image, while in the proposed algorithm is computed for each pixel, as follows.

Introducing a weight $\alpha_{x,y}$ on the variability of the intensity of the pixel (x, y):

$$\alpha_{x,y} = \frac{1}{max(1, \sigma(x,y))} \cdot \left(1 - \frac{1}{\gamma} \frac{\sum_{i=1}^{T} M_{x,y}(i)}{T}\right), \tag{4}$$

where the fraction $\frac{1}{\gamma}$ is typically around $\frac{1}{3}$, and a weight $\beta_{x,y}$ on the number of changed pixels:

$$\beta_{x,y} = \frac{1}{\gamma} \cdot \left(\frac{\sum_{x,y} M_{x,y}}{\text{number of pixels in the image}} + 1\right), \tag{5}$$

we compute the threshold $\phi_{x,y}$ as

$$\phi_{x,y} = (\alpha_{x,y} - \beta_{x,y}) \cdot U \tag{6}$$

Equations (4) and (5) use the instantaneous change of pixel (x, y), represented by the binary matrix $M_{x,y}(t)$ computed as follows:

$$M_{x,y}(t) = \begin{cases} 1 & \text{if } \Delta \geq \tau \text{at time t} \\ 0 & otherwise \end{cases} \tag{7}$$

Thus, if $FC_{x,y} > \phi_{x,y}$ the pixel in the background is considered to be changed and hence its histogram model should to be updated. Moreover, if the model is changed, the background image should be reconstructed from the histogram model.

The matrix NFC is also used for another background maintenance problem. Over long acquisition time, if a pixel has small variations under the threshold ϕ, it can have changed its value. So, if NFC is greater than 100 times U, the background image is computed from the histograms model even for unchanged pixels.

This algorithm offers some improved features with respect to EHB. First of all, the algorithm is capable to adapt the background to the gradual changes of lights that happens at different hours and weather conditions during the day, as the histograms are continuously updated, and is capable to adapt single parts of the background image taking into account the different dynamics of the changes in different regions of the grabbed image. The proposed algorithm is also well suited to face the problem of sudden light changes, as when a light is turned on or when sun appears among the numbs, choosing accordingly the parameter U. Moreover, one can expect a reduced number of I/O operations due to the reduced updates of the background image. Some other features are in common to EHB, such as the absence of a training phase and the fact that it can work properly when the start grabbed image has foreground elements already present.

4   GPU-Based Implementation

GPU computing turns the massive floating-point computational power of a modern graphics accelerator's shader pipeline into general-purpose computing power. When utilizing a GPU there are several things that must be considered, as the internal structure of the GPU is completely different from the internal structure of CPUs (Fig. 3).

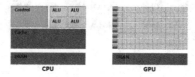

Fig. 3. Quick comparison between CPU and GPU.

First of all, the execution model of GPUs is really different from CPUs. GPUs employ massive parallelism and wide vector instructions, executing the same instruction for more elements at a time. Without designing algorithms that take this into consideration, the performance will be only a small fraction of what the hardware is capable of. Fig. 4 shows how a multithreaded program can easily adapt to different GPU structures.

Another thing to consider is that the GPU is on a separate circuit board, the graphic card, that is connected to the rest of the computer through a PCI express slot (as shown in Fig. 5), which implies that all data transfer between the CPU and the GPU is relatively slow. On the basis of this considerations, it is only through an accurate understanding of the architecture that we can develop and implement efficient algorithms.

5   Parallelization of the Proposed Histogram-Based Algorithm for Moving Object Segmentation

The proposed approach has been implemented on GPU: each acquired image is divided into 8x8 pixel blocks and for each block a thread pool of independent threads is instantiated.

A big amount of memory is required because, inside the GPU, for each concurrent thread several data structure have to be stored for each pixel, namely the three histograms H^c, M, FC and NFC. A schema of the data structure is represented in Fig. 6.

Each thread updates the model of a single pixel of the background. As the pixels are update by independent threads, this approach does not require inter-thread communication to synchronize the thread operations. A schematic representation of the overall parallelized algorithm is reported in Fig. 7.

6   Experimental Assessment and Analysis

The results described in this section have been computed on one core of an Intel Core 2 Quad Q9550 CPU running at 2.83 GHz and will be used to evaluate the

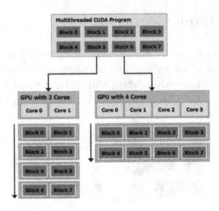

Fig. 4. Execution of parallel threads on different GPU architectures.

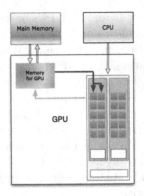

Fig. 5. Architecture of the system GPU and CPU.

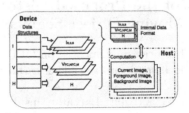

Fig. 6. Data structure used in the parallelized algorithm.

GPU speedup. We implemented on GPUs the proposed algorithm and the EHB algorithm. In the following, the performance in terms of computational time are presented. In Table 1 the time required for the computation on two different GPU architectures is reported: a single GPU board (NVIDIA GeForce 9800 GT with 512 MB) and a dual GPU board (GTX 295 with 1024 MB).

A typical measure used to evaluate the scalability of parallel algorithms is the speedup, defined as the ratio of the CPU time over the GPU time. In Fig. 8 the speed-up of the proposed algorithm is reported for different dimensions of

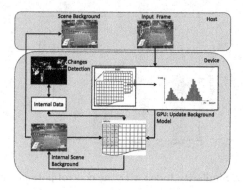

Fig. 7. Data management in the parallelized algorithm.

the image: the nominal resolution of the images on the camera used is 320x240 pixels, corresponding to 76800 pixels on the abscissa of Fig. 8. The GPU time is computed on an NVIDIA 9800 GTX.

Table 1. Computational time [ms] on different GPUs

Algorithm	GTX 9800 time [ms]	GTX 295 (single GPU) time [ms]	GTX 295 (dual) time [ms]
EHB	17	13.25	6.72
Proposed	13.6	9.65	4.90

In Fig. 9 we report the similarity of the proposed algorithm vs. the control parameter U (described in Sect. 3). As the frame rate increases, the image precision can reach a higher value, and more computational effort is required. This improvement is due to the fact that the background is updated more frequently and it can allow to observe fast event as quickly moving objects, fast changes and light variations. If the update frequency is too low, when an event occurs among two update time instants, it will not be recorded.

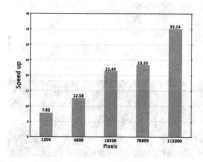

Fig. 8. Speed-up evaluated on a Nvidia 9800 GTX.

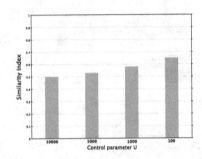

Fig. 9. Similarity Index over the control parameter U.

Fig. 10. Results using a simple average algorithm implemented on CPU.

Fig. 11. Results using the proposed algorithm implemented on GPU.

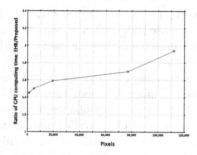

Fig. 12. Ratio of the GPU computing time between EHB and the proposed algorithm.

Finally, we evaluated the quality of the background model computed by GPU. This is in general difficult to perform as it would require ground truth background models. Hence, we compare the background model generated by GPU with the one generated by the CPU version, computing the average difference AD described in Eq. (8) as proposed in [22]:

$$AD = 2 \cdot abs \left(\frac{I_{GPU} - I_{CPU}}{I_{GPU} + I_{CPU}} \right) \tag{8}$$

The average difference AD, evaluated on the same 13000 frames on GPU and CPU, is 0.5 % and the variance is 0.5 %. Thus, we can conclude that GPU and CPU versions are providing the same results.

7   Concluding Remarks and Future Work

It is worth noting that the background can be estimated, as in Yu-Medioni [22], with a simple average of previous frames. This average approach is faster. However, its performance are very poor, as shown in Fig. 10.

Figure 10 shows, from the top, the same complex scenes reported in Fig. 1. From the top, we see the grabbed image, the reconstructed background in the middle, and, at the bottom, the difference image D obtained with the average approach used in Yu-Medioni [22]. It is clear that in the difference image D there are many ghosts which make impossible to determine the moving objects.

On the other hand, in Fig. 11 the same scenes are processed with the proposed algorithm implemented on the GPU. It is evident from Fig. 11 that the algorithm implemented on GPU gives the same results of the algorithm implemented on CPU, as reported in [4]. Moreover the algorithm leads to a much better results than the average approach used by Yu-Medioni because the reconstructed backgrounds are cleaner (middle panel) and the difference images (on the bottom) allow a much more precise determination of moving objects.

Finally, it is important to note that the proposed algorithm is well tailored to parallel implementation. In fact, Fig. 12 shows that on GPU the improved background quality of the proposed algorithm is obtained with low computational time. In Fig. 12 we report the ratio of the computation time between EHB and the proposed algorithm versus different image resolutions. For the considered image dimensions, the proposed algorithm scales very well as the number of pixels increases.

As the evolution of video camera technology provides more powerful devices, the resolution of the acquired image becomes higher and higher to provide better definition of details. In the video surveillance field, higher resolutions allow to zoom a region of an image without sacrifice spatial resolution. It is worth noting that the proposed algorithm is well suited for high resolution images, as it presents a linear speedup as the number of pixel increases. Moreover, the proposed algorithm can manage high frame rate in real-time, and it is suited for video tracking of rapidly moving objects.

At current state of the art, full HD videos can be managed in real-time using the current generation of GPU. The proposed parallel algorithm slightly depends on the particular GPU architecture adopted, so it might operate properly on future generation GPUs. Other interesting extensions of the overall framework concern with: (*i*) studying how *fragmentation techniques* (e.g., [2,7]) can be integrated as to improve the efficiency of our framework; (*ii*) moving towards the *Big-Data's philosophy* (e.g., [5,6,21]), as moving objects naturally generate big data sets; (*iii*) exploring *privacy-preservation issues* (e.g., [8–10]), which are now becoming more and more critical for image processing research (e.g., [12,17,19]).

References

1. •, Cuda c programming guide. http://developer.nvidia.com/cuda/nvidia-gpu-computing-documentation
2. Bonifati, A., Cuzzocrea, A.: Efficient fragmentation of large XML documents. In: Wagner, R., Revell, N., Pernul, G. (eds.) DEXA 2007. LNCS, vol. 4653, pp. 539–550. Springer, Heidelberg (2007)
3. Cucchiara, R., Grana, C., Piccardi, M., Prati, A.: Detecting moving objects, ghosts, and shadows in video streams. IEEE Trans. Pattern Anal. Mach. Intell. **25**(10), 1337–1342 (2003)
4. Cuzzocrea, A., Mumolo, E., Moro, A., Umeda, K.: Effective and efficient moving object segmentation via an innovative statistical approach. In: Proceedings of International Conference on Complex, Intelligent, and Software Intensive Systems (2015)
5. Cuzzocrea, A.: Analytics over big data: exploring the convergence of dataware-housing, OLAP and data-intensive cloud infrastructures. In: 37th Annual IEEE Computer Software and Applications Conference, COMPSAC 2013, Kyoto, Japan, July 22–26, 2013, pp. 481–483 (2013)
6. Cuzzocrea, A., Bellatreche, L., Song, I.-Y.: Data warehousing and OLAP over big data: current challenges and future research directions. In: Proceedings of the Sixteenth International Workshop on Data Warehousing and OLAP, DOLAP 2013, San Francisco, CA, USA, October 28, 2013, pp. 67–70 (2013)
7. Cuzzocrea, A., Darmont, J., Mahboubi, H.: Fragmenting very large XML data warehouses via k-means clustering algorithm. IJBIDM **4**(3/4), 301–328 (2009)

8. Cuzzocrea, A., Russo, V.: Privacy preserving OLAP and OLAP security. In: Encyclopedia of Data Warehousing and Mining, 2nd edn., vol. 4, pp. 1575–1581 (2009)
9. Cuzzocrea, A., Russo, V., Saccà, D.: A robust sampling-based framework for privacy preserving OLAP. In: Song, I.-Y., Eder, J., Nguyen, T.M. (eds.) DaWaK 2008. LNCS, vol. 5182, pp. 97–114. Springer, Heidelberg (2008)
10. Cuzzocrea, A., Saccà, D.: Balancing accuracy and privacy of OLAP aggregations on data cubes. Proceedings of the DOLAP 2010, ACM 13th International Workshop on Data Warehousing and OLAP, Toronto, Ontario, Canada, October 30, 2010, pp. 93–98 (2010)
11. Griesser, A., De Roeck, S., Neubeck, A., Van Gool, L.: Gpu-based foreground background segmentation using an extended colinearity criterion. In: Proceedings of Vision, Modeling and Visualization
12. Donghui, H., Bin, S., Zheng, S., Zhao, Z.-Q., Xintao, W., Xindong, W.: Security and privacy protocols for perceptual image hashing. IJSNet **17**(3), 146–162 (2015)
13. Cheng, L., Gong, M.: Real-time foreground segmentation on gpus using local online learning and global graph cut optimization. In: ICPR
14. Wolf, M., Poremba, M., Xie, Y.: Accelerating adaptive background subtraction with gpu and cbea architecture. In: Proceedings of the IEEE Workshop Signal Processing Systems
15. Ohmer, J.F., Perry, P.G., Redding, N.J.: Gpu-accelerated background generation algorithm with low latency. In: Proceedings of the Conference of the Australian Pattern Recognition Society on Digital Image Compression Techniques and Applications
16. Pham, V., Phong, V.D., Hung, V.T., Bac, L.H.: Gpu implementation of extended gaussian mixture model for background subtraction. In: Proceedings of the IEEE International Conference on Computing and Communication Technologies, Research, Innovation, and Vision for the Future
17. Squicciarini, A.C., Lin, D., Sundareswaran, S., Wede, J.: Privacy policy inference of user-uploaded images on content sharing sites. IEEE Trans. Knowl. Data Eng. **27**(1), 193–206 (2015)
18. Toyama, K., Krumm, J., Brumitt, B., Meyers, B.: Wallflower: principles and practice of background maintenance. In: The Proceedings of the Seventh IEEE International Conference on Computer Visio
19. Wang, C., Zhang, B., Ren, K., Roveda, J.: Privacy-assured outsourcing of image reconstruction service in cloud. IEEE Trans. Emerging Topics Comput. **1**(1), 166–177 (2013)
20. Medioni G., Qian, Y.: A gpu implementation of motion detection from a moving platform. In: CVPR
21. Yu, B., Cuzzocrea, A., Jeong, D.H., Maydebura, S.: On managing very large sensor-network data using bigtable. In: 12th IEEE/ACM International Symposium on Cluster, Cloud and Grid Computing, CCGrid 2012, Ottawa, Canada, May 13–16, 2012, pp. 918–922 (2012)
22. Qian, Yu., Medioni, G.: A gpu-based implementation of motion detection from a moving platform. In: IEEE Computer Society Conference on Computer Vision and Pattern Recognition Workshops, CVPRW 2008, pp. 1–6 (2008)

Advanced Networking

Hardware-Assisted IEEE 802.15.4 Transmissions and Why to Avoid Them

Andreas Weigel[✉] and Volker Turau

Institute of Telematics, Hamburg University of Technology, Hamburg, Germany
{andreas.weigel,turau}@tuhh.de

Abstract. 6LoWPAN's fragmentation mechanism enables transport of IPv6 datagrams with the required minimum MTU of 1280 bytes over IEEE 802.15.4-based networks. Testbed experiments showed disastrously bad datagram success rates for a collection traffic scenario with large, 6LoWPAN-fragmented datagrams, which significantly differed from the simulation results for a comparable scenario. In this paper we present an experimental setup that enables capturing the MAC and transceiver states of participating nodes in realtime. The results of our experiments show, that for the given fragmentation/collection scenario, the usage of the extended operating mode of the transceiver hardware, which provides CSMA/CA, ACKs and retransmissions in hardware, is responsible for nearly all datagram losses. Therefore, we strongly advise against using such hardware-assisted modes of operation in similar traffic scenarios.

Keywords: 6LoWPAN · 802.15.4 · Forwarding · Fragmentation · TX_ARET · Extended operating mode · Internet of things

1 Introduction

With the proposal of 6LoWPAN, RPL and CoAP [7, 8, 12], several efforts towards an IP-based standard protocol stack for low-power, lossy and wireless networks have been carried out in the recent years, creating a major building block for the vision of the Internet of Things. The physical and data link layers of these networks are usually realized according to the IEEE 802.15.4 standard [2]. Considering the small payload size of 127 bytes for 802.15.4 data frames, 6LoWPAN provides header compression and datagram fragmentation mechanisms to mitigate the otherwise large overheads caused by IP headers and to fulfill the minimum MTU demands of 1280 bytes of IPv6, respectively.

Many envisioned traffic scenarios for applications based on a 6LoWPAN stack mainly consider only small payloads which fit into single 802.15.4 data frames. Smart metering, on the other hand, is an example for applications which can necessitate much larger datagrams, e.g., to communicate detailed load profiles up to several kilobytes [10]. Another such example is structural health monitoring for buildings [3]. Therefore, we argue, that the transport of large 6LoWPAN-fragmented datagrams is relevant enough to justify an investigation of its performance.

© Springer International Publishing Switzerland 2015
G. Di Fatta et al. (Eds.): IDCS 2015, LNCS 9258, pp. 223–234, 2015.
DOI: 10.1007/978-3-319-23237-9_20

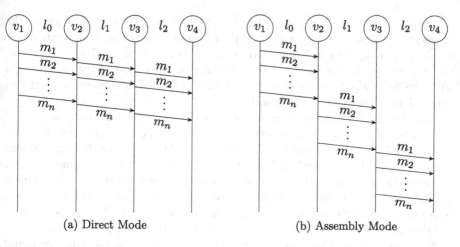

(a) Direct Mode   (b) Assembly Mode

Fig. 1. Sequence chart of messages sent in direct and assembly modes; l_k denotes the l-th link, m_i the i-th fragment

With 6LoWPAN, there are two possible approaches to the forwarding of fragments of a datagram:

- Reassembling the whole datagram at each hop (**Assembly** mode)
- Getting the next hop from the IP layer in a cross-layer fashion and directly forwarding each fragment without reassembling the datagram at intermediate hops (**Direct** mode)

The Direct mode can reduce the buffer space needed for datagrams in transit and potentially decreases the end-to-end delay on longer paths (see Fig. 1). Sticking to a completely standardized approach, we consider only these two route-over approaches in this paper and do not evaluate any mesh-under schemes.

The different forwarding techniques were evaluated by Ludovici et al. [4] and Weigel et al. [11] in simulations and testbeds for data collection scenarios in nonbeacon-enabled IEEE 802.15.4/6LoWPAN network. Both found that the average datagram success rate for the Assembly mode was higher than that of the Direct mode. The testbed used by Weigel et al. had up to six hops and consisted of 13 ATmega256RFR2 nodes. One striking observation was, that using the Direct mode, the average datagram success rate was extremely low, especially for nodes farther away from the data sink (approaching 0 %). The authors especially could not satisfyingly explain the significant differences of the success rates between testbed and simulation.

There are several reasons why a fragment transmission can fail even in the presence of retransmissions. Hidden nodes can cause collisions which cannot be completely prevented by the CSMA/CA mechanism of 802.15.4. Especially in the Direct mode, the transfer of multiple fragments directly one after the other creates potential for a large number of such collisions as illustrated in Fig. 1a. Those collisions, though, are also reflected in the presented simulation model. Effects that are not modeled in simulation, are interference by other networks in the 2.4 GHz band, i.e., 802.11 wireless LAN and changes in the physical environment (people moving, doors opening and closing) of the testbed, which may change the link quality over time and lead to frame losses. However, these effects would also have a strong influence on the results of the experiments with the Assembly forwarding mode, for which the results between testbed and simulation did not differ significantly.

Another, less obvious, significant difference between the simulation model and testbed was the use of the transceiver's extended operating mode in the testbed. This extended operating mode offers the two additional states RX_AACK and TX_ARET [1]. The former handles automatic frame filtering and transmission of acknowledgements while the latter executes the complete CSMA/CA mechanism plus necessary retransmissions in hardware. Apart from making the overall (software) implementation of the data link layer less complex, this feature potentially reduces the needed program and data memory[1], the use of peripherals (timer) and the load of the CPU. Additionally, the hardware processing is faster and thereby can slightly speed up the overall transmission process of a frame, e.g., by sending ACKs faster. Similar hardware support is offered by other transceivers as well, e.g., Microchip's MRF24XA [6]. Such hardware-supported operating modes, however, currently work by putting the radio hardware into a state, in which the transceiver is unable to receive any messages once the automatized transmission process (TX_ARET) has started.

We suspected this property of the extended operating mode to be mainly responsible for the observed differences in performance. In this paper, we present an experimental setup to observe the states of each wireless node during the transmission of a large fragmented datagram. We found that in IEEE 802.15.4 nonbeacon-enabled networks the hardware-supported operating mode strongly degraded the performance of data collection of large 6LoWPAN-fragmented datagrams over multiple hops. Section 2 introduces two different data link implementations and their corresponding state machines. Section 3 describes our testbed, and the results of the experiments are evaluated in Sect. 4. Section 5 concludes the paper.

2 Capturing Node State in Realtime

Three approaches can be applied to evaluate the extended operating modes' impact on the overall performance:

- An analytical approach, based on a model similar to the one proposed by Ludovici et al. [5], but extended to a multi-hop scenario.
- A simulative approach, using a model which captures the behavior of such an extended operating mode.
- An approach comparing two implementations in a testbed, with the possibility to capture the sequence of states of each node's MAC layer.

---

[1] Of the implementations described in Sect. 2, the AACK MAC is smaller than the Software MAC by 5280 bytes ROM and 578 bytes RAM.

We decided to adopt the third approach to be able to eliminate any inaccuracies and limitations of the other models. As representative for the extended operating mode, we use the MAC layer implementation for the ATmega256RFR2 that is included in CometOS[2] [9], a lightweight runtime environment for developing communication protocols for different hardware platforms and the OMNeT++ simulator[3]. We call this implementation "AACK MAC" in the remainder of the paper. As a reference, we ported the radio stack for the ATmega128RFA1 (which is nearly identical to the ATmega256RFR2) of TinyOS[4] to CometOS. We used the TinyOS radio stack because it is widely used and modularized. This layer implements the control of the transmission process comprising acknowledgements, retransmissions, backoffs and clear-channel assessment in software. We also created an alternative backoff layer, which implements the unslotted CSMA/CA of 802.15.4 and replaces the default TinyOS backoff mechanism. This implementation is referred to as Software MAC throughout the paper.

Keeping track of the accurate sequence of states of each node's MAC layer poses two major difficulties. First, the memory needed to store a large number of state changes is not available on the resource-constrained nodes which already contain a complete IPv6/6LoWPAN stack plus a parallel stack to control the execution of experiments. Secondly, time synchronization with the accuracy of some μs between nodes is necessary to accurately interpret state sequences locally. To achieve such a synchronization, additional frames on the wireless channel are necessary, interfering with the data frames of the experiment. For those reasons, we pursued a different approach and instrumented both MAC layer implementations to encode all relevant events as a 4 bit value and signal them to another microcontroller using plain GPIO ports.

We decided to directly output the present event instead of keeping track of the complete state machine within a node throughout the different layers of the radio stack. This was done in order to make the instrumentation of code as non-intrusive as possible. In consequence, only four CPU cycles (250 ns) are needed to update the value of the GPIO port to signal a new event.

We took two steps to arrive at a simplified state machine that contains all the relevant information about the MAC layer's state of each node. First, we identified the events and states necessary to unambiguously reconstruct the sequence of states from a sequence of events and created a detailed state machine for each of the two implementations (Figs. 2 and 3). Secondly, several states of the detailed versions were subsumed under a smaller subset of states relevant to the evaluation. Our goal is to especially recognize the occurrences and results of situations, in which a sender transmits, while the destination node is in a backoff phase.

For the Software MAC we therefore distinguish between "normal" RX states and those RX states, during which the transceiver is processing a transmission request as well (marked by a _TX_PD suffix in Fig. 2) and subsumed the latter under an RX_TX_PENDING state. Additional subsumed states for both

---

[2] http://www.ti5.tu-harburg.de/research/projects/cometos/.

[3] http://omnetpp.org.

[4] http://www.tinyos.net/.

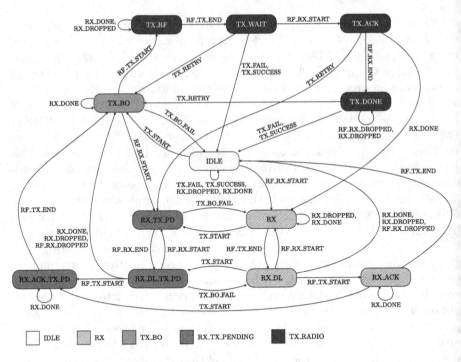

Fig. 2. State machine for software MAC

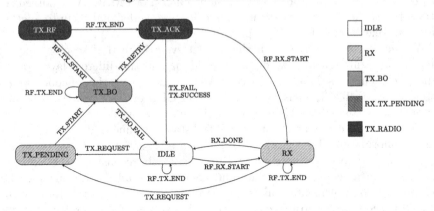

Fig. 3. State machine for AACK MAC and legend for aggregated states

implementations are IDLE, TX_BO (CSMA backoff), RX (receiving) and TX_RF (sending). Those are represented by different shades/patterns in Fig. 2. Note that for the AACK MAC there is no straightforward way to determine if a started reception has been successfully finished. This also includes the reception of frames not destined for this node – in both cases, there is only the absence of an interrupt. Therefore, nodes are often recorded to remain in an "RX" state after an unsuccessful or discarded (filtered) reception, instead of going back to IDLE.

3   Experimental Setup

The actual testbed consisted of four ATmega256RFR2 nodes (labelled 105, 10E, 10D and 10 F in Fig. 4) in a single large room, spaced about two to three meters from each other. Customized Cat5 patch cables were used to connect the transceiver's GPIO ports to 16 pins of PORT C of an ARM Cortex-M4 on Freescale's FRDM-K64F evalution board, as shown in Fig. 4. The Cortex-M4 executed a simple application with two chained timers, configured to yield a combined timer precision of $266\frac{2}{3}$ ns. This application sampled the state of the 16 input pins in a busy loop and stored every stable (constant for one tick of the timer) change of their value with the corresponding timestamp. The CPU ran at 120 MHz, which was fast enough to sample the input port several times per timer tick. The chosen timer precision, in turn, ensured that no event was missed[5]. Upon another GPIO signal, results were sent via UART to a PC and the memory was reset. This signal was generated by the actual base station controlling the traffic generator for the experiment and forwarded via TCP to a Raspberry Pi, which drove the pin.

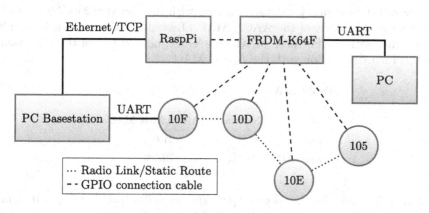

Fig. 4. Schematic diagram of experimental setup

The nodes used a static routing table to forward the IP datagrams. Only node 105 sent 20 datagrams of 1200 bytes payload to the PC base station. Thereby, additional cross-interference between fragments of datagrams originating at different nodes was eliminated from the experiment. The sending interval was fixed to 4 s, which is more than twice the maximal observed end-to-end delay for a datagram to arrive (or fail). The transmission power of the transceivers was set to the minimal value of −16.5dBm to realize multiple radio hops between the nodes. Other 802.15.4 MAC parameters were kept constant at values of the former experiments by Weigel et al. (Table 1). Nodes were configured to use the unslotted CSMA-CA mechanism.

Apart from the Direct mode, the former experiments also evaluated a so-called Direct-ARR mode, which dramatically improved the reliability for large

---

[5] The minimum duration between two events was observed to be larger than 4 μs.

Table 1. 802.15.4 MAC parameters for all configurations

minBe	maxBe	csmaBackoffs	maxFrameRetries	CCA mode	CCA threshold
5	8	5	7	0	-90 dBm

datagrams. It works by adding an adaptive delay after the transmission of each fragment at the 6LoWPAN layer. The delay is set to an average of three times the average transmission time to prevent self-induced collisions with formerly forwarded fragments. To gain insight into the influence of rate-restriction at the 6LoWPAN layer, for each MAC layer implementation we carried out experiments using the normal Direct forwarding mode and the Direct-ARR forwarding mode, resulting in four different configurations. All experiments were repeated 50 times.

4   Evaluation

4.1   Direct Mode

The overall success rate for datagrams sent with the Software MAC is dramatically better than that of the AACK MAC (Table 2). In comparison to a 97 % success rate with the Software MAC, on average, only 21.6 % of the datagrams reached their destination with the AACK MAC.

Table 2. Average success rate of datagrams

Mode	Software MAC	AACK MAC
Direct	97 %	21.6 %
Direct-ARR	99.6 %	79.5 %

The main reason for the observed performance is illustrated in Fig. 5. It shows the (aggregated) sequence of states all nodes pass through during a complete transmission of a datagram. As expected, during the transmission of the 18 fragments, a situation occurs in which the next receiver on the path (node 0x10E) enters the TX_ARET state for long enough, that the sending node unsuccessfully tries to send a frame to it – recall that during TX_ARET, the transceiver is not able to receive any frame. This pattern can be observed in slight variations for most of the datagrams in all runs for the AACK MAC in Direct mode.

The Software MAC's superior performance can be mainly attributed to the different behavior concerning the reception of frames while being in some TX state (Fig. 6). The occasions in which a node received frames while being in a back-off state for it's own transmission are marked as RX_TX_PENDING in the plot. It can be seen that allowing these receptions of frames does not lead to any losses of frames pending for transmission, but on the contrary significantly reduces the number of necessary retransmissions for the sending node.

Departing from individual datagrams to a more general view, the number of fragments in certain combinations of events at the sending node and state at

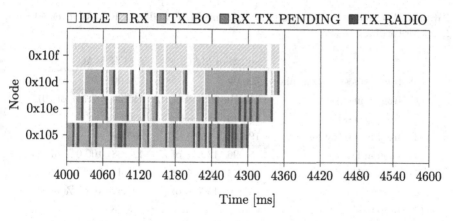

Fig. 5. Sequence of states; AACK MAC, direct mode, run 0, datagram 1

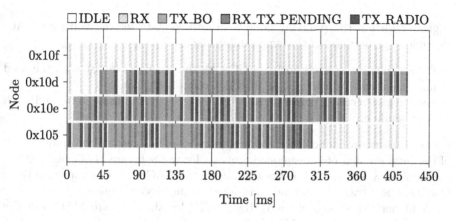

Fig. 6. Sequence of states; Software MAC, direct mode, run 0, datagram 0

the receiving node were extracted from the experiment data. Table 3 shows the summed up and averaged results for the first two nodes of the path (105, 10E).

Comparing these data, it can be observed that the number of total fragments sent (fragRequests) reaches only 57.7 % of the number of fragments needed for a complete transmission (fragRequests (max)) of the datagram, because often senders had to give up the transmission due to a completely failed transmission of a fragment. Furthermore, there is a difference in the relative and absolute number of retries and transmission failures caused by frames which were transmitted to a sender which was in some TX state (TX_BO or TX_RF), denoted as fragFailDstTx. For the AACK MAC, nearly all (99 %) failed frame transmissions are caused by such frames, compared to 77.8 % for the Software MAC. Also, for the Software MAC, the ratio of failed transmissions with receiver-TX and receiver-non-TX states (fragFailDstNonTx) against their respective totals (fragDstTxTotal, fragDstNonTxTotal) are not far apart from each other: 13.6 % vs. 10.6 %. This suggests that the probability of a successful transmission is only

Table 3. Average fragment counts of Software MAC and AACK MAC over 50 runs; direct forwarding mode

		Software MAC		AACK MAC	
(0)	fragRequests (theo. max)	720.00		720.00	
(1)	fragRequests	717.10	99.6 % of (0)	415.30	57.7 % of (0)
(2)	fragSuccessDstTx	518.48		0	
(3)	fragSuccessDstNonTx	198.38		398.76	
(4)	fragFailDstTx	81.96	13.6 % of (7)	423.08	100.0 % of (7)
(5)	fragFailDstNonTx	23.44	10.6 % of (8)	4.44	1.1 % of (8)
(6)	fragFailTotal	105.40	14.7 % of (1)	427.52	102.9 % of (1)
(7)	fragDstTxTotal	600.44		423.08	
(8)	fragDstNonTxTotal	221.82		403.20	

slightly higher if the receiving node is in an idle state for the Software MAC. Possible explanations for this small difference are:

- A Transmission started during a CCA by the receiver are lost with the used implementation (during CCA, SHR detection is disabled).
- Sender and receiver perform their CCA at nearly the same time and both start sending.

Much more pronounced is the overall number of failures, which is only 14.7 % of the total number of transmission requests for the Software MAC, but 102.9 % for the AACK MAC. This means that, using the AACK MAC, on average there is about one retransmission for every initial transmission request.

A higher percentage of fragFailDstNonTx for the Software MAC over the AACK MAC (10.6 % vs 1.1 % of all fragments with the receiver in a non-TX state) is observable. A possible explanation can be found in the fact that, with the Software MAC, on average more fragments reach the nodes farther down the path and thereby increase the number of collisions due the hidden terminal problem, which is not captured by selected metrics.

4.2 Direct-ARR

Using adaptive rate restriction increases the average datagram success rate of the Software MAC slightly, that of the AACK MAC greatly (Table 2).

Figures 7 and 8 show the sequences of states with AACK MAC and Direct-ARR mode for a successful and an unsuccessful datagram transmission, respectively. Figure 7 illustrates how the additional delay of the Direct-ARR mode mitigates the risk of deaf receivers. However, due to the inherent random nature of the length of backoffs in 802.15.4 and random failures on the wireless channel, the delay mechanism does not completely prevent situations, in which again the sender tries to get its fragment to a receiver in TX_ARET state, as shown in Fig. 8.

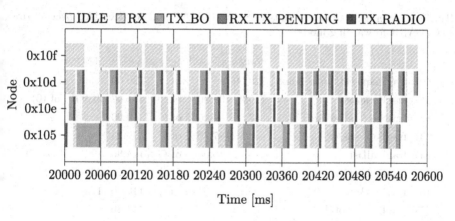

Fig. 7. Sequence of states; AACK MAC, Direct-ARR mode, run 0, datagram 5

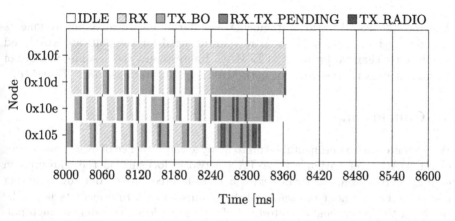

Fig. 8. Sequence of states; AACK MAC, Direct-ARR mode, run 0, datagram 2

Observing the results of 50 runs, we find that the by far dominating cause for losses and retransmissions for the AACK MAC are again those fragments, which where lost due to the sender being in TX_ARET state (Table 4). As for the Direct mode, the number of transmission failures caused by a receiver-TX state is two orders of magnitude larger than that of transmission failures with a receiver-non-TX state.

However, the relative (in comparison to the number of fragments transmissions requested in total) and absolute number of transmission failures is greatly reduced by the Direct-ARR mode, from 427.52 (102.9 %) to 116.5 (17.6 %). Considering the simple traffic scenario with a single sender and only four hops, the performance of the AACK MAC can still be regarded as disastrous, especially compared with the 99.9 % achieved by the Software MAC.

Most clearly, the effect of the rate restriction is shown by rows (7) and (8) of Table 4. Apart from preventing hidden-terminal collisions, it also reduces the number of occasions during which senders transmit toward a receiver in TX state.

Table 4. Average fragment counts of Software MAC and AACK MAC over 50 runs; Direct-ARR forwarding mode

		Software MAC		AACK MAC	
(0)	fragRequests (theo. max)	720.00		720.00	
(1)	fragRequests	719.92	99.99 % of (0)	661.62	91.90 % of (0)
(2)	fragSuccessDstTx	87.80	12.20 % of (1)	0.00	
(3)	fragSuccessDstNonTx	632.10	87.80 % of (1)	657.28	
(4)	fragFailDstTx	16.72	16.00 % of (7)	114.80	100.00 % of (7)
(5)	fragFailDstNonTx	42.44	6.30 % of (8)	1.70	0.26 % of (8)
(6)	fragFailTotal	59.16	8.20 % of (1)	116.50	17.60 % of (1)
(7)	fragDstTxTotal	104.52		114.80	
(8)	fragDstNonTxTotal	674.54		658.98	

Thereby, the overall ratio of fragments sent during receiver-TX and fragments sent during receiver-non-TX is more than inverted for the Software MAC and significantly changed for the AACK MAC. Interestingly, the absolute number of fragments is nearly the same for both MAC implementations (rows (7) and (8)).

5   Conclusion

We presented an experimental setup to analyze the sequence of events and states of the MAC layer within a 6LoWPAN network, focusing on the transmission of fragmented large datagrams with a cross-layered direct route-over routing approach, i.e., without reassembling datagrams on each intermediate hop. The results of the experiments in a testbed of four nodes forming a simple line topology have shown, that the extended operating mode of the hardware transceiver is responsible for the bad performance and the observed difference to the results from simulation. Additional mechanisms like rate restriction can significantly improve the performance by preventing situations in which packet losses typically occur, but an implementation using the extended operating mode is still not competitive.

Although only a small testbed was evaluated, it is obvious that the degradation of performance can not be less severe in larger networks and/or networks with a larger diameter. Application scenarios that involve consecutive transmissions of multiple frames along the same route employing an unslotted CSMA/CA mechanism therefore should avoid using hardware-assisted transmissions in their current state.

References

1. Atmel Corporation: 8-bit AVR Microcontroller with Low Power 2.4GHz Transceiver for ZigBee and IEEE 802.15.4: ATmega256RFR2, September 2014, rev. C

2. Institute of Electrical and Electronics Engineering: IEEE 802.15.4-2011 - IEEE Standard for Local and Metropolitan Area Networks– Part 15.4: Low-Rate Wireless Personal Area Networks (2011)
3. Kim, S., Fonseca, R., Dutta, P., Tavakoli, A., Culler, D., Levis, P., Shenker, S., Stoica, I.: Flush: a reliable bulk transport protocol for multihop wireless networks. In: Proceedings of the 5th International Conference on Embedded Networked Sensor Systems, pp. 351–365, SenSys2007 (2007)
4. Ludovici, A., Calveras, A., Casademont, J.: Forwarding techniques for IP fragmented packets in a real 6LoWPAN network. Sensors 11(1), 992–1008 (2011)
5. Ludovici, A., Marco, P.D., Calveras, A., Johansson, K.H.: Analytical model of large data transactions in coap networks. Sensors 14(8), 15610–15638 (2014)
6. Microchip Technology Inc.: Low-Power, 2.4 GHz ISM-Band IEEE 802.15.4 RF Transceiver with Extended Proprietary Features: MRF24XA, April 2015, rev. C
7. Montenegro, G., Kushalnagar, N., Hui, J., Culler, D.: Transmission of IPv6 Packets over IEEE 802.15.4 Networks. RFC 4944, September 2007. http://www.rfc-editor. org/rfc/pdfrfc/rfc4944.txt.pdf
8. Shelby, Z., Hartke, K., Bormann, C.: The Constrained Application Protocol (CoAP). RFC 7252, June 2014. http://www.ietf.org/rfc/rfc7252.txt
9. Unterschütz, S., Weigel, A., Turau, V.: Cross-platform protocol development based on OMNeT++. In: Proceedings of the 5th International ICST Conference on Simulation Tools and Techniques, SIMUTOOLS 2012, pp. 278–282, March 2012
10. Weigel, A., Renner, C., Turau, V., Ernst, H.: Wireless sensor networks for smart metering. In: 2014 IEEE International Energy Conference and Exhibition (ENERGYCON), May 2014
11. Weigel, A., Ringwelski, M., Turau, V., Timm-Giel, A.: Route-over forwarding techniques in a 6lowpan. EAI Endorsed Trans. Mob. Commun. Appl. 14(5) (2014)
12. Winter, T., Thubert, P., Brandt, A., Hui, J., Kelsey, R., Levis, P., Pister, K., Struik, R., Vasseur, J.P., Alexander, R.: RPL: IPv6 Routing Protocol for Low-Power and Lossy Networks. RFC 6550, March 2012. http://www.ietf.org/rfc/rfc6550.txt

Containment of Fast Scanning Computer Network Worms

Muhammad Aminu Ahmad[✉] and Steve Woodhead

Faculty of Engineering and Science, University of Greenwich, Greenwich, UK
{m.ahmad,s.r.woodhead}@gre.ac.uk

Abstract. This paper presents a mechanism for detecting and containing fast scanning computer network worms. The countermeasure mechanism, termed NEDAC, uses a behavioural detection technique that observes the absence of DNS resolution in newly initiated outgoing connections. Upon detection of abnormal behaviour by a host, based on the absence of DNS resolution, the detection system then invokes a data link containment system to block traffic from the host. The concept has been demonstrated using a developed prototype and tested in a virtualised network environment. An empirical analysis of network worm propagation has been conducted based on the characteristics of reported contemporary vulnerabilities to test the capabilities of the countermeasure mechanism. The results show that the developed mechanism is sensitive in detecting and blocking fast scanning worm infection at an early stage.

Keywords: Worm detection · Malware · Cyber defence · Network security

1 Introduction

Malicious software (malware) [1] is a generic term for any software that enters a computer system without the authorisation of the user to perform unwanted actions. Such software is a significant risk to the security of computer systems, with those connected to the Internet being at particular risk. Self-propagating malware (termed a worm) is a particular class of software which is rare, but particularly dangerous, because of its highly virulent nature. Fast scanning computer network worms are a particularly dangerous sub-class of such software.

The Internet has experienced a number of notable worm outbreaks (e.g. Slammer, Code Red and Witty [2]) that caused disruption of services and significant financial losses to government, transportation and other institutions [3]. However, the number of computer network worm outbreaks reduced significantly until the return of similar characteristics in the Stuxnet [4] outbreak that targeted industrial control systems in order to cause damage [5], which led to the release of other variants such as Duqu , Flame and Gauss for cyber espionage [4]. Vulnerabilities that can be exploited by a worm continue to be published by system vendors including the Microsoft RDP vulnerability (CVE-2012-0002) of

© Springer International Publishing Switzerland 2015
G. Di Fatta et al. (Eds.): IDCS 2015, LNCS 9258, pp. 235–247, 2015.
DOI: 10.1007/978-3-319-23237-9_21

2012, and the ShellShock (CVE-2014-6271) and Drupal (CVE-2014-3704) vulnerabilities of 2014. The present threat of such an event therefore remains clear.

Previously reported research work used behavioural detection and suppression techniques at the host [6], local network and network perimeter [7] levels to counter the propagation of fast scanning computer network worms. However, there are limitations and shortcomings in the reported techniques. These limitations and shortcomings involve ineffectiveness in detecting worms, resource consumption, delay in deployment and detection, management overhead and computational complexity, and in most cases the techniques only slow, rather than stop worm infections [2,8]. The previously reported research work can be categorized into signature-based and anomaly-based detection systems. The signature-based detection system maintains a database of signatures for previously known attacks and raises an alarm if a datagram in the network matches a signature in the database. Anomaly-based detection systems examine network traffic in order to build a profile of the normal behaviour and then raise an alarm for events that deviate from the normal profile. In contrast to signature-based systems, anomaly-based systems can detect new attacks. Anomaly-based detection systems look for deviations from the normal profile, based on the datagram-header information, payload information or both [9]. Datagram-header based anomaly detection systems use datagram header information to detect worm propagation. The focus of this paper is to develop an anomaly-based detection scheme using datagram-header information.

This paper presents a mechanism that uses two approaches for detecting and containing fast scanning computer network worms (abbreviated as fast scanning worms hereafter), which we have termed NEDAC (NEtwork and DAta link layer Countermeasure). NEDAC uses detection and containment techniques to defend against fast scanning worm attacks, which operate at the network level and data link level respectively. The detection part of the mechanism observes DNS activities to detect absence of DNS lookup in newly initiated outgoing connections. The containment part of the mechanism blocks outgoing traffic from a host that has been identified as infected, using data link access control.

The remainder of the paper is presented as follows. Section 2 presents related work on worm detection and containment systems. Section 3 presents an overview of wormable vulnerabilities. Section 4 presents the description of the developed countermeasure mechanism. Section 5 presents the experimental evaluation of the reported mechanism using a developed prototype. Section 6 concludes the paper and discusses possible future work.

2   Related Work

Significant research efforts have been devoted to the development of anomaly-based network intrusion detection systems, which have led to the existence of numerous approaches [8]. A number of these approaches [9] use datagram header information to identify the presence of computer network worms. Among these approaches are those that monitor source and destination IP addresses of datagrams, such as the work reported by Williamson [6]. Williamson [6] proposed a detection and suppression technique that uses the source and destination IP addresses of the host making a request to detect an attack. Whenever a request is made, the approach checks the newness of the host making the request by comparing the destination of the request to a short list of recently made connections. If the host is new it is then delayed, otherwise it will be processed as normal. However, many fast scanning worms (TCP-based) initiate connection requests to randomly-generated IP addresses, which results in a number of failed connections [2]. As a result, in addition to monitoring source and destination IP addresses, some approaches use the status of connection requests to detect worm behaviour such as the work of Jung et al. [10], Weaver et al. [11] and Rasheed et. al [12]. This technique uses the count of successful and failed connection attempts to determine the presence of worm scanning.

Furthermore, some detection approaches such as those reported by Gu et. al [13] and Mahoney and Chan [14] monitor source and destination ports and the Ethernet header fields. The work of Gu et al. [13] uses source and destination IP addresses and source and destination ports to detect fast scanning worms. This algorithm termed Destination Source Correlation (DSC), correlates incoming and outgoing traffic and keeps track of SYN datagrams and UDP traffic of the source and destination. Thus, if a host received a datagram on port i, and then starts sending datagrams destined for port i, it becomes a suspect. Then if the immediate outgoing scan rate for the suspect host deviates from a normal profile, the host is considered to be infected. Mahoney and Chan [14] developed the Packet Header Anomaly Detection (PHAD) technique, which learns the normal ranges of values for each datagram header field at the data link (Ethernet), network (IP), and transport/control layers (TCP, UDP, ICMP). PHAD uses the probability of rate anomalies in detection mode, based on the rate of anomalies observed during the training phase; the rarer the detected anomalies, the more likely they are to be hostile.

Another detection approach is to use DNS activities of hosts to detect worm propagation. Whyte et al. [7] and Shahzad and Woodhead [15] used DNS-based rate limiting to suppress fast scanning worms in an enterprise network. The observation was scanning worms often use numeric IP addresses instead of the qualified domain name of a system, which eliminates the need for a DNS query. In contrast, the vast majority of legitimate publicly available services are accessed through the use of DNS protocol; the network service that maps numeric IP addresses to corresponding alphanumeric names. Therefore the main idea behind this technique is that the absence of DNS resolution before a new connection is considered anomalous. This notion was first proposed by Ganger et al. [16], and if is implemented properly, it will impose severe limitations on worm traffic. This forces scanning worms to either probe DNS namespace or issue a DNS query for each IP address, which significantly reduces the speed of worm propagation [17]. The mechanism presented in this paper builds on the DNS-based detection scheme.

3   Wormable Vulnerability

According to Tidy et. al [5], a vulnerability is said to be wormable if it is network reachable, provides remote code execution, provides network access, and does not require human interaction once exploited.

Individual vulnerabilities can be researched through a number of online sources that provide details of identified vulnerabilities such as the Common Vulnerabilities and Exposures (CVE) system [18]. The CVE system focuses on providing details for a range of vulnerabilities and keeps notes of whether a vulnerability is network reachable or requires human interaction if exploited. Additionally, Symantec Connect [19] provides working exploits for some vulnerabilities. These details provide the necessary information for assessing the wormability of many vulnerabilities. Some of the reported contemporary wormable vulnerabilities include Microsoft RDP (CVE-2012-0002) of 2012 and ShellShock (CVE-2014-6271) of 2014 [18].

4   Worm Countermeasure System

The proposed detection and containment mechanism uses DNS-based anomalies to detect the propagation of fast scanning worms in enterprise networks. Many fast scanning worms generate pseudo-random IPv4 addresses directly, without undertaking a DNS query. This behaviour obviates the need for DNS lookup, which is abnormal for the vast majority of legitimate publicly available services and is therefore a tell tale sign of scanning worm propagation [16]. Using a classification developed by Whyte et al. [7], the main focus of this paper is to detect worm propagation where the infection source is from local to remote and local to local using a detection system working at the network layer and a containment system working at the data link layer.

The NEDAC mechanism consists of two main sub-systems that work together to provide a countermeasure solution. The first system is the network layer detection system and the second system is the data link layer containment system, with a connection maintained between the two components to enable continuous data transmission. The detection system keeps track of all outgoing new TCP SYN and UDP datagrams by correlating them with a DNS resolution cache to determine the absence of DNS lookup. When a datagram is transmitted to a destination address without prior DNS lookup, the source IP address is maintained in a cache and its corresponding counter is incremented. The counter is incremented subsequently for every distinct datagram sent by a host without a prior DNS lookup. A threshold value, v, is set in order to assign a maximum number of distinct IP addresses a host can attempt to contact without a prior DNS lookup per time duration, t. Upon reaching the value, v, the detection system will mark the behaviour as worm propagation and therefore invokes the countermeasure by sending the MAC address of the source host to the containment system. The data link containment system listens on a TCP port for incoming connection from the detection system in order to block outgoing traffic from an infected host. Upon the receipt of a host MAC address from the detection system, the containment system will generate an access control update to block all datagrams originating from the specified host.

The design of the NEDAC mechanism is presented in Fig. 1. Figure 1a shows the flow diagram of the network layer detection system and Fig. 1b shows the flow diagram of the containment system.

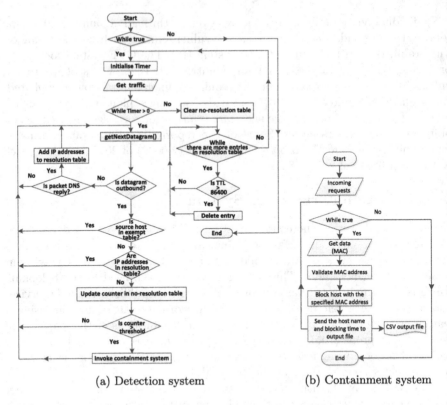

(a) Detection system   (b) Containment system

Fig. 1. Flow diagram of the NEDAC mechanism

The detection system initialises a timer and then monitors TCP SYN and UDP datagrams. The detection system uses two caches, namely the resolution table and no-resolution table. Upon encountering a DNS response datagram, the algorithm records the host that made the DNS resolution and the resolved address in the resolution table. For outbound datagrams, the algorithm determines whether the source host is white-listed by checking the exempt table. The exempt table elements are a combination of IP addresses and port numbers that are exempt from the detection algorithm for known systems that legitimately communicate using IP addresses directly. If there is a miss, the algorithm determines whether there is a recent DNS query prior to sending the datagram by checking the resolution table. If there is a miss, the algorithm then increments the host's counter in the no-resolution table and determines whether the entry exceeds a threshold. Upon exceeding a threshold, the system invokes the countermeasure solution by sending the source host MAC address to the containment system. After the expiration of the predefined timer, the system clears the entries in the no-resolution table, and then checks the resolution table in order to remove entries with expired TTL values.

The containment system receives MAC address of an infected host from the detection system and then blocks all traffic originating from the host. Finally, the system logs the host details and timestamp.

The NEDAC mechanism has been implemented as a software prototype using the C programming language. The C language provides low level programming support for network traffic using open source libraries such as *libpcap* [20] and *pjproject* [21], which facilitate traffic analysis.

5 Evaluation

This section presents an evaluation of the NEDAC mechanism. Firstly, analytical results of the number of susceptible hosts for the candidate contemporary vulnerabilities were presented. Then a description of the methodology used to evaluate NEDAC using developed worm outbreak scenarios was also presented. Finally, the section details the parameters used for the worm outbreak scenarios and the experimental results obtained.

The experiments reported in this paper use the Microsoft RDP (CVE-2012-0002) and ShellShock (CVE-2014-6271) contemporary vulnerabilities to develop potential worm outbreak scenarios for the evaluation of the NEDAC prototype. An initial challenge for the work was determining the values of the susceptible populations for these vulnerabilities. As a result, the CAIDA Internet Topology Data Kit (ITDK) [22] was used as a sample to determine the susceptible population values. The CAIDA ITDK includes passive traffic trace files for two Equinix backbones based in Chicago and San Jose in an anonymised format. Two trace files were collected from each centre. The four trace files, dated 20/03/2014, comprised approximately 47.85 million datagrams across a one minute period. The trace files were analysed and divided into two separate files containing datagrams originating from Windows hosts and from Linux hosts based on the reported IP header TTL of the datagram using Wireshark and Tshark [23]. The filters used to determine whether a datagram originated from a Windows or Linux host are "ip.ttl>64 && ip.ttl<129" and "ip.ttl<65" respectively.

Microsoft RDP protocol and mod_cgi are the main infection vectors for the Microsoft RDP and ShellShock vulnerabilities respectively. The mod_cgi is required by the popular host management tools Parallel Plesk and cPanel for certain modules, and so if it is possible to estimate the total number of hosts with these tools installed, this could act as a lower bound value for the number of Linux hosts with the module that could be susceptible to ShellShock. Such an estimate was developed by filtering datagrams with a destination TCP port equal to the management interface ports of the Plesk (8834) and cPanel (2083, 2082), compared to overall Linux hosts. However, RDP datagrams were filtered using TCP/UDP port 3389, compared to overall Windows hosts. The filtration of the datagrams was achieved using "tshark -r <.pcap> -T fields -e ip.dst | sort | uniq | wc -l", where the "sort", "uniq" and "wc -l" commands provide a count of the unique IP addresses that offer a particular service. The analysis further extrapolated the figures to determine a representative value of the entire IPv4 address space using $S_p = r * m * u_{ip}$, where S_p is the susceptible population, r is the ratio determined for each vulnerability from the dataset, m is the market share [24] of the target operating system, and u_{ip} is the routable IP address space; $3,673,309,759$ [25]. The market shares of Windows-based hosts and Linux-based hosts are 75% and 5.4% respectively of connected hosts on the Internet [24], therefore the average susceptible population values of RDP and Plesk/cPanel were estimated as 16.48 million and $42,533$ respectively.

To estimate the worm datagram sizes for experimentation, proof of concept exploits were collected from Symantec vulnerability database [19] for the Microsoft RDP and ShellShock vulnerabilities. The result of this estimation process was datagram sizes of 3.8 kb and 2 kb for RDP and ShellShock vulnerabilities respectively. These were used to configure the reported worm propagation experiments.

5.1   Experimental Methodology

The NEDAC prototype was deployed and tested in a virtualised network environment. The virtualised network environment comprises two personal computers with Intel Core i7 (12 virtual cores at 3.20 GHz) processor, 64 GB of RAM and 2 TB of hard disk storage capacity. The computers use VMware ESXi 5.5 [26] server to provide virtualization services, which enable the development of virtual networks on each computer in order to form a virtualised enterprise network. VMware ESXi has been chosen due to its strong performance in terms of the utilization of CPU, memory, disk I/O and network I/O [27]. The developed virtualised enterprise network of each computer comprises LANs with a DHCP server for IP address management, a DNS server for name resolution, an NTP server to provide a time synchronization service for the virtual hosts, a logging server to keep a record of worm infection activities and routers for internal routing services. Both internal and external routers have been implemented using the Quagga routing suite [28]. The detection system was installed on the gateway of each virtualised LAN and the containment system on the virtual switches of the virtual enterprise networks. Figure 2 depicts the logical and physical architecture of the virtualised environment.

Worm propagation behaviour was experimented using a worm daemon [29] that has been developed with the capabilities of facilitating a worm attack event using chosen worm characteristics. The worm daemon system consists of both client and server modules capable of sending and receiving UDP datagrams. The client module is used to initiate a worm attack against the desired targets. Virtual hosts are made susceptible by running the server module, which listens on a specific UDP port and then, after receiving an "infection" datagram, continuously transmits "infectious" UDP datagrams. Upon infection, a susceptible host will send its time stamp and IP address information to the logging server for record management. The logging server has been configured with a logging daemon that keeps the details of infected host addresses and infection time. This process will continue until full infection is achieved based on the details recorded on the logging server. Finally, the experiment used Damn Small Linux (DSL) [30] as the operating system for the virtual machines. Furthermore, initiating a worm outbreak experiment involves creating the required number of virtual machines by cloning a base virtual machine that has been configured with the correct worm

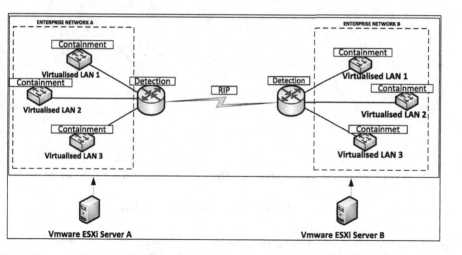

Fig. 2. Virtual environment for countermeasure testing

daemon. The virtual machines will then be powered to automatically synchronize their time with the NTP server, and then wait for inbound datagrams. The worm infection event is then initiated by sending a UDP datagram to one of the susceptible virtual machines in one of the virtualised LANs. A UDP-based worm has been chosen due to its higher rate of propagation compared to a TCP-based counterpart. UDP-based worms require no acknowledgement and cannot be detected by mechanisms that rely on number or state of failed connection attempts.

5.2 Experimental Parameters

The average susceptible population of hosts for each of the two candidate contemporary vulnerabilities and the size of routable IPv4 address space $(3,673,309,759$ [25]) were used to determine the number of susceptible hosts per million Internet hosts for each vulnerability using $P_m = \left[\left(\frac{S_p}{R_{ip}}\right) * 1,000,000\right]$, where, P_m denotes the value of susceptible hosts per million Internet hosts, S_p denotes the absolute number of hosts susceptible to the vulnerability and R_{ip} denotes the number of routable IPv4 addresses. The results were 4454 and 12 susceptible hosts per million for the RDP and ShellShock vulnerabilities respectively.

Another input value required by the worm daemon is the scan rate of the worm. The scan rate for each of the contemporary worm candidates has been determined using $\beta = \frac{U_{ip}}{S_p}$, where β denotes the scan rate. The resulting scan rates were 223 and 86364 "infectious" datagrams per second for RDP-based and ShellShock-based worms respectively.

5.3 RDP-Based Worm Behaviour

The RDP-based worm experiment was conducted using 4454 susceptible hosts per million in a single class B size network, and therefore contained

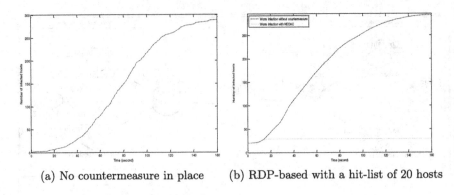

(a) No countermeasure in place   (b) RDP-based with a hit-list of 20 hosts

Fig. 3. RDP-based worm propagation behaviour

$\left[2^{16} * \left(\frac{4454}{1000000}\right)\right] = 292$ susceptible hosts. The daemon was configured to listen on UDP port 3389 and then transmits UDP datagrams to port 3389 at a scan rate of 80 "infectious" datagrams per second, once "infected" using random seed. The scan rate was scaled down to 35% of the calculated value in order to avoid overloading server resources.

Five RDP-based worm experiments were conducted using one initially infected host without any countermeasure in place. Figure 3a shows the average result of the five experiments. The RDP-based experiment was repeated with NEDAC mechanism in place using a range of threshold values of 10, 20, 50, 100, 200, 400, 500 and 800 distinct IP addresses contacted without prior DNS lookup. NEDAC was configured to invoke the containment system if a threshold is exceeded within time duration of 10 s. The worm infection was detected and contained by the NEDAC mechanism with no further infection across the entire range of NEDAC experiments conducted.

The RDP-based worm experiment was also conducted with a hit-list [31] of 10 and 20 hosts in order to further evaluate the capability of the NEDAC mechanism. The hit-list behaviour was tested using threshold value of 800 and a time duration of 10 s. The worm propagation was also detected and contained with zero and nine further infections for the hit-list of 10 and 20 hosts respectively. Figure 3b shows the results of worm propagation using a hit-list of 20 hosts with and without the NEDAC mechanism.

5.4   ShellShock-Based Worm Behaviour

The ShellShock-based worm experiment was conducted using 12 susceptible hosts per million in a single class A size network, and therefore contained $\left[2^{24} * \left(\frac{12}{1000000}\right)\right] = 203$ susceptible hosts. The daemon was configured to listen on UDP port 8080 and then transmits UDP datagrams to port 8080 at a scan rate of 86 "infectious" datagrams per second, once "infected" using random seed. The scan rate was scaled down by a factor of 1000 $\left(\frac{86,364}{1,000}\right) = 86$ in order to avoid overloading server resources.

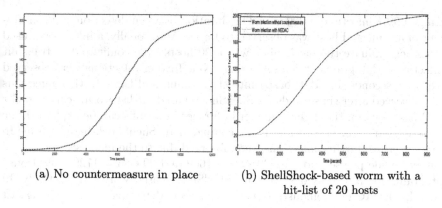

(a) No countermeasure in place   (b) ShellShock-based worm with a
                                         hit-list of 20 hosts

Fig. 4. ShellShock-based worm propagation behaviour

As with the RDP experiments, five ShellShock-based worm experiments were conducted using one initially infected host without any countermeasure in place. Figure 4a shows the average result of the five experiments. The ShellShock-based experiment was repeated with NEDAC mechanism in place using a range of threshold values of 10,20, 50, 100, 200, 400, 500, 800 and 860 distinct IP addresses contacted without prior DNS lookup. The worm infection was detected and contained by the NEDAC mechanism with no further infection across the entire range of NEDAC experiments conducted.

The ShellShock-based worm infection experiment was repeated with a hit-list [31] of 10 and 20 hosts in order to further evaluate the capability of the NEDAC mechanism. The hit-list behaviour was tested using a threshold value of 860 and a time duration of 10 s. The worm propagation was detected and contained with zero and three further infections for the hit-list of 10 and 20 hosts respectively. Figure 4b shows the results of worm propagation using a hit-list of 20 hosts with and without the NEDAC mechanism.

5 Conclusion and Future Work

This paper has presented a mechanism, which comprises a DNS-based anomaly detection system and a data link layer containment system to counter the propagation of worms. The empirical results of the experiments conducted showed that the mechanism can detect and completely contain fast scanning worm including hit-list worm propagation scenario. This is due to the containment techniques employed in the data link layer that isolates a given infected host from the network and therefore ends the worm propagation.

The experimental results for the RDP-based worm experiment without a countermeasure show attainment of 99% infection in 2 min. Thus using 224 scans per second for the RDP-based worm, the susceptible population of 294 hosts in a class B network could be infected in $\left[160\ sec * \left(\frac{35}{100}\right)\right] = 56$ s. However, despite the low population of susceptible hosts for the ShellShock-based worm compared to the RDP-based worm, the experimental results for ShellShock-based worm attained 99% infection in 200 min. The duration between detection and containment of an infected host was observed to be 1 s. Additionally, a hit-list was used to further evaluate the mechanism where 20 hosts were configured to transmit "infectious" datagrams at the same time. Nine further infections were observed after four seconds for RDP-based hit-list scanning and three further infections were observed after six seconds for ShellShock-based hit-list worm scanning. For RDP-based worm, the higher number of further infections can be explained due to large number of susceptible hosts compared to ShellShock-based worm. In both scenarios, further infections were observed due to the increased number of contacts made per second, i.e., $20 * 80 = 1600$ and $20 * 86 = 1720$ "infectious" datagrams for RDP-based worm and ShellShock-based worms respectively. In general, NEDAC has demonstrated effectiveness in detecting and containing fast scanning worms at early stage.

Furthermore, the speed of Internet connection available for an infected host and the worm datagram size determine how fast a worm can send datagrams. The Internet connection speed was estimated to be within the range10 Mbps to 1000 Mbps [32]. Using the Internet connection speed and a worm datagram size, the time T, required for a single worm instance, with size M (in bytes), to send datagram to a single IP address over a C megabits Internet connection can be determined using $T = \frac{M}{C} * 8$. Using 10Mbps Internet connection speed as a lower bound, the times required to transmit single datagram by RDP-based and ShelShock-based worms are 3 and 2 ms respectively. Using 1000Mbps as an upper bound, the times required are 0.03 and 0.02 ms for RDP-based and ShellSock-based worms respectively. Therefore the RDP-based worm can transmit 333 datagrams and 33, 333 datagrams using 10 Mbps and 1000 Mbps connections speeds per second respectively. Similarly, the ShellShock-based worm can transmit 500 datagrams and 50, 000 datagrams using 10 Mbps and 1000 Mbps connections speeds per second respectively. Thus, with these scan rates, NEDAC can detect and contain these contemporary worms in one second depending on the threshold value used, because a reasonable threshold value should not exceed 300 scans per second.

As future work, we plan to optimise the mechanism, particularly the detection scheme. It is believed that proper implementation of the DNS-based detection scheme will impose severe restriction on scanning worms. The mechanism will further be evaluated using a range of diverse worm scanning techniques such as stealthy scanning, local-preference scanning, topological scanning and evasive scanning. The effect of background traffic will also be tested to further evaluate the effectiveness of the mechanism and determine false alarms. The complexity of the detection system will be evaluated and then a comparative evaluation of the overall mechanism will be conducted.

References

1. Niemelä, J., Palomäki, P.: Malware detection and application monitoring, November 2013

2. Li, P., Salour, M., Su, X.: A survey of internet worm detection and containment. IEEE Commun. Surv. Tutorials **10**(1), 20–35 (2008)
3. Fosnock, C.: Computer worms: past, present, and future, August 2005
4. Bencsáth, B., Pék, G., Buttyán, L., Félegyházi, M.: The cousins of stuxnet: Duqu, flame, and gauss. Fut. Int. **4**(4), 971–1003 (2012)
5. Tidy, L.J., Shahzad, K., Muhammad, A., Woodhead, S.: An assessment of the contemporary threat posed by network worm malware. In: The Ninth Internation Conference on Systems and Networks Communications (ICSNC 2014), October 2014
6. Williamson, M.M.: Throttling viruses: restricting propagation to defeat malicious mobile code. In: Proceedings of the 8th Annual IEEE Computer Security Applications Conference, pp. 61–68 (2002)
7. Whyte, D., Kranakis, E., Van Oorschot, P.C.: Dns-based detection of scanning worms in an enterprise network. In: NDSS, February 2005
8. Jyothsna, V., Prasad, V.R., Prasad, K.M.: A review of anomaly based intrusion detection systems. Int. J. Comput. Appl. (0975–8887), **28**(7), 26–35 (2011)
9. Cheema, F.M., Akram, A., Iqbal, Z.: Comparative evaluation of header vs. payload based network anomaly detectors. In: Proceedings of the World Congress on Engineering, vol. 1, pp. 1–5, July 2009
10. Jung, J., Paxson, V., Berger, A.W., Balakrishnan, H.: Fast portscan detection using sequential hypothesis testing. In: Proceedings of the 2004 IEEE Symposium on Security and Privacy, pp. 211–225. IEEE (2004)
11. Weaver, N., Staniford, S., Paxson, V.: Very fast containment of scanning worms. In: Proceedings of the 13th USENIX Security Symposium (2004)
12. Rasheed, M.M., Norwawi, N.M., Ghazali, O., Kadhum, M.M.: Intelligent failure connection algorithm for detecting internet worms. Int. J. Comput. Sci. Netw. Secur. (IJCSNS) **9**(5), 280 (2009)
13. Gu, G., Sharif, M., Qin, X., Dagon, D., Lee, W., Riley, G.: Worm detection, early warning and response based on local victim information. In: 20th Annual IEEE Computer Security Applications Conference, pp. 136–145 (2004)
14. Mahoney, M., Chan, P.K.: Phad: Packet header anomaly detection for identifying hostile network traffic. Technical report, Florida Institute of Technology technical report CS200104 (2001)
15. Shahzad, K., Woodhead, S.: Towards automated distributed containment of zeroday network worms. In: 2014 International Conference on Computing, Communication and Networking Technologies (ICCCNT), pp. 1–7. IEEE (2014)
16. Ganger, G.R., Economou, G., Bielski, S.M.: Self securing network interfaces: What, why and how? Technical report, Carnegie Mellon Univ Pittsburgh Pa School of Computer Science (2002)
17. Wong, C., Bielski, S., Studer, A., Wang, C.-X.: Empirical analysis of rate limiting mechanisms. In: Valdes, A., Zamboni, D. (eds.) RAID 2005. LNCS, vol. 3858, pp. 22–42. Springer, Heidelberg (2006)
18. CVE. Common Vulnerabilities and Exposures (2014). https://cve.mitre.org/. Accessed on 19 October 2014
19. S. Connect. Vulnerabilities. http://www.securityfocus.com/. Accessed on 12 November 2014
20. Garcia, L.M.: Programming with libpcap sniffing the network from our own application. In: Hakin9-Computer Security Magazine, pp. 2–2008 (2008)
21. PJPROJECT LIBRARY. http://www.pjsip.org/
22. CAIDA, The Internet Topology Data Kit. http://www.caida.org/data/passive. Accessed on 11 November 2014

23. Combs, G.: Tshark-the wireshark network analyser. http://www.wireshark.org
24. W3schools os statistics. http://www.w3schools.com. Accessed on 12 November 2014
25. Cotton, M., Vegoda, L.: Special use ipv4 addresses. Technical report, BCP 153, RFC 5735, January 2010
26. Lowe, S.: Mastering VMware vSphere 5. Wiley (2011)
27. Hwang, J., Zeng, S., Wood, T.: A component based performance comparison of four hypervisors. In: 2013 IFIP/IEEE International Symposium on Integrated Network Management (IM 2013), pp. 269–276, May 2013
28. Ishiguro, K., Takada, T., Ohara, Y., Zinin, A.D., Natapov, G., Mizutani, A.: Quagga routing suite (2007)
29. Shahzad, K., Woodhead, S.: A pseudo-worm daemon (pwd) for empirical analysis of zero-day network worms and countermeasure testing. In: 2014 International Conference on Computing, Communication and Networking Technologies (ICCCNT), pp. 1–6. IEEE (2014)
30. Damn Small Linux. http://www.damnsmalllinux.org/. Accessed 19 October 2014
31. Staniford, S., Vern, P., Nicholas, W.: How to own the internet in your spare time. In: USENIX Security Symposium, pp. 149–167, August 2002
32. Net Index. http://www.netindex.com/. Accessed 16 November 2014

Fragmented-Iterated Bloom Filters for Routing in Distributed Event-Based Sensor Networks

Cristina Muñoz[✉] and Pierre Leone[✉]

Computer Science Department, University of Geneva, Carouge, Switzerland
{Cristina.Munoz,Pierre.Leone}@unige.ch

Abstract. In this research, we propose the construction of a new architecture of Fragmented–Iterated Bloom Filters (FIBFs) to redirect complex events in a distributed event-based sensor network. We introduce two novel structures of Bloom Filters (BFs): Fragmented BFs (FBFs) and Iterated BFs (IBFs). The aim of IBFs is to discard single events that do not match any subscription. Then, FBFs deal with conjunctive and disjunctive set of events. Whether a match is found at the FBFs the publication is forwarded. Our strategy is theoretically and practically compared to the use of Standard BFs. The results show that FBFs lead to save memory and computational resources at the membership test. Moreover, we show that there is no memory cost for dividing a BF in smaller BFs using the same: (1) number of elements to insert and (2) probability of false positives. Then, we prove that FBFs may use fast hash functions that present a complexity of $O\left(\log_2\left(x\right)\right)$ while Standard BFs use hashes with a complexity of $O\left(\left(\log_2\left(y\right)\right)^2\right)$. The hash output is represented by $x, y \in \mathbb{N}$ so that $x < y$. Additionally, it is shown that the use of the double hashing technique does not improve the computational complexity. Finally, we show that the construction of a structure of IBFs using an Iterated Hash Function (IHF) reduce the complexity because smaller filters and less hash functions are required.

Keywords: Distributed event-based system · Bloom filter · Sensor network · Iterated hash function

1 Introduction

The dissemination of sensing data requires the use of different sources and destinations. Typically, in an ubiquitous sensing scenario some nodes provide data and other nodes use these data as actuators. Then, a distributed event-based system may be used to exchange information. In such a system, publishers and subscribers do not have any information about each other. They depend on the event notification service to match publications with subscriptions. In distributed networks, this service is implemented using a network of brokers nodes. A broker node is any node in the network that has information about any single or set of subscriptions. Publishers must contact a broker node to route events. Similarly, subscribers rely on broker nodes to save subscriptions. The selection of

© Springer International Publishing Switzerland 2015
G. Di Fatta et al. (Eds.): IDCS 2015, LNCS 9258, pp. 248–261, 2015.
DOI: 10.1007/978-3-319-23237-9_22

broker nodes requires the use of an overlay layer on the top of the network layer. Distributed Hash Tables (DHT) [3] construct the overlay layer mapping a key to a particular node with storage location properties. Other techniques select broker nodes that isolate a part of the network as cluster heads [2]. Furthermore, brokers can be selected on a tree or a set of independent trees [11]. All these techniques need a network protocol to provide point-to-point communication on the network layer. Recently, it has been proposed [9] to merge the network and the overlay layers of distributed event-based systems so that no other network protocol is needed. The advantage of this strategy is that it is no necessary to maintain the network topology. The main consequence is that nodes, which do not actively participate in the system, do not keep any information about topology. This leads to save energy and computing resources in those devices. Paths between publishers, subscribers and brokers are well-defined using an efficient variation of random walks.

In this paper, we propose to implement a new architecture of Bloom Filters (BFs) at broker nodes of [9]. Each broker node implements Fragmented–Iterated Bloom Filters (FIBFs) at each interface of communication. FIBFs save effectively a set of subscriptions that use conjunctive and disjunctive operations. When a publication arrives to a certain interface, the corresponding FIBFs are checked to decide if it has to be forwarded or not. A publication will be forwarded if there are any subscribers behind that interface, which are waiting for that specific type of events. It is out of the scope of this paper to specify the distance–vector routing protocol for updating brokers.

The dispatching algorithm proposed at individual brokers works in two steps: first, a Validation Table (VT) is used to discard individual events that do not match any subscription. Second, a Routing Table (RT) for each outgoing interface is used to match event conjunctions against subscriptions. The VT reduces the number of combinations to produce conjunctions.

Our system is focused on the use of constrained devices as sensor motes. Nevertheless, the system could be used on other type of networks that require limited devices or to optimize the use of available resources. Our approach is compared theoretically and practically, using three different wireless sensor motes, with the use of Standard BFs. The results show that complexity and memory are reduced.

The rest of this paper is organized as follows: Sect. 2 details the research problem. Section 3 points out related work. Section 4 describes the design of FIBFs. Section 5 analyzes theoretically and practically the performance of our design. Finally, Sect. 6 summarizes our proposal.

2 Problem Statement

We present a system based on [9], which uses a distributed notification service composed of several broker nodes. With the aim to fragment the load and exploit locality in the event delivery process, broker nodes are located at intersections of Directional Random Walks forming local networks. Their main objective is to efficiently save sets of subscriptions corresponding to the subscribers that can be reached through them. Each interface of a broker implements an independent structure of FIBFs. This implies that at each interface a different set of subscriptions is saved using and efficacious data structure.

An example of a possible scenario is shown at Fig. 1. Six local networks are connected using broker nodes. We observe, that there exist as many interfaces at a broker as networks directly connected to it. Broker 1 (B1), is the only broker which connects three different networks. It must be remarked that there exists no possible link between networks already connected to the system. So that it is not possible to have a fifth broker (B5) in our system to connect networks 1 (N1) and 5 (N5). Figure 1 shows the set of subscriptions that should be saved at each interface. We observe that a broker should be able to reach all networks using all its interfaces.

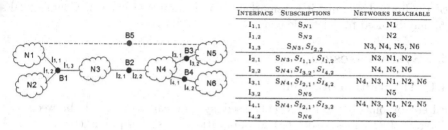

Interface	Subscriptions	Networks reachable
$I_{1,1}$	S_{N1}	N1
$I_{1,2}$	S_{N2}	N2
$I_{1,3}$	$S_{N3}, S_{I_{2,2}}$	N3, N4, N5, N6
$I_{2,1}$	$S_{N3}, S_{I_{1,1}}, S_{I_{1,2}}$	N3, N1, N2
$I_{2,2}$	$S_{N4}, S_{I_{3,2}}, S_{I_{4,2}}$	N4, N5, N6
$I_{3,1}$	$S_{N4}, S_{I_{2,1}}, S_{I_{4,2}}$	N4, N3, N1, N2, N6
$I_{3,2}$	S_{N5}	N5
$I_{4,1}$	$S_{N4}, S_{I_{2,1}}, S_{I_{3,2}}$	N4, N3, N1, N2, N5
$I_{4,2}$	S_{N6}	N6

Fig. 1. Example of a possible scenario.

The complexity of the research problem is increased when defining subscriptions. In our system we accept a set of conjunctions and disjunctions as predicates of subscriptions. In this paper each predicate is identified as an object of a JSON file (see Sect. 4.1). A possible subscription may be defined as follows:

$$(object1) \lor (object2 \land object3) \lor (object4)$$

In our design every single object corresponding to a subscription is saved in the VT. Then, conjunctions of objects are saved separately at the RT.

A publication is composed of different objects. When receiving a certain publication through an interface a broker node checks the publication at the rest of interfaces using the appropriate structure of FIBFs. At an interface each object of the publication is checked at the VT. If an object is not located inside the VT it is discarded. Objects which pass the VT test are combined between them to form conjunctions. If any conjunction is found at the RT the publication is forwarded through that interface.

3 Related Work

Bloom filters [12] have been widely studied, mainly because they effectively group information. A few event-based systems use BFs. In Lipsin [7] events use BFs to save link identifiers instead of saving subscriptions. The weakest point of this solution is that the topology of the network must be previously discovered in order to build a tree matching publications with subscriptions. In [6] BFs are used to discover the identification of specific subscribers. The main drawback of this approach is that combinations of predicates need to be saved separately and using a certain branch of the tree. Furthermore, we do not route publications but we finally get the ID of subscribers, so that we need other protocol in order to route the publication. The use of attenuated BFs has been proposed [13] in order to attract events in a network. Nevertheless, the model works with a certain probability, so that it is not guaranteed that a publisher matches all subscribers. Content-based information can also use Hierarchical BFs [14] to self-organize information. Hierarchies are established using geographic data and BFs save information of each partition at a cluster head device. This strategy is mostly focused on the network model and the discussion about the implementation of BFs is limited. Finally, it is remarkable to mention that efficient Counting BFs [5] may be used to delete elements.

4   System Design

4.1   Description of Events

Filters of our distributed event-based system can distinguish between two different JSON files associated to publications or subscriptions (see Fig. 2). A publication or a subscription is defined by a set of different objects or arrays of objects. An object, which represents a certain membership or event, can be considered as a tree of different pairs of name/value called strings. In our examples we can distinguish objects because they begin and end with braces: {...}. Arrays of objects begin and end with brackets: [...].

Moreover, there are two different cases to take into account for subscriptions: we consider ANDs (conjunctions) of objects and ORs (disjunctions). Figure 2b, shows an example in which conjunctions and disjunctions are used.

First of all, two different sub–subscriptions are taken into account: (1) *Sub–Subscription 1* considers the conjunction of certain values for *sensor* and *location*, (2) *Sub–Subscription 2* considers only a certain value for *sensor*, composed of two strings. The final subscriber expects to receive events from: (1) sensors at windows measuring light located at lab1 in the hall of building A in the university campus OR (2) events from sensors detecting presence at doors.

4.2   Overview of the Dispatching Algorithm

Firstly, we design a Validation Table (VT) using the properties of Iterated Hash Functions (IHFs) [1]. The VT is used to discard single objects (events) in a publication that do not match with any subscription saved. Afterwards, the Routing Table (RT), which is efficiently constructed using Fragmented BFs (FBFs), is used to check the appropriate conjunctions associated to a publication.

```
{
  "PUBLICATION":{

    "sensor":[
      {
        "place":"window",                      {
        "type":"light",                          "SUB-SUBSCRIPTION1":{
        "value":"0"
      },                                            "sensor":{
                                                      "place":"window",
      {                                               "type":"light",
        "place":"door",                               "value":"0"
        "type":"presence",                          },
        "value":"35"
      },                                            "location":{
                                                      "zone": "university",
      {                                               "building":"A",
        "type":"accelerometer",                       "floor":"hall",
        "value":"2"                                   "specificpath":"lab1"
      }                                             }
    ],                                            },

    "actuator":{                                "SUB-SUBSCRIPTION2":{
      "place":"window",
      "type":"presence",                          "sensor":{
      "value":"true"                                "place": "door",
    },                                              "type": "presence"
                                                  }
    "location":{                                }
      "zone": "university",
      "building":"A",                         }
      "floor":"hall",
      "specificpath":"lab1"
    }
  }
}
```

| a) Publication | b) Subscription |

Fig. 2. JSON files.

4.3   Validation Table: Iterated BFs (IBFs)

All objects related to subscriptions are saved in the VT separately and iteratively. In Sect. 4.1 we pointed out that each object is composed of different strings. We consider that the final hash of an object is the output of the Iterated Hash Function (IHF) of all strings. Besides this, the VT is used to check for single objects corresponding to a publication. This step is used to discard objects that must not be checked on the RT.

Design of the Validation Table. Let s be a string member of the set S of strings that are part of an object. $|S|$ denotes the total number of strings for a certain object. Each $s \in S$ is iteratively hashed until arriving to the last string of the object. The VT is composed of a set of Standard BFs classified by levels. In the first level the hash of the first string of the object is saved. In the second level, the iterative hash of the second string with the previous one is saved and so on. If $k_{opt} \geq 3$, where k_{opt} denotes the optimum number of hash functions, then two different IHFs will be used for the first two hashes. Afterwards, the double hashing technique [8] may be used to speed up the process.

We can save computational resources as shown in Sect. 5.1. The methodology consists on fragmenting each filter assigned to a level in several filters that group objects of the same nature.

Example of a Subscription. Figure 3 shows the construction of the VT for the subscription described at Fig. 2b. The different strings of each object are iteratively hashed and saved at the corresponding position of the Iterated BFs (IBFs). For example, the object of type *sensor* formed by three strings: *window/light/0* is hashed string by string. The other two objects corresponding to the subscription are also iteratively hashed and saved. The VT can be simple or fragmented. A Simple VT is composed by one filter per level (see Fig. 3a). As previously mentioned, we improve the efficiency of our system by using fragmented VTs (see Fig. 3b). In this case, we implement one filter per type of object at each level (*sensor, location*).

Example of a Publication. When a publication is received all objects are checked on the VT. In our example at Fig. 2a we have a total of five objects to check. The objects of type *sensor*: *window/light/0* and *door/presence/35* and the object of type *location*: *university/A/hall/lab1* pass the test. For simplification, we have excluded the management of values. In these cases, a pointer from the last iterative hash to a memory position will be used to save the range of values accepted by subscribers.

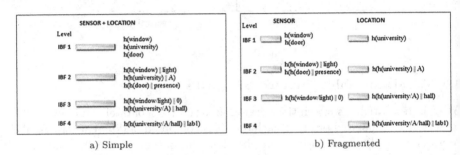

a) Simple   b) Fragmented

Fig. 3. Validation table for the subscription of Fig. 2.

4.4   Routing Table: Fragmented BFs (FBFs)

The purpose of the RT is to efficiently save conjunctions associated to the objects of subscriptions. Besides this, publications check the RT to find a match with subscribers and forward the object or event.

Design of the Routing Table. The RT is divided in levels. Each level is related to the way in which subscriptions are saved. Level 1 groups together filters which save objects of a certain type in a single way. This means that subscriptions are grouped using disjunctions. The following levels are related to the way that conjunctions of different type of objects are grouped. e.g. Level 2 groups different combinations of the conjunction of two objects of different types, etc. In Sect. 5.1 we study different ways to fragment filters at each level. The exact FBFs to check are known because they are identified depending on the type of objects they save (i.e. sensor, location, ...).

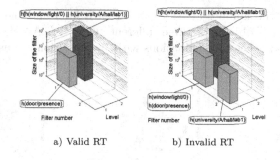

a) Valid RT   b) Invalid RT

Fig. 4. Routing table for the subscription of Fig. 2.

Example of a Subscription. Following our example of Fig. 2b, the three objects of the subscription must be saved in the RT. The subscription is divided in two sub-subscriptions: in the first one an object of type *sensor* must be combined, using a conjunction, with an object of type *location*. This means that both events must be assured to redirect the publication. For this reason, we do not have individually the final output of the hash of both objects but the conjunction of them at a level 2 BF. The second sub-subscription contains only one object or event to be assured so that the final hash of the object is saved individually at a filter of level 1. Figure 4a shows the resulting RT. We also illustrate that a RT that contains all individual hashes, as shown in Fig. 4b, is not valid for this example.

Example of a Publication. The matching operation that takes place when a publication is received only considers the three objects that already passed the validation test. Afterwards, the available filters that compose the RT are checked. In our example there is no filter to check for type of objects *location* (no filter at position 2 of level 1), so that the individual hash of this type of objects that passed the validation test are also discarded for the membership test. Finally, we check for the matching of: $h(door/presence)$ and $h(h(window/light/0) \| h(university/A/hall/lab1))$. The membership test starts at level 1 and if no matching is found the subsequent levels are checked. In this example, a match is found at level 1 for the value of $h(door/presence)$ so that the membership test results positive without further checking and the publication is forwarded.

5 Evaluation

5.1 Theoretical Evaluation of Fragmented BFs

In order to discuss the performance of FBFs we consider different distributions of the overall memory. This implies that we use a different number of BFs of different sizes depending on the distribution used. Moreover, it must be taken into account that we also divide the FBFs in groups depending on the level. Each set of objects of the same type is represented using a letter (A, B or C).

Figure 5 details the number of BFs used at each level and the different sizes for combinations of objects of three different types (i.e. A-sensor, B-location, C-actuator). From level 2, combinations without repetition are used.

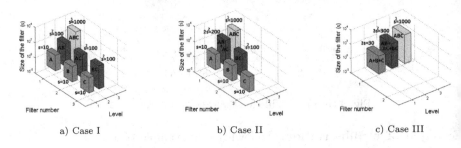

a) Case I   b) Case II   c) Case III

Fig. 5. Routing table for 3 type of objects.

Three different distributions are proposed:

- *Case I:* The overall memory is uniformly fragmented at each level. Figure 5a shows how sizes and combinations of type of objects are distributed.
- *Case II:* Filters referred by this distribution fragment uniformly the overall memory at the first level, taking into account sets of objects of the same type. In the following levels the size of BFs changes depending on the number of combinations of different type of objects contained. In the example shown at Fig. 5b, the biggest filter of level 2 contains all possible combinations of objects of type A with objects of type B and C. The rest of BFs of this level discard all possible combinations with A. In this case, as we only have three different type of objects, the second BF of level 2 contains the combination of B and C. If we had more type of objects we would discard A and also B, for the combinations of the following BFs.
- *Case III:* It corresponds to the use of Standard BFs (see Fig. 5c). Memory is divided depending on combinations and there is one filter per level.

The number of filters used increases exponentially for case I. The number of filters for cases II and III increases constantly. Case III uses less filters but their size is the biggest. Case I uses more filters per level of a smaller size.

Evaluation of the Publication Membership Test. We intend to show that by fragmenting BFs, memory and resources used for checking elements inside the RT can be saved. For this purpose, we are going to use an example in which a group of events are classified in six different types: $G = \{A, B, C, D, E, F\}$.

Subscriptions received are related to types of object A and the combination of objects of type $\{A, D\}$, $\{B, E\}$, $\{B, C, D\}$, $\{B, E, F\}$, $\{B, C, E, F\}$ and $\{A, B, C, D, E, F\}$. This implies that not all possible BFs per level are used. Figure 6 compares full RTs with the resultant RT of our example. For case I 7 BFs and a total of 1.012.210 memory positions are used. Case II and case III use 6 and 5 BFs but the overall memory positions used are larger, 1.046.910 and

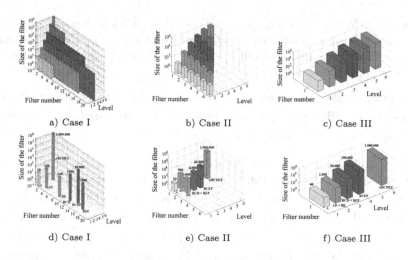

Fig. 6. Routing table for 6 type of objects: (a, b, c) Full (d, e, f) Not full.

.171.560 respectively. In case that the combination $\{A, B, C, D, E, F\}$ would
be outside the set of subscriptions, the difference would be higher. Moreover,
as mentioned at Sect. 4.4, before checking a certain level of the RT we discard
making combinations with validated objects when there is no BF in the appropriate position saving computational resources.

Memory Cost for Fragmenting a BF. We intend to show that memory
requirements do not change when using different distribution of BFs, which
occupy the same positions in memory. So then, for saving the same number of
elements the same number of memory positions are needed in Case I, II and III.

Theorem 1. *Given a k_{opt}, optimum number of hash functions, we state that to
insert n elements we select to our convenience the total number of BFs to use by
distributing the n elements, maintaining the same probability of false positives f
and the same overall m bit memory positions in use.*

Proof. It is well-known [12] that given a k_{opt}, optimum number of hash functions,
we can fix the number m of memory positions for a given n number of elements
and a certain f probability of false positives: $m = -\frac{n \ln f}{(\ln 2)^2}$. Then $m \propto n$, so that
we can state that for inserting n elements we can use a big filter of m positions
or a certain f; or we can use different filters of different m' positions for the
same f, where each $m' < m$, by appropriately distributing between the smaller
filters the total n elements to insert.

e.g. For inserting 400 elements with $f = 0.0073$ using a $k_{opt} = 7$ we could use:
one filter of 4096 bits or sixteen filters of 256 bits and a capacity for 25 elements.

Improvement on Computational Complexity. In this research, we have
studied the performance of our system using two different hash functions:

Fowler–Noll–Vo hash functions (FNV) [4] and Pearson hash functions [10]. Moreover, we demonstrate that complexity is reduced when using smaller bit length outputs. This means that filters of Case I are the best in terms of computational complexity and filters of Case III are the worst.

Lemma 1. *A filter which uses FNV hash functions presents a complexity of* $O\left((\log_2(y))^2\right)$. *Where y represents the hash output in $\mathbb{N}$ and $\log_2(y)$ is the bit length of the hash code that may correspond to 32, 64, 128, 256, 512 or 1024.*

Proof. A multiplication of order $\log_2(y)$ is done at the beginning of the FNV hash function. By applying the rule of product to the multiplication we get that the computational complexity for this operation is $O\left((\log_2(y))^2\right)$. After this, the result is XORed with an octet. The computational complexity for this operation is $O\left(max\left(\log_2(y),(\log_2(y))^2\right)\right) = O\left((\log_2(y))^2\right)$. The iterative process results in k iterations which yields a final algorithm complexity of $O\left((\log_2(y))^2\right)$.

Lemma 2. *A filter which uses Pearson hash functions presents a complexity of $O(\log_2(x))$. Where x represents the hash output in $\mathbb{N}$ and $\log_2(x)$ is the bit length of the hash code that corresponds to 8.*

Proof. An XOR is computed at the beginning of the Pearson hash function. The computational complexity for this operation is $O(\log_2(x))$. After this, the result is rotated with the use of a pre-established table. The computational complexity for this operation is $O(max(\log_2(x),1) = O(\log_2(x))$. The iterative process results in k iterations which yields a final algorithm complexity of $O(\log_2(x))$.

Theorem 2. *The computational complexity needed for inserting elements in a BF of p_1 positions is smaller than for a BF of p_2 positions if $p_1 < p_2$.*

Proof. Using Lemma 1 we can state that the smaller the hash output the smaller complexity presents a FNV hash function. Moreover, when comparing FNV hash functions with a simpler hash function as the Pearson, we can state using Lemmas 1 and 2 that simpler hash functions reduce the complexity because they use smaller bit lengths and because more complex operations are avoided.

Lemma 3. *The double hashing technique presents a complexity of* $O\left((\log_2(n))^2\right)$. *Where n represents the hash output in $\mathbb{N}$ of h_1 and h_2 and $\log_2(n)$ is the bit length of the hash code.*

Proof. The double hashing technique [8] uses three operations. First of all, the multiplication of i and h_2 is done. Afterwards, the result is added to h_1. Finally, a modular operation of order n is implemented. Clearly, this last operation limits the upper bound of the double hashing technique. Then, the computational complexity is $O\left((\log_2(n))^2\right)$.

Theorem 3. *The upper bound of a FNV hash function and the double hashing technique coincide when using the same bit length for the hash code.*

Proof. Lemmas 1 and 3 show that the upper bounds of a FNV hash function and the double hashing technique coincide.

5.2   Practical Evaluation of Fragmented BFs

For measuring the performance of our solution we have selected three different type of motes that use the low power consumption IEEE802.15.4 standard at 2.4 GHz: Advancticsys XM1000, Zolertia Z1 and Crossbow TelosB. The microprocessors of XM1000 and Z1 offer similar performance whereas the microprocessor of TelosB shows more limitations in terms of frequency and flash storage. All motes have been programmed in C using the Contiki version 2.6 OS.

Table 1. Execution time for inserting one subscription on a standard BF and a FBF.

	PEARSON HASH		FNV 32 HASH		FNV 64 HASH	
	16 FBFs		1 Standard BF		1 Standard BF	
CONFIGURATION						
Array per bits (m/n)	256/25	256/25	4096/400	4096/400	4096/400	4096/400
Overall n° of subscriptions	400	400	400	400	400	400
Probability of false positives (f)	0.0073	0.0073	0.0073	0.0073	0.0073	0.0073
N° of hash functions (k_{opt})	7	7	7	7	7	7
Double Hashing (DH)	No	Yes	No	Yes	No	Yes
N° of hashes implemented	7	2+5DH	7	2+5DH	4	1+6DH
EXECUTION TIME (μs)						
Advancticsys XM1000	0	0	7812	7812	31250	31250
Zolertia Z1	0	0	15625	15625	31250	31250
Crossbow TelosB	0	0	23437	23437	78120	78120

The execution time shown at Table 1 is provided in μs. We observe that in all cases TelosB motes are slower. This is due to the fact that they are equipped with more limited microprocessors. Besides this, XM1000 and Z1 motes provide similar execution times taking into account that the first one is slightly quicker. Moreover, as expected by Theorem 3 the use of the double hashing technique when working with fast hash functions does not reduce the execution time in any case. Finally, we observe as shown at Theorem 2 that hashes that output less bits reduce the execution time. In our experiments, Pearson hash functions take even less than one clock tick. Furthermore, as shown at Lemma 1 FNV hash functions that produce a smaller number of bits at the output improve the computational complexity. In this case the execution time is smaller for FNV of 32 bits than for FNV of 64 bits even if FNV of 64 bits implement less hashes.

5.3   Theoretical Evaluation of Iterated BFs

Improvement on the Number of Hash Functions Using IBFs. We intend to show that by using IBFs the optimum number of hash functions is decreased.

Theorem 4. *Given n elements to insert (1) in a Standard BF using m bit positions or (2) in a set d of individual BFs that use m' bit positions, where $m' = m/d$; then the k_{opt}, optimum number of hash functions, is smaller when using d individual BFs.*

Proof. It is known [12] that $k_{opt} = \frac{m}{n} ln2$. Then, for inserting n elements in a filter of m bit positions we use $k_{opt} = \frac{m}{n} ln2$. While for inserting the same number of elements in a smaller filter of m' bit positions, where $m' = m/d$, we use $k'_{opt} = \frac{m/d}{n} ln2$. Then, we can state that $k'_{opt} < k_{opt}$.

Improvement on Computational Complexity Using IBFs. We intend to show that by using IBFs we are able to reduce the computational complexity achieving the same performance than with a single Standard BF in terms of: (1) number of elements to insert to the filter, (2) overall size and (3) overall probability of false positives.

Theorem 5. *We define a single Standard BF with a probability of false positives f that contains n elements using m positions and k_{opt} hash functions. Then, we define a set d of individual BFs with an independent probability of false positives f', where each filter uses m' memory positions and k'_{opt} hash functions. A number n of elements are inserted at each filter. We can state that the structure of individual BFs improves the computational complexity needed by: (1) reducing the size of individual filters and (2) benefiting from the properties of IHFs.*

Proof. The overall probability of IBFs is f due to $f = \prod_{i=1}^{d} f'_i$. Then, we can state that to occupy the same overall number of bit positions m individual BFs use m' bit positions, where $m' = m/d$. Therefore, by using more filters with higher individual f' we save computational complexity due to the fact that $m' < m$ (see Theorem 2) and $k'_{opt} < k_{opt}$ (see Theorem 4). Moreover, it must be remarked that IHFs reuse the previous hashes in order to get a new hash. This implies that the overall number of iterations is the same for the computation of (1) the hash for a single Standard BF and (2) all hashes needed for IBFs.

5.4   Practical Evaluation of Iterated BFs

We have assessed the motes used at Sect. 5.2 to measure the execution time obtained by IBFs. We have conducted experiments for accepting up to 100, 200 and 400 subscriptions using the same number of bit positions in all cases. This means, that the probability of false positives and the number of hashes to insert per subscription are different in each case. As shown in Table 2 using the same array per bits (m/n) the probability of false positives increases as the number of accepted subscriptions grows. On the contrary, the number of hash functions used decrease as the number of subscriptions accepted grows.

Table 2. Execution time for inserting one subscription on a standard BF and IBFs.

SUBSCRIPTIONS	400 SUBSCRIPTIONS				200 SUBSCRIPTIONS				100 SUBSCRIPTIONS			
HASH FUNCTION	PEARSON		FNV 32		PEARSON		FNV 32		PEARSON		FNV 32	
TYPE OF BF	Iterated		Standard		Iterated		Standard		Iterated		Standard	
N° OF BFs (d)	16		1		16		1		16		1	
CONFIGURATION												
m/n	256/400		4096/400		256/200		4096/200		256/100		4096/100	
Individual f	0.7353		0.0073		0.5407		$5.3294 \cdot 10^{-5}$		0.2923		$2.8403 \cdot 10^{-8}$	
False positives (f)	0.0073		0.0073		$5.3294 \cdot 10^{-5}$		$5.3294 \cdot 10^{-5}$		$2.8403 \cdot 10^{-8}$		$2.8403 \cdot 10^{-8}$	
N° hashes (k_{opt})	1		7		1		14		2		28	
DH	No	YES	No	YES	No	YES	No	YES	No	YES	No	YES
Hashes tested	1	1	7	2+5DH	1	1	14	2+12DH	2	2	28	2+26DH
EXECUTION (μs)												
XM1000	0	0	7812	7812	0	0	7812	7812	0	0	7812	7812
Z1	0	0	15625	15625	0	0	15625	15625	0	0	15625	15625
TelosB	0	0	23437	23437	0	0	23437	23437	0	0	23437	23437

The results shown at Table 2 for execution times measured in μs are similar than in Sect. 5.2. TelosB motes provide again the worst results due to their limited microprocessor. In this case the difference between the processors of XM1000 and Z1 motes is perceived in all cases. In addition, we observe again as shown in Theorem 3 that the double hashing technique does not improve the execution time. Finally, the experiments conducted using IBFs take less than one clock tick while experiments using Standard BFs take more time. This is due to the fact that IBFs require less hashes and a simpler function that reduces the computational complexity.

8   Conclusion

In this paper, we propose a new architecture of FIBFs to be implemented at broker nodes of a distributed event-based system. The main purpose is to effectively route events in a sensing network that uses constrained devices. Events are classified using conjunctions and disjunctions, which leads to a combinatorial problem. Our protocol uses a Validation Table that uses Iterated BFs to discard events that do not match any subscription. Then, validated events are combined to search for a matching in the Routing Table composed of FBFs. If a matching is found the publication is forwarded. Our strategy is theoretically and practically compared to the use of Standard BFs.

First of all, we justify the benefits obtained by using FBFs. The use of FBFs leads to save memory and computational resources at the membership test. Furthermore, it is proved that there is no memory cost for fragmenting a filter in smaller filters for the same number of elements and a given probability of false positives. Then, we prove that smaller filters reduce the computational complexity because of the use of simpler hash functions. Besides, we prove that the double hashing technique does not improve the complexity.

Moreover, we justify the improvements obtained using IBFs. The use of IBFs leads to use less hashes and smaller filters so complexity is reduced.

Finally, the evaluation of these strategies using wireless sensor devices shows that the execution time is reduced when using FBFs and IBFs.

Acknowledgments. We thank the comments of Dr. Eduardo Solana, especially those concerning the use of hash functions. This work has been developed as part of the POPWiN project that is financially supported by the Hasler Foundation.

References

1. Backes, M., Barthe, G., Berg, M., Gregoire, B., Kunz, C., Skoruppa, M., Beguelin, S.: Verified security of merkle-damgård. In: IEEE Computer Security Foundations Symposium, pp. 354–368 (2012)
2. Fang, Q., Gao, J., Guibas, L.J.: Landmark-based information storage and retrieval in sensor networks. In: In The 25th Conference of the IEEE Communication Society (INFOCOM06), pp. 1–12 (2006)
3. Fersi, G., Louati, W., Jemaa, M.B.: Distributed hash table-based routing and data management in wireless sensor networks: a survey. Wirel. Netw. **19**(2), 219–236 (2013)
4. Fowler, G., Noll, L.C., Vo, K.-P., Eastlake, D.: The FNV Non-Cryptographic Hash Algorithm. Internet Draft (2015)
5. Huang, K., Zhang, J., Zhang, D., Xie, G., Salamatian, K., Liu, A., Li, W.: A multi-partitioning approach to building fast and accurate counting bloom filters. In: IEEE 27th International Symposium on Parallel Distributed Processing, pp. 1159–1170 (2013)
6. Jerzak, Z., Fetzer, C.: Bloom filter based routing for content-based publish/subscribe. In: Proceedings of the Second International Conference on Distributed Event-based Systems, pp. 71–81 (2008)
7. Jokela, P., Zahemszky, A., Rothenberg, C.E., Arianfar, S., Nikander, P.: Lipsin: line speed publish/subscribe inter-networking. In: Proceedings of the ACM SIGCOMM 2009 Conference on Data Communication, SIGCOMM 2009, pp. 195–206 (2009)
8. Kirsch, A., Mitzenmacher, M.: Less hashing, same performance: building a better bloom filter. In: Azar, Y., Erlebach, T. (eds.) Algorithms-ESA 2006, pp. 456–467. Springer, Heidelberg (2006)
9. Muñoz, C., Leone, P.: Design of a novel network architecture for distributed event-based systems using directional random walks in an ubiquitous sensing scenario. Intl. J. Adv. Netw. Serv. **7**(34), 252–264 (2014)
10. Pearson, P.K.: Fast hashing of variable-length text strings. Commun. ACM **33**(6), 677–680 (1990)
11. Shi, K., Deng, Z., Qin, X.: Tinymq: a content-based publish/subscribe middleware for wireless sensor networks. In: The Fifth International Conference on Sensor Technologies and Applications, pp. 12–17 (2011)
12. Tarkoma, S., Rothenberg, C., Lagerspetz, E.: Theory and practice of bloom filters for distributed systems. IEEE Commun. Surv. Tutorials **14**(1), 131–155 (2012)
13. Wong, B., Guha, S.: Quasar: a probabilistic publish-subscribe system for social networks. In: Proceedings of the 7th international conference on Peer-to-peer systems, pp. 2–2 (2008)
14. Yu, Y.T., Li, X., Gerla, M., Sanadidi, M.: Scalable vanet content routing using hierarchical bloom filters. In: 2013 9th International Wireless Communications and Mobile Computing Conference (IWCMC), pp. 1629–1634, July 2013

Big Data and Social Networks

Fast Adaptive Real-Time Classification for Data Streams with Concept Drift

Mark Tennant[1]([✉]), Frederic Stahl[1], and João Bártolo Gomes[2]

[1] University of Reading, PO Box 225, Whiteknights, Reading RG6 6AY, UK
m.tennant@pgr.reading.ac.uk, F.T.Stahl@reading.ac.uk
[2] Institute for Infocomm Research (I2R), A*STAR,
1 Fusionopolis Way Connexis, Singapore City 138632, Singapore
bartologjp@i2r.a-star.edu.sg

Abstract. An important application of Big Data Analytics is the real-time analysis of streaming data. Streaming data imposes unique challenges to data mining algorithms, such as concept drifts, the need to analyse the data on the fly due to unbounded data streams and scalable algorithms due to potentially high throughput of data. Real-time classification algorithms that are adaptive to concept drifts and fast exist, however, most approaches are not naturally parallel and are thus limited in their scalability. This paper presents work on the Micro-Cluster Nearest Neighbour (MC-NN) classifier. MC-NN is based on an adaptive statistical data summary based on Micro-Clusters. MC-NN is very fast and adaptive to concept drift whilst maintaining the parallel properties of the base KNN classifier. Also MC-NN is competitive compared with existing data stream classifiers in terms of accuracy and speed.

Keywords: Data stream classification · Adaptation to concept drift · High velocity data streams

1 Introduction

The work presented in this paper focuses on some of the challenges associated with the *velocity* aspect of Big Data [4]. Velocity in Big Data Analytics refers to data instances that arrive at a very high speed and thus challenge our computational capabilities in processing data [6]. Data stream classification trains a classifier in real-time on incoming data instances with a known classification, in order to enable the classification of previously unseen data instances. It is important that the classifier adapts to changes in the pattern encoded in the stream in order to keep the model accurate over time. Such changes in the pattern are also called concept drifts [5]. Some applications of data stream classification include sensor networks; Internet traffic management and web log analysis [8]; intrusion detection [9]. It is not feasible to capture, store and process data streams; as data streams are potentially infinite. Hence, algorithms are needed that can analyse data on the fly as it is being generated. Systems that make use of such algorithms are of great importance to applications such as the ones described above.

© Springer International Publishing Switzerland 2015
G. Di Fatta et al. (Eds.): IDCS 2015, LNCS 9258, pp. 265–272, 2015.
DOI: 10.1007/978-3-319-23237-9_23

n the past two decades various data stream classifiers have been published, such
s Hoeffding Trees [3], G-eRules [10], Very Fast Decision Rules (VFDR) [7] etc.
These algorithms induce a classifier and adapt to concept drifts with only one
pass through the data, making them relatively fast. This research paper proposes a new adaptive computationally efficient data stream classifier. The new
classifier proposes a Micro-Cluster based data structure with Variance based
splitting. This Micro-Cluster structure is coupled with a K Nearest Neighbour
(KNN) classifier approach termed MC-NN. Variance based Micro-Clusters continuously adapt to concept drifts through updating statistical summaries of data
instances from the data stream and are robust to noise. KNN has been used as
a base classification approach, as KNN is naturally parallel and thus allows for
future works to be applied in a parallel framework.

This paper is organised as follows: Sect. 2 describes the MC-NN algorithm
whereas Sect. 3 provides an empirical evaluation of MC-NN and a comparison
against existing data stream classifiers. Conclusions are discussed in Sect. 4.

2 Adaptive Micro-cluster Nearest Neighbour Data Stream Classification

2.1 Micro-cluster Based Nearest Neighbour

In the authors' previous feasibility study [12], a parallel real-time classifier was
implemented based upon KNN. In KNN a data instance is assigned the class
that is most common amongst its K nearest neighbours. The basic approach of
the real-time KNN is to keep a sliding fixed size time window of the most recent
data instances and execute KNN from the sliding window set. Real-time KNN
retrains on recent instances whilst older instances are deleted. However, real-
time KNN is computationally slow with faster data streams [12]. To overcome
the computational bottleneck of real-time KNN and the problems associated
with the sliding window, the here presented classifier adapts Micro-Clusters.
Micro-Clusters, originally developed for data stream clustering [1] in order to
provide a summary of the locality of the data are of the form:

$$< CF2^x, CF1^x, CF2^t, CF1^t, n > .$$

The sum of the squares of the attributes are maintained the vector $CF2^x$,
the sum of the values in vector $CF1^x$; the sum of time stamps in vector $CF1^t$;
and the number of data instances is stored in scalar n. $CF2^x$ and $CF1^x$ can
be used to calculate the locality and boundary of the Micro-Clusters whereas
$CF2^t$ and $CF1^t$ can be used to determine the *recency* of the data summarised
in the cluster. MC-NN adapts Micro-Clusters to compute nearest neighbours for
classification. The Micro-Cluster structure has been extended by terms CL for
the cluster's class label, ϵ as error count, Θ as error threshold for *splitting*, α as
initial time stamp and Ω as a threshold for the Micro-Cluster's performance:

$$< CF2^x, CF1^x, CF1^t, n, CL, \epsilon, \Theta, \alpha, \Omega >$$

The centroid of the Micro-Cluster can be calculated by $\frac{CF1^x}{n}$. In order to classify a new data instance from the stream the MC-NN classifier calculates the Euclidean distances between the data instance and each Micro-Cluster centroid and the class label of the nearest Micro-Cluster is assigned to the data instance. ϵ of a Micro-Cluster is initially 0 and incremented by 1 if the Micro-Cluster is used for classification and missclassifies the data instance. Likewise ϵ is decremented by 1 if the Micro-Cluster is involved in a correct classification. Θ is a user defined upper limit of acceptable ϵ. It is expected that a low Θ will cause the algorithm to adapt to changes faster, but will be more susceptible to noise. A larger Θ value will be more tolerant to noise but may not 'learn' as fast. As more labelled

---

Algorithm 1. Training the MC-NN classifier

Data: Train Instance
Result: Re-Positioned Localised sub-set of Micro-Clusters
Remove Micro-Clusters with poor performance (under Ω value)
foreach *Micro-Cluster in LocalSet* **do**
| Evaluate Micro-Cluster against NewInstance;
end
Sort EvaluationsByDistance();
if *Nearest Micro-Cluster is of the Training Items Class Label* **then**
CorrectClassification Event
NewInstance is Incremented into Nearest Micro-Cluster Nearset Micro-Cluster Error count (ϵ) reduced.
else
MisClassification Event
2 Micro-Clusters Identified:
1) Micro-Cluster that should have been identified as the Nearest to the New Instance of the same Classification Label.
2) Micro-Cluster that incorrectly was Nearest the New Instance.
Training Item incrementally added to Micro-Cluster of Correct Classification Label.
Both Micro-Clusters have internal Error count (ϵ) Incremented
foreach *Micro-Cluster Identified* **do**
| **if** *Micro-Cluster Error count (ϵ) exceeds Error Threshold (θ)* **then**
| | Sub-Divide Micro-Cluster upon attribute of largest Variance
| **end**
end
end

---

instances are received for learning they will change the distribution of the Micro-Clusters. According to Algorithm 1 two scenarios are possible after the nearest Micro-Cluster has been identified when a new training instance is presented to the classifier:

Scenario 1: If the nearest Micro-Cluster is of the same label as the training instance, then the instance is incrementally added to the Micro-Cluster and ϵ is decremented by 1.

Scenario 2: If the nearest Micro-Cluster is of a different class label, then the training instance is incrementally added to the nearest Micro-Cluster that matches the training instance's class label. However, the error count ϵ of both involved Micro-Clusters is incremented.

If over time a Micro-Cluster's error count ϵ reaches the error threshold Θ then the Micro-Cluster is *split*. This is done by evaluating the Micro-Cluster's dimensions for the size of its variance, which can be calculated using Eq. (1), where x denotes a particular attribute. The splitting of a Micro-Cluster generates two new Micro-Clusters, centred about the point of the parent Micro-Cluster's attribute of greatest variance; while the parent Micro-Cluster is removed. The assumption behind this way of splitting attributes is that a larger variance value of one attribute over another indicates that a greater range of values have been seen for this attribute. Therefore the attribute may contribute towards miss-classifications. This splitting of a Micro-Cluster causes the two new Micro-Clusters to separate and better fit the underlying concept encoded in the stream. Once the attribute of largest variance has been identified, the two new Micro-Clusters are initially populated with the parent's internal mean / centre data $CF1^x$). The split attribute (with the largest variance), is altered by the variance value identified in the positive direction in one of the new Micro-Clusters and negatively in the other. This ensures that future training will further re-position the two new Micro-Clusters better than the parent could alone.

$$Variance[x] = \sqrt{\left(\frac{CF2^x}{n}\right) - \left(\frac{CF1^x}{n}\right)^2} \tag{1}$$

When a Micro-Cluster has a new instance added to it, it's internal instance count n is incremented by 1 and the sum of time stamps($CF1^t$) is incremented by the new time stamp value(T). The *Triangle Number* $\Delta(T) = ((T^2 + T)/2)$ of this time stamp will give an upper bound to the maximum possible value of $CF1^t$. Therefore, if all instances were entered into this Micro-Cluster $CF1^t$ would be equal to the triangular number of T. The lower the value of $CF1^t$ is from the *Triangular Number* the poorer the Micro-Cluster has been participating in the stream classification. The use of Triangular Numbers give more importance to recent instances over earlier ones added to the Micro-Cluster, as the time stamp value (T) is always increasing and MC-NN uses the sum of these incremental values. Triangular numbers assume that all Micro-Clusters were created at time stamp 1. To counter this each Micro-Cluster keeps track of the time stamp when it was initialised (α). The Micro-Cluster's real $\Delta(T)$ can be calculated by $\Delta(T) - \Delta(\alpha)$. Any Micro-Clusters that fall under a pre-set threshold value of Ω) are deleted as they are considered old. For the rest of this paper a value of 10 % was given to all Micro-Cluster Ω values as it seemed to work best for most classification problems.

Evaluation

This Section evaluates MC-NN in terms of accuracy, adaptivity to concept drifts and computational efficiency on a quad core 'Intel core' I5 processor with 8 Gb RAM. All classifiers and data stream generators are implemented in the Massive Online Analysis (MOA) framework. Three data streams have been utilised: The **SEA data stream** [11] contains three continuous attributes and two class labels. A class label of *True* is given only if the Threshold level of a preset value is surpassed by summing two of the attributes, otherwise class label *False* is given. Arbitrarily function 1 (value 8) was chosen for the initial concept and function 3 (value 7) for the concept change. The **Random Tree Generator** [2] creates a random tree with each leaf node randomly assigned a class label. In our experiments the random tree(s) comprise ten continuous attributes and three class labels. A drift is achieved by simply generating a different random tree. Both, the Random Tree and the SEA datastreams generated 35,000 instances. The concept drift begins at instance 10,000 with a gradual change over 1,000 instances to the second stream. The **Hyperplane generator** creates a linearly separable model. A Hyperplane in 'D' dimensions slowly rotates continuously changing the linear decision boundary of the stream. The experiments using the Hyperplane generator created 10 million data instances, with five numerical attributes and two classes. In order to add an additional challenge 10 % noise was generated as well with probability $P(0.75)$ chance of reversing the direction of the rotation causing an 'Oscillation' effect. A version of the stream with probability $P(0)$ chance of reversing the direction of the concept drift was also created. MC-NN was compared against Hoeffding Trees [3], incremental Naïve Bayes and real-time KNN classifier [12]. Each instance was tested upon the classifier to log the classifier's performance before being used for training: this is also know as prequential testing.

Adaptation to New Concepts: Two MC-NN classifiers were created, one with $\Theta = 2$ (error threshold) and the other with $\Theta = 10$. Table 1 compares MC-NN against other stream classification algorithms on the SEA and Random Tree data streams. Please note that for real-time KNN several experiments have been carried out and only the experiments with the best setting for K are included in the table. The results show that real-time KNN's results are competitive to the Hoeffding Tree and Naïve Bayes classifiers. MC-NN achieves accuracies close to all competitors, while clearly outperforming real-time KNN in terms of runtime. Regarding accuracy MC-NN is similar to Hoeffding Trees and Naïve Bayes. It is also noticeable that a larger Θ results in a shorter runtime of MC-NN. This can be explained by the fact that when Θ is larger it will take more time for a Micro-Cluster to reach Θ and thus it will perform splits less frequently.

Table 1. Accuracies and runtime of MC-NN compared with other data stream classifiers. Accuracies are listed in percent and runtime is listed in seconds. Θ denotes the error threshold used in MC-NN

Algorithm	SEA accuracy(runtime)	Random Tree accuracy(runtime)
Naïve Bayes	94.40(0.11)	64.17(0.10)
Hoeffding Tree	95.96(0.19)	69.88(0.28)
real-time KNN	97.17(24.73) K=5000	71.34(9.04) K=2000
MC($\Theta = 2$)	94.03(0.28)	70.30(2.02)
MC($\Theta = 10$)	92.99(0.03)	60.99(1.49)

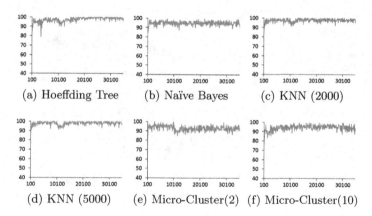

(a) Hoeffding Tree   (b) Naïve Bayes   (c) KNN (2000)

(d) KNN (5000)   (e) Micro-Cluster(2)   (f) Micro-Cluster(10)

Fig. 1. Concept drift adaptation on the SEA data stream. Accuracy is plotted along the vertical axis, instance stream is plotted along the horizontal axis.

Figures 1 and 2 illustrate the same experiments as listed in Table 1, the accuracy is displayed over time. For SEA it can be seen that all classifiers achieve relatively high accuracy at any time and only show a slight deterioration in accuracy during the concept drift (instances 10,000 - 11,000). For the Random Tree it can be seen that Hoeffding Tree and Naïve Bayes classifiers are clearly challenged with adapting to the concept drift as they need a long time to fully regain their previous classification accuracy level. The real-time KNN classifer also have a noticeable deterioration of their classification accuracy during the concept drift but recover much faster compared with Hoeffding Tree and Naïve Bayes. However, they do not reach the same level of classification accuracy as Hoeffding trees and Naïve Bayes. The results of MC-NN clearly show the lowest classification accuracy deterioration and almost recover instantly. MC-NN is able to reach the same classification accuracy levels as Hoeffding tree and Naïve Bayes, whereas real-time KNN performs poorly.

The Results in Figs. 3 and 4 show the total accuracy of the different classifiers evaluated on the Hyperplane data streams with their runtime in brackets. In terms of classification accuracy it can be seen that MC-NN(10) achieves second highest accuracy, but only 0.04 % behind Naïve Bayes on the stream with no oscillation. On the stream with oscillation effect MC-NN(10) clearly outperforms all its competitors. Please note that the Figures display only the runtime for the best configurations with real-time KNN. In terms of runtime, MC-NN is faster than Hoeffding Trees and achieves a similar speed to that of Naïve Bayes. However, MC-NN is approximately 30 times faster than real-time KNN. Please note that for the larger Θ MC-NN performs slightly faster, which can be explained by MC-NN being less likely to perform Micro-Cluster splits which consume some of the runtime. Figure 3 shows the experiments for the Rotating Hyperplane data stream over time for all 10 million data instances. All classifiers need some initialisation phase before producing a stable classification accuracy. Overall MC-NN(10) achieves a similar performance to Naïve Bayes and

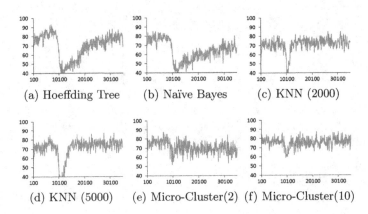

Fig. 2. Concept drift adaptation on the Random Tree data stream. Accuracy is plotted along the vertical axis, instance stream is plotted along the horizontal axis.

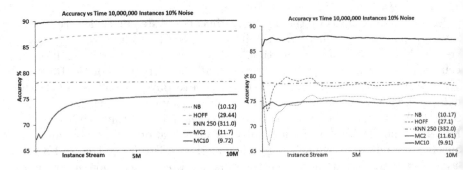

Fig. 3. Concept Drift adaptation on the Hyperplane with Rotating Boundary.

Fig. 4. Concept drift adaptation on the hyperplane with oscillating boundary.

outperforms is predecessor real-time KNN clearly. Figure 4 shows the experiments for the Oscillating Hyperplane data stream over time for all 10 million data instances. MC-NN(10) remains stable and clearly outperforms all its competitors. Both Naïve Bayes and the Hoffeding Tree classifiers suffer at the beginning of the data stream with a negative accuracy trend. This is due to the overlapping data values that are contradicting each other due to oscillation. Overall MC-NN achieves a similar performance compared with well established data stream classifiers in terms of accuracy and runtime and clearly outperforms its predecessor MC-NN is more robust in terms of adaptation to concept drifts, especially complex continuous concept drifts. Moreover MC-NN is naturally parallel and thus has the advantage to be scaled up to high speed data streams.

4   Conclusions

This paper presents the development of the novel MC-NN data stream classifier that is competitive with popular existing data stream classifiers in terms of accuracy and adaptability to concept drifts, but is also computationally efficient and potentially scalable to parallel computer architectures. The developed classifier is based on a nearest neighbour approach for classification and on a novel kind of Micro-Cluster for classification purposes to maintain a recent summary of the data observed and its performance. MC-NN has been compared empirically with Hoeffding tree, Naïve Bayes for streaming data and its predecessor real-time KNN. Empirical results show that MC-NN achieves similar or better accuracy, adaptability to concept drifts and shorter runtime compared with its competitors. Notably MC-NN is very robust when confronted with continuously changing concepts and noise. The paper also points out that MC-NN is naturally parallel as Micro-Clusters can be distributed over multiple computational nodes in a computer cluster. Therefore ongoing work comprises the implementation and empirical evaluation of a new parallel MC-NN classifier.

References

1. Aggarwal, C., Han, J., Wang, J., Yu, P.: A framework for clustering evolving data streams. In: Proceedings of the 29th VLDB Conference, Berlin, Germany (2003)
2. Domingos, P., Hulten, G.: Mining high-speed data streams. In: KDD, pp. 71–80 (2000)
3. Domingos, P., Hulten, G.: Mining high-speed data streams. In: Proceedings of the Sixth ACM SIGKDD International Conference on Knowledge Discovery and Data Mining, KDD 2000, pp. 71–80. ACM, New York, NY, USA (2000)
4. Ebbers, M., Abdel-Gayed, A., Budhi, V., Dolot, F.: Addressing Data Volume, Velocity, and Variety with IBM InfoSphere Streams V3.0. (2013)
5. Gaber, M.M., Zaslavsky, A., Krishnaswamy, S.: A survey of classification methods in data streams. In: Aggarwal, C.C. (ed.) Data Streams. Advances in Database Systems, vol. 31, pp. 39–59. Springer, New York (2007)
6. Gaber, M.M., Zaslavsky, A., Krishnaswamy, S.: Mining data streams: a review. ACM SIGMOD Rec. 34, 18–26 (2005)
7. Gama, J., Kosina, P.: Learning decision rules from data streams. In: Proceedings of the Twenty-Second International Joint Conference on Artificial Intelligence - Volume Two, IJCAI 2011, pp. 1255–1260. AAAI Press (2011)
8. Gama, J.: Knowledge Discovery from Data Streams. Chapman and Hall / CRC, London (2010)
9. Jadhav, A., Jadhav, A., Jadhav, P., Kulkarni, P.: A novel approach for the design of network intrusion detection system (NIDS). In: 2013 International Conference on Sensor Network Security Technology and Privacy Communication System (SNS PCS), pp. 22–27 (2013)
10. Le, T., Stahl, F., Gomes, J.B., Gaber, M.M., Di Fatta, G.: Computationally efficient rule-based classification for continuous streaming data. In: Bramer, M., Petridis, M. (eds.) Research and Development in Intelligent Systems XXXI, pp. 21–34. Springer International Publishing, Switzerland (2014)
11. Street, W.N., Kim, Y.S.: A streaming ensemble algorithm (SEA) for large-scale classification. In: Proceedings of the Seventh ACM SIGKDD International Conference on Knowledge Discovery and Data Mining, pp. 377–382 (2001)
12. Tennant, M., Stahl, F., Di Fatta, G., Gomes, J.: Towards a parallel computationally efficient approach to scaling up data stream classification. In: Bramer, M., Petridis, M. (eds.) Research and Development in Intelligent Systems XXXI, pp. 51–65. Springer International Publishing, Switzerland (2014)

Omentum – A Peer-to-Peer Approach for Internet-Scale Virtual Microscopy

Andreas Barbian[1,2(✉)], Dennis Malenica[2], Timm J. Filler[1],
and Michael Schoettner[2]

[1] Department of Anatomy, University of Duesseldorf, Duesseldorf, Germany
andreas.barbian@hhu.de
[2] Department of Computer Science, University of Duesseldorf,
Duesseldorf, Germany

Abstract. Virtual microscopy is increasingly used for e-learning and medical online exams at universities. Traditional client-server systems support up to a few hundred of users accessing more than 10.000 large microscopic images (each several Gigabyte) and each being able to make interactive annotations. We have developed the first peer-to-peer based solution bringing virtual microscopy to an Internet-scale community. We address data distribution and replication by a novel overlay called Omentum, which is based on a random-graph architecture. Omentum uses a lightweight messaging service for peer communication and supports traffic-free routing-path calculation. Based on the directed random graph the system achieves path compression by walking along inbound links during the actual routing phase. The evaluation shows the efficiency and scalability of the Omentum overlay network, its replication strategy and an administrative communication overhead for creating new replicas around 0.06 %.

1 Introduction

A virtual microscope is in general referred to as an application for exploring digitalized, high-resolution microscopic images. These whole slide images (WSI) are commonly several Gigabytes in size and contained in proprietary image containers [8]. In the past decade several supplements were contributed to enhance the capabilities of many virtual microscopes as compared to standard light microscopes, such as textual or drawn annotations.

For the presented application "Omentum", the proprietary image containers have been converted into JPEG images and have been reorganized to a pyramid like structure. Each image has a fixed size and represents a distinct part, a tile of the original slide. As different magnification levels are available in most WSI each layer in the JPEG pyramid contains the same tiles with a lower resolution compared to the layer below [7].

The WSI conversion allows reproducible partitioning for easier distribution. As an additional benefit, Omentum does not depend on any proprietary format

© Springer International Publishing Switzerland 2015
G. Di Fatta et al. (Eds.): IDCS 2015, LNCS 9258, pp. 273–284, 2015.
DOI: 10.1007/978-3-319-23237-9_24

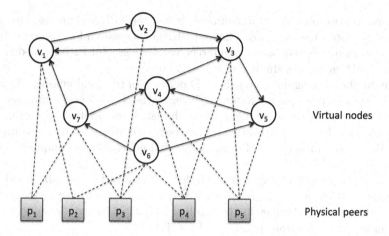

Fig. 1. Simplified node distribution in the Omentum overlay.

nd can be easily extended to a diversity of data types, e.g. different scanner
manufacturers or DICOM[1] datasets to include further areas of medical images.

Omentum exists as an implementation in Java and is used for medical educa-
on. Although, it is not designed as a licenced medical application to constitute
rofessional consultation on medical images of individual users. It is a distrib-
ted approach to browsing and annotating a high quantity of high-resolution
'SI with an Internet-scale community. Therefore, we restricted the storing of
ew images in the network to only specific peers at numerous medical faculties.
evertheless, publishing user-generated content, e.g. links and annotations, is
ot limited in any way.

We conclude that the number of available slides does not change as frequently
s new annotations are created due to the relatively small number of peers
lowed to contribute new images. An essential cornerstone of our overlay is thus
e prompt communication of any updates to the list of slides to any connected
ode. Apart from that, updates to annotations are forwarded to responsible
plica holders only, and queried via searches.

The overlay network presented in the next section uses two pseudo random
umber generators for construction and is mainly inspired by PathFinder [4]. It
atures a novel replication model using automatic load balancing based on peer
rformance monitoring. An additional challenge is the distributed storage and
plication of interactively generated annotations.

Omentum: Overlay Architecture

mentum's overlay connects different data partitions, which represent virtual
des hosted by one or more peers (see Fig. 1).

Digital Imaging and Communications In Medicine.

Therefore, two pseudo random number generators (PRNG) are used to create its random-graph-based overlay. The first PRNG generates a Poisson-distributed number of neighbors that a new node receives. The second PRNG, seeded with the node's ID, generates the IDs of its neighbors.

The number of neighbors and their ID depend on the total number of virtual nodes present in the system. Referring back to the low-latency communication mentioned before, each peer knows about the latest metadata (update) of each available slide. Hence, as virtual nodes represent partitions of the pre-computed slides, the maximum number of available virtual nodes can be computed locally by each peer.

Choosing a proper expectancy value for the size of the neighborhood is as important as limiting the degree of each node. Both values have a strong influence on the number of edges in the random graph but do not increase routing performance after a certain point (ref. Sect. 4).

Partitioning the WSI increases the number of objects that have to be stored and replicated in the system. Moreover, it should decrease the overall load on each peer serving a particular partition, as the amount of data is significantly lower compared to a whole slide.

Any client needs to be able to calculate the number of partitions each slide has. This is addressed by determining T_0 as the number of tiles in the most magnified layer from the slides' width w and height h, as well as the known dimension of each tile.

$$T_0 = \left\lceil \frac{w}{t_x} \right\rceil \cdot \left\lceil \frac{h}{t_y} \right\rceil \tag{1}$$

The maximum number of partitions Π can be calculated as the quotient of T_0 and n_0, the maximum number of tiles in the deepest layer each partition is responsible for. To simplify computation, n_0 should be a power of 2.

$$\Pi = \frac{T_0}{n_0} \tag{2}$$

The number of tiles a partition has in the most magnified layer is given by Eq. (3).

$$T_0(P) = w_0 \cdot h_0, w_0 = \left\lceil \frac{w}{t_x \sqrt{n_0}} \right\rceil \wedge h_0 = \left\lceil \frac{h}{t_y \sqrt{n_0}} \right\rceil \tag{3}$$

The total number of tiles in any partition can be aggregated by Eq. (4) as the number of virtual zoom levels z is known from the WSI generation process.

$$T(P) = \sum_{i=0}^{z} \left(\frac{1}{2^i} \cdot |P_0| \right) \tag{4}$$

From this, the starting tile T_S in any partition P_k with $k \in \Pi$ can be calculated by Eq. (5).

$$T_S(P_k) = ((k \cdot \sqrt{n_0}) \div w_0) \cdot h_0 + ((k \cdot \sqrt{n_0}) \bmod w_0) \tag{5}$$

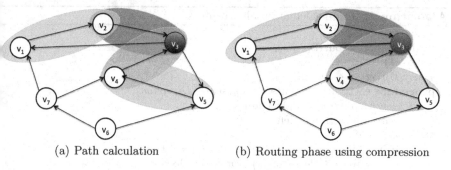

(a) Path calculation   (b) Routing phase using compression

Fig. 2. Visualization of routing calculation between virtual nodes 1 and 5.

After enabling each peer to obtain the number of partitions in any slide and
ts starting tile, slides can be split to be distributed on a fine grained level.

Additionally, with the rounding in Eq. (3), the upper most layers are most
requently distributed. In particular, this process is beneficial for effective pre-
iew caching, as the images of the pyramid's upper layers are requested most
ommonly. We were able to validate this type of behavior based on recorded
ata of a sample of more than 400 real users in classroom. Almost every partici-
ant used a low magnification of the WSI to gain an overview of a slide prior to
iew the slide at maximum magnification for a detailed impression of potentially
nteresting parts.

With the approach presented before, nodes are able to calculate the ID of
specific partition P_k containing a requested tile. This is done by summing up
he number of partitions for all slides with a lower ID than the requested one.
Afterwards, the partition of the tile within the requested slide is calculated and
dded to the previously calculated sum. This leads to the ID of the virtual node
esponsible for the requested tile.

Virtual nodes maintain a list of their neighbors, including inbound and out-
ound links. This is necessary to implement path compression during the routing
hase (ref. Sect. 2.1).

Importantly, all servers (for instance from different universities) are continu-
usly connected to the network and are responsible for creating the initial overlay
hilst no other peers are connected. The servers are connected to each other in a
eparate neighborhood. This allows fast propagation of new slide insertions and
consistent level of information for the overlay creation phase.

.1   Routing

he virtual node responsible for the requested data has to be determined. All
outing information can be computed without any network traffic. Therefore, a
RNG is seeded with the ID of this target node to calculate its neighbors. The
ame is done with a second PRNG seeded with the ID of the starting node. The
alculation of the routing path is done by increasing the search distance for each
irtual node and calculating their neighbors respectively (see Algorithm 1).

Algorithm 1. Route calculation algorithm

s : starting vNodeID
d : destination vNodeID
$way \leftarrow \{\}$
$searchDirection \leftarrow$ right
procedure CALCULATEPATH($s, d, way, searchDirection$)
    if $searchDirection =$ right **then**
        $searchDirection \leftarrow$ left
        $way.\text{add}(s)$
        if Neighbors(s) $\cap$ (Neighbors(d) $\cup \{d\}$) $= \emptyset$ **then**
            for all $n \in$ Neighbors(s) : $\nexists n \in way$ **do**
                return CALCULATEPATH($n, d, way, searchDirection$)
            end for
        else
            return way
        end if
    else
        process the other direction accordingly
    end if
end procedure

Figure 2a shows an example for routing from node v_1 to node v_5 using the previously given node distribution.

As the random graph is directed, only outbound edges can be calculated by the algorithm. After the second routing step in the given example, node v_3 is found as the connecting node between v_1 and v_5.

After the calculation, the actual routing phase starts. In this phase v_1 takes the routing list containing the nodes v_2, v_3, v_4 and v_5 and checks his inbound links for possible path compressions starting at the end of the list. As v_3 has an inbound edge on v_1, the beginning of the list is truncated and given to v_3 containing v_4 and v_5 only. Node v_3 executes the same algorithm now and routes to v_5 directly, due to an existing outbound link. Instead of using the calculated path with length 4 via v_2, v_3 and v_4 to v_5, the routing is done directly via v_3 to v_5 with a length of 2 (see Fig. 2b).

The ability to compress a path during the actual routing phase reduces the average path length between nodes. Its efficiency mainly depends on the degree of the virtual nodes. An additional aspect is, that each peer may be responsible for more than one virtual node. In this case, the routing calculation is executed using multiple starting points.

As each peer keeps track of the routing information to nodes he contacted at least once, the speed of consecutive calculations can be increased significantly.

Retrieving tiles from computable partitions is executed like a data lookup in a DHT with a hash function referencing the connection between slide, partition and tiles. As user-generated content always is associated to a slide, the retrieval of annotations can be achieved relying on the same routing information.

The annotations are connected to a separate partition associated to each slide. This limits the number of hosts to query for user generated content, thus enabling fast exhaustive searches.

8 Replication

The overlay has to handle different types of data, which can be divided into two categories. The first category contains static objects, representing all tiles, partitions and slides. The second category contains dynamic objects, that are subject to frequent changes and represents any kind of user-generated annotations. Both categories need their own algorithms.

In general, static objects do not change but can be removed from the system. Their replicas need to be handled accordingly. This class of objects represents the images and constitute the largest amount of traffic in the network.

Dynamic objects have to be considered separately regarding replication. They are divided into four distinct classes: instant, temporary, managed and persistent.

Objects classified as *instant* have a very short lifetime and are neither replicated nor updated. Typical examples of this class include queries and heartbeats.

Members in the class of *temporary* objects may have a longer but still finite lifetime and may be replicated, but the replicas will not be maintained and therefore fade over time. Examples include requests for assistance triggered by poor node performance and context updates of other users observing the same area.

Managed objects are strongly connected to the creating node. They are not replicated and have to disappear in case the connected node leaves the network. The list of connected nodes or neighbors are typical examples for this class.

Objects are classified as *persistent* if they need to be available even after the creating host leaves the network. To ensure this, a distinct number of replicas has to be maintained for each object. Any published annotation generated by users belongs to this group.

As annotations are stored in a separate partition for each slide, the replication is similar to static objects. Nevertheless, their updates are still more expensive regarding traffic, as the updated information has to be distributed among the responsible replicas. This does not constitute much traffic compared to the static image objects, as annotation are internally represented as compressed Strings and not graphical objects.

8.1 Replicas as Virtual Neighborhoods

A virtual node represents a single data partition. It is a physically not existing construct of a group of replicas hosted on multiple peers. All replicas for a virtual node are connected to each other in a separate virtual neighborhood. In this neighborhood information about the individual performance of each peer is shared. Performance parameters of each peer are aggregated by fuzzy logic to create an indicator, which reflects usage of hardware resources as well as the available bandwidth. This value is appended as a single byte to most messages transmitted between communicating replicas.

The neighborhood is organized as a list that each peer maintains. The list is sorted by intent, as the oldest replica is the first entry. The administrative overhead to manage these list on involved peers includes inserts and removals of replicas. As these peers communicate on a regular basis, node failures can be discovered and handled quickly by adapting the neighborhood list.

Any new replica is added to the end of the list. This enables each peer to compute the number of active replicas simply by querying the size of this list.

Only the last replica in this list may ask for leaving the virtual neighborhood. This decreases the administrative overhead for avoiding multiple simultaneous leaves triggered by high performance of the virtual node (ref. Sect. 3.3).

During a recovery from node churn, re-joining nodes are explicitly allowed to resume their position in the network. Therefore, they try to connect to previously known virtual nodes and re-join their virtual neighborhood. If the appropriate replicas are unavailable, normal joining occurs. After this, the new peers, responsible for the previously shared virtual node, are informed, that a replica can be resumed.

3.2 Creating Replicas

New replicas are created dynamically according to the rules described below. The most obvious reason is undercutting the minimal quantity of copies for a virtual node. In this case, the last node in the replica neighborhood starts the creation process for a new replica.

Additionally, the performance of a virtual node can be considered as a reason to create new replicas despite the number of already existing copies. Therefore a virtual neighborhood of replica holders can decide to ask for another host replicating their data. As each peer hosting a virtual node keeps track of the replicas, the performance indicators of all replicas are known. The performance indicator enables any peer in his virtual neighborhood to delegate requests to more performant peers. In case that any replica is already at or above its defined load threshold, the last peer in the neighborhood can start the creation process for a new replica.

Delegating this task to only a single peer removes the overhead in timely coordination of replica creation requests. In case the last node can no longer accomplish this task, e.g. due to heavy load or even failure, this task is assigned to the next peer in the list.

The peer than informs the neighborhood about starting its search for a new peer.

Omentum allows several implementations of node selection strategies. For example preferring performant nodes. Therefore, peers can create a *temporary* request, which lives for a designated number of hops. Any receiving peer may answer to this request and the most performant one is chosen by the initiating peer.

Other strategies are possible as well. For stronger randomness, nodes can be selected by random walks in the overlay graph. As the random walk leads only to another virtual host, its replicas have to be queried to take over the additional data.

Additionally, Geo-location algorithms can be used to decrease the overall number of hops.

After a responsible peer has found a potential new replica location, the joining data is transferred. This data consists of the replica list and a list of files forming the virtual node. With this list, the joining peer contacts any existing replica in the neighborhood and requests the node's content from multiple sources.

Replicas can be resumed, e.g. after node churns or intentional leaves. Solely data for different or missing checksums are transmitted.

5.3   Removing Replicas

To dissolve a replica, two criteria have to be matched. At first, the performance of a virtual node, meaning the average performance of its replica holders, has to be high enough. Additionally, the minimum quantity of available replicas has to be exceeded. Therefore, the last replica in the neighborhood periodically checks its performance values and the list of active replicas. To prevent unintended removals due to temporary performance peaks, a dissolving peers has to wait for an adjustable period time before leaving the neighborhood. The shorter this period is, the faster the system reorganizes itself and the more affectable it is to avoidable copy operations.

Prior to leaving, the replica has to inform his neighborhood about the removal. Each replica than removes the dissolved peer from the list of replicas and recalculates the virtual node's performance index.

In case a peer simply leaves the network and the performance of the neighborhood undercuts a given performance or quantity threshold, a new replica has to be created.

Evaluation

The simulation compares Omentum's overlay for different network sizes, ranging from 10K to 10 million nodes. The simulations were performed on a Intel® Quad-core i7 with 16 GB RAM. Due to seeded PRNGs any result is reproducible and does not depend on hardware specifications.

The number of edges in the random graph has a strong influence on the resilience in case of node churn, but increases the administration complexity for each node. At some point the beneficial aspects (connectivity and path compression) no longer exceeds the administration Overhead (see Fig. 3). Therefore, we limited the maximal expectancy value for a node's degree to 20. This provides sufficient flexibility for node connection in different overlays sizes and limits administration overhead in very large overlays.

The distribution of edges in the overlay after limiting the expectancy value for any nodes interconnection is shown in Fig. 4.

Reducing the actual routing path during the routing phase is a two-step process and provides a significant optimization on the number of hops needed for a specific path. At first, the inbound links are considered as shortcuts to

Table 1. Omentum's administrative overhead for a network with 10 million virtual nodes, 2 million peers and an average partition size of 307.2 MiB.

Message	Traffic (MiB)	Payload (%)	Overhead (%)
VNodeJoinRequest	460		0.243 %
VNodeJoinAccept	460		0.243 %
PeerJoinRequest	76		0.040 %
PeerJoinAccept	100		0.053 %
PeerDataRequest	86,016		45.388 %
PeerDataTransmit	307,200,000	100.000 %	54.033 %
Summary	307,389,512	99.938 %	0.062 %

later notes in the routing list. The compression achieved depends on the size of the overlay (see Fig. 5). As only five percent of randomly chosen node pairs are examined, effective path compression drops with increasing the number of nodes in the overlay.

Secondly, any routing information gained during consecutive routing operations is cached for a configurable number of nodes (currently 5.000) to increase shorten paths in future calculations.

Regarding the administrative overhead, Omentum's overlay proves to be very effective. Table 1 shows an in-depth analysis of the traffic distribution for creating an equally distributed and equally filled overlay with 10 million virtual nodes and 2 million participating peers. The average partition size is around 300 MiB.

5   Related Work

There are numerous solutions for virtual microscopy [5,6,10,12], but only a few of them allow the simultaneous examination of multiple slides [11]. Although most solutions features an implementation relying on web deployment, we stick to a platform independent application as this allows the usage of peer-to-peer technology.

The variety of existing structured and unstructured overlays for peer-to-peer systems is overwhelming [1–3,9,13,16], but none has been used for virtual microscopy. The difficulty for Omentum was that DHT-like functionality was needed to easily retrieve requested image parts while providing exhaustive searches for user generated annotations that may contain free text. The development of Omentum has been mainly inspired by PathFinder [4] and BubbleStorm [15] as they use a random-graph based overlay allowing traffic-less calculation of routing paths. In contrast to PathFinder, that replicates random objects on newly joining nodes or replicates new objects to random nodes, we developed a novel, application-suitable replication strategy that allows load balancing based on individual peer performance. This performance respects computation power as well as the available bandwidth, whilst achieving an adjustable number of

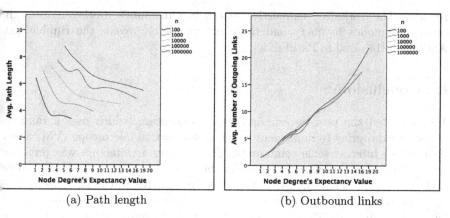

(a) Path length   (b) Outbound links

Fig. 3. Dependency of edge distribution on the expectancy value for the node degree.

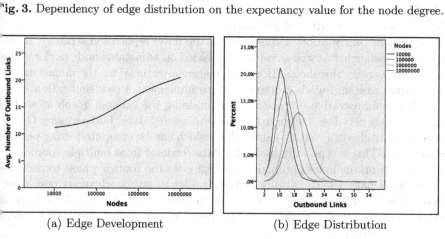

(a) Edge Development   (b) Edge Distribution

Fig. 4. Development and distribution of edges in networks of various sizes.

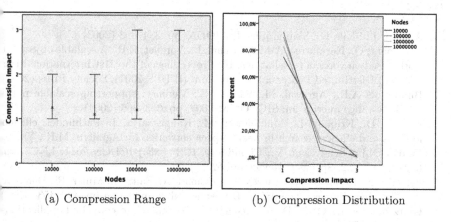

(a) Compression Range   (b) Compression Distribution

Fig. 5. Impact of path compression on various network sizes.

replicas. The optimized exhaustive search in Omentum's overlay reduces the number of nodes to query and therefore completely avoids the BubbleCast-Algorithm [14] used in PathFinder.

6 Conclusion

We presented the peer-to-peer application Omentum, which uses a random-graph-based overlay to implement a distributed virtual microscope (VM) accessible by an Internet-scale community. The overlays architecture was preferred over a DHT implementation because of the traffic-less routing path calculation and the very efficient exhaustive search. An interactive VM used to access tens of thousands of high-resolution microscopic images and their numerous annotations generates a significant amount of traffic on a university's infrastructure. The growing user base with a strong need for off-campus teaching initiated the development of a distributed approach.

The main contribution of this paper is the novel replication strategy. It features load balancing as well as replication based on adjustable node performance and data quantity thresholds. Both parameters are crucial for the demonstrated application case and made it mandatory to implement a new replication strategy. The administrative overhead for maintaining the random graph as well as the replicas is very low, compared to the transmitted data. Furthermore, Omentum avails traffic-less routing calculation, which can be computed using parallel algorithms. This is especially useful for data retrieval from multiple sources.

Future work includes optimizing strategies for the routing phase to decrease the average path length. Additionally, we plan to study advanced peer selection strategies during the creation of new replicas. This includes the reduction of physical hops between peers and a probably increased bandwidth between connected replicas.

References

1. Aspnes, J., Shah, G.: Skip graphs. In: SODA, pp. 384–393 (2003)
2. Beaumont, O., Kermarrec, A-M., Marchal, L., Voronet, É.R.: A scalable object net work based on voronoi tessellations. In: Proceedings of the 21st International Parallel and Distributed Processing Symposium (IPDPS 2007), Society Press (2007)
3. Bharambe, A.R., Agrawal, M., Seshan, S.: Mercury: supporting scalable multi attribute range queries. In: SIGCOMM 2004, pp. 353–366 (2004)
4. Bradler, D., Krumov, L., Mühlhäuser, M., Kangasharju, J.: Pathfinder: efficien lookups and efficient search in peer-to-peer networks. In: Aguilera, M.K., Yu, H. Vaidya, N.H., Srinivasan, V., Choudhury, R.R. (eds.) ICDCN 2011. LNCS, vol 6522, pp. 77–82. Springer, Heidelberg (2011)
5. Ferreira, R, Moon, B., Humphries, J., Sussman, A., Saltz, J., Miller, R., Demarzo A.: The virtual microscope. In: AMIA Annu Fall Symposium pp. 449–453 (1997)
6. Glatz-Krieger, K., Glatz, D., Mihatsch, M.J.: Virtual microscopy: first applications Pathologe **27**(6), 469–476 (2006)

7. Jaegermann, A., Filler, T.J., Schoettner, M.: Distributed architecture for a peer-to-peer-based virtual microscope. In: Dowling, J., Taïani, F. (eds.) DAIS 2013. LNCS, vol. 7891, pp. 199–204. Springer, Heidelberg (2013)
8. Rojo, M.G., García, G.B., Mateos, C.P., García, J.G., Vincente, M.C.: Critical comparison of 31 commercially available digital slide systems in pathology. Int. J. Surg. Pathol. 14(4), 285–305 (2006)
9. Rowstron, A., Druschel, P.: Pastry: scalable, decentralized object location, and routing for large-scale peer-to-peer systems. In: Guerraoui, R. (ed.) Middleware 2001. LNCS, vol. 2218, pp. 329–350. Springer, Heidelberg (2001)
10. Saeger, K., Schmidt, D.: Digital slide training portal. training slides available on the internet from the german division of the iap. Pathologe 27(6), 477–480 (2006)
11. Sander, B., Golas, M.M.: An interactive e-learning platform facilitating group and peer group learning. Anat. Sci. Educ. 6(3), 182–190 (2013)
12. Schmidt, C., Reinehr, M., Leucht, O., Behrendt, N., Geiler, S., Britsch, S.: Mymicroscope-intelligent virtual microscopy in a blended learning model at ulm university. Ann. Anat. 193(5), 395–402 (2011)
13. Stoica, I., Morris, R., Karger, D., Kaashoek, M.F., Balakrishnan, H.: Chord: a scalable peer-to-peer lookup service for internet applications. In: SIGCOMM 2001, pp. 149–160 (2001)
14. Terpstra, W.W., Kangasharju, J., Leng, C., Buchmann, A.P.: Bubblestorm: resilient, probabilistic, and exhaustive peer-to-peer search. In: SIGCOMM 2007, Kyoto, August 2007
15. Terpstra, W.W., Leng, C., Buchmann, A.P.: Bubblestorm: analysis of probabilistic exhaustive search in a heterogeneous peer-to-peer system. Technical report TUD-CS-2007-2, Technische Universität Darmstadt (2007)
16. Zhao, B.Y., Kubiatowicz, J., Joseph, A.D.: Tapestry: an infrastructure for fault-tolerant wide-area location and routing. Technical report UCB/CSD-01-1141, Computer Science Division, University of California, April 2001

Using Social Networks Data for Behavior and Sentiment Analysis

Barbara Calabrese, Mario Cannataro[(⊠)], and Nicola Ielpo

Department of Medical and Surgical Sciences, Magna Græcia
University Viale Europa, 88100 Catanzaro, Italy
cannataro@unicz.it

Abstract. With the advent of social networks, a huge amount of information is generated and stored every day. The social networks therefore represent a potentially infinite source of user data, usable both for scientific and commercial applications. Specifically, they store a lot of data regarding the single individual and behavior, as well as information related to individuals and their relationship with other individuals, i.e. a sort of collective behavior. The combination of behavior and sentiment analysis tools with methodologies of affective computing could allow the extraction of useful data that convey information for different applications, such as detection of depression state in psychology, political events, stock marketing fluctuations. The paper surveys some data extraction tools for social networks and emerging computing trends such as behavior analysis, sentiment analysis and affective computing. Then the paper proposes a first architecture for behavior analysis integrating those tools.

Keywords: Social network · Behavior analysis · Sentiment analysis · Affective computing

1 Introduction

In recent years, social networks have seen an exponential increase and now they store a lot of data regarding individuals and their relationship with other individuals as well as data regarding groups or communities of users. Thus, analyzing social network data may be helpful to detect behaviour and emotions of individuals as well of communities.

Social networks provide some interfaces that allow to access to the data of its members in respect of their privacy. However, since they base their own business model on this data, consequently the (legal) access modes to the data and the amount of data extracted from the social network are very low. Alternatively there are other methods for extracting data from social network associated with the Web Scraping [1–3].

The aim of the paper is to provide an overview of the methods for data extraction from social networks and to discuss issues related to the integration of

© Springer International Publishing Switzerland 2015
G. Di Fatta et al. (Eds.): IDCS 2015, LNCS 9258, pp. 285–293, 2015.
DOI: 10.1007/978-3-319-23237-9_25

ocial networks, behavior analysis, sentiment analysis and afffective computing. Specifically, the paper contains an initial proposal relating to a possible system hat integrates the described methodologies.

The paper is organized as follows: Sect. 2 describes the main features and he APIs (Application Programming Interfaces) for data extraction from Facebook and Twitter; Sect. 3 presents the main issues and some examples of systems in the fields of behavior and sentiment analysis, and affective computing; Sect. 4 proposes an integration scheme of the previously described methodologies with social networks and, finally, Sect. 5 concludes the paper, highlighting future works.

2 Social Networks: A Main Data Source for Detecting Behaviors and Emotions

Social networks are the most representative models of Graph Databases. In social networks [4], the nodes are people and groups, while the links show relationships or flows between the nodes. Some examples are the friendships, business relationships, research networks (collaboration, co-authorship), recordings of communications (mail, phone calls, etc. ...), computer networks, national security. There is an increasing activity in the field of social networks analysis, visualization and data processing in such networks.

To analyze social networks data the following main tasks need to be performed: social network data extraction (e.g. through the APIs provided by major social networks providers); data storage (e.g. through the emerging NoSQL databases well suited to store graph-based data); data analytics (to discover behaviors and emotions), eventually coupled with complementary approaches such as affective computing, eye movement and facial movement detection.

In the following, the main features of the two most popular social network, Facebook and Twitter, are described.

2.1 Facebook API

Facebook is a social network that allows registered users to create their own profile to upload photos, videos and send messages, in order to keep in touch with friends, family and colleagues. It also has the following features: groups, events, pages, chat, marketplace and privacy manager. In order to try to extract information from a user, you must be registered to the social network. If the user belongs to my friends network then I can have access to all the information that he/she has made available on his/her user profile. Instead in the case in which he/she is not my friend, the data that I might be able to collect depend entirely on how he/she has set the privacy for his/her profile. So with regard to Facebook, finding information about a user that is not in our friends network turns out to be a very complicated operation and appears to be influenced by the level of privacy that this user has set for himself/herself. Generally, most of the registered users on Facebook do not change these settings and leave the default ones that allow the tracing of the person on the search engines and leave public the basic information of the profile.

Facebook is characterized by the social graph, the graph in which nodes represent entities (such as people, pages or applications) and arcs represent entities connections. Therefore each entity or object is a node in the social graph and every action of an entity is an arc. It is possible to interact with the social graph in a unique way, i.e. through HTTP calls to the Facebook API [5]. The interaction involves two main components: the Graph API for reading and writing of the social graph and the OGP (Open Graph Protocol), which is the protocol that allows you to insert any object in the social graph by simply entering within it the meta-data RDFa (Resource Description Framework in Attributes).

The Graph API allows to have a uniform view of the Facebook social graph through simple HTTP calls; it provides, therefore, a subset of the nodes and connections of the graph. Each entity of the social graph has a unique identifier; then the properties of the object can be tracked at $https://graph.facebook.com/<id>$. Alternatively, all entities with a $username$ field (such as user profiles and pages) are accessible using this field instead of the id. HTTP calls return a response message with a well-defined structure (XML or JSON); the latter is the most widely used format for response messages of Web Services because it is lighter than XML. It is possible to examine the connections between the various objects of the social graph using the following URL structure $https://graph.facebook.com/<id>/connection\_type$.

The Graph API therefore allows to easily access all public information of an object; in case you wish to obtain additional information, you need permission of the entity that owns them.

Facebook and Twitter (described in the next paragraph) provide APIs with the OAuth authentication mechanism. The purpose of this protocol is to provide a framework for the verification of the identity of the entities involved in secure transactions. Currently, there are two versions of this protocol: OAuth 1.0 [6] and OAuth 2.0 [7]. Both versions support two-legged authentication, in which a server is guaranteed about the user identity and three-legged authentication in which a server is guaranteed by an application about the user identity. This type of authentication requires the use of the access token and it is currently implemented by the Social Network.

The Facebook authentication mechanism is based on OAuth 2.0 protocol, which provides for the acquisition of an access token. There are different ways of acquiring the access token; the easiest one is to go into the Graph API Explorer and press the "Get Access Token". Then you will need to select the permissions you are interested in, by selecting the appropriate boxes. Of course this can also be done via HTTP, just hanging to the query string of the API HTTP address the access_token parameter ($https://graph.facebook.com/me?access\_token = ...$)

The Graph API provides three types of permits: base permits (it does not require any access token); user data and friends data permits (they are designed to restrict access to personal data of users); extended permits (required for publication and access to sensitive data). So, the access token is a mechanism whose aim is to provide a temporary and limited access to the Facebook API. Graph

API calls return most of the properties of the object of the social graph related to the query sent; to select the parameters that you want returned, you must enter the fields parameter in the search string of the API call.

2.2 Twitter API

Twitter is a service of micro-blogging with two main characteristics: its users send messages (tweets) of 140 characters usually compounds by keywords (in the form of hashtags), natural language and common abbreviations; moreover, each user can follow other users so that his/her timeline is populated by their tweets. It is much easier to obtain user data because the profiles are public and can be viewed by anyone. As for Facebook, there is the ability to change the settings relating to privacy so that a user can see the profile of other users, only after they have accepted his/her request. Even in this case, however, users who choose this route about privacy are few; moreover also any person not registered in Twitter can access to user profiles.

Compared to Facebook, Twitter connections are bidirectional: there is an asymmetric network consisting of friends, that is the accounts that a user follow, and followers, that is the accounts that follow the user. The timeline of a user that you can trace in the home consists of a real-time stream containing all the tweets of his/her friends.

As Facebook provides the Graph API Explorer useful to explore the API, Twitter provides the Twitter Console; generally Twitter offers an extensive collection of APIs, all based on HTTP [8]. Twitter supports two authentication methods based on the OAuth protocol: the first one based on OAuth 1.0a related to the user and the second one based on OAuth 2.0 related to an application.

The first mode, defined application-user authentication, includes an HTTP authorization request that communicates what application is making the request, on behalf of which user the application is making the request, if the user has authorized or not the application and if during transit the request has been tampered by third parties.

In the second mode, defined application-only authentication, the application encodes its consumer key and its secret key in a set of encoded credentials and then performs an HTTP POST request to endpoint OAuth2/token to exchange these credentials with a bearer token. The bearer token obtained is used to authenticate the application that it represents in the REST API. The latter approach is much simpler because it is not required that the call is signed.

The typology of the Twitter API end-point is the following:

$https://api.twitter.com/1.1/ <resource>/<action>$.

The Twitter API include 16 resources: timeline, tweet, search, streaming, direct messages, friends and followers, users, user suggested, favorites, lists, saved search, places, trends, spam reporting, OAuth, help. The Twitter Search API allows the execution of real-time queries on recent tweet. In particular, the query must be simple, limited to a maximum of 1000 characters, including operators and it is always required some form of authentication. In this case the only available resource is the tweet. The Twitter Streaming API allows a real-time update of information relating to specific resource, thereby eliminating the need to repeatedly call at regular intervals (polling) its REST end-point.

2.3   NoSQL Databases

The increase of the volume of data to be stored and the need to process large amounts of unstructured data in a short time, is a continuous trend; therefore we are observing the emerging of a new model of data management that moves away from the relational model: the NoSQL model. It provides four main families of database: Key-Values stores; Column-oriented databases; Document databases and Graph databases [9]. Graph databases have become a topic of interest in the last years, mainly due to the large amount of data modeled as a graph introduced by web. A graph, the key element of the Graph database, is defined as a simple mathematical structure that consists of nodes and arcs connecting the nodes. More formally, a graph is an ordered pair of sets G = (V, E), with V a set of nodes and E a set of arcs, such that the elements of E are elements of V pairs [10].

3   Emerging Computing Trends

3.1   Behaviour Analysis

With the rise of social media, users are given opportunities to exhibit different behaviors such as sharing, posting, liking, commenting, and befriending conveniently. By analyzing behaviors observed on social media, it is possible to classify these behaviors into individual and collective behavior. Individual behavior is exhibited by a single user, whereas collective behavior is observed when a group of users behave together [11].

In [12], the authors investigated whether posts on FB would also be applicable for the prediction of users' psychological traits such as self-monitoring (SM) skill that is supposed to be linked with users' expression behavior in the online environment. They present a model to evaluate the relationship between the posts and SM skills. First, they evaluate the quality of responses to the Snyder's Self-Monitoring Questionnaire collected via the Internet; and secondly, explore the textual features of the posts in different SM-level groups. The prediction of posts resulted in an approximate 60 % accuracy compared with the classification made by Snyder's SM scale. They concluded that the textual posts on the FB Wall could partially predict the users' SM skills.

Zhang et al. propose a socioscope model for social-network and human behavior analysis based on mobile-phone call-detail records [13]. They use multiple probability and statistical methods for quantifying social groups relationships, and communication patterns and for detecting human-behavior changes. They propose a new index to measure the level of reciprocity between users and their communication partners. For the validation of their results, they used real-life call logs of 81 users which contain approximately 500,000 hour of data on users' location, communication, and device-usage behavior collected over eight months at the Massachusetts Institute of Technology (MIT) by the Reality Mining Project group.

3.2   Sentiment Analysis

Sentiment analysis aims to analyze people's sentiment, opinions, attitudes, emotions. Different techniques and software tools have been developed to carry out Sentiment Analysis. Most of works in this research area focus on classifying texts according to their sentiment polarity, which can be positive, negative or neutral. Therefore, it can be considered a text classification problem, since its goal consists of categorizing texts within classes by means of algorithmic methods.

The paper [14] offers a comprehensive review about this topic and compares some free access web services, analyzing their capabilities to classify and score different pieces of text with respect to the sentiments contained therein.

In the last years, thanks to the increasing amount of information delivered through social networks, many researches have been focused on applying sentiment analysis to these data [15,16]. Sentiment analysis aims at mining users opinion and sentiment polarity from the posted text on the social network.

In [17], the authors apply data mining techniques to psychology, specifically to the field of depression, to detect depressed users in social network services. They create an accurate model based on sentiment analysis. In fact, the main symptom of the depression is severe negative emotions and lack of positive emotions.

In [18], a new method for sentiment analysis in Facebook has been presented aiming: (i) to extract information about the users' sentiment polarity (positive, neutral or negative), as transmitted in the messages they write; and (ii) to model the users' usual sentiment polarity and to detect significant emotional changes. The authors have implemented this method in SentBuk, a Facebook application [19]. SentBuk retrieves messages written by users in Facebook and classifies them according to their polarity, showing the results to the users through an interactive interface. It also supports emotional change detection, friend's emotion finding, user classification according to their messages, and statistics, among others. The classification method implemented in SentBuk follows a hybrid approach: it combines lexical-based and machine-learning techniques. The results obtained through this approach show that it is feasible to perform sentiment analysis in Facebook with high accuracy (83.27 %).

3.3   Affective Computing

Affective Computing is computing that relates to, arises from, or deliberately influences emotion or other affective phenomena [20]. Existing emotion recognition technologies include physiological signals recording, facial expression and/or voice analysis [21,22]. Physiological emotion recognition is based on obtrusive technologies that require special equipment or devices, e.g. skin conductance sensors, blood pressure monitors, ECG and/or EEG recording devices. Facial expressions and voice systems for emotion recognition, instead, use devices that should be positioned in front of the face of the user or should always listen to the voice of user [23]. In the following, some examples of emotion recognition systems are reported and discussed.

C. Peter et al. proposed wearable system architecture for collecting emotion-related physiological signals such as heart rate, skin conductivity, and a skin temperature of users [24]. They developed a prototype system, consisting of a glove with a sensor unit, and a base unit for receiving the data transmitted from the sensor unit. S. V. Ioannou et al. realize an emotion recognition system based on the evaluation of facial expressions [25]. They implemented a neuro-fuzzy network based on rules which have been defined via analysis of facial animation parameters (FAPs) variations of users. With experimental real data, they also showed acceptable recognition accuracy of higher than 70 %. A. Batliner et al. presented an overview of the state of the art in automatic recognition of emotional states using acoustic and linguistic parameters [26]. They summarized core technologies such as corpus engineering, feature extraction, and classification have been used for building emotion recognition systems via the speech analysis.

In [23], the authors present a machine learning approach to recognize emotional states through the acquisition of some features related to user behavioral patterns (e.g. typing speed) and the user context (e.g. location) in the social network services. They developed an Android application that acquires and analyzes these features whenever the user sends a text message to Twitter. They built a Bayesian classifier that recognizes seven classes: one neutral and six relative to basic emotions with an accuracy of 67,52 %.

The paper [27] describes an intelligent and affective tutoring system designed and implemented within a social network. The tutoring system evaluates cognitive and affective aspects and applies fuzzy logic to calculate the exercises that are presented to the student. The authors use Kohonen neural networks to recognize emotions through faces and voices and multi-attribute utility theory to encourage positive affective states.

4   Towards an Integration of Existing Approaches

Social networks user often expresses her/his feeling or emotional states with written text or by using emoticon. However, some users have difficulties to express their feelings or can simulate. These limits could be exceeded by adopting emotion recognition technologies related to affective computing and combining them with typical text-mining methodologies of behavior and sentiment analysis.

Specifically, the affective computing research has focused on the detection of facial expressions since the signal is very easy to be captured by camera. Moreover, microphones are commonly equipped for computers, smartphones, etc. to record speech and vocal expressions. Pressure sensors on pad, keyboard, mouse collect posture and gesture patterns. According to specific recorded signals, different methods and tools could be combined with text-mining methodologies to detect affect, sentiments and behaviors.

The Fig. 1 represents a scheme of a system for the integration of data extracted from social networks and other data coming from external sensor devices (e.g. eye detectors, facial movements detectors, etc.). The collected data need to be stored in appropriate databases (e.g. SQL and/or NoSQL) for further analysis and investigations.

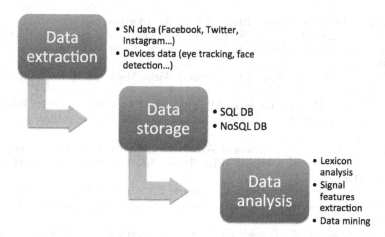

Fig. 1. Block diagram of an integrated system for sentiment and behavior analysis from social networks and sensors devices.

Conclusions and Future Works

Today, new computing technologies permit the detection and analysis of behavior, sentiment and affects. Specifically, the application of behavior and sentiment analysis on data social networks and the integration with affective computing methodologies offers the possibility to increase information and realize novel applications in different fields. The paper surveys some data extraction methods for social networks (Facebook and Twitter) and emerging computing trends such as behavior analysis, sentiment analysis and affective computing. The paper proposes a first architecture for behavior analysis integrating those tools. A detailed implementation of the different modules (data extraction, storage and analysis) will be presented as future work.

References

1. Catanese, S.A., De Meo P., Ferrara, E.: Crawling facebook for social network analysis purposes. In: Proceedings of the International Conference on Web Intelligence, Mining and Semantics (2011)
2. Traud, A.L., Kelsic, E.D., Mucha, P.J., Porter, M.A.: Comparing community structure to characteristics in online collegiate social networks. SIAM Rev. **53**(3), 17 (2008)
3. Traud, A.L., Mucha P.J., Porter, M.A.: Social Structure of Facebook Networks. CoRR: 82 (2011)
4. Hanneman, R.A.: Introduction to Social Network Methods. Technical report, Department of Sociology, University of California, Riverside (2001)
5. Facebook. Graph API - Facebook Developers, March 2012. https://developers.facebook.com/docs/reference/api/
6. Hammer-Lahav, E.: The OAuth 1.0 Protocol. RFC 5849, April 2010
7. Hardt, D.: The OAuth 2.0 Authorization Framework. RFC 6749, October 2012

8. Twitter API. https://dev.twitter.com/overview/documentation
9. Eifrem, E.: A nosql overview and the benefits of graph databases. Nosql East (2009)
10. Trudeau, R.J.: Introduction to Graph Theory. Dover Publications, New York (1994)
11. Zafarani, R., Liu, H.: Behavior Analysis in Social Media. IEEE Intell. Sys. **29**(4), 9–11 (2014)
12. He, Q., Glas, C.A.W., Kosinski, M., Stillwell, D.J., Veldkamp, B.P.: Predicting self-monitoring skills using textual posts on Facebook. Comput. Hum. Behav. **33**, 69–78 (2014)
13. Zhang, H., Dantu, R., Cangussu, J.W.: Socioscope: human relationship and behavior analysis in social networks. IEEE Trans. Sys. Man Cybernetics Part A Sys. Hum. **41**(6), 1122–1143 (2011)
14. Serrano-Guerrero, J., Olivas, J.A., Romero, F.P., Herrera-Viedma, E.: Sentiment analysis: a review and comparative analysis of web services. Inf. Sci. **311**, 18–38 (2015)
15. Go, A., Bhayani, R., Huang, L.: Twitter sentiment classification using distant supervision. Technical report. Stanford University, Stanford Digital Library Technologies Project (2009)
16. Pak, A., Paroubek, P.: Twitter as a corpus for sentiment analysis and opinion mining. In: Proceedings of the Seventh Conference on International Language Resourcesand Evaluation, pp. 1320-1326 (2010)
17. Wang, X., Zhang, C., Ji, Y., Sun, L., Wu, L., Bao, Z.: A depression detection model based on sentiment analysis in micro-blog social network. In: Li, J., Cao, L., Wang, C., Tan, K.C., Liu, B., Pei, J., Tseng, V.S. (eds.) PAKDD 2013 Workshops. LNCS, vol. 7867, pp. 201–213. Springer, Heidelberg (2013)
18. Ortigosa, A., Martin, J.M., Carro, R.M.: Sentiment analysis in Facebook and itsapplication to e-learning. Comput. Hum. Behav. **31**, 527–541 (2014)
19. Martin, J.M., Ortigosa, A., Carro, R. M.: SentBuk: sentiment analysis for e-learning environments. In: International Symposium on Computers in Education (SIIE 2012), pp. 1–6. IEEE (2012)
20. Picard, R.: Affect. Comput. Cambridge MIT Press, Cambridge (2000)
21. Armony, J.L.: Affective Computing. Trends Cognitive Sci. **2**(7), 270 (1998)
22. Calvo, R.A., D'Mello, S.: Affect Detection: an interdisciplinary review of models methods, and their applications. IEEE Trans. Affect. Comput. **1**(1), 18–37 (2010)
23. Lee, H., Choi, Y.S., Lee, S., Park, I.P.: Towards unobtrusive emotion recognition for affective social communication. In: 9th Annual IEEE Consumer Communications and Networking Conference, pp. 260–264. IEEE (2012)
24. Peter, C., Ebert, E., Beikirch, H.: A wearable multi-sensor system for mobile acquisition of emotion-related physiological data. In: Tao, J., Tan, T., Picard, R.W (eds.) ACII 2005. LNCS, vol. 3784, pp. 691–698. Springer, Heidelberg (2005)
25. Ioannou, S.V., Raouzaiou, A.T., Tzouvaras, V.A., Mailis, T.P., Karpouzis, K.C. Kollias, S.D.: Emotion recognition through facial expression analysis based on neurofuzzy network. Neural Netw. **18**(4), 423–435 (2005)
26. Batliner, A., Schuller, B., Seppi, D., Steidl, S., Devillers, L., Vidrascu, L., Vogt, T. Aharonson, V., Amir, N.: The automatic recognition of emotions in speech. Emot. Oriented Sys. **2**, 71–99 (2011)
27. Barrón-Estrada, M.L., Zatarain-Cabada, R., Beltrán V., J.A., Cibrian R., F.L. Pérez, Y.H.: An Intelligent and affective tutoring system within a social network for learning mathematics. In: Pavón, J., Duque-Méndez, N.D., Fuentes-Fernández R. (eds.) IBERAMIA 2012. LNCS, vol. 7637, pp. 651–661. Springer, Heidelberg (2012)

Sentimental Preference Extraction from Online Reviews for Recommendation

Nieqing Cao, Jingjing Cao$^{(\boxtimes)}$, Panpan Liu, and Wenfeng Li$^{(\boxtimes)}$

School of Logistics and Engineer, Wuhan University of Technology,
Wuhan 430077, China
NieqingCao@126.com,
{bettycao, liupanpan, liwf}@whut.edu.cn

Abstract. With booming electronic commerce, online reviews are often created by users like who buys a product or goes to a restaurant. However, littery and unordered free-text reviews make it difficult for new users to acquire and analyze useful information. Thus, recommendation system plays an increasingly important role in online surfing. Nowadays, it has been proved that recommendation system based on topics is an available method in the theory and practice. However, there is little study to extract preferences from the perspective of sentiment. The method we proposed is to combine the topics and sentiments for generating a user's preference from the user's previous reviews. According to the degree of similarity with public's preference, recommendation system we proposed would judge whether it should recommend the new products to this user. The empirical results show that the recommendation system we proposed can make accurately and effectively recommend.

Keywords: Topic extraction · Sentiment analysis · Recommendation system · User preference

Introduction

The recent development of Web 4.0 has enlarged people's ability of expressing their thought and preference for the product/service they bought in the market. Followed by this, a huge amount of data has been coming which makes a lot of burden for people to quickly get the effective information. In this area, recommendation systems (RS) are widely popular. They are aiming at recommending items to users according their preferences. On the whole, recommendation systems mainly consist of content-based and collaborative filtering(CF) based approaches. Content-based RSs make use of the items' similarity to give some advice to a user. Collaborative filtering based RSs depend on users' similarity to find out the user models who have the same preference for product and then recommends another user's interested items to the target user. However, the users' preferences not only performed in the rating of products they purchased, but also existed in the attitude tendency (sentiment) for those products.

Recently, a hot direction is to define the sentiment polarity as positive or negative of a given review. Usually, the subjective views are utilized for sentiment classification. Users' behaviors and public opinions are more likely to be found and organized by

Springer International Publishing Switzerland 2015
, Di Fatta et al. (Eds.): IDCS 2015, LNCS 9258, pp. 294–303, 2015.
DOI: 10.1007/978-3-319-23237-9_26

sentiment classification. To classify sentiments of reviews not only can help enterprises to understand users' opinions but also can give a great influence on user's purchase intentions.

For exacting preferences of customers, the method we proposed is to combine the topics which the customers pay close attention to with the customers' emotional tendency to these topics. When we recommend a new product to a user, we would first check the user's reviews for other products and then we would identify the topics he or she concentrates on and the sentiment analysis for these topics. In this paper, we manage to utilize the recommendation system based on topics and sentiments to recommend customized new products to users. Two main contributions have been made and described as follows: the first contribution is that our work combines the topics and sentiments in the reviews to make analysis and recommendations. The other contribution is that we get the user's preferences from his or her previous reviews which are compared with public preferences to determine whether the system should recommend the new products to the users.

This paper is structured as follows. We report on related work in the Sect. 2. In Sect. 3, we will give a detailed description of our algorithm to solve the user cold start problem and our experiments on the real data set will be given in Sect. 4. In Sect. 5, we will make some conclusion about this study.

2 Related Work

Recommendation system is a useful tool to ease customers' burden to get the available information in the vast amounts of data and message. Lee et al. [1] proposed a novel recommender system which only uses positively rating items in users' profiles to make an effective recommendation based on graph. Yung-Ming Li et al. [2] integrate preference similarity, recommendation trust and social relations to make a social recommender system that can generate personalized product recommendations. Dooms et al [3] partition the complete calculation process into any number of jobs by implementing an in-memory, content-based recommendation algorithm.

There is a great amount of literature for Recommender System concentrated on different topics, such as e-commerce [4, 5], e-learning [6], music [7, 8], books [9], television [10] and web search [11], among others.For example, Konstantinos Christidis and Gregoris Mentzas [12] proposed an innovative recommender system to exploit the hidden topics found in auction marketplaces across the web in order to support these functions.

Apart from topics, sentiment analysis [13] is a good way to extract users' opinions. We can get positive or negative attitudes, emotions and views from sentiment analysis. P. Venkata Krishna et al. [14] illustrated an approach for a recommendation system using Learning automata (LA) and sentiment analysis. Their experiments show that their approach based on sentiment analysis improves the efficiency of the recommender system.Michael K.S. Park and Namme Moon [15] aim to improve the effectiveness of the music recommender systems and one of their methods is to analyze the personal sentiments and contexts.Recently, Tian Pingfang et al. [16] proposed a method based on the sentiment analysis for semantic recommendation mechanism which are more accurate than other compared methods. In their study, they expanded the expression sentiment base and collected all kinds of hot words. And there are many studies confirmed that Integrating some methods and sentiment analysis is a good way to enhance the effectiveness of experiments. For example, Leung, C. W. et al. [17] integrated collaborative filtering and sentiment analysis for their approach and preliminary results validated the effectiveness of various tasks in the proposed framework.

In our study, our proposed algorithm makes the topics and sentiment in a review together to seek out a user's preference and make a recommendation for him/her.

3   Algorithm

The recommendation system we proposed consists of two phases: combining topics and sentiments, and extracting users' preferences and the degree of similarity with popular preferences. The process is expressed in Fig. 1.

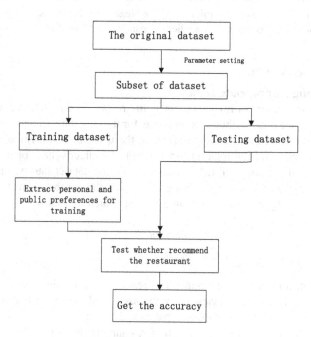

Fig. 1. The algorithm process

3.1   The Topics and Sentiments Phase

The first phase is composed of three parts, which are selecting topics, dividing sentiments and combining topics with sentiments. During the first part we need to select several topics. In this paper, we choose six typical topics from our restaurant data set. These topics are food, service, price, ambience, anecdotes and miscellaneous. Then, during the second part, we should divide the sentiment analysis into four polarities, that, positive sentiment, negative sentiment, neutral sentiment and conflict sentiment. This four polarities can effectively express one's attitude to the corresponding item. During the third part, we would combine the six topics with the four sentiments. Adding the six topics and the four sentiments itself, there are thirty-four (4*6 + 4+6) features all. For example, *food positive* can express positive attitude for one restaurant' food. All features would be listed in Table 1.

Table 1. Topics and sentiments

	Food	Service	Price	Ambience	Anecdotes	Miscellaneous
Positive	Food positive	Service positive	Price positive	Ambience positive	Anecdotes positive	Miscellaneous positive
Negative	Food negative	Service negative	Price negative	Ambience negative	Anecdotes negative	Miscellaneous negative
Neutral	Food neural	Service neutral	Price neutral	Ambience neutral	Anecdotes neutral	Miscellaneous neutral
Conflict	Food conflict	Service conflict	Price conflict	Ambience conflict	Anecdotes conflict	Miscellaneous conflict

3.2   The Preference Phrase

3.2.1   Selecting Appropriate Data

There are various amount of reviews in the entire restaurant data set. We would choose a part of appropriate data to obtain experiments for training data set and testing data set. In this paper, we would find the data in which the user has commented x restaurants, where $x \in [m, n]$ and find the relationship between the effectiveness of the recommendation system and the range of x. We would divide the dataset into two parts, one for training and the other for testing. Among these data, the number of restaurants which has been reviewed by one user for training is calculated as follows:

$$trainNum = ceil(x/2)$$
$$x \in range[m, n] \ and \ x \in N^+$$

(1)

This means that, for one user, the number of restaurants for training is the ceil number of one half of all restaurants reviewed by the user. And the rest restaurants would be used for testing. For example, suppose that m = 2 and n = 4, we would choose those data in which the users has reviewed 2 to 4 restaurants. In these selected data, if one user has reviewed 3 restaurants, that, x = 3, the restaurants for training would be two and the rest restaurant would be used for testing.

3.2.2   Transforming Information

In order to process files with textual data, one should transform the texts into numerical data which can be recognized by computer. In this study, we define score to describe the importance of sentences proportion labeled features in a review. This method can effectively decrease misjudgements thanks to a user's tirade for one aspect. The score can be calculated as follows:

$$\text{score} = \frac{\text{the number of sentences with feature}}{\text{the number of sentences in a review}} \tag{2}$$

It should be noted that some sentences are annotated with multiple sentiments or topics. In this case, one should redistribute the weight of the sentences. For example, a sentence is annotated as positive, neutral and food, and there are four sentences in the review. The score of feature food positive would be calculated as $(1/4)/2 = 0.125$, equal to the feature neutral food.

3.2.3 Training

Notational conventions. U, R and F denote the training data set used to create the model. The labels in this set are known. There are n users in training data set and they are denoted U_i, $i = 1,2,...,l,...,n$. A restaurant is denoted as R_j and $j = 1,2,...,m$. There are k features in the study. F_{jk} indicates the user's score for the j restaurant and the k feature.

The whole process is carried out iteratively for each user. In the interest of clarity, the process described below is only for one user$_l$ in the training dataset even though the process is also repeated for the other users. The process for one user is as follows:

Firstly, get the preferences (P_{jk}) for each restaurant of this user$_l$.

$$P_{jk} = F_{jk}^l - \frac{1}{n-1}\left(\sum_{i=1}^{n} F_{jk}^i - F_{jk}^l\right) \tag{3}$$

$$(k = 1,..., K)$$

And then, get the features that the user$_l$ concentrates on. We should set a threshold θ_1 as a critical value. The value of θ_1 can be defined by ourselves in experiments. For those preferences for the restaurant we calculated before, we select those preferences which are greater than θ_1 as 1. And we select those preferences which are less than or equal to θ_1 as 0. In order to clearly denote the process, we would install a variable L_{jk} for user$_l$. L_{jk} can make it clearer that which preferences the users *concentrates on*. This procedure can be described as follows:

$$L_{jk} = \begin{cases} 1 & p_{jk} \geq \theta_1 \\ 0 & p_{jk} < \theta_1 \end{cases} \text{ and } L = \{L_{jk}\} \tag{4}$$

After that, we need to calculate the total value for every feature. If

$$\sum_{j=1}^{m} L_{jk} > \frac{m}{2} \tag{5}$$

Then the Feature k would be selected into a set (S) as one concerned feature. Otherwise, Feature k is discarded. And

$$S = \left\{ k' \left| \sum_{j=1}^{m} L_{jk'} > \frac{m}{2} \right. \right\} \tag{6}$$

We denote it as $S_{k'}$.

User$_l$'s final preferences(Q) to the concerning features are shown as follows:

$$Q_{k'} = \frac{1}{|S|} \sum_{j=1}^{m} P_{jk'} \tag{7}$$

For those features which are not defined as a concerning features, their final preferences would be labeled as 0. The details are listed in the Table 2.

Table 2. Finding features the user concentrate on

Table Head	Food positive	Food negative	...	Miscellaneous conflict
Restaurant1	1	0		0
Restaurant2	0	1		0
...				
Total value				

3.2.4 Testing

In the extracted data before, one part for training, remaining part for testing. This means that we would use the remainder restaurants of the user reviewed to test the user and determine whether we should recommend or not. According to the well-known results, we can get accuracies of recommendation. The testWeight is denoted as a degree of similarity for a user and public.

$$testWeight = \frac{Feature_B(A \cap B)}{Feature_B B}$$

$$A = \{x \in S_{k'}\} \text{ and } B = \{x \in F_B, x > 0\} \tag{8}$$

The higher the value of testWeight, may indicates two aspects:One possible reason is that there are many high concerning features that the user and the public common concerned. Another reason is that although their common concerns may be not greatly repeated, the features that the user and the public common concerned are very live.

We would decide whether recommend the restaurant to the user by the value of testWeight. And we would set an another threshold θ_2 to compare with the value of testWeight. if the value of testWeight is greater than θ_2, it means the user's preferences is similar to the popular preferences. According to the good or bad public reviews, we would recommend or not recommend the restaurant to the user. If the value of testWeight is less than θ_2, it means the user's preferences is different from the public preferences. And the recommending condition would be an inverse relationship to previous point.

4 Experimental Design and Results

In the following section, we conduct some empirical experiments based on our proposed algorithm.

4.1 Data Set and Experimental Setting

We conduct our experiments with a restaurant review data set that is RED[1] data set [18]. It contains reviews from users on items, trust values between users, items category, categories hierarchy and users expertise on categories. For our experiments, we mainly extract the corpus of over 50000 restaurant reviews from Citysearch New York in the data set. The corpus contains 5531 restaurants, with associated structured information (location, cuisine type) and a set of reviews. There are 52264 reviews, of which 1359 are editorial reviews and the rest are user reviews. The average user review has 5.28 sentences. The reviews are written by 32284 distinct users, for whom we only have unique username information. For each review, there are six categories (Food, Service, Price, Ambience, Anecdotes, and Miscellaneous) identified in the data set. In addition to sentence categories, sentences have an associated sentiment: Positive, Negative, Neutral, or Conflict [19].

The experimental settings are divided into three sections. During the first section, we need to determine the range of the selected data. In our study, we choose m = 2 and n = 4. We select the data in which the user has reviewed two or three or four restaurants from the whole data set. During second section, we need to determine the two value of thresholds, θ_1 and θ_2. We let $\theta_1 = 0$, this means that if a feature's personal preference is greater than 0, the feature would be a common concern. And we would set θ_2 in different values to observe the influences brought by the variation of θ_2. During third section, we would determine the way of performance evaluation. Final, we would calculate the accuracy of our recommendation system by using testing data set.

4.2 Experimental Results and Analysis

Tables 3 and 4 summarize the average accuracies based on different value of θ_2. From these Tables, we can easily see that the accuracies of $\theta_2 = 1/(10*n)$ is equal to the accuracies of $\theta_2 = 1/(2*n)$ when n = 2. This phenomenon indicates that their test-Weights are all greater than $\theta_2 = 1/(2*2)$. And we can also find that $\theta_2 = 1/(10*n)$ always performs better than $\theta_2 = 1/(2*n)$ in the case of n = 3 and n = 4. This result shows that we can conjecture that higher accuracies can be obtained under $\theta_2 = 1/(10*n)$ with the growth of n rather than $\theta_2 = 1/(2*n)$.

Beyond that, we can clearly find the differences between different ranges of data extraction from Fig. 2. The horizontal axis denotes the values of θ_2, and the vertical axis denotes the accuracies of recommendation system. The blue color bar represents the accuracies of the case 1: the number of the reviews is selected in [3, 4]; whereas the

---

Table 3. The average accuracies of $\theta_2 = 1/(10*n)$

$\Theta_2 = 1/(10*n)$	m = 3	m = 4	m = 5	m = 6	m = 7	m = 8	m = 9	m = 10	m = 11
n = 2		0.7863	0.7987	0.8066	0.8099	0.8155	0.8154	0.8169	
n = 3			0.8066	0.8049	0.8029	0.8040	0.8041	0.8076	0.8114
n = 4			0.8085	0.8082	0.8090	0.8084	0.8093	0.8112	0.8160

Table 4. The average accuracies of $\theta_2 = 1/(2*n)$

$\Theta_2 = 1/(2*n)$	m = 3	m = 4	m = 5	m = 6	m = 7	m = 8	m = 9	m = 10	m = 11
n = 2		0.7863	0.7987	0.8066	0.8099	0.8155	0.8154	0.8169	
n = 3			0.7788	0.7496	0.7206	0.7040	0.6928	0.6923	0.6910
n = 4			0.7118	0.7249	0.7304	0.7352	0.7396	0.7435	0.7482

red color bar means the case 2: the number of the reviews is selected in [3, 10]. The figure shows that the performance of case 1 is better than the performance of case 2 because in case 2, it contains more training samples. However, the summation execution time of all θ_2 in case 1 is much faster than case 2, which are 5.4262 s and 16.2167 s respectively.

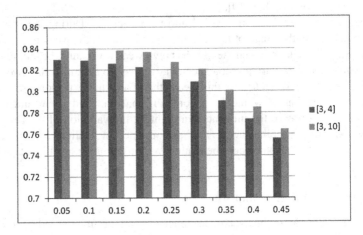

Fig. 2. Accuracies of recommendation for different cases

5   Conclusions and Directions

With the rapid development of website, the more user-generated contents, the more important for effective recommendation system. How to effectively and accurately recommend products to a new user has been a hot topic in recent years. Under the typical restaurant review data set, we combined topics with sentiments. Based on experiments, we recommend products to new users according to their previous reviews for other restaurants. The final results indicate that the recommendation system we proposed can effectively and accurately achieve recommended functionality. This means that the system we proposed can be an available method for recommending.

In future, there are several directions for us to study. Firstly, we can use other typical review data sets. Our restaurant review data set cannot represent the whole aspect. Secondly, we can continue studying the option of threshold and the extraction of data set.

Acknowledgements. This work was supported by the Fundamental Research Funds for the Central Universities (WUT:2014-IV-054).

References

1. Lee, K., Lee, K.: Escaping your comfort zone: A graph-based recommender system for finding novel recommendations among relevant items. Expert Syst. Appl. **42**(10), 4851–4858 (2015)
2. Li, Y.-M., Chun-Te, W., Lai, C.-Y.: A social recommender mechanism for e-commerce: Combining similarity, trust, and relationship. Decisi. Support Syst. **55**(3), 740–752 (2013)
3. Dooms, S., Audenaert, P., Fostier, J., De Pessemier, T., Martens, L.: In-memory, distributed content-based recommender system. J. Intel. Inform. Syst. **42**(3), 645–669 (2014)
4. Huang, Z., Zeng, D., Chen, H.: A comparison of collaborative filtering recommendation algorithms for e-commerce. IEEE Intel. Syst. **22**(5), 68–78 (2007)
5. Castro-Sanchez, J.J., Miguel, R., Vallejo, D., López-López, L.M.: A highly adaptive recommender system based on fuzzy logic for B2C e-commerce portals. Expert Syst. Appl. **38**(3), 2441–2454 (2011)
6. Bobadilla, J., Serradilla, F., Hernando, A.: Collaborative filtering adapted to recommender systems of e-learning. Knowl. Based Syst. **22**, 261–265 (2009)
7. Lee, S.K., Cho, Y.H., Kim, S.H.: Collaborative filtering with ordinal scale-based implicit ratings for mobile music recommendations. Inform. Sci. **180**(11), 2142–2155 (2010)
8. Tan, S., Bu, J., Chen, C.H., He, X.: Using rich social media information for music recommendation via hypergraph model. ACM Trans. Multimedia Comput., Commun. Appl. **7**(1), Article 7 (2011)
9. Núñez-Valdéz, E.R., Cueva-Lovelle, J.M., Sanjuán-Martínez, O., García-Díaz, V., Ordoñez, P., Montenegro-Marín, C.E.: Implicit feedback techniques on recommender systems applied to electronic books. Comput. Hum. Behav. **28**(4), 1186–1193 (2012)
10. Barragáns-Martínez, A.B., Costa-Montenegro, E., Burguillo, J.C., Rey-López, M., Mikic-Fonte, F.A., Peleteiro, A.: A hybrid content-based and item-based collaborative filtering approach to recommend TV programs enhanced with singular value decomposition. Inform. Sci. **180**(22), 4290–4311 (2010)
11. Mcnally, K., O'mahony, M.P., Coyle, M., Briggs, P., Smyth, B.: A case study of collaboration and reputation in social web search, ACM Trans. Intel. Syst. Technol. **3**(1), Article 4 (2011)
12. Christidis, K., Mentzas, G.: A topic-based recommender system for electronic marketplace platforms. Expert Syst. Appl. **40**, 4370–4379 (2013)
13. Li, X., Murata, T.: Customizing knowledge-based recommender system by tracking analysis of user behavior. In: Proceedings of the IEEE 17th International Conference Industrial Engineering and Engineering Management (IE&EM), pp. 65–69 (2010)
14. Krishna, P.V., Misra, S., Joshi, D., Obaidat, M.S.: Learning automata based sentiment analysis for recommender system on cloud. In: 2013 International Conference on Computer, Information and Telecommunication Systems (CITS), pp. 1–5. IEEE, May 2013

15. Park, M.K., Moon, N.: The Effects of personal sentiments and contexts on the acceptance of music recommender systems. In: 2011 5th FTRA International Conference on Multimedia and Ubiquitous Engineering (MUE), pp. 289–292. IEEE, June 2011

16. Tian, P., Zhu, Z., Xiong, L., Xu, F.: A recommendation mechanism for web publishing based on sentiment analysis of microblog, wuhan university. J. Nat. Sci. **22**(2), 146–152 (2015)

17. Leung, C.W., Chan, S.C., Chung, F.L.:. Integrating collaborative filtering and sentiment analysis: A rating inference approach. In: Proceedings of the ECAI 2006 Workshop on Recommender Systems, pp. 62–66, August 2006

18. Meyffret, S., Guillot, E., Medini, L., Laforest, F.: RED: A Rich Epinions Dataset for Recommender Systems. Université de Lyon (2012)

19. Ganu, G., Elhadad, N., Marian, A.: Beyond the stars: Improving rating predictions using review text content. In: Proceedings of the 12th International Workshop on the Web and Databases (2009)

Author Index

Printed in the United States
By Bookmasters